Forensic Photography

Forensic Photography

A Practitioner's Guide

Nick Marsh

Consultant Forensic Practitioner, UK

WILEY Blackwell

Library of Congress Cataloging-in-Publication Data applied for.

Hardback ISBN: 9781119975823

A catalogue record for this book is available from the British Library.

Wiley also publishes its books in a variety of electronic formats. Some content that appears in print
may not be available in electronic books.

Set in 10.5/12.5pt Times Ten by Aptara Inc., New Delhi, India
Printed and bound in Singapore by Markono Print Media Pte Ltd

1   2014

Contents

Foreword

Of all the forensic disciplines forensic photography is the most misunderstood and the least recognised. In this book Nick Marsh, one of the world's leading professional forensic photographers, sets the record straight. From the perspective of a practitioner he manages to convey the significant contribution that forensic photography makes to the investigation of crime and the administration of justice. Forensic photography is an area of expertise that, as with other forensic disciplines, can make or break a case and it has a critical role in other visual forms of forensic evidence such as fingerprints, footwear and tool mark examination. No amount of expertise in these other disciplines can compensate for a poor source image for comparison. Forensic photography is one of the most challenging forensic disciplines and Nick shows how a detailed understanding of light, digital imaging and a problem-solving approach is at the heart of this profession. The move to digital capture, rather than wet film, only changes the tools available to the forensic photographer not the inherent expertise and skill that is required to recover forensic evidence through photography.

I have had the pleasure to work with Nick and to support his development of this important area. I commend this text to all those involved in the forensic profession with the hope that it provides the basis to establish forensic photography as a specialist field in its own right.

Gary Pugh, OBE
Director of Forensic Services
Metropolitan Police Service

Preface

The last 10 years has seen a massive surge of interest in forensics, due to the CSI effect both in television and film. [1] This is generally focused on pathologists, crime scene examiners or investigating personal. Unfortunately, the forensic photographer is often portrayed in these programmes as an extra, running around in the background, their input reduced to providing a few background flashes to the story line.

I hope that within the confines of this book, and I can fly the flag for the forensic photography within the evidential environment, and also share my passion for forensic photography as a very particular and important line of work.

I will point out at this point that I am not an academic, nor a teacher; I am a practitioner, so this book is based on the personal experiences of last 25 years of forensic photography and observations from an operational perspective. It is aimed, I hope, at readers who already have a general interest in forensic photography or are studying it. Those of you who wish to improve your techniques or are involved in imaging, and finally those of you that use forensic imaging to support your casework, such as Crime Scene Managers or Senior Investigating Officers.

I will go into depth where needed and lay out ground rules. But this book should not be seen as a replacement for Langford's basic or advanced photography.[1] Also, any opinions expressed are purely my own and not necessarily those representing the Metropolitan Police or others within the photographic industry. I apologise in advance for any technical mistakes within the text, as although every attempt is made to ensure facts are correct, mistakes sometimes happen. Finally the illustrations and guidance within this book are based on my own experiences; therefore your own agency may undertake or approach casework in a different way. The important thing to remember is we are all trying to achieve the same end result.

---

[1] *Langford's Basic Photography: The Guide for Serious Photographers* by Michael Langford, Anna Fox and Richard Sawdon Smith.

A bit about me: I studied Scientific and Technical photography at Berkshire College of Art and Design in Reading in the early 1980s. After taking a year or so out, working in the 'real world', an ex student colleague of mine suggested I apply to the Metropolitan Police where he was now working. Although I did not like the sight of blood, I somewhat reluctantly applied, was interviewed, and in March 1986 I joined the Metropolitan Police photographic branch based at Scotland Yard.

Over these past 25 years plus, I have photographed or been involved in many of the highest profile cases in London and at least seven bombings, including the Bishopsgate bombing.[2] I have also worked on many major incidents and disasters, such as the Clapham rail accident and Windsor Castle fire, through to the more recent – the 7/7 suicide bombing scenes. I have also attended well over 1000 murder scenes or post mortems and have attended more assault, fatal accident and other types of scenes than I care to consider.

I am currently the Consultant Practitioner of the Evidence Recovery Unit, co-running a team of 18 photographers, undertaking evidential photography, particularly in use of specialist light sources for the retrieval of latent evidence. I have also undertaken casework and training in countries as far flung as St Vincent's in the Caribbean, to Hanoi in Vietnam. I give numerous talks a year to a variety of audiences as diverse as the Forensic Science Society, universities and secondary schools, through to other police forces and government agencies. I often host visitors from imaging units and forensic units both within the UK and overseas, and am also listed on the Centrex database at the National Policing Improvement Agency (NPIA) as a contact for forensic imaging and specialist lighting for the detection of latent evidence. I have also written or contributed to a number of published papers, articles and books on various photographically related subjects.

It is safe to say that when I started my photography career in the 1980s I had no idea of the route in which it would take me. During my career I have had a remarkable and unrepeatable journey through forensic photography, not only in London but also all round the world. This book has been written drawing on those experiences.

I certainly don't know it all, and after 20 years I'm still learning, but I am a problem solver and, more importantly, I have empathy for what the customer requires and how to photographically achieve it.

It is sad to say that with the advent of digital capture in the United Kingdom, photography seems to have taken a back step in the forensic strategy and now stands at a crossroads. Film in its many guises had been the preserve of the trained photographer, but as Sandford L. Weiss points out in his book,

---

[2] The Bishops Gate Bombing: on the 24th April 1993 the Provisional Irish Republican Army (IRA) detonated a truck bomb on Bishopsgate, a major artery road, through the city of London. The bomb killed one person injured 44 others and caused over 1 million pound worth of damage.

Forensic Photography: The Importance of Accuracy,[3] digital imaging is the way of today's world. You do not often hear officers asking specifically for the photographer, now they are more likely to ask for a Crime Scene examiner who has a camera. This is understandable and in many circumstances common sense, after all it is questionable as to whether you need a professional photographer to photograph a car in car pound. Indeed this crossover of basic skills is a necessity of modern policing; hence I am also trained in the relevant skills of scene examination.

The problem as I see it, however, is that this scaling down of skills has had the effect that the photographer's knowledge and all he or she has to give is lost over time. Indeed within many forces, the simple use of cross-polarising filters for the removal of reflections or enhancing an injury, a bread and butter technique for us, has virtually died out. This I believe has led to a misconception that a trained and skilled photographer is no longer required within the policing arena. Yet photography is a science, when scrutinised, it relies on the principles of light and physics and is repeatable time and time again. No court would dream of allowing a non-qualified practitioner to comment on blood pattern distribution or DNA analysis. Because photography is now perceived as a mass media product, it is taken for granted that any images produced must be a representation of reality. But I would argue in many cases that this couldn't be further from the truth. Indeed, in the last few years I have been involved in a number of cases from the high courts, where it could be argued that the quality of photography was directly contributable to questionable judicial findings.

In today's world, the forensic photographer's skills lie well beyond just recording the crime scene; it should be instrumental and woven into the investigation. We provide the visualisation of both visible and invisible evidence, from the recording of latent finger marks, to the infrared capture of the blood on the clothing.

A senior member of staff once told me that my work was not as important as my colleagues, the forensic scientists, because I don't produce a 20-page statement. He is right, I don't normally produce a 20-page statement, but as the saying goes 'a picture says a thousand words' and in a court trial an album of accurately taken photographs can and does have far more impact than any number of hesitant or mumbling expert witnesses.

Regardless of your imaging background, or level of photographic knowledge, I hope that by writing this book, I can underpin your understanding of the importance of forensic photography and support those of you who wish to build on, or increase, your knowledge in this field.

On a number of occasions during the compilation of this book, I have been asked why I should bother to write a book on forensic photography. After all

---

[3] *Forensic Photography: The Importance of Accuracy* Sandford L Weiss, Pearson Prentice Hall.

there are plenty of photography books and websites dedicated to photography out there already. If I walk into my nearest bookshop, there are numerous books on how to take good photographs. Many are written by acclaimed academics or professional photographers and all have something to offer. I believe, however, that in the main they are aimed towards recreational and artistic demands. They are trying to be creative, innovative and more importantly to produce a pleasing image on the eye. You never see a photograph in a book that doesn't look artistically constructed, correctly colour balanced and most importantly interesting. Indeed if they weren't, they wouldn't sell any books. Yet forensic photography isn't about creating pleasing images (although that is a bonus if you can achieve it), it is about either trying to capture the moment as it exists, warts and all or revealing evidence which the eye cannot see, such as a fluorescent finger mark at a murder scene.

Within this book I clearly cannot cover all the disciplines that a forensic photographer may require over his professional career, and to some extent these will be driven by your own force's requirements. Indeed, technology is changing so fast that some topics covered within this book may be obsolete or undertaken in a radically different way within a few years. I am, however, going to look at those techniques and skills which I believe are the most useful to all.

I have had the privilege of delivering training both here in the UK and on occasions overseas and have witnessed the enthusiasm of staff when they learn the impact of a new technique. I have also realised, though, that unless the technique is practised is can be quickly forgotten. So I have written this book as a practical support to problems, for those working in the field.

As I have already stated, this is not a book on the photographic principles, though I have tried to explain some of the technical topics in depth where applicable. It is, however, beyond the limitations of this book to go into great technical detail on all subjects. Where possible I will point you towards other publications or websites that offer good, sound advice. Nor will I cover the history of forensic photography, there are plenty of books that will do that for you and far more eloquently than I could. There are also numerous websites are dealing with everything from lens tests, to depth of field. I have therefore limited my comments to convey the basic ideas, but have not necessarily looked at the minutia of an issue. This I hope is made up for in the diversity of the subjects covered. Also, as much as I regret it, I will not spend much time looking at traditional 'film' apart from in passing and as reference. Space is limited and technology is forever moving on. Indeed by the time this book is finally finished, I doubt there will be a police agency in the world using wet film. The other topic I won't specifically be covering is why 'X' camera is better the 'Y' camera. This is for two good reasons: one, by the time this book comes out any camera recommended will be out of date and two, I believe cameras are to some extent a personal choice.

One last comment, for those of you hoping to see lots of blood and gore, I am sorry to disappoint. Unlike some countries, where images seem to go into the public domain for all to see after a trail, here in the United Kingdom images are still closely guarded and are difficult to acquire. I have therefore decided to illustrate the book with 'mock ups' so as not to cause offence and to let me demonstrate points more accurately.

I hope that you enjoy the book and I hope that it encourages you to look more deeply at the skills you have, or ones you would like to develop in this field.

Finally, the techniques I explain within the book may be done in different ways by different forces or agencies, or following alternative ideas in books by other authors. The important issue is that we all are working towards a common goal of quality and reliability in the courtroom.

To paraphrase Quincy MD[4]

'You are about to enter the most fascinating theatre of police work, the world of forensic photography.'

Reference

(1) 'CSI Effect: Popular Fiction about Forensic Science Affects the Public's Expectations about Real Forensic Science', Schweitzer, N. J.; Saks, Michael J. 47 *Jurimetrics* 357 (2006–2007). And 'Investigating the 'CSI Effect' Effect: Media and Litigation Crisis in Criminal Law', Simon A Cole & Rachel Dioso-Villa *Stanford Law Review* Vol. 61, No 6 (2009).

---

[4] Quincy, or Quincy ME, was a US television series made by Universal Studios and was based on a forensic pathologist; it ran on NBC for 6 years.

Acknowledgements

This book would not be possible without the input of the following people who have been good enough to give up time to either read this, help me prepare images or provide ideas.

The first thing I must do is to thank the publishers, for giving me the opportunity to write about one of the most impacting, but often overlooked, areas of police casework, that of forensic imaging.

I would also like to thank John Smith, co-author of the digital process chapter. John is Senior Lecturer in Imaging Science in the Faculty of Media, Arts and Design at Westminster University. His research interests include applications of imaging, development of forensic imaging techniques and integration of imaging with other forensic disciplines. Simon Moore contributing author to the use of the immersive and interactive 360 imaging. Bernard Hogan-Howe, The Commissioner Metropolitan Police, (and his predecessors) who has given me the opportunities over the last 25 years.

Gary Pugh, Director of Forensic Services, who has always supported the use of skilled professionals, when other forces have lost their specialists. Chris Porter, Head of the Specialist Forensic Services, for allowing me to use the department's equipment. Nick Bishop, Senior Forensic Practitioner (imaging) the best latent mark photographer I know, for teaching me the key skills required over the past 25 years and his support through the good times and the bad. Michael Sisterson, Senior Forensic Practitioner (imaging), my right hand man. All of the staff in the ERU, for their patience when I kept saying, 'did you know I am writing a book'. Ian Jakeman Scientific Support Manager for Dorset Police, who has given me so many ideas and kindly agrees to peer review much of this book. Steve Bleay, CAST (Centre for Applied Science and Technology, Home Office Research) who has often corrected or encouraged some of my stranger ideas over the years and has been kind enough to peer review much of this book. Peter Goby-Watt, Metropolitan Police training school for his guiding support and the use of the Crime Academy facilities and for the loan of some of their source training material.

Also, I would like to give special thanks to Eric Pascoe and Frank Blackwell (retired) from Berkshire College of Art and Design for kick-starting my career in scientific and technical photography, and to Tony Rider and Ken Creer, who unknowingly started me on this journey all those years ago when I joined the Metropolitan Police. Little did they or I know what, what started as a job between jobs would turn into!

Mark Enticknapp for suggesting I join the Metropolitan Police in the first place.

My mother who supported me through college and ensured I got to the train on time!

And finally to Fiona, my wife, for putting up with my early morning tapping at the keyboard and to my girls Philippa and Hannah for keeping their dad supplied with tea during those long days when the words or images just didn't flow.

Nick Marsh
April 2013

About the Companion Website

This book is accompanied by a companion website:

www.wiley.com/go/marsh/forensicphotography

The website includes:

- A chapter on Post-Production which is only available on the companion website
- Powerpoints of all figures from the book for downloading
- PDFs of all tables from the book for downloading

1
Image Processing

1.1 Introduction

In the past there was only one choice of recording medium, 'Film'. It was available in a number of sizes normally $10'' \times 8''$ and $5'' \times 4''$ sheet film, 120 and 220 roll film and of course 35 mm. This was then available in a various emulsions: colour negative, reversal, black and white and in a number of speeds (sensitivity). Although limited film stocks are still available in small numbers, film no longer has a mass-market appeal and more importantly, is no longer be used by law enforcement agencies.

Today the advent of the digital sensor has made all these 'film' choices and more, available at the touch of a few buttons. Yet it could be argued that instead of making the task easier, it has made the choice harder. For example, todays camera manufacturers not only produce various size sensors, but each has its own particular sensor design and its own in-house post production software.

As a forensic photographer the question is how we decide which system is fit for purpose and to answer that question, we must have an understanding of the very heart of modern camera technology, the sensor and the digital process.

I shall start with definitions of the digital image and an explanation of digital image acquisition; then I will discuss some simple examples of things we commonly do to images that might not be thought of as image processing, which will introduce the fundamental concepts of what image processing is about. I'll consider both the reactive and proactive uses of image processing – put another way, examples of restoration processes and enhancement processes – and along the way we'll encounter analysis processes and synthesis processes. All these terms will be defined, but it may be more understandable if their explanation comes after some practical examples.

Forensic Photography: A Practitioner's Guide, First Edition. Nick Marsh.
© 2014 John Wiley & Sons, Ltd. Published 2014 by John Wiley & Sons, Ltd.

Image processing is a term that covers a very large number of operations that may be performed on an image, some of which the photographer will have control of, some of which a technician may have control of, and some of which will be dictated by the equipment therefore in practice, may be out of the control of those using it. Image processing occurs at every stage between exposing a photograph and finally presenting it to the end user. It is, therefore, unavoidable. At the very least a basic understanding of image processing is essential, even if only to assist with choosing from the many settings in a digital camera's set up and shooting menus. Many users may not even consider the latter as image processing, as the term is more commonly applied to the treatment of images once they have been captured. With some relatively simple processes astonishing results may be achieved from photographs that may initially appear of limited use. An advanced knowledge of image processing options may even revolutionise how you approach photography from the outset. Although the broad term *image processing* also applies to analogue photography (for example various different film developers may be chosen for different effects, such as high contrast or high acutance (sharpness)) we will only consider *digital* image processing here. In a small volume such as this, we can only scratch the surface of this vast subject with its myriad options. I will introduce the fundamental concepts common to all digital imaging: the digital image, the imaging chain, the classes of operations and examples of where in the imaging chain they may be encountered. In the forensic context the integrity and reliability of images is of the utmost importance, particularly when images provide primary evidence. So we must consider ways to ensure integrity and prove reliability: I will discuss the concepts of workflow, the audit trail, archiving and storage and direct you to published best practice guidelines and further reading. When discussing post-capture software I will most often refer to Adobe Photoshop because it is the most widely used application, but the principles apply to all image processing software.

1.2   The digital image

What is a digital image? It's a question I often ask photographers. The replies are many and varied but rarely do I receive a response similar to 'it's a set of binary numbers representing a scene', because that's not how people perceive images. We can see images, can't we? A set of binary data is altogether more abstract. But for the digital image on your memory card, or on your hard drive, or in the ether between your wireless devices: can you see it? No, you'll need a monitor or a printer to display it first. The camera's optics project a pattern of light onto an array of electronic sensors; the electronics convert the response signals into a set of binary data and, in the simplest concept, a monitor's electronics will convert the binary data into electrical signals, which are then sent to an array of, say, light emitting diodes (LEDs) to display as a pattern of light. The result will be a likeness of the thing photographed, a *representation* of the *scene*. Once it is accepted that the digital image is data

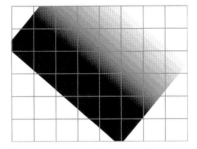 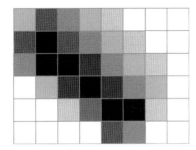

Figure 1.1   Left: Image of object (smooth edges, continuous tone) projected onto array of square pixels. Right: digitised image after sampling and quantisation. Sampling leads to 'blocky' edges; quantisation produces discrete levels of grey and leads to blurred edges because the resulting grey level is a function of the average intensity at each pixel.

and that we can't see data and therefore need some device in order to see the image, I suggest we can consider two important concepts: one, we can free ourselves of presumptions that an image appearing on one device, say, 'computer screen A', is any truer a representation than its appearance on another device, say, 'computer screen B', (unless both screens are calibrated to some independent standard), and two, the necessity for image processing, or data manipulation[1] becomes apparent.

1.3   Image acquisition

Although the digital camera is the most common device for acquiring a digital image, digital images may originate from other devices such as scanners, frame-grabbers from analogue video, and so on. Scanners, whether specialist film scanners or flat-bed desk-top scanners, are regularly used to digitise photographic negatives and prints in a hybrid workflow. Whatever the device, the fundamental processes of digital image acquisition are similar.

All processes of digital image acquisition involve two basic operations: sampling (measuring light intensity) and quantisation (assigning a discrete value to that measurement) (Figure 1.1). The number of locations at which light intensity can be measured (sampled) is set by the number of pixels a device has, which is usually stated as the pixel count. The convention is for cameras to be specified as, for example, 4000 × 3000 pixels, or '12 megapixels', where a megapixel is one million pixels. For scanners, the figure is stated as pixels per inch, both horizontally and vertically. The number of pixels largely defines

---

[1] The term *manipulation* is generally avoided when discussing forensic image processing as it is considered to imply malicious intent. The Oxford English Dictionary, however, also defines *manipulate* as 'handle, treat, or use, especially skilfully'. I sometimes use the term provocatively to remind people that image data must be processed to be displayed and we need to consider the steps we have little control over (such as printer drivers) as well as those we have much control over (such as the use of Photoshop).

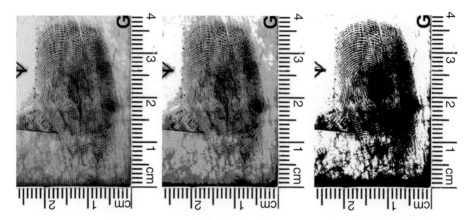

Figure 1.2 Images of finger mark, recorded with bit depths of (left) 8, (middle) 2, and (right) 1, giving 256, 4 and 2 grey levels respectively. In order for us to perceive a monochrome image as having continuous tone, 8-bits are required, allowing 2^8, that is 256, discrete values or grey levels. I will discuss file formats later in the chapter but it is worth noting here that different file formats may have, or allow, different bit depths. It is common for raw formats to utilise 10, 12 or 14 bits; TIFF may allow 8 or 16 bits, whilst JPEG is limited to 8 bits. Are extra bits necessary if we can't perceive the difference between several different values? Maybe (more on this later).

the spatial resolution of the resulting image (other factors include the optics employed in the formation of the image).

The number of values used to represent the light intensity at each location is limited by the *bit depth* of the device. *Bit* is an abbreviation of *binary digit*; the number of possible values will be a power of two. A 1-bit image can have only two possible pixel values: 0 or 1, that is black or white and nothing in between (Figure 1.2).

1.4   Colour images

In practice most of us use colour cameras. Pixels can't inherently 'see' colour. To record colour information individual pixels are overlaid with coloured filters, most commonly the three additive primary colours: red, green and blue (RGB), the filters being arranged in a regular mosaic pattern or *colour filter array* (CFA). Each individual pixel is therefore only able to respond to part of the colour spectrum. But when we look closely at the resulting image we find each pixel has values for each of the three primaries. The process of deriving the 'missing' two colour values for each pixel is called demosaicing[2] and is one of the first instances of image processing in the imaging chain. The result is, in

---

[2] Demosaicing involves processes of interpolation, 'filling in the gaps', and is common to the vast majority of colour cameras. Some people argue strongly that interpolation must be avoided, whilst being apparently oblivious to the fact that by their own definition two-thirds of every photograph they take is 'made up'! Cameras employing Foveon X3 sensors, where demosaicing is not necessary, are

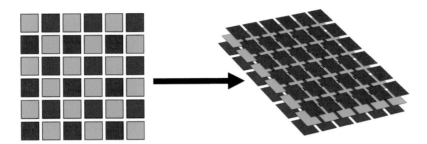

Figure 1.3   A typical Bayer colour filter array, laid over the sensor, means that each pixel only records part of the colour spectrum (left); full colour information for each pixel results from demosaicing (right).

effect, three overlaid monochrome images. Therefore colour images require 3 × 8 (24) bits, or 3 × 16 (48) bits, and so on (Figure 1.3). To add to the confusion, 24-bit colour images are often referred to as '8-bit'; 48-bit colour images '16-bit', and so on.

Whether we're dealing with greyscale or colour images, the outcome of the image acquisition process is a two-dimensional matrix of binary integers representing the scene photographed, where each integer represents a grey level (or each set of RGB integers represents a colour) and each position in the matrix represents a geometric location. Again, this concept of the digital image should assist the understanding of all that follows.

1.5   The imaging chain and workflow

The *imaging chain* is the series of devices between image acquisition, or capture (input), and final display (output) and workflow is the *direction of travel* through the imaging chain. If you take a photograph with a digital camera the chances are the first time you see the resulting image is on the screen on the back of the camera. The light projected onto the sensor by the lens has been sampled and quantised; the resulting digital image has been processed in-camera and signals sent to the camera screen. Already there are three links in the chain: image sensor, camera processor, camera screen. The chain can be considered to be made up of a series of links, where each link is 'input–process–output' and where the output of one link is the input to the next link. A simple, practical, scenario may involve taking a photograph and saving it in raw format, converting it to TIF format on a computer whilst viewing it on screen, and then printing it on a desktop printer. This involves the four major links of camera, computer, screen and printer.

---

notable exceptions. Demosaicing could be considered to be a restoration process, but I suggest by strict definition it is a synthesis process.

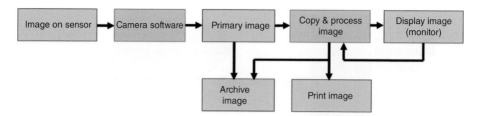

Figure 1.4   A typical imaging chain and workflow.

Each device will have its particular characteristics in terms of how it repro-duces and displays the image data, and each device will therefore require the data to be processed somehow. Mostly this is done by the electronics and drivers associated with each device, over which the user has little control, though in many cases some control may be exerted via, say, an on-screen dialogue box. Possibly the simplest to understand (yet the most important) attribute of images is the reproduction of tones (brightness, contrast) and the most common image processes involve adjusting brightness and contrast in some way. An analogy with film photography is the two-link negative–positive black and white print process: the first link is the production of a negative image, where the tones of the *subject* are reversed; the second link is the pro-duction of a positive print, where the tones of the *negative* are reversed: the contrast and brightness are controlled at each stage by the level of exposure, the development conditions and the choice of emulsions of suitable grade (contrast); the reproduction of tones is described by a material's character-istic curve. In comparison, a digital imaging device's tone reproduction may be described by its transfer function although, in contrast to film manufactur-ers, the manufacturers of digital imaging devices rarely publish transfer func-tions. Resulting images may be modified by adjusting brightness and contrast or using levels or curves functions. Colour balance is maintained by treating each of the RGB images separately whilst aiming for neutral tones without colour casts. Even if our only concern is to maintain 'correct' tone and colour, some adjustment throughout the chain will be inevitable, especially if the final output is a print. Processing is necessary because of device-dependent colour reproduction characteristics. The RGB primaries of a computer screen are unlikely to match exactly those of the camera sensor, and neither will match the printer, which will print in the subtractive primaries of cyan, magenta and yellow (CMY),[3] at the very least, and may include several more colours. Many potential problems of colour reproduction can be avoided by employing good colour management. In simple terms, colour management is the prac-tice of ensuring that the colour you see on screen is the most accurate repre-sentation of the colour the camera recorded, and that your resultant print is

---

[3] To push the previous point about interpolation, the conversion from RGB to CMY will involve the recalculation of *every* pixel value and, by definition, the alteration of *every* colour.

similarly colour-accurate. Detailed discussion of colour management is outside the scope of this volume, but the importance of maintaining accurate colour should be obvious. We should, however, consider the relatively simple question of how to achieve correct white balance.

1.6 White balance

When we look at a scene we have a remarkable ability to compensate for changes in the colour of the illuminant. I often use a piece of A4 white paper to illustrate the point to students in a room illuminated with a combination of fluorescent strip lights on the ceiling and diffuse daylight through the windows. I'll hold the paper in a corner of the room where it is lit mostly by the fluorescent lights and ask, 'what colour is the paper?' The answer, of course, is 'white'. I'll then move to the window, where the paper is lit almost exclusively by diffuse daylight and ask again, 'what colour is the paper?' Again, the answer is 'white'. The colour of the paper hasn't changed and we know that, but we do compensate for changes in the colour of the illuminant: daylight is relatively more blue and fluorescent lighting relatively more yellow. In effect, our brain equips us with an automatic white balance similar to the camera function of the same name. But whereas we experience a scene in the context of its full environment, the camera captures an image that becomes abstracted from that environment and viewed at some future time, most likely under different conditions. If we photograph the paper in the two locations, and we want the paper to appear white in both photographs, then we need to adjust the camera's white balance accordingly otherwise the paper may appear yellow or blue in one of the photographs. It is good practice to match the camera's white balance to the illuminant by choosing one of the standard presets so that the camera maintains neutral colour reproduction without colour casts. When we change the camera's white balance setting we are telling the camera's software to process the image so that colours in the image appear as we see them. Cameras' automatic white balance can be remarkably adept, but where colours are critical it is best to include a reference colour scale within the original image and choose a suitable white balance pre-set. The colour scale then provides an objective, device-independent reference, which can be relied upon and can aid colour correction (Figure 1.5). Colour correction may be considered a restoration process.

Where workflow is fully colour managed, it should be possible to rely on the tones and colours of images at each stage, but my experience of forensic photography in practice suggests fully colour-managed workflow is the exception. In many practical scenarios it is very difficult to maintain control of the full imaging chain: what happens to those carefully exposed and colour balanced crime scene images once they're burnt to a CD and sent out to the investigating officer; who is ensuring the accuracy of the officer's computer screen and printer? Again, this illustrates why it is useful to include a reference colour scale. Photoshop offers a couple of very useful quick fixes for images that have

Figure 1.5   Colour scales (and linear scales) provide standard references, against which objects in the image may be compared.

minor exposure and colour errors: the levels and grey-picker tools. Before discussing them, we should stop to consider the image histogram.

1.7   Image histogram

The histogram is a graphical representation of the distribution of grey levels within an image (and is an example of the output of an analysis process). It is an excellent aid for judging exposure and I recommend selecting an image review mode on the camera to display the overall histogram (or, better still, the RGB histograms) along with the image. The horizontal axis represents the available grey levels from black, at the far left, to white, at the far right, and the vertical axis represents the number of pixels that possess each value. The histogram can therefore be used to judge whether an image is under-, over- or correctly-exposed: a 'good' histogram will show a wide distribution of grey levels (Figure 1.6).

Histograms that show bunching of grey levels towards the extremes of the scale suggest some subject details have not been captured. If detail has not been captured it cannot be recovered, but in some circumstances detail may have been recorded that is not visible in the initial image.

1.7.1   Levels and grey-picker tools

Where the only error is a minor exposure error, use Photoshop's levels tool. When this is chosen, the image histogram is displayed, directly under which are three small triangles representing the black-, mid-grey- and white-points. These points may be moved along the scale by clicking and dragging to redistribute the grey levels (Figure 1.7).

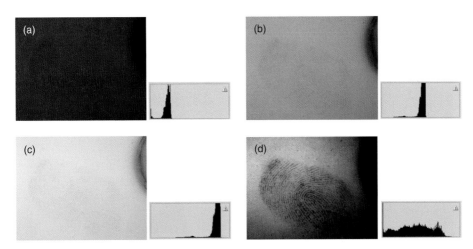

Figure 1.6 (a) Dark, low contrast image and associated histogram. (b) Low contrast image and associated histogram. (c) Bright, low contrast image and associated histogram. (d) High contrast image and associated histogram.

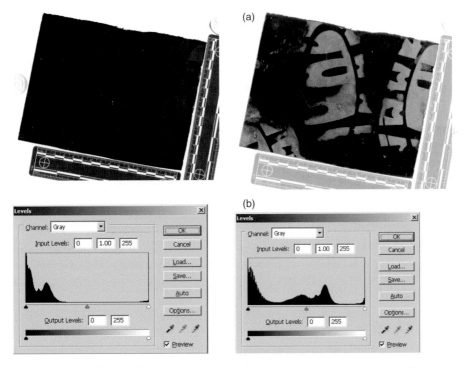

Figure 1.7 Use of levels function. (a) The image as captured and the associated histogram. (b) Image processing using the level to enhance contrast and associated histogram.

(a)

(b)

Figure 1.8   (a) Original image and histogram. The point in the image chosen to represent a neutral grey is indicated here by an 'X', near the centre of the image. (b) Image and histogram after colour adjustment using the grey picker.

Where the problem is one of colour balance, use the grey-picker tool: first choose 'levels', then click on the grey-picker, and then choose a point in the image that ought to be mid-grey and click on that point. The result should be similar to having had the white balance on the camera set correctly in the first place (Figure 1.8).

Note that these quick fixes, and similar operations, should not be considered as replacements for choosing correct settings before taking photographs: the 'corrected' or 'restored' image comes at the expense of losing some image data and results may be inconsistent.

We have established the fundamental properties of digital images, the imaging chain and workflow. We have already covered some important image processing concepts, but in order to explore image processing in more depth let's move onto what we may want to do with our images. I tend to classify forensic photography into two types: *reactive* (documentary) photography and *proactive* (examination-quality) photography. The former includes general crime scene photography and the photography of exhibits (items): the aim is to produce a 'true to life' record of the scene, as seen, that is with correct lighting, perspective, colour balance, contrast, and so on. The latter includes marks photography (finger marks, footwear marks, etc.), where the aim may be to produce the clearest possible image of a finger mark, distinct from the background surface on which it is deposited. The two classes are not mutually exclusive. Blood pattern analysis, bite marks by reflected ultraviolet radiation, night-time CCTV under infrared radiation, crash reconstruction via photogrammetry: these are just a few examples where the two-dimensional image may be analysed to provide three-dimensional information, and/or where we rely on photography to provide an accurate record of the inherently invisible. Conversely, it can be extremely important to demonstrate, via photographs, the accurate visual appearance of marks, for example finger marks in blood. But to keep things simple during further discussion, I will concentrate on fairly standard examples of documentary and examination-quality photography.

In an ideal situation the photographer will have a comprehensive understanding of how an image is processed at every stage throughout the imaging chain and will be able to exert full control of every process in order to produce the best possible outcome. In practice this is difficult, if not impossible, to achieve. The digital camera market is highly competitive and manufacturers tend not to publish every detail of the processing that occurs even before the primary image is produced. Forensic photographers form a very small part of the range of users; we use cameras that are designed for the much larger market of commercial and amateur photography, which includes press, landscape, portrait, sports, weddings, and so on. One only has to browse reviews of cameras in the photography press or on-line to find examples where differing results are produced by cameras employing exactly the same imaging sensor to appreciate the point (in some ways it was the same with film: one film might have been aimed at portrait photographers, giving pleasing skin tones and relatively low contrast, while another might have been aimed at landscape photographers, giving more saturated blue skies and lush greens). Possibly the best we can hope for is for photographers to understand which image processes they can control and which processes they cannot control to enable them to make informed decisions at each stage. It is unacceptable for a photographer to neither understand nor control the processes. At best, that would lead to blind faith that the primary image produced by a camera, or the

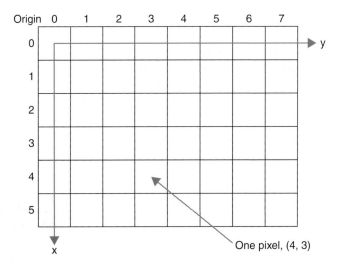

Figure 1.9 The digital image as an indexed two-dimensional array of values, showing pixel location.

modified image at any subsequent stage in the chain, is inherently objective and therefore 'truer' than one to which expert control has been applied. At worst, lack of awareness may result in images that are misleading because of the introduction of imaging artefacts.

A process may be defined as 'a course of action or a procedure, especially a series of stages' (*OED*), a definition well-suited here. Following the definition of the digital image, it is most useful to conceptualise the digital image as a regular, two-dimensional, mathematical matrix of discrete numbers. The position of a number within the matrix represents the geometric position of the sample (pixel) to which it relates, and the value of the numbers ('pixel values', or 'digital values') represents its intensity (brightness) and colour. If this sounds complicated, it's not! Open an image in Photoshop; display also the *info* window; move the cursor around over the image and see what happens in the info window: the X and Y values give a pixel's location and the R, G and B values give the pixel values (remember, a colour image is composed of three overlaid greyscale images). This is about as close to seeing the image data as we can get, but this is accessible only once the image has been saved in a format exportable from the camera and readable by Photoshop (Figure 1.9).

1.8   Image processing terminology

Various terms may be used to describe what, in the general sense, may be done to an image, and why. The following terms are useful in describing the various concepts of image processing, though I should note they are not universally adopted and different terms and classifications may be found. For example, there is debate over whether *enhancement* may somehow imply an image has been materially altered, never mind *manipulation*! Once again, you may ultimately have to explain your methods in court, so choose language that you are comfortable with; language that accurately describes what you have done, and why.

- *Enhancement*: the objective improvement of visibility. Examples include improving the contrast of a finger mark and suppressing background texture or noise.
- *Restoration*: the objective removal of artefacts. Examples include: reducing image noise; correcting geometric distortion.
- *Reconstruction*: the objective compositing of a new, single, image of a scene. Examples include: combining several images of a subject that was impossible to light in one photograph.
- *Synthesis*: the production of photograph-like images from data, where the data do not originate from a digital photograph. Examples include: text annotations, computer graphics.
- *Compression*: the reduction of size of an image file.
- *Analysis*: the extraction of information. Examples include: automatic fingerprint identification systems (AFIS), automatic number plate recognition (ANPR), photogrammetry.
- *Manipulation*: it simply means 'handling' but is widely considered to imply subjective, or even malicious, alteration and is therefore generally avoided in the forensic context.

It is worth noting here that increasingly complex signal- and image-processing may be performed in-camera, some of which may even be 'hard wired' into the imaging chip, so it is getting increasingly difficult for a camera user to access image data that are truly 'raw'. This is not the case for all cameras, however: whilst most colour cameras and DSLRs will process image files before export, alternatives are available. Scientific (often monochrome) charge-coupled device (CCD) cameras offer the best option for critical work. A good example is the Home Office's IRIS (Integrated Rapid Imaging System) of the late 1990s, which was a finger mark imaging workstation specified with such a camera. In practice, and especially in the field, the DSLR dominates; the least-processed image file available will be the proprietary 'raw' format.

I will structure the following discussion in terms of the common classes of operation (the individual actions or procedures), illustrating the concepts with common examples. I will follow with some discussion about their combination into series of stages, which will involve looking again at the imaging chain, and I will end with a return to the concepts of the audit trail and best practice guidelines. I will use Photoshop to illustrate many of the operations because it is so widely used and because of its versatility. Some people consider other applications are more suited to forensic image processing, and there may well be good arguments for the likes of MATLAB, Image Pro, V++, and so on. On the other hand, some practitioners may not have access to specialist or expensive applications. There are some very good free applications available for download from the web, most notably (in my opinion) ImageJ, Irfanview and GIMP. Applications included as part of the suite that comes with any PC or Mac may be of some, possibly limited, use. And of course every camera and scanner manufacturer supplies proprietary software for interfacing with scanners, the management of raw files, and so on. Oh, and then there are plenty of other options such as Adobe Lightroom and Apple Aperture. If the range of possible applications is large, consider the various permutations that could be implemented! It is, therefore, practically impossible to state what should and shouldn't be used; where, and in which order; for this type of image or that. I often quote the maxim, 'it's not what you have but the way that you use it', and I reiterate my points that individuals and organisations need to establish local SOPs and responsibilities. Whatever the application, and wherever the processes are applied, all image processes share similar principles, which is where we shall start.

1.9   Digital image processing operations

To keep things simple I will concentrate on 8-bit monochrome (greyscale) images, that is images with 256 possible grey levels. It is conventional for the minimum value, 0, to represent black and the maximum value, 255, to represent white. I will make reference to colour images and images with greater bit depths where appropriate.

1.9.1   Image cropping

Image cropping, if done at all, is usually performed mid-way through, or near the end of the imaging chain to remove unnecessary portions of an image. If we simply crop off a portion of an image we'll leave the remainder unaltered (Figure 1.10).

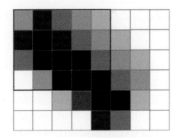 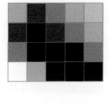

Figure 1.10   Image cropping. An area is selected and the rest of the image is cropped out leaving the remaining portion unchanged.

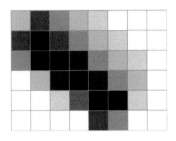 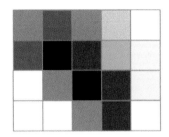

Figure 1.11 Image resampling. In this example, the image is resampled from 8 × 6 pixels to 5 × 4 pixels; every pixel value must be recalculated, resulting in increased blockiness and blurring.

1.9.2 Image resampling (resizing)

Image resampling may be performed at many stages of the imaging chain. Demosaicing involves resampling; unless an image is viewed pixel-for-pixel on a screen it will need to be resampled; printing almost always involves resampling. If we resize an image from its native dimensions then we'll be either adding or removing pixels. In the simplest case, if we reduce the image dimensions by half then the value of each 'new' pixel will be the average of the two 'old' pixels it replaces (Figure 1.11).

If we increase the image dimensions by a factor of two, the simplest method is to just double up every pixel. This method is called nearest neighbour interpolation, and the results can look blocky, or pixellated. Bilinear interpolation calculates each new, intermediate, pixel value as an average of the four (two vertical and two horizontal) surrounding original pixel values and produces smoother looking results; bicubic interpolation follows a similar procedure based on sixteen surrounding original pixel values and produces even smoother results.

When images are resized by any factor other than $^1/_2$ or 2, similar functions to those described are applied but the maths is a little more complicated than simply averaging the values of two, four or sixteen original pixels.

1.9.3 Image flipping and rotation

If we simply want to produce a mirror image of an image, for example 'flipping' a footwear mark on a non-transparent transfer medium, the process is a simple transformation: each pixel will 'land' in a geometric location that is precisely in line with the initial matrix and no recalculation or interpolation will be necessary. If we use software to rotate a digital image by a multiple of 90° then, likewise, no recalculation or interpolation will be necessary. If, however, we rotate the image by any other angle then the pixels won't 'land' in locations consistent with the matrix and therefore every single pixel value will

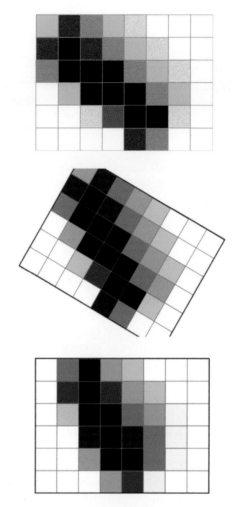

Figure 1.12   Image rotation. The image (top) is rotated clockwise by approximately 30° (middle) and resampled to fit the rectangular matrix (bottom image), resulting in increased blockiness and blurring.

need to be recalculated by the software (Figure 1.12). The process will involve some form of interpolation.

These processes of resampling are examples of geometric transformations. Other geometric transformations include digital zoom, scaling (stretching the image in one direction), warping, correction of lens distortion and perspective correction. All of these employ one, or a combination, of the processes described above. If multiple geometric transformation processes are applied, their effects will be cumulative. If geometric transformation processes are necessary they should be applied towards the end of any image processing sequence where possible. Any image output from a device such as a camera or scanner that differs in pixel resolution from the optical resolution of the device, will have been processed with some form of interpolation. For example, a scanner may have an optical resolution of 1200 ppi but the user may require images of 1000 ppi, an output resolution that can only be obtained by recalculating every pixel value. Photoshop's crop tool is very useful for resampling, resizing, rotating and even correcting perspective distortion, and the beauty of the crop tool is that it does this in one step.

Where geometric transformations involve resampling, any resulting pixel value that is not an integer between 0 and 255 will need rounding to the nearest value, which will introduce a small amount of noise. In addition, once the transformation has been applied and the pixel values recalculated, we can't get back to the original image simply by applying a reverse transformation because we're effectively applying two separate transformations and their effects will be cumulative. This problem can be avoided by using software that allows 'multiple un-dos' by saving previous versions of images in buffer memory *and* not saving and closing images part way through processing. I recommend exploring options afforded by Photoshop's history functions when multiple processes are used.

1.9.4 Linear scales

When performing geometric transformations, whether simply rotating or resizing/resampling, or complicated distortion corrections, it is imperative to use only known control points in the image. Proper use of linear scales allows this and should give you the confidence to demonstrate, if necessary, that your application of processes has been objective and is reproducible and you have not, for example, warped the crime scene mark to match the suspect's print! Although it can be argued that linear scales are unnecessary for all documentary photos, they are certainly useful in some. Whilst someone viewing an image of, say, the exterior of a house may be able to make some assumptions about scale and perspective (is it a real house or a doll's house?) the same may not be true of more abstract documentary photos. The knife photographed against a plain, white, lab bench: is the blade 15cm or 30cm in length? A linear scale will avoid ambiguity. Linear scales are essential with images of marks. It is best practice to photograph marks from a position perpendicular to the mark so that the image magnification is uniform across the whole image, in which case only one linear scale may be necessary. But it is better to include both a horizontal and a vertical linear scale in an image to allow accurate scaling along both dimensions. In circumstances where a geometric transformation such as perspective correction will be used, it is even better to include linear scales along all four sides. The most useful scales are the specific L-shaped forensic scales, which include useful features such as accurate 90° corners, circles and crosses; ideally they should be at least as long as the area of interest; they must be legible in the image to be of use (Figure 1.13).

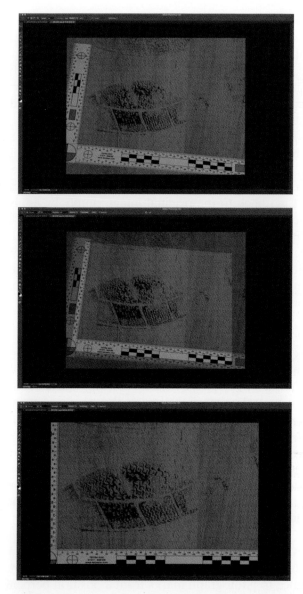

Figure 1.13   Photoshop's crop tool allows resampling, resizing, rotation and perspective correction to be performed all together. Image (top) suffers from perspective distortion and is not at a scale suitable for comparison. The user may select the desired output size and resolution before placing and dragging a box (middle, highlighted section), which then becomes the output image (bottom). In this example the perspective correction is only approximate; it would have been much better to have included a second L-shaped scale to fully bound the mark, allowing reliable and accurate correction.

1.10   Classes of operations

1.10.1   Point processing

Point processes are the simplest of processes. They are processes where the output value for each pixel location depends only on the application of some mathematical function to its input value, not on the values of any other pixel location, and each output pixel is in exactly the same geometric location as its associated input pixel. The simplest cases are those where the four basic mathematical operations are applied to a single image: addition, subtraction, multiplication and division. Another approach to point processing employs the *look up table* (LUT), which, as the name suggests, is not necessarily based on any mathematical function but may simply be a list of arbitrary output values relating to possible input values, for example 'if input pixel value = 0, output pixel value = 5; if input pixel value = 1, output pixel value = 7' and so on; potentially any available output value can be assigned to any input value.

1.10.2   Addition

If 0 represents black and, as pixel values increase, the greys become lighter until the maximum value of 255, white, is reached, it should be straightforward to imagine that, if we were to add exactly the same value to every pixel in an image, the result would simply be a lighter image. Adding a small value, say 5, to every pixel will result in a slightly lighter image; adding a much larger value will result in a much lighter image. It's a simple concept, but already you might spot a problem: what happens to those pixels whose values are already close to 255? If we added 10 to every pixel, then where we previously had some distinction between the very light greys of 245 and 255, all would now be 255 and we will have lost any information those levels may have contained. This is known as *clipping* in the *highlights* (Figure 1.14).

1.10.3   Subtraction

Conversely, if we subtract the same value from every pixel, the result will be a darker image, and if we lose the ability to discriminate between pixels whose initial values were close to 0 then, once again, we will lose information: this time the *shadows* will be clipped (Figure 1.15).

   Basic brightness adjustments rely on the application of addition and subtraction. If an image is badly underexposed or overexposed there are initially unlikely to be grey levels close to 255 or 0 respectively, so the crude application of addition or subtraction may not result in clipping.

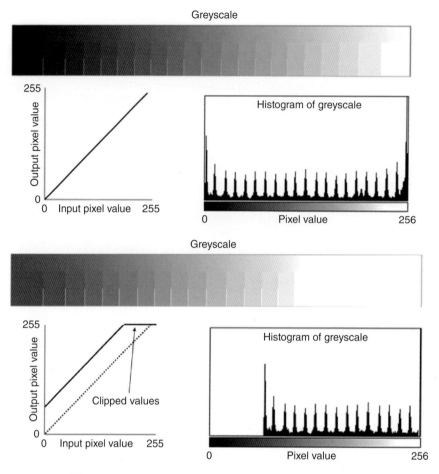

Figure 1.14   Addition. Top: image of grey scale, graph of input pixel values versus output pixel values and associated image histogram before simple brightness adjustment. Bottom: resulting image of greyscale, graph of input pixel values versus output pixel values and associated image histogram after simple brightness adjustment (lightening). Note the loss of discrimination in the highlight region.

1.10.4   Multiplication and division

Division is simply multiplication by a value less than 1, so we can consider them together. If we multiply the value of every pixel by, say, 2, what will be the result? $0 \times 2 = 0$; $1 \times 2 = 2$; $2 \times 2 = 4$ and so on: the result will be an image that has twice the contrast of the original.[4] And once we get to mid grey (128) in the original, we'll get clipped highlights in the copy. So simple

---

[4] The correct term is *gamma*, rather than *contrast*, but the latter is widely used to mean the former.

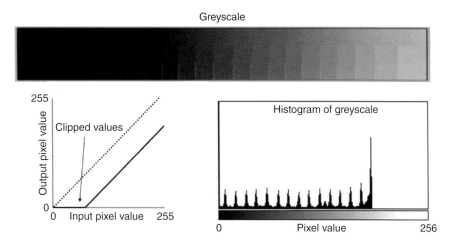

Figure 1.15   Subtraction. Starting from the same point as in figure 1.14, top, above: resulting image of greyscale, graph of input pixel values versus output pixel values and associated image histogram after simple brightness adjustment (darkening). Note the loss of discrimination in the shadow region.

multiplication (by numbers greater than 1) gives an increase in contrast and a higher chance of clipped highlights. If we multiply every pixel value by 0.5 (the same as dividing by 2) it follows that we'll get a reduction in contrast. And we'll encounter a new problem: what happens to pixel values that initially were odd? Remember, we're dealing with binary data, so we can't have a resulting value of, say, 67.5; it will need to be rounded to 67 or 68.

In my multiplication by 2 example, the mid grey of the original becomes white in the copy; in the multiplication by 0.5 the white of the original becomes mid grey in the copy. So, as well as a change in contrast, there is a change in brightness in each case. As above, we can alter brightness by addition or subtraction so, to maintain image brightness whilst altering contrast, multiplication *and* addition or multiplication *and* subtraction are applied together. The potential for clipping remains, only now it may affect both the highlights and the shadows. The problem of rounding also remains.

I have chosen to describe these operations with reference to simple, fundamental maths for two reasons. First, the alteration of brightness and contrast in various combinations is so widely used that, to those new to the concepts of image processing, it can be quite a surprise; and even to those familiar with their common incarnations the potential power of such fundamentally simple processes can be truly astonishing: therein lies the good news! Second, the simple examples above or, more specifically, the problems they introduce – clipping and rounding – nicely illustrate further associated problems: noise and artefacts: therein lies the bad news! What would you like first, the good news or the bad news? Let's start with the bad.

1.10.5   The bad news: artefacts

Anything introduced into an image, which results in the image not being a true representation of the scene, is an artefact. The definition includes lens flare, dust, and so on, but I'll restrict the discussion here to digital imaging artefacts. There are many ways artefacts can be introduced into digital images, including the use of long exposures, high ISO sensitivity, sharpening, compression, image rotation and so on. Once an artefact has been introduced its effect and visibility may be increased during subsequent processing, with obvious detrimental results. On the other hand, if artefacts are identified in an image, there may be a suitable process to remove or suppress them. And, as should be clear by now, the order in which a series of processes is applied can have considerable bearing on whether the problem of artefacts is worsened or lessened. By now I hope you will be wondering how it is possible to tell whether or not something, possibly unexpected, appearing in an image is an artefact, and whether or not a person processing the image will simply be removing artefacts or will be unwittingly manipulating the image. These are not trivial questions. Awareness of the appearance of artefacts, knowledge of suitable suppression techniques, skill in their application and, of course, experience will help. This applies whether you're working on images on the computer or explaining your methods in court.

1.10.6   The good news: versatility

White balance, colour correction, contrast, brightness, levels, curves, invert, threshold, the channel mixer, 'calculations', layers, layer blend options, high dynamic range (HDR) imaging: all of these tools employ one, or a combination of, the basic mathematical functions of addition (and subtraction) and multiplication (and division) and/or utilise LUTs. Now you should appreciate just how powerful and versatile are a few simple operations. Do, though, be aware of the potential for clipping and rounding errors and the introduction of noise and artefacts.

1.11   Noise reduction

One of the most common artefacts is image noise. In digital imaging we try to make a distinction between image noise and image artefacts, but it could be argued that any artefact is noise and vice versa. With forensic marks photography, we often encounter textured or patterned backgrounds, which may disrupt or hide detail in the mark, and we may consider such backgrounds to be subject noise. In practice it can be difficult, if not impossible, to distinguish between image noise and subject noise, especially if the individual examining or processing the image is not familiar with either the original mark or the characteristics of the image capture device used. When processing an image

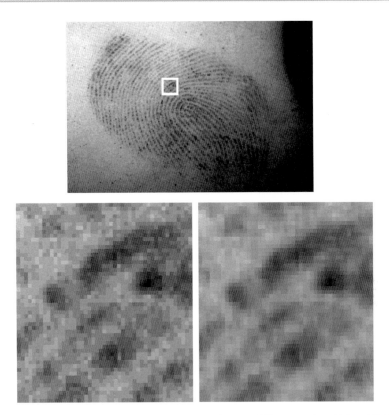

Figure 1.16 Noise reduction with blur filter. Top: image of finger mark, which exhibits contouring and noise as a result of extreme contrast enhancement. Bottom, left: close up of section
indicated by white box. Bottom, right: same area after simple blur filter. Note: the original image
was captured in JPEG format, which accounts for the poor quality. The amount of blur can be
increased by either applying the same process multiple times or by increasing the size of the
neighbourhood (group) to, say, five by five or seven by seven pixels.

to reduce noise, best practice should be followed, that is keep a copy of the
un-processed image and keep a record of the processing.

The simplest noise reduction filter is the blur filter which, in contrast to the
point processes outlined above, is a neighbourhood process. With neighbourhood processes, the output value for any pixel depends on functions applied
to a group of pixels centred on the input pixel. The simplest blur filter takes a
group of three pixels by three pixels and calculates their average (mean) value
to produce the central output value (Figure 1.16).

A slightly different filter is the median filter. As the name suggests, rather
than calculating the mean value of the neighbourhood, the median value of
the neighbourhood becomes the central output value (the median value of a
group of numbers is the middle value when they're rearranged in ascending
order).

A third type is the Gaussian blur, which is similar in operation to the simple blur filter. The significant difference is that the Gaussian blur filter gives more weight to the central input pixel value and gradually less weight to those nearer the periphery of the neighbourhood when calculating the output pixel value. The effect of the Gaussian blur filter is closer to the effect of lens blur than other noise reduction filters.

Some noise reduction filters allow the user to choose radius and threshold values. The radius value determines the size of the neighbourhood (one pixel radius equates to a three by three neighbourhood; two pixels radius to five by five and so on). The threshold value sets a minimum difference, below which an input pixel value will not be altered when calculating the output value.

More advanced noise reduction filters are available but their operation is likely to be based on one, or a combination of the three, of those described here. The general aim is to reduce noise whilst preserving detail, especially edges, but there's always a trade-off. The results of using any noise reduction filter on any image may be better or worse than the results of using another noise reduction filter. I recommend experimenting with the various filters and options at your disposal on a variety of different images and looking closely at, and comparing, the results. In practice I find myself using the Gaussian blur filter the most as its operation is more easily understood and explained than 'smart blur' type filters and it generally gives me better results than simple blur filters.

1.12   Sharpening filters

Sharpening filters also use neighbourhood processing operations but, in simple terms, the aim is almost the opposite to that of blur filters. The result of applying a sharpening filter is an image that appears crisper, with more prominent edges. Although fine detail may be more visible (which is why we use them) it is just an optical illusion, though an effective one. The basic sharpening filter simply increases the contrast between adjacent pixels of different value. Where there is an area of one tone, that is no difference between adjacent pixels, there will be no difference in the output image, but where there is a change in tone, for example at an edge, the contrast of the edge will be increased in the output image, hence it will appear sharper. No detail is added to the image but the detail present becomes more apparent. The basic sharpening filter does not distinguish between edges and other changes in pixel values so it will also accentuate noise. More advanced sharpening filters are available that are better at sharpening edges without increasing noise. Again, some filters allow the user to choose various values, for example amount, radius and threshold. Again, the radius value determines the size of the neighbourhood (one pixel radius equates to a three by three neighbourhood; two pixels radius to five by five and so on). The threshold value sets a minimum difference below which an input pixel value will not be altered when calculating the

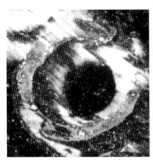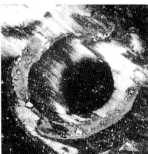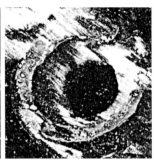

Figure 1.17   Images of a 2 cm² section of a footwear mark. Left: before sharpening; middle: after USM, amount 100, radius 1.5, threshold 0; right, after USM, amount 200, radius 5.0, threshold 0.

output value. The amount sets the proportion by which the contrast of pixels is increased. The unsharp mask (USM) filter is such a filter, allowing a lot of control of the results, and it is the one I use the most. Again, I recommend trying the various options yourself and comparing the results (Figure 1.17).

If sharpening filters are over-applied they introduce artefacts: not only do they accentuate noise but they can add a halo effect to edges.

It is impossible to say that this filter or that filter will give the best results; results are scene dependent. For example, a small amount of blur may improve the visibility of finger mark ridges against a noisy background by effectively suppressing the appearance of the noise but at the expense of blurring some features of the finger mark ridge edges (Figure 1.18). If a sharpening filter were applied to the same original image it could make the noise more prominent and the finger mark ridges less visible. Conversely, a finger mark on a plain background is likely to become clearer with a little sharpening and less clear with a little blurring.

I should point out that as well as being scene-dependent, neighbourhood processes such as blurring and sharpening are only really effective on an image at a given resolution. Here's an example: say we use a modern DSLR to photograph a finger mark, filling the frame and using the full resolution of the camera. We might obtain an image that has an effective resolution of, say, 3000 ppi. It is rather pointless producing the visibly best image at 3000 ppi and then resampling the image down to 1000 ppi for the fingerprint bureau, because the result of resampling in this example will be to remove fine detail, which is analogous to blurring. The image should be resampled to the required resolution first and then processed to produce the visibly best image. Additionally, when processing images using neighbourhood processes, it is important to be viewing the images at a suitable resolution on screen. I always view my images at a scale of 100% and from a distance of about 50 cm – any smaller scale or any greater distance and the effect of the process may not be visible. Unfortunately there are even further complications, at both ends of the imaging chain.

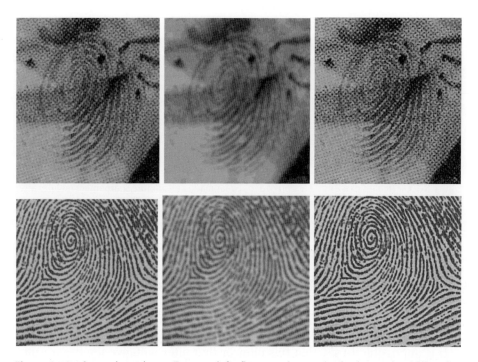

Figure 1.18   Scene dependency. Top row, left: finger mark on noisy background; middle: after a medium amount of blurring; right: after a medium amount of sharpening. Bottom, left: finger mark on plain background; middle: after a medium amount of blurring; right: after a medium amount of sharpening. The amounts of blurring and sharpening in each example are similar. Note how the visibility of finger mark ridges is improved by a different filter in each case.

Cameras generally offer image sharpening and noise reduction options in their shooting menus to be applied to images before they are saved. JPEG compression introduces both noise, in the form of blocky compression artefacts, and sharpening to enhance edges. Printer drivers and software may further process images to produce 'better' prints. Several times I have found that an image that looks perfect on screen looks far from perfect once printed. It must be accepted that there will be some difference in appearance between screen and print because they employ such fundamentally different technologies. The pragmatic solution involves trial and error, examination of results, tweaking of settings and gaining of experience with whatever workflow one uses. Examination of results should be suitable for the given application, for example if the final prints will be examined by a fingerprint examiner using a magnifying glass, then use a magnifying glass to examine your prints; if your final prints are general crime scene documentary photos to be viewed at arms length by an investigating officer, then why examine them with a magnifying glass?

My advice is to apply sharpening only as a final step on an otherwise 'finished' image, and only where it improves the visual quality of the image. This is more important with images that will undergo significant brightness, contrast or colour adjustment through the chain, and more important with images of marks, where edge detail is so important. The reason, if it is not already obvious, is because sharpening increases contrast locally; brightness, contrast and colour adjustment further down the chain will all affect subsequent contrast, both globally and locally; most images will be subject to some form of geometric transformation at some stage in the chain; the effect of multiple processes is cumulative; and sharpening is only really effective when applied to an image at its output resolution.

My advice regarding noise reduction is not so straightforward and may even sound contradictory! In my experience many in-camera noise reduction filters do a better job during the fraction of a second it takes the camera to process the image than I have been able to do during several minutes with Photoshop. My current opinion is that the camera engineers have done an excellent job of designing noise reduction functions that perform well with their systems.

1.13   History log

Photoshop provides an excellent tool that helps with the audit trail: the history log. It allows a record of all that is done to the image in Photoshop to be saved, either as part of the image file or as a separate text file. It is not automatically activated; you'll need to make a few choices in the preferences menu. Go to Edit/Preferences/History and select the detailed history log option. Choose a number of stages large enough to cover all possibilities. I recommend choosing the option that saves the history to the image file's metadata, which means the record becomes part of the same file as the image data and is always associated with the image. There may be circumstances in which you wish to save the history also as a separate text file. Bear in mind the history only records anything done in Photoshop and not other processing software.

1.14   Layers

I recommend you investigate the functionality provided by Photoshop's layers. The basic concept of a layer is analogous to an overlay over a conventional print but layers are so much more versatile than anything physical could hope to be. I will give a couple of examples to illustrate the versatility of layers.

1.14.1   Adjustment layers and layer masks

Rather than performing adjustments directly on an image, if you use an adjustment layer the underlying image does not change but its appearance does, in accordance with whatever adjustment you have applied to the adjustment layer. It's similar with layer masks: rather than making a direct selection of a section of the image, a layer mask allows you to select an area to which to apply an adjustment. Advantages of using layers include: the underlying image does not change; they can help demonstrate the important conditions of transparency and reproducibility; layers can be 'switched' on and off, which can aid image interpretation; they can allow processes to be undone in a way that can't otherwise be achieved; they allow images to be saved and closed part way through processing, and later opened again, whilst retaining all of the previous advantages. Disadvantages of layers are that images can only be saved in the proprietary Photoshop file format and their use can greatly increase file sizes.

1.14.2 Composite images

I use layers a lot in the production of composite images, especially when photographing luminol reactions, so I will use my method as an example. Capture two images, one of the luminol reaction in otherwise total darkness and one of the scene or item (background) in normal room light. Process each image differently: process the image of the luminol reaction to best show the detail and process the background image to best show the item. Then copy the luminol image and paste it onto the background image so that the luminol image becomes the upper of two layers. Then adjust the opacity of the luminol image to show the contextual information of the background without losing any of the detail of the luminol image. If necessary the image can then be 'flattened', that is reduced to a single layer, so that it can be saved as either a TIFF or JPEG. Obviously, it is extremely important to ensure accurate alignment of the two layers. This can be achieved by taking great care at the time of photography not to alter the position or focusing of the camera between shots and by closely examining the composite image, switching between layers and checking the alignment of any landmarks across the entire image area. When producing composite images such as these, it is important that every image used in the composite is of exactly the same dimensions and orientations, otherwise they will not align.

The use of layers to apply adjustments and masks can be considered similar to the use of raw file conversion software: in both cases the underlying image data are not altered but the way that data are processed and displayed is modified by the choices made by the user. Layers, therefore, should offer some benefits. For example, cascading multiple processes to avoid cumulative rounding errors, which should be especially useful when dealing with images that require considerable processing, especially with 8-bit images and especially with compressed images such as JPEGs if compressed images are ever unavoidable.

1.15 Bit depth and dynamic range

Now seems an appropriate time to return to the subject of bit depth. I previously stated that 2^8, or 256, grey levels were required in order to produce a continuous-tone image, without noticeable changes in adjacent grey levels.

Whilst that may be true, and fine for images where only small adjustments will be required later, imagine what happens if we need to greatly increase (amplify) the contrast of a faint finger mark, for example: two adjacent grey levels that were imperceptibly different may now become obviously different and the resulting image may exhibit contouring and increased noise, both image artefacts. Now imagine that instead of the original two, imperceptibly different, grey levels we had several grey levels to describe the same small transition in lightness. If we perform the same amplification to the image then the 'top' and 'bottom' grey levels will be stretched apart, just as before, but the extra levels in the middle might still allow the appearance of continuous tone and lower noise in the output image. In general terms, more grey levels equals more discrete steps (e.g. a 16-bit image can represent 2^{16} or 65 536 levels) so rounding errors will be smaller, allowing multiple processes to be applied without resulting in so many image artefacts. Bit depth is related to, but is distinct from, dynamic range.

A further distinct advantage of having a higher bit depth is that it is possible to extend the effective dynamic range of an image. Dynamic range relates to the overall range of exposure that may be recorded, whereas bit depth relates to the number of separate levels that maybe coded within that range. This is one of the advantages of raw file formats, and why they allow the user to correct for white balance and small errors in exposure without losing details in highlights and shadows because of clipping.

1.16 File formats

DSLR cameras allow images to be saved in various file formats, most commonly JPEG (.JPG) (Joint Photographic Experts Group) and raw (the general term for proprietary raw formats although each has its own, e.g. Nikon's .NEF and Canon's .CR2). Other digital imaging devices, such as scanners, may allow images to be saved in a wider choice of file formats, some of which are more suited to desktop publishing and graphics applications than the photographic formats. In addition to JPEG and raw TIFF (.TIF) (Tagged Image File Format) is the most commonly used and JPEG2000 (.JP2) is useful in some situations.

1.17 Image compression

Image compression refers to the process of reducing file size by discarding data. *Lossless compression* means data are discarded with no loss of information, that is the pixel values of each and every pixel will be exactly the same after decompression as they were before compression. Lossless compression is achievable only at small compression ratios, typically up to 3:1. *Lossy compression* allows higher compression ratios; the higher the ratio, the more data that are discarded, with a subsequent loss of information, that is the pixel values of every pixel will not be the same after decompression as they were before compression.

At relatively low compression ratios, JPEG and JPEG2000 will produce images that are perceptibly identical to uncompressed images. In some cases, even high compression ratios can be achieved before any visible difference is perceptible. This may be extremely useful towards the end of an imaging chain, for example to save transmission time over a wireless network. In other instances this apparent strength is a major weakness. Consider a faintly fluorescing finger mark on a disruptive background. The resulting image may have low contrast, poor colour definition, high noise content and so forth. In such a case it is precisely the initially imperceptible differences that, for example, a 12-bit raw file will record, that may later be revealed by image processing. The raw image can be enhanced to a far greater extent to reveal far more information than if the image had been saved initially as a JPEG. It is a case of not being able to recover data once they are discarded. When, and why, data are discarded; and where, and why, in the imaging chain any particular file format is chosen, are issues that should be considered.

1.18   Image processing at image capture

This is something that is often overlooked but, just as with the choice of file format at image capture, decisions made at the capture stage can affect the content of the image and may limit the potential for image processing further along the chain. The single biggest choice is usually, JPEG or raw? I suggest you first familiarise yourself with the effects of any choices that can be made in, for example, the camera shooting menu. Examples of settings that can affect the appearance, and therefore the content, of resultant images include (but are not limited to):

- Image size: any setting other than the 'native resolution' (the number of pixels specified on the sensor) will involve some form of resampling.
- Image quality: there is usually a choice of 'low, medium, high' or similar, often with the option of 'raw' and often with the option of raw plus low, medium or high. The choice is between saving captured images at one of three levels of JPEG compression, or raw, or both. Choose one, or a combination, suitable for the task.
- White balance: as discussed previously, it is usually best to choose a pre-set to match the lighting conditions at the time of capture.
- Colour space: sRGB is designed for on screen work; Adobe RGB is designed for more demanding work and allows a wider gamut (range) of colours to be coded.
- Colour saturation: affects the appearance of colours; in most forensic work a 'neutral' setting is most appropriate.

- Sharpening: affects the crispness of edges, as explained earlier. For images that will undergo minimal further processing, some sharpening can be useful, but for marks photography I recommend switching it off.
- ISO setting: in simple terms it is a misconception that raising the ISO raises a camera's sensitivity to light. Unlike film, which is available in different types and is removable, a camera's sensor is integral to the camera. Raising the ISO setting means having to squeeze more image signal out of an otherwise underexposed image and therefore noise will also be amplified.
- Noise reduction (NR): there are often several options, maybe 'off/low/high' for both 'high ISO NR' and 'long exposure NR' and different methods are used in different instances and/or in different cameras. High ISO NR aims to reduce the effects of amplifying weak image signals. A common method to reduce noise associated with long exposures is for the camera to automatically take another exposure of the same length, but without opening the shutter, to obtain a blank reference image, which is then subtracted, in-camera, from the real image.
- 'Dynamic range optimisation', 'D-lighting', or similar: a way of producing, in-camera, an image that makes better use of the camera's dynamic range than 'standard' image capture. It can be very effective with dark or very contrasty subjects.

If shooting in any format other than raw, all user-chosen settings will be applied to the image at the point the file is first saved and cannot be undone

1.19   Properties of common formats

Raw: A 'raw' file is unprocessed or minimally processed data from the image sensor. A raw file format is proprietary to the manufacturer and the imaging system and may need to be converted to a non-proprietary format for viewing, editing, printing, and so on. Shooting in raw format allows most settings to be applied later, at the point of conversion from raw to another format. Indeed, raw files are essentially 'digital negatives': different versions can be derived from the same raw file, using different choices if desired, which is a distinct advantage. So long as the image file is not actually converted to a different file format using raw conversion software, the software does not change the actual image data, which is a further benefit of the format. Proprietary converters apply the manufacturer's decoding when opening raw files; non-proprietary converters may use a different decoding algorithm, resulting in an image with a different appearance. Similarly, no changes are made to the file when editing: editing information is carried in an associated but separate file, that is image data remain unchanged but the 'instructions' for how to display the data change. Raw files tend to have greater bit depth and greater dynamic range than other file formats.

TIFF: files are generally uncompressed, although the standard does allow for certain types of lossless compression. TIFF files may be either 8-bit or 16-bit. When a TIFF file is edited the image data are changed and, once saved, the changes cannot be undone.

JPEG: files are compressed using lossy compression, which may result in the loss of relevant information. Generally, JPEG files are 8-bit colour images, so any JPEG originating from a device with a higher bit depth will already be compressed by a reduction in dynamic range and bit depth. JPEG images may display characteristic 'blocking' artefacts as a result of the compression algorithm. There are 12-bit and 'lossless' options defined in the JPEG standard, however these not widely supported in products.

JPEG2000: is fundamentally different from JPEG. A different compression algorithm is employed, which has similarities to that of the Wavelet Scalar Quantisation (WSQ) file format, which was specifically designed for fingerprint images. JPEG2000 is considered suitable for some finger mark applications because it allows higher compression ratios with fewer perceptible artifacts than JPEG. JPEG2000 compression does not result in blocking artefacts.

Each file format has its strengths and weaknesses. None of the formats need necessarily be avoided but it is imperative that users are aware of the strengths and weaknesses of the common file formats. It is easily argued that in forensic contexts we should choose raw formats by default. After all, the camera captures the same initial image data whether we choose to save the image as raw or decide to throw away maybe 90% of the data, manipulate the remaining 10%, and save it as JPEG. The major drawbacks of raw relate to file handling and data storage. The IT systems of many agencies don't support raw file formats, nor do many software applications. A pragmatic solution may be to choose the 'high quality JPEG + raw' quality setting, save the raw files locally and use JPEGs for networked distribution.

Bear in mind that it is possible, and easy, to open an image file of one format in an image processing application such as Photoshop and save it in a different file format: don't assume that an image with the suffix .tif was always an uncompressed TIF! Once again, the exceptions are raw files, for reasons mentioned above.

1.20   Image archiving and the audit trail

Discussion of the pros and cons of the various file formats leads us on nicely to the subjects of archiving, image handling, and how to document image handling, including image processing.

1.20.1   Best practice and the audit trail

In the days before digital photography, things were much simpler. With black and white film we might note the development conditions; with colour film we used standardised, quality-controlled processes; all film was labelled in some way by the manufacturer and the image on the film was a physical entity. It was not necessary to keep detailed records because the processed film itself gave most of the clues one would need to ensure accurate reproduction. It is a very different story with digital photography. The proliferation of digital photographic devices and the nature of digital images mean we must pay very close attention to every detail of our digital workflow. Major considerations for forensic photography include traceability, reproducibility, authenticity and integrity.

Traceability: An *audit trail* should make it possible to trace any forensic photograph to a specific day, time, place; the individual who took the photograph; the camera with which the photograph was taken and many of the camera settings. The audit trail should be maintained from the time that the image is captured to the time it is transferred to the end user and is essential for evidential purposes. Digital cameras facilitate much of this by storing a lot of useful information in the metadata, such as the time at which the photo was taken, exposure settings, white balance and so on. Date and time data will only be reliable if the photographer ensures they are set correctly before photography. The audit trail should also include the method(s), conditions and equipment used to photograph the subject, including camera, lens, lighting, and the nature and order of any post-capture processing functions (including change in file format) that have been applied to the image. Image management: Must include assurance that the relevant data are not lost or otherwise compromised. For example, non-image data are not generally transferred to the hard copy when an image is printed.

Reproducibility: It should be possible for a similarly skilled practitioner to end up with similar results by following the audit trail. It should be possible to demonstrate that the working copy can be repeatably obtained from the master copy by following the audit trail and therefore accurate recording of these data is essential.

Authenticity: this should be established by the credentials of the organisation (police, forensic science institute), and individuals (police photographer, forensic scientist) and documented standard operating procedures (SOPs).

Integrity: ultimately, this is the responsibility of the individual photographer! With the best will in the world, any system is ultimately fallible to a determined, malicious individual.

Exactly how these things are achieved will vary between organisations. Some choose to have prescriptive documented SOPs, maybe allowing very little alteration of images. Some organisations may allow CSIs little control but allow specialist photographers a lot of control. Some organisations rely heavily on written audit trails, while some rely more on electronic systems. Whatever system you operate within, be sure to follow correct procedures and do not do anything to your images that you cannot explain and defend in court. SOPs ought to be written with authority, at least in part to protect lesser-skilled practitioners so that, for example, a non-specialist CSI can stand in court and state 'I was following procedures established by my organisation'. And then, if necessary, those who wrote the SOPs can be brought to court to explain things in more detail. There exist several publications, available on the web, which every photographer should be aware of. The prime reference is the Home Office Digital Imaging Procedure, the benchmark document, recognised around the world as best practice. It explains in detail how general workflow should be managed and documented. The essential points of the guidelines are:

- Every aspect of the process including photography, image processing, storage and archiving should be carried out by suitably trained and authorised operators.
- The audit trail must be established from the outset. This includes correctly setting the date and time on the camera (date and time data will be embedded within every image file as part of the metadata).
- After photography, transfer image files to permanent, read-only media at the earliest opportunity.[5]
- Protect the *original images* and work only on *working copies. Original images* must not be modified.
- Limit access to image files to authorised personnel only.

Terminology[6]

- *Primary Image*: digital photography is distinctly different from film photography. With the latter, the image is directly recorded onto the (removable) film, which is later processed and archived. With a digital camera the sensor remains in the camera and the digital image is first available when it is stored on a removable memory card or the computer's hard drive if the camera is tethered to, and controlled from, a computer. There will only be *one* primary image.
- *Master Image*: the authenticated, archived bit-for-bit copy of the primary image, for example, that which is on a signature-sealed CD, filed away. The master copy must not be capable of being modified or overwritten and is kept to act as a reference image if digital evidence is ultimately presented in court.

---

[5] This is a guideline to insure integrity. In practice many organisations have moved away from the use of CDs and DVDs and instead use secure servers. There are arguments for and against each method of storage.

[6] These definitions are based on the Home Office Digital Image Procedure and precise definitions may differ locally.

- *Original Image*: any bit-for-bit copy of the primary image. There may be any number of copies of the original image.
- *Working Copy*: this may be an exact copy or a modified copy of the original image. Any modifications should be documented in the audit trail. An advantage of using raw files is that this is produced automatically during processing and kept in a separate associated file.

1.21 Printing images

Consideration needs to be given to printing digital images, where necessary. For example, very few digital printers are able to reproduce finger mark images at 500 pixels per inch at a scale of 1:1, which is the requirement for input to the UK national database. The resolution of most printers is in the range 300–400 dots per inch, so printed images will exhibit a loss in image quality. Much higher dpi figures may be quoted, particularly by inkjet printer manufacturers, partly because different printing technologies require different numbers of dots to reproduce similar detail. Tests should be conducted using a selection of representative images to determine what detail is being lost with any printer and, therefore, the printer's suitability for the task.

1.22 Image storage

When storing images as permanent records, other considerations become important, such as the longevity of the image file format, the longevity of the medium on which it is stored, and the means of archiving images. It is here that raw formats may show their weakness, whilst more widely adopted formats, such as JPEGs, may be continue to be widely supported. It is anticipated that stored images will be reviewed after periods of time dictated by the nature of the crime and decisions made regarding their retention or disposal. These considerations are more fully covered in the Home Office Digital Imaging Procedure and the NPIA Police Use of Digital Evidence documents.

1.23 Summary

Where possible, the 'best' image should be obtained at the time of capture by use of appropriate lighting and camera settings. Image processing offers many possibilities for further enhancement but it must be seen as a complement to, rather than a replacement for, the skilled control of lighting. We've only covered some of the basics in this chapter. For example, we looked at simple blur filters for background suppression. More advanced tools, such as the Fast Fourier Transform, are available. Whilst basic enhancement functions may be applied by those with a basic knowledge of image processing, advanced processing functions should only be carried out by imaging specialists who are trained and competent in their use. Local SOPs should be drafted to adequately cover the roles and responsibilities of individuals, any processes employed, the documentation of processing, the style and format of the audit trail and so on. The Home Office's Digital Imaging Procedure is augmented by useful guidelines published by The Scientific Working Group on Imaging Technologies (SWGIT).

Many image processes are involved throughout the imaging chain, often as an automatic part of capture, display or output. Image processes often involve quite simple arithmetic operations on pixel values. Commonly, several different methods or orders of separate processes may be followed to achieve similar results. Understanding the methods can help in understanding the implications of their application and preventing unwanted quality loss. Artefacts may be produced as a result of processes, particularly when over-applied, and some processes are applied simply to correct for the artefacts produced by other processes!

I always end my discussions of image processing with the phrase, 'work backwards!', or maybe that should be 'think backwards!' The point is that because decisions made at each stage of the imaging chain have an impact on later stages, it is useful – if not essential – to consider your final output requirements BEFORE image capture (if possible): will you be able to meet your output requirements, and how will you do so? Consider what stages of the imaging chain you can control and if you can't control certain stages, what limits are imposed? And finally, beware (i.e. avoid!) capturing images which will be processed and analysed in JPEG format.

2
Cameras and Lenses

2.1 Overview

As we saw in Chapter 1, the world of photography is now almost exclusively digital, and for practicality and consistency within this book I have chosen to use the Digital Single Lens Reflex Camera (DSLR) as my point of reference. That is not to say that other types of cameras cannot be used, such as high-end compact cameras.[1] However, in the following chapters we will need to cover the use of a camera in many varied scenarios, which unfortunately means that compact cameras, or those with fixed non-interchangeable lenses, do not allow the full combination of accessories, functions or techniques to be undertaken. However, do not worry if we are not using the latest camera or kit. This book is, I hope, about thought processes and techniques, not the latest gizmos or adaptation.

Forensic photography is, to my mind, based around constructive thought processes, problem solving and occasionally inspiration, not the specific camera we hold in our hand.

I have to admit that in today's world technology is moving at such a pace that, by the time you read this chapter and regardless of all my best intentions, it will probably be out of date. I feel sure that within five years any cameras mentioned here now within this text will be as old and dusty a memory as the Kodak Box Brownie[2] and the Nikon F3[3] are today.

---

[1] Compact cameras are also referred to as point-and-shoot cameras. They generally contain a zoom lens and flash and tend to be fully automatic, but are still small enough to fit into a small pocket, hence the name.

[2] The box brownie was the first popular and mass produced camera, introduced by Eastman Kodak in 1900 at the cost of $1.

[3] Nikon F3 was introduced as a replacement for Nikon F and F2 in 1980. It was a very popular professional 35 mm camera. Designed by Giorgetto Giugiaro it was the first to have the now distinctive red strip, deviations of which are now indicative of the Nikon range.

Forensic Photography: A Practitioner's Guide, First Edition. Nick Marsh.
© 2014 John Wiley & Sons, Ltd. Published 2014 by John Wiley & Sons, Ltd.

Although the choice of camera can be important for some specific applications, as we shall see later, you do not need to have the top of the range kit in order to work professionally and accurately. My colleague, Nick Bishop, one of the best latent mark photographers that I know, can achieve the same results equally as well with a basic manual camera as with the most complicated Nikon D3. The important thing to remember is that the fundamental of capturing and recording light will remain the same no matter what camera you use.

That said, to have a true understanding of forensic photography one must have an understanding of how our equipment works, whether it is the camera, lenses or processing software. Once in court there are no excuses for an absence of understanding, indeed a whole trial could hinge on your level of knowledge or lack of it.

Before we look at cameras, however, now is probably a good time to make a comparison with our own vision system, the eye and brain, as opposed to what a camera might see or record.

Although I don't want to dwell on this, it is important that we have some basic understanding of the mechanics of both, as on face value both would appear to be very similar:

- The eye has a pupil the camera has an aperture.
- The eye has an iris the camera has a shutter.
- The eye has a retina the camera has a sensor.
- Both have lenses.
- The eye has a brain to process the image and the camera has image development software.

Unfortunately things are far more complicated than they might at first appear. Not only do we need to look at why our eyes work the way they do, but also how a camera sees light.

Our eyes are amazing instruments, as we look round a scene they are constantly changing as we focus or look at areas of highlights or shadow. All this is done without us giving any thought to the process, which means they are more akin to a video camera than a still one. I don't want to dwell too much on the mechanics of the eye, but we should address one or two issues

First is the issue of resolution and detail.

We have already seen that the camera's sensor is made up of light sensitive pixels, which are uniformly laid across the whole surface of the sensor, the colour being artificially created using a Bayer or mosaic filter. In the human eye the retina contains two distinct photoreceptors: the rod and cones. The rods are far more numerous, some 120 million, and are far more sensitive than the cones. However, they are not sensitive to colour. Colour vision is provided by the 6 to 7 million cones which are concentrated in a central area called the macula, at the centre of which there is a 0.3 mm, very densely packed, area called the fovea centralis.

It is currently accepted that these 6–7 million cones are divided into three groups as follows, approximately: 64% 'red' cones, 32% 'green' cones and 2% 'blue' cones. Even the distribution of the cones is uneven, with the red and green ones concentrated in the fovea centralis whilst the blue cones lie mostly in fovea.

The 120 million rods, on the other hand, have no sensitivity to colour but are more sensitive to light and are responsible for our dark adapted or scotopic vision.

Digital cameras tend to have a file size of between 5–20 megapixels, which is often said to be less than the human eye. This is based on the fact that a person with 20/20 vision is able to resolve detail equivalent to a 52 megapixel camera with a 60% field of view.

This, however, is misleading; as we saw above the rods and cones are not evenly distributed. This means that it is only our central portion of vision that can resolve at this resolution, the further we are from the centre, the more it dissolves. For example, if we look at the areas just 20% off-centre we can only resolve one-tenth as much detail and, at the edge, we can only detect large-scale contrast and colour. It could therefore be argued that our eyes can only perceive detail comparable to a 5–15 megapixel camera (depending on one's eyesight), but our eye is not seeing it pixel by pixel, it is seeing it as texture, colour and contrast. This means that it is effectively painting our perception of the image as our eyes look round a scene memorising the pertinent areas of interest.

There are a number of other advantages our eyes have in regards to resolution and detail, such as low light adaptation: when the illumination is moonlight or starlight our eyes automatically see in monochrome relying mainly on the rods, and the centre of our vision actually sees less than our slightly off-centre peripheral vision. This is why, when we are searching at scenes, we often see very faint but useful fluorescing marks in our peripheral vision rather than when we are looking straight ahead.

The other area where the eye wins hands down is in the dynamic range, it is estimated that under typical conditions our eye can see a dynamic range of 10–14 f-stops, compared to a DSLR, which has a range of 8–11 f-stops. This allows us to create a mental picture of a scene, balancing all the light levels within it within milliseconds.

Clearly, one area where the camera wins is in their variable sensitivity with regard to their ability to resolve faint or fast moving subjects. DSLR cameras can turn up their ISO sensitivity allowing high shutter speeds to be used, freezing movement. Conversely they can be lowered allowing long exposures, letting the image build up on the sensor, which the human eye cannot.

The second major factor is the angle of view.

With camera lenses, this is a pretty straightforward concept: the longer the focal length of the lens, the narrower the angle view (as we shall see later in the chapter). Our eye, technically, has a focal length of approximately 22 mm, but unfortunately this is misleading as:

- The back of our eye is curved.
- The periphery of our eye has progressively less detail than the centre.
- Any view we see is generated by using both eyes.

This means that each eye has a field of view, depending on the individual, of between 120–200°. This depends on how you define objects as being seen, with the overlap between the two eyes being around 130°, which is very close to a fisheye lens.

At these extreme angles, though, evolution has dictated that our peripheral vision can only see large objects or detect movement. If this field of view were captured with a stills camera it would produce a very distorted view of the world.

The central 30–40% of our field of view has the most impact on our perception, which is approximately equivalent to 50 mm lens on a full size 35 mm sensor. (To be absolute accurate it should be equivalent to a 43 mm lens, but industry has accepted 50 mm.) Although the 50 mm lens does not give the same field of view as the eye, it does replicate the perspective.

If our angle of view with the lens is too wide, the relative sizes of objects captured are exaggerated and objects near the edge of the frame become distorted. Conversely with a narrow field of view, such as a focal long lens, the opposite happens and similar objects lose their sense of depth. Our eye, on the other hand, has no issue with a wide and distorted view of the world, as our brain processes the image to make it distortion free.

The reality is that both systems operate to different standards, with our eyes relying on the brain to correct, interpret and feedback what they are seeing, whereas a digital camera can only see the raw data for what it is. It is important, therefore, to ensure it is recording exactly what you require. After all, when we look at a photographic print it is no longer 3D interpretation of the scene, but a flattened 2D one, so it needs to have focus, depth of field, colour balance and contrast if it is to look natural for our brains to interpret.

2.2   Cameras

For many years, cameras came in all shapes and sizes but the one consistency was that they all used standard size films. Also, because film was a light sensitive recording medium covered in grains of silver, it made sense that the larger the film format, the better the image you would capture. Within the Metropolitan Police, the standard scene-going camera from the 1950s was the 5 × 4

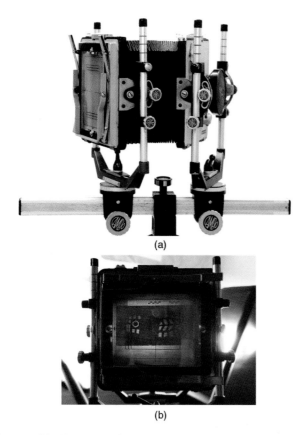

(a)

(b)

Figure 2.1 Photographic illustration of 'k'. (a) A Cambo 5 × 4 camera demonstrating the separate movement of the front lens panel and the rear film plane. (b) The image projected onto the rear ground glass focusing screen.

Cambo (Figure 2.1) and the MPP.[4] With the improvement in roll film, this changed to the Pentax 6 × 7 in the early 1970s, and later the Bronica 6 × 7.[5] These were still the mainstay, until their recent replacement with digital in around 2003 (35 mm[6] was reserved mainly for publicity and surveillance photography and for some types of fingerprint photography).

---

[4] The Cambo 5 × 4 is a monorail camera, first built in the Netherlands in 1947. It is referred to as a 5 × 4 because of the physical size of the film it: used 5 inches by 4 inches (102 mm by 127 mm). The MPP (Micro precision products) was a British copy of the Linhof Super Technika and was a compact 5 × 4 camera, where the lens and bellows folded back into its own body.

[5] The Asahi Pentax was first built in 1969 and looked and operated like an oversized 35 mm camera. The Bronica (first introduced in 1982), on the other hand, looked and operated like a medium format camera and could be used at either waist level or with an AE head at eye level. Both use a negative which is 6 cm by 7 cm hence 6 × 7 in the names.

[6] 35 mm film was first introduced in 1892 for use in both still and motion pictures, it get its name from being cut into strips about 1 3/8 inches wide or 35 mm wide.

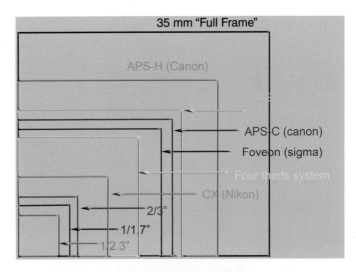

Figure 2.2   Illustration of sensor sizes. Note, even with APS there are differences in size between manufactures.

For practicality's sake, this meant that once you had invested in a camera system it would last for years, indeed we had a Nikon F3 on a copy set that was there for over 15 years.

So, if I know I need a DSLR, can I just go out and purchase one? Unfortunately it is still not that simple, we need to look at another set of factors that may control our choice of camera. These are the sensor size, sharpness and acutance; they are important as they are the factors which help to govern the image quality.

Although we looked at image size in terms of megabytes in the previous chapter, we have not yet looked at the sensor's physical size. Does it matter?

Most manufacturers produce sensors that are smaller than traditional 35 mm film and are often referred to as APS-C (Advanced Photo System-Classic) or DX sensors; this is in reference to a film size created in 1996 which became very popular with certain manufacturers in pocket cameras. It is 25.1 mm × 16.7 mm as compared to 35 mm film, which is 36 mm × 24 mm (Figure 2.2). This would not be an issue, apart from the fact that Canon and Nikon also have full size sensors – referred to as FX sensors – in their range of cameras, allowing the sensor to be bigger and faster. The issue for us, as we will see when we look at lenses, is that the size of the sensor directly alters the standard lens's focal length.

Resolution, as the name suggests, is related to the camera's overall (sensor, lenses, image processing software etc.) ability to resolve information. While acutance refers to the lens's ability to render the sharp edge of an object as a sharp edge in the photograph. In reality it is referring to the clear and defined edge of one object in relation to another.

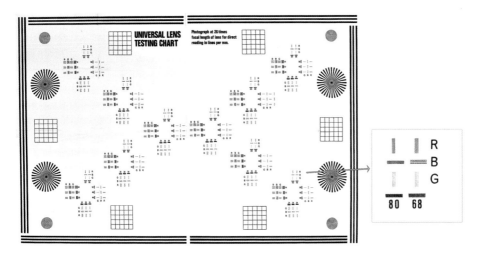

Figure 2.3 An old style lens resolution chart produced in the 1980s taken on a Nikkor 105 mm macro lens. On the right you can see an enlargement showing 60 and 80 line pairs.

This is normally tested using a resolution chart (Figure 2.3). These charts contain black and white line pairs, which become increasingly thinner and closer together. When the camera system can no longer separate the line pairs, they will become less distinct and show as grey.

These charts come in a variety of forms and can be used to make any comparison you require between cameras and lenses.[7]

Every month there seems to be a new camera being launched; as I write the long awaited Nikon D800 and D4[8] and the Sigma SD1[9] have just arrived. Each claims to offer greater resolution pixel count, HD video and new multipoint metering modes or colour resolution.

At the end of the day, however, they are all designed to undertake one function: that of capturing a set amount of light, or 'exposure', in order to reproduce an image. No matter how clever the camera appears, this function remains the same.

2.3 Exposure

So what is the correct exposure? According to the *OED*[10] exposure is the quantity of light reaching a photographic film, as determined by shutter speed and lens aperture.

---

[7] For examples try http://www.aig-imaging.com/mm5/merchant.mvc or www.graphics.cornell.edu/westin/misc/res-chart.html

[8] www.nikon.co.uk

[9] www.sigma-imaging-uk.com

[10] Oxford dictionaries: http://oxforddictionaries.com/definition/exposure

To enable us to achieve the above, we need to look at three distinct functions: ISOs, apertures and shutter speeds, which are often referred to as the exposure triangle. This is because the adjusting of any one value affects the other two, which we shall look at in a moment.

With today's sophisticated camera technology, the correct exposure is now almost taken for granted by most amateur camera users, regardless of lighting conditions. But to achieve it, you must delegate some, if not all, of your technical responsibility to the camera. Depending on its software brain and the mode it is set in, it will choose to alter one of these three factors, the aperture, shutter speed, or the ISO. Hence the numerous functions buttons seen on most cameras (Figure 2.4). Each function mode will make exposure

Figure 2.4   The common camera mode settings available on most digital cameras.
Auto: The camera automatically adjusts all the settings to produce the optimal results.
Portrait mode: Shoots portraits with the background in soft focus using large apertures, it also changes the colour balance to give natural looking skin tone. Landscape mode: Enhances colour balance to enhance the scene, switches of built-in flash and auto-assist focus.
Close up mode (macro): The camera automatically focuses on the subject in the centre focus area. Small apertures are used with slow shutter speed; the use of a tripod is recommended.
Sports mode: High shutter speeds, automatically switches off the flash and auto focus-assist light.
Night landscape mode: Uses slow shutter speed and increased colour saturation and ISOs; a tripod is recommended.
Night portrait mode: Balances background illumination with fill-in flash in the foreground. Can increase colour saturation and ISOs.
Manual: Allows the user to select any ISO, aperture or shutter speed. Aperture priority: Allows the operator to select the required aperture whilst the camera adjusts the shutter speeds.
Shutter speed priority: Allows the operator to select the shutter speed, whilst the camera adjusts the aperture.
Program: Similar to auto, where the camera controls the shutter speed and aperture whilst the user can control other settings.

compensations that are preferable for that type of photography. So, for example, if you choose the 'running man' symbol, the emphasis will be on the camera ensuring a high shutter speed at the expense of the aperture. Or, conversely, if you chose the 'A' setting for aperture priority, it will change the shutter speeds to compensate. There is always a trade-off: the forensic photographer, however, needs to have an understanding of this and use it to their advantage.

As this is not an instruction book on general photography, I am not going to go into depth on the camera functions. For those of you who already know about them, it would be a waste of valuable space, and for those that have had their curiosity engaged, there are plenty of web sites and books that are far better at explaining this than me. I am, however, going to give what I hope will be enough information to get us going.

2.4 ISOs

I remember once being in a well known electronics shop and overhearing the assistant replying to a customer enquiry with 'ISO, I'm not sure but, I think it's got something to do with the flash'; clearly an assistant who was never going to be a photographer. For the forensic photographer, the control and understanding of ISO is important in achieving accurate end results, whether it's in surveillance or scene photography.

So what does ISO mean? If we look back at film, its sensitivity was measured by the 'ASA' American Standards Association or '*Din*' Deutsches Institutfür Normung number. Now all digital camera manufacturers have adopted 'International Organization for Standardization', or ISO, from the Greek word 'isos' meaning equal.[11]

In simplistic terms, the ISO is a measure of the camera sensor's sensitivity to a given amount of light.

The exposure value, or EV, is a photographic scale for the amount of light that passes through the lens and hits the sensor. The exposure value is a combination of both the aperture and shutter speed and is an absolute exposure value. The ISO defines EV 0, at an aperture size of 1 and 1 second of exposure time, based on a film sensitivity of 100 ISO.[12]

The same correct exposure can be achieved with other pairs of numbers like f1.4 and 2 seconds. By closing the aperture to f1.4, the area of the aperture hole is halved, so by doubling the exposure time, you let the same amount of light through.

The use of EV has become unfashionable due to the use of automatic light meters. However, nearly all DSLR's still have an EV adjustment setting often displayed as $-/-/0/+/++$ EV.

---

[11] http://www.iso.org/iso/home.html
[12] http://www.ansi.org. BS ISO12232:2006 – Determination of exposure index, ISO speed rating, standard output sensitivity and recommended exposure index.

A practical example of correct exposure was traditionally expressed as taking a photograph at 100 ASA, at 1/125 s at f16, on a bright sunny day, giving you a correctly exposed image. Although this scenario can still be used, I have foud that most digital cameras have a response nearer to 200 ASA.

Most digital cameras have the ability to adjust the ISO from around 100 to 1600, although in professional DSLRs, this may be considerably higher.

The lower the ISO number, the slower the sensor's response to light; the higher the ISO number, the faster the sensor's response to light, thus each doubling in ISO setting doubles its response to any given amount of light.

So, if we take our example above and increased the ISO to 200, our new exposure would now be either 1/250 s at f16, if we change the shutter speed, or 1/125 s at f32 if we change the aperture, but we still get the same end exposure.

Digital cameras have now far exceeded the limited response of film, with the Nikon D4 achieving an ISO of 204 800 on its H4 setting.

As in all things, however, there is a trade-off: as traditional film speeds increased and thus became more light sensitive, they produced visible grain. This was because the silver halides needed to be bigger to respond more quickly to the light. So it is with digital, but in this case the grain is replaced by electronic noise, which is generally seen in the shadow areas (see Chapter 1).

2.5   The shutter

All cameras have to have a system for stopping or allowing the light to reach the sensor of film plane. In its simplest form on a pinhole camera the shutter is merely removing black tape from over the hole and leaving it for a few hours before replacing it; basic but it worked. Today's cameras are fitted with focal plane shutters; this means the shutter is fitted directly in front of the focal plane of the sensor or film.

There are two distinct types, the vertical-travel and the two-curtain shutter. The two 'curtain' shutter, as the name suggests, uses two curtains made from an opaque rubberised fabric. When the exposure is made, the first curtain moves across the film plane revealing the sensor, generally from right to left. After the desired shutter speed has passed, the second curtain travels in the same direction as the first, covering the sensor back up. Faster shutter speeds are achieved by closing the second curtain before the first one is fully open; this creates a vertical slit that travels horizontally across the sensor or film. When the exposure is completed, the shutters are rewound back to their start positions, ready to fire again.

Most modern DSLRs, however, use the vertical-travel shutter. These work in the exactly the same way as the curtain shutter, but instead of a rubberised horizontal moving curtain, as above, they use vertical moving metal blades. This means that the distance that the shutter blades physically move is reduced from 36 mm to 24 mm, as they can travel across the focal plane in a much faster time. This means that not only can they reach speeds of 1/8000th of a second, but also can achieve higher flash sync speeds typically to around 1/250th of a second.

The shutter speed refers to the amount of time the shutter is open to allow light to hit the camera sensor. Thus, a 1 second exposure will open the shutter for 1 second and 1/125 will open the shutter for just 1/125th of a second.

On the film cameras of the past, the shutter speed differences were in one stop increments (see f-stops below): Bulb, 1 s, 1/2 s, 1/4 s, 1/8 s, 1/15 s, 1/30 s, 1/60 s, 1/125 s, 1/250 s, 1/500 s, 1/1000 s, 1/2000 s. However, most digital cameras now have a far greater choice of shutter control. My Nikon D80[13] has a range going from:

Bulb*, 30, 20, 15, 10, 8, 6, 4, 3, 2, 1.5, 1, 3/4, $^1/_2$, 1/3, 1/4, 1/6, 1/8, 1/10, 1/15, 1/20, 1/30, 1/45, 1/60, 1/90, 1/125, 1/180, 1/250, 1/350, 1/500, 1/750, 1/1000, 1/5000, 1/2000, 1/3000, 1/4000 s. (The term bulb is still used to refer to when the shutter is held open by the photographer for long exposures. This is believed to have originated from the use of pneumatically actuated shutter releases when squeezing an air 'bulb' that would fire the shutter. Although these were later generally replaced in by metal cable releases, the term has remained. Many older cameras still have a screw thread in the shutter release button to accept a bulb or cable release. Indeed they were still standard issue with our Pentax 6 × 7 kits. However, nearly all digital cameras now require an electronic release system, the use of which is to be encouraged.)

2.6   F-stops and apertures

In photography f-stops are used as a unit to quantify ratios of light or exposure, with a 'stop'* meaning a factor of two, or one half. One-stop is also known as the Exposure Value or (EV) and each stop is marked on a ring around the lens, with its corresponding f-number.

Within any lens there is a diaphragm: this is a set of blades connected to the ring, which restricts the light passing through it. As the f-number above is selected, the blades open or close, forming a circular opening, to let more or less light through. (The term 'stop' comes from early days of photography, where instead of a using an adjustable aperture, cameras used wooden panels with holes drilled through them to adjust the light levels; these panel literally stopped light.)

The 'aperture' is the physical size of the opening. When the aperture is increased in size it is often referred to as 'opening up' and when decreasing the aperture size, it is referred to as 'stopping down' (Figure 2.5).

---

[13] The D80 was launched in 2006 as a replacement for the D50.

Nikkor 50 mm 1.8 lens

Figure 2.5   A Nikkor 50 mm 1.8 lens with the diaphragm in various aperture settings. Note that opening or closing the lens by one stop will double or halve the light passing through the lens. For example, changing the aperture from f8 to f5.6 will let twice the amount of light in, whereas changing it from f8 to f11 will halve the light passing through the lens.

The f-stop in reality is a fraction of the focal length of the lenses being used and relates to the size of the aperture opening. Modern lenses use an f-stop scale, which is based on a geometric sequence of the powers of the square root of 2, which are rounded off to produce: f1, f1.4, f2, f2.8, f4, f5.6, f8, f11, f16, f22, f32, f45, f64, f90, f128, f245, and so on; they are in reality fractions, so f4 is really 1/4.

This can be expressed as:

Focal length of the lens ÷ The f-stop selection = Diameter of diaphragm

or

Focal length of the lens ÷ Diameter of diaphragm = f-stop

F-stops can cause some confusion with new photographers, as an apparently larger number, such as f45, represents a smaller aperture, whilst a smaller number such as f2 creates a large one. Therefore, I find it useful to always remember that the f-stop is a fraction, it is easy to understand that f45 is not a large number, but a 1/45th fraction of the focal length of the lens, whilst f2 is not small but represents $\frac{1}{2}$ the focal length.

For example, a 100 mm focal length lens with an aperture of f8, will have a pupil diameter of 12.5 mm. On a 200 mm focal length lens, the pupil diameter would be 25 mm, but both would produce the same luminance in the focal plane when imaging an object of a given luminance.

The important factor here is that, just like shutter speed, opening or closing the aperture (changing the f-stop) halves or doubles the light entering the lens to the sensor. Although, on the face of it, f-stops do not appear as numbers that can be doubled or halved, we will explore this further when we look at the inverse square law.

2.7 So what is the correct exposure?

There are some complicated scientific equations we can carry out, but for prac-ticality at a scene the correct exposure is generally when the image looks nor-mal, neither too light nor too dark, with details in both the highlights and the shadows. This can be seen visually and reviewed on the LCD monitor on the camera, or more accurately by looking at the cameras histogram (see Chap-ter 1). To some extent, though, it really does depend on what you are pho-tographing, some subjects require that they are overexposed (given too much light) or underexposed (not given enough light), such as fluorescing latent marks or luminal, rather than the exposure indicated in the camera meter, as we will see later.

As said above, photographers traditionally talk of exposure in 'stops' with the correct or optimal exposure being '0'. This can be observed when you look through the viewfinder at the exposure meter in most DSLR cameras (see exposure values).

When the camera is activated it detects the light hitting the sensor plane and gives a reading, indicating over- or underexposure; by adjusting the aperture or shutter it should be possible to get that reading to zero.

So, for example, if our given exposure reading is 1/30 s at f16, but I make the exposure at 1/30 s at f22, I would have exposed it at −1 stop, or 'one stop underexposed'. Conversely, if I change my exposure to 1/30 s at f8 I would now be + 1 on the exposure, so I would be 'one stop overexposed'. This is often a generalisation harking back to film, as many digital cameras have almost fluid aperture controls making quarter or half stop adjustments possible.

With experience you will soon find that just by looking at an image on the camera screen, or its histogram, it is possible to see a half stop under- or over-exposure. The important rule is the more accurate the exposure, the less time you will have to spend in post-production. This is particularly important if you are shooting jpegs and not RAW or TIFF files (see chapter on image quality).

Ok, so we now hopefully have an overview and understanding of the expo-sure triangle, but how do we work out how much light there is in the first place? For that we need some form of light meter.

2.8   Metering modes

Correct exposure can be measured in a number of ways, either in the camera or through external devices. Although all digital cameras have advanced metering systems, they rely on the light being reflected back from the subject. But what do they use as a standard?

In college I was taught that this was based on the fact that, in a 'normal' scene, taking into account all the variances of colour shade and light, an average scene will reflect 18% of the light falling on it. Any photographer will tell you this can then be represented by an 18% grey card; this logically is a card that reflects 18% of the light hitting it. In reality, not many people carry around a grey card with them when out on a shoot. With experience you can meter off other surfaces, for example green grass is also around 18% reflective, along with many road surfaces. Depending on your skin tone, you can meter off your hand, mine is conveniently around 36% reflective, which would produce a 1 stop underexposure, that is more light than is required. So I would need to open up 1 stop. However, in researching this book, it was brought to my attention that in fact I had been working for the past 20 years under false guidance. The origins of the grey card are in fact shrouded in mystery. In the 1941 Kodak reference handbook, it recommends using the 'yellow' paper packet to determine exposures for kodachrome. To quote from the handbook

An Eastman photographic paper envelope should be put in front of the subject, facing the camera. A reading is made by holding the meter close to the envelope without shading it. For average subjects the indicated exposure should be doubled.

It is a reasonable substitute for an incident light reading where exposure is keyed to the highlights. But, in reality, it appears to just be there for the photographer to take a light reading without being influenced by the colour of the subject.

I have also since found out that Nikon meters are actually working to the American National Standards Institute (ANSI) standard which uses a luminance value of 12% as a guide. But I still find 18% a good ballpark figure.

2.8.1   Measuring the light

There are a number of ways in which you can take this all important meter reading and, as we will see below, each will have its own advantages and disadvantages. If possible, however, I would still encourage you to have in your kit bag a hand held incident light meter for those critical exposure problems.

2.8.2   Camera meters

Matrix meters: here multiple light reading are taken in a grid across the viewfinder, the camera's on board computer assesses the light falling on it and then adjusts for what it perceives as the correct exposure. This is good for general scene work and covers many scenarios.

Centre-weighted: because the area of interest is normally to be found in the centre of the image, this area is sometimes defined in the viewfinder as a circle. The camera will assess the light falling in the centre of the sensor and make an exposure based on this reading. This is good for ensuring the main area of interest is correctly exposed.

Spot metering: here the exposure is worked out based on the very centre of the viewfinder; this is useful for when a critical exposure is required, such as a fluorescing mark, where you would want to meter for the mark but not the darkened background.

2.8.3   Incident light meters

For a more accurate exposure, many professionals will use an incident light meter, off camera. Incident light meters measure the light falling on the target; this is a far more accurate way of recording the light values and is why professional photographers are often seen with using handheld light meters. The incident light meter is held over the target and the exposure is read on the display and then transferred to the camera. This is often seen at weddings, where a white dress can throw centre-weighted metering off balance, causing underexposure of the scene. This is a particularly useful technique where the photographer is placing lights to illuminate an exhibit, or where multiple studio or flash units are used.

2.9   Getting the right exposure

Most cameras have the ability to operate in three main exposure modes, manual, aperture priority and shutter priority.

Manual: allows the forensic photographer to independently choose, in any combination, the required ISO, shutter speed and aperture, and allows complete control over the exposure.

Aperture priority: in this mode, you choose the f-stop the camera is to use. To achieve correct exposure the camera will change the shutter speeds. This is no problem on a bright sunny day, but in shadows or when photographing an interior shutter speed will fall. This can create two issues; firstly, you may not be able to hold the camera without causing camera shake. Secondly, anything moving within the area of interest may have motion blur. Both these issues can be rectified quite simply by the use of a tripod (of which I will say more later) and supplementary lighting such as electronic flash. A tripod will offer a solid camera platform and also has a secondary function, meaning you don't have to put the camera down in the blood-stained crime scene. Electronic flash will not only give a bright source of illumination but, because its burst is so short, it will freeze any movement within the scene.

Shutter priority: in this mode you choose the shutter speed that the camera will use. To ensure correct exposure the camera will change the f-stop. This means that you can safely set a shutter speed which you know you can physically hold still, say 1/60th. However, the trade-off here is that your depth of field may suffer. Again, in bright daylight this won't be an issue, but in shadows, or inside, you may find that you have no depth of field. This can be rectified as above by firstly using a tripod or secondly by the use of electronic flash.

As we saw above, many cameras have lots of other modes, such as Program, Close up, Action, Landscapes and so on. I would strongly advise against using these modes for forensic applications, as it is important for you to make the right exposure choice, balanced against what is going to be sacrificed in terms depth of field, shutter speed, or noise if we increase the ISO. Also, many of these programs add extra digital enhancements, such as sharpening and colour saturation, which may not be desirable or forensically sound in our finished image.

2.10   Dynamic range

All recording mediums, be it film or digital, have a limited dynamic range. This is the range of luminosity that can be reproduced accurately. This can be seen when highlights are rendered as white and shadows as just black with no detail. The loss of shadow detail is not abrupt with film or with a digital sensor. But highlight burn out on digital sensors can be very abrupt and highlight detail can be lost. This can lead to a gross hue or saturation shift, as the colours saturate in turn (see Chapter 1).

Most DSLR cameras allow the blown highlight areas to be seen on the image review screen, normally as a flashing area allowing you to adjust your exposure accordingly. The Fuji sensor deals with this situation in a different way by allocating the extra photodiodes: the so-called 'R' pixel. This is of a lower sensitivity and retains detail in the highlights.

This leads on to another technique which is used and has some dramatic effects, that of HDRI (high dynamic range imaging). Rather than trying to capture the scene in one shot using one exposure, here a number of exposure are taken across a broad range, normally around four stops under and four stops over, these images are then merged using software such as picturenaut[14]

---

[14] http://www.hdrlabs.com/picturenaut

and this allows the highlight in the underexposed images to be merged with the overexposed shadow areas from another image to create a perfectly exposed image or to boost images to create a new effect.

This is not commonly used in the forensics arena; however, it has the ability to be very useful in some situations, such as a dark arson scene with large windows and strong sunlight. Provided a proper audit trail is in place, it should not dissuade an operator from using it.

Above and in the previous chapter we looked at the basics in camera functions and at achieving the right exposure. But this only gives you part of the picture, so to speak, as there is no point in having a correctly exposed image if it appears that is out of focus or lacks depth of field, and much of this is reliant on the lenses we are going to use.

2.11   Depth of field and focus

So what is depth of field?

Before we look at the focusing techniques, it's important to have an understanding around another factor that is highly important to attaining a perception of a sharp image, that of depth of field (DOF)

Simply put, it is the distance between the nearest and the farthest objects within the image that look sharp and are in focus. The objective in nearly all forensic photography is to ensure that the whole area of a photograph is as sharp as possible.

There are three factors that affect DOF, the f-stop the lens is set to, the choice of lens and the camera-to subject distance.

The general guideline is the smaller the aperture the greater the depth of field.

For example, if we consider the normal lens with an f-stop range of f3.5 to f22, the DOF will increase as we stop down from f3.5 to f22 (Figure 2.6).

Examples:
It is possible to calculate the depth of field using the near focus distance and the far focus distance

$$NF = (HF \times D)/(HF + (D\text{-}L))$$
$$FF = (HF \times D)/(HF\text{-}(D\text{-}L))$$
$$DOF = FF\text{-}NF$$

Where

NF = is the near focus limit (mm)
FF = is the far focus limit (mm)
HF = is the hyperfocal distance
D is the focused distance of the lens in mm
L is the focal length of the lens

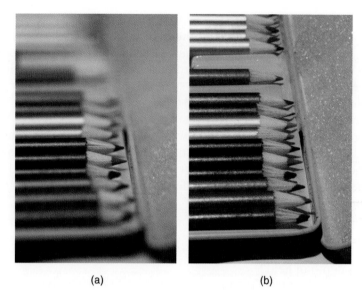

(a)   (b)

Figure 2.6   shows the use of the aperture to control the depth of field. (a) The aperture wide open at f2.8. (b) The aperture closed to f22.

For those of you who own an Apple iPhone, there is a download available at Apple iTunes which makes it all very easy.[15]

Another way to remember the relationship between the aperture and the depth of field is to visualise it as a ball of plasticine, as we can see in Figure 2.7. This ball represents the set amount of light required for our given exposure. If we flatten the ball out it makes a disk with a larger diameter, but it is thin. This represents a large aperture producing a shallow depth of field. If, however, we roll the same ball into a long sausage shape we get a small diameter. This represents a small aperture, with an increased depth of field.

Control over the f-stops on the camera is critical for the forensic photographer as it is possible to maximise or minimise the depth of field, but does lens choice affect my depth of field?

The answer is yes, DOF is a function of the focal length of the lens being used; the rule of thumb being, the shorter the focal length the greater the DOF with any given f-stop. Figure 2.9 shows the relationship between the focal length and the DOF.

All f/stops have a relationship to the focal length of the lens if:

- FFL equals the focal length of the lens,
- f-stop is the particular f-stop, and
- DOD is the diameter of the diaphragm inside the lens

---

[15] http://itunes.apple.com/app/dofwizard

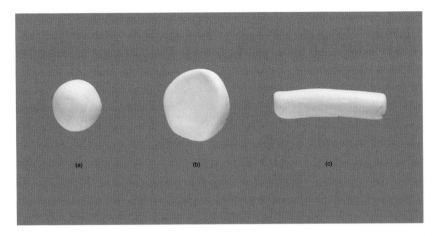

Figure 2.7   (a) Our set amount of light represented by a ball of plasticine. (b) The plasticine flattened to produce a large flat disk, representing a large aperture but shallow depth of field. (c) The plastic rolled into a sausage shape, representing a small aperture and large depth of field.

Which can written as FFL / f-stop = DOD

- The diameter of the diaphragm can be calculated by dividing the FFL by the f-stop.
- The f-stop can be calculated by dividing the FFL by the size of the lens opening.
- The FFL is a calculated by multiplying the f-stop number and the size of the lens opening.

So a 24 mm lens at F16 =1.5 mm
A 200 mm lens at F16 = 12.5 mm

So the next question is: what else affects the DOF?

2.11.1   Lens choice

Clearly the choice of f stop has a relationship to the focal length of the lens as it can be expressed as the equation.

The focal length of the lens divided by the f/stop number gives the diameter of the diaphragm or lens opening

It can also be expressed as the focal length of the lens divided by the diameter of the diaphragm = f/stop.

The diameter of the diaphragm can be determined by dividing the focal length by the f/stop.

The f/stop can be derived from dividing the focal length by the size of the lens opening.

The focal length is achieved multiplying the f/stop and the size of the lens opening.

In practicality if we look at depth of field as a function of our lens choice we would see that the shorter the focal length of the lens the greater the depth of field.

2.11.2   Distance to the subject

I must at this point make a comment around a perception that has sprung up that digital cameras, especially pocket cameras, have greater depth of field than the equivalent 35 mm focal length lenses. In reality the shorter the focal length the greater the depth of field at any given fixed f-stop still holds true. So, if the sensor is 1/4 the size of 35 mm film, through a lens that is correspondingly 1/4 the focal length, the depth of field increases 4 times from a comparison of image's perspective.

2.11.3   The rule of thirds

This is the way that I subconsciousl deal with DOF issues. You may have noticed in the previous examples that the DOF is not split evenly behind and in front of the plane of focus. Often it is given as a rule of thumb that DOF extends two-thirds behind the focus plan and one-third in front of the focal plane. However this is actually incorrect, if you look at the hyperfocal focusing (below) you can see that the DOF range behind the actual point of focus is more than double the DOF field range in front of it. This is also true of zone focusing when the background is at a distance of 9 m or beyond, where it works out at a 1/6 to 5/6 ratio. If, however, the distance is between 1.5 m and 6 m then the ratio does work.

When working at distances of less than a metre the ratio approaches half and half, so care must be given when undertaking critical work which requires a good depth of field.

The other scenario in which the rule doesn't work is if you are using a microscope, here the rule almost reverses, with two-thirds in front of the plane of focus and one-third behind.

You will have noticed in all the illustrations I have been using small apertures f32, f22, f16. This is ok on a fine, sunny day, but not so easy on dark, wintery days in central London. However this a good time to mention the 'T' word again; although no longer fashionable, the tripod does offer us a stable platform that allows us to slow the shutter speed down, so we can achieve f22 without any problem.

2.11.4   Focus

When I started learning scientific and technical photography back in the 1980s, the standard camera we used at college was an old Cambo 5 × 4. Here there was no option but to focus the lens by hand racking the lens panel backwards or forwards. This was a time consuming event, which involved putting a black cloth over your head and using a magnifying loop on the fresnel focusing screen (see Figure 2.1). It may have taken time, but there were a number of lessons to be learnt, including that just getting the point of interest sharp isn't the only consideration when focusing.

With today's cameras, there is a tendency to rely on the auto focus settings on camera: after all the manufacturers have spent many hours of research to ensure that they function correctly. Yet, why is it that I see so many photographs that are out of focus or have no depth of field?

It is useful for the forensic photographer to have an understanding of the principles of manual focusing, depth of field, pre-focusing, hyperfocal focusing and finally zone focusing.

Many cameras have complex matrix focusing systems or even face recognition, and that's great for parties and holiday snaps. But the problem tends to be that they focus just on that, the main point of interest. This in itself is not a problem and can be very useful, but for the forensic photographer this isn't always appropriate. For example, I have seen a number of examples of photographs taken at large arson scenes, where the scene is pitch black.

In these situations auto focus may or may not work, even if the camera has a focus-assist light or is infrared guided. Often the camera will lock onto an object in the middle of the field of view, such as a fallen beam or chair. Unfortunately, linked to auto exposure, using a wide aperture means that there is no depth of field and the actual seat of fire is out of focus. The other good example is photographing a finger mark on glass, particularly at scene. Auto focus just doesn't have clue, but you will get some nice images of the backgrounds! (See Figure 7.21 in finger and shoe mark photography.)

Before we look at focus, we need to have an understanding of what the perception of focus is. You will often hear photographers saying how sharp an image is in reference to focus, but this relies on the resolution and acutance of both the lens and camera sensor.

Resolution What do we actually mean when we talk of resolution?

Resolution is the ability of the camera lens and software to resolve an image; this is normally tested using alternate black and white line pairs and is traditionally measured using a resolution chart.

The line pairs get progressively thinner and closer together, eventually they will become less distinct and will blur into grey. It is this ability to distinguish the fine detail that gives a camera its line pair resolution.

Using a resolution chart is a good way to compare different lenses, particularly between zoom lenses and prime lenses and camera bodies.

I feel at this juncture I should say that there is no point in comparing film with digital. We must be practical and not sentimental about this, even if some people still claim that film has the greater resolution, we are in reality never going to return to it.

There is no question that all of today's digital cameras have sufficient quality to capture a general scene, but for the forensic photographer the question we need to ask of the digital camera is: does it provide sufficient resolution to accurately allow the capture and subsequent representation of finger, shoe, tyre and injury marks?

Acutance   Above we saw that resolution is measured by how small a detail the digital sensor can measure, but with acutance we need to look at the lowest tone a lens can resolve. For example, a lens with a high resolution may resolve lots of detail but if it, or the sensor, has low acutance this may be seen as a flattening of the tone curve, giving a muddy or flat look; in effect acutance is the edge contrast of an image.

To some extent acutance can and is increased by using an un-sharp mask, here we increase the brightness between adjacent areas. The size of this increase is proportional to the existing differences. For example, a completely uniform area will not be affected at all. But an area of high contrast will be affected the most. To determine this effect it looks at three parameters: the amount, radius and threshold. The amount is by how much the un-sharp changes the contrast. The radius looks at how far from each pixel to make the adjustment. Finally, the threshold looks at how much difference to make any change at all. Therefore each picture will be changed in a unique and specific way. As long as the detail was captured, that is the tonal difference was above the minimum that the system can record, it can be enhanced. However, overuse of the un-sharp mask will cause sharpening halos, aliasing or other unwanted side effects (see previous chapter on digital workflow).

2.11.5   Manual focus

There are only a few occasions that my lenses are not set to manual focus, the photography of finger, shoe and latent evidence is often done in low lighting conditions or under adverse conditions, which often cause issues for the auto focus. I also like to control the region of focus in the images I take. Interestingly, if you ask a colleague to look through the camera, I will guarantee that they will inevitably and subconsciously refocus the lens.

Focus is generally carried out by looking through the viewfinder and turning the focusing ring until the area of interest is sharp and clear. This works equally well with prime focus lenses (a prime lens is photographic lens whose focal length is fixed) or when using a zoom lens (a lens with a variable focal length). It is worth noting that if you are having difficulty focusing on the area of interest, that if you focus at the maximum zoom magnification, (giving greater clarity of the area of interest) then zoom back to your desired viewing angle, the area of interest will stay in focus without the need to readjust.

There are, however, some very useful variants on manual focusing which the photographer can use to their advantage for difficult situations or in particular applications.

Pre-focus Pre-focus is handy for undertaking photography where image size ratios might need to be controlled, for example in fingerprint or injury photography. Here the lens will be set to the required setting, say its 1:1 mark, and presented to the mark. Instead of focusing using the lens, the camera is moved backwards and forwards until the image is sharp. If this is on a copy type set up, multiple marks can be photographed all at exactly the same scaling. I also use this technique for victim photography when doing the reference and cross-polarised photography. The lens is kept at the same position and I will physically move backwards and forwards until the image is sharp. Again, this ensures that the two shots are at identical magnification for comparison.

Another example is at an arson scene, where it may be too dark to see when the area of interest is in focus, which has been very useful on a number of occasions. Here the distance to the area of interest can be set using the markings on the lens barrel. Saying that, it is worth noting here, that, unfortunately, many new digital lenses don't have these markings, making this technique impossible.

Hyperfocal distance The hyperfocal distance is the closest point at which a lens can be focused whilst keeping objects at infinity acceptably sharp. In other words, the focus distance with the maximum depth of field. If the lens is focused at this distance, all objects from half the hyperfocal distance to infinity will be acceptably sharp.

This sounds a mouthful, so what do we actually mean? Clearly, at a crime scene it is our responsibility to ensure that we are able to see as much as possible, sharp and in focus. Hyperfocal distance is about maximising our depth of field when the background is deemed to be infinity, as shown on the lens barrel represented as '∞' (the lemniscate symbol '∞' is used to indicate infinity on all lenses).

If you look Figure 2.8 you will see a 70–210 mm zoom lens and around the lens barrel are two rows of numbers indicating the distance in feet and metres. You will also notice that as you turn the focus left to right the numbers appear to get closer together until you get to infinity ∞. Interestingly, as far as the lens is concerned, infinity is no more than 20–30 metres away.

Hyperfocal distance is useful in three categories of scenario:

- Large scenes where infinity is the backdrop, a park or open space.
- Scenes where infinity is not the backdrop, like a view across the road looking towards a building,
- Close ups of exhibits, like a knife on the pavement.

If our primary concern is the need to get infinity in focus, you may be tempted to focus on infinity. But all that means in reality is that infinity is in focus, and there is no guarantee for the rest of the field of view. If you look at Figure 2.8 again, you will see that just below the distance markings on the barrel itself is another set of numbers on either side of the focusing point. These indicate the

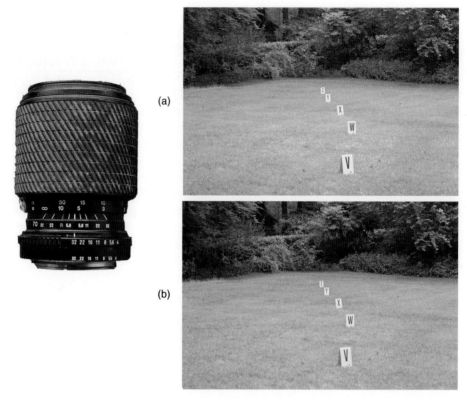

Figure 2.8   An example of hyperfocal distance. (a) Focused using the hyperfocal distance (note that all the letters are acceptably in focus). (b) Focused on infinity, although the letters Z, Y and X are acceptably sharp, W and V are both soft.

depth of field scale (DOF scale).This scale is really useful, but unfortunately not all lenses are now marked in this way.

As we saw above, the DOF is a scale which allows us to work out the depth of field (i.e. the area which is in focus) with any given aperture at any given distance. Don't forget though that when looking through the camera you will only see one point of focus.

If you look at Figure 2.8, you will see a zoom lens set to 80 mm. If you look at the depth of field indicator on the lens and read off the distances you will see that at

- f32 DOF will go from approximately 3 m to ∞ image (a)
- f22 DOF will go from 4 m to 30 m
- f5.6 DOF will go from 5 m to 8 m.

To get the hyperfocal distance to work to our advantage, we now need to know what aperture you will be shooting at. Let's say it's a bright sunny day and we can use f32. Now rotate the focus so the ∞ symbol lines up with your chosen aperture marking, in this case f32 (as seen in Figure 2.8). You will see that you should have from infinity (∞) to 3 m in focus.

If we had focused on infinity, you would get from infinity to only approximately 7 m in focus. This process can be repeated for any other aperture, say f11. If the lens was focused at infinity it would give us a depth of focus from approximately 20 m to infinity. But if the ∞ is positioned at f11, it would give a depth of focus from 8 m to infinity: an extra 12 metres of depth of field.

It is therefore important, when using this technique, to switch the camera to manual focus. If you do not the camera will determine the area of focus, and if it is looking across an area of open space, this will probably end up as infinity: the very issue we are trying to avoid.

So, as you can see, there are a number of ways of using DOF to our advantage but only by using the hyperfocal distance will we ensure that infinity is in focus. By using the hyperfocal distance we have also maximised our depth of field focus and our depth of field.

I said before that not all lenses are now marked with DOF scales, yet clearly for the forensic photographer it is imperative that we can use this to our advantage. If your lens doesn't have a DOF scale it is still possible to use the rule because lens construction is now so uniform.

$$\text{Hyperfocal distance} = \frac{\text{focal length} \times \text{focal length}}{\text{Circle of confusion} \times \text{f-stop}}$$

The focal length will be different in each case, if you are using a zoom lens the focal length can be read off the lens barrel.

As for the 'circle of confusion', for our purposes you need to know that this constant differs depending on the camera you are using and the acceptable sharpness on a 10 × 8 print viewed at a normal viewing distance. For a digital DX SLR this is around 0.02 and for 35 mm, or for an FX DSLR it is around 0.03.

The f-stop will be your chosen aperture, generally around f16 or f22. (Many landscape photographers prefer to shoot wider at f11 as the lens gives less diffraction, but this will depend on the lens you are using.)

Using the above formula we can work out the hyperfocal distance for any given lens aperture, so let's say we are photographing a road traffic accident with infinity as the backdrop. Our choice of lens will be a 50 mm to ensure that the perspective is correct and we will choose f11 because it is slightly overcast.

$$\text{Hyperfocal distance} = \frac{50\,\text{mm} \times 50\,\text{mm} = 2500}{0.03 \times 110.33\,\text{mm}} = 7.5757\,\text{mm}$$

Therefore the hyperfocal distance will be 7.5 m.

Table 2.1   Quick guide for a FX DSL.

f-stop	Focal length				
	24 mm	35 mm	50 mm	75 mm	100 mm
f2.8	6.8 m	14.6 m	29.8 m	67 m	119 m
f4	4.8 mm	10.2 m	20.8 m	46.8 m	83.3 m
f5.6	3.6 m	7.6 m	15.6 m	35 m	62.5 m
f8	2.4 m	5 m	10.4 m	23.4 m	41.7 m
f11	1.7 m	3.7 m	7.5 m	17 m	30.3 m
f16	1.2 m	2.5 m	5.2 m	11.7 m	20.8 m
f22	0.87 m	1.8 m	3.7 m	8.5 m	15.1 m

Now you need to focus on an object at this distance, or set the lens to that distance. Everything from this focusing point (the hyperfocal distance) and halfway between this point and the camera will be sharp.

Although this a bit of a chore to undertake each time, once you have calculated these distances you can keep them handy and apply them when required.

Below I have created a quick guide for a FX DSL (Table 2.1).

You will see that the shorter the focal length the greater the hyperfocal distance that is achievable using a known aperture. This relationship between the sensor size, aperture and focal length of lens also explains why the hyperfocal distance on compact cameras is so good. Even though I have supplied the above table, you may notice on many modern lenses that the focus distance indicators often go from around 3 m straight into infinity. This means that, provided you are stopped down, you will by default end up with the maximum hyperfocal distance, provided you do not focus on an area closer than the maximum known distance listed on the lens, or on infinity.

Zone focusing   As described in Scenario 'b' above, these are scenes where infinity is not the backdrop, say a view across the road looking towards a building. Often it is just an area that needs highlighting, so how do you ensure DOF is correct when infinity is not an issue?

Again we need to determine the f-stop required by taking an exposure reading. We then need to ascertain what in the background of our photograph is normally the point furthest away.

With zone focusing it is necessary to know the distance to the background object. Use the lens to focus manually on this object and note the distance down. If there is no obvious back marker to your composition, use the area at the top of your frame and measure that distance. Now swing the camera up so that this area is now in the middle of the frame and focus. (If you are using a zoom lens you can zoom in to check your focus.) Then look at your depth of field scale again. Set the distance we just measured to the top of the frame and set it to the f-stop you intend to use. You will now see that at f-22 the range

Figure 2.9 In this example of zone focusing we can see that the markers are in focus but infinity is not. (In this case infinity is indicated by the tree line.)

will be from 3.5 m to 20 m. Now simply recompose your image so the bottom of the field of view matches the closest DOF number. This is a good way of maximising the DOF when infinity is not in view (Figure 2.9).

Clearly, situations will arise when you cannot ensure the whole scene is covered by the DOF, but this at least ensures that the main areas are. Aesthetically it is better for the DOF to drift out at the top of the frame rather than the bottom, so if you are using this technique always ensure that nothing is in frame that is nearer that the closest DOF for that aperture.

Again, as I have said above, many lenses do not have comprehensive distances marked on them. In these cases, apply the smallest aperture you can and use the rule of thirds as a guide. Always check the review screen to ensure that the key area of interest is in focus; if it is not, adjust your focus point.

Camera to subject distance We have already discussed that we can achieve a pretty good depth of field using our hyperfocal distance or through zone focusing, but what happens when we are asked to undertake macro photography of a small exhibit? Can we use our depth of field guide? I am afraid

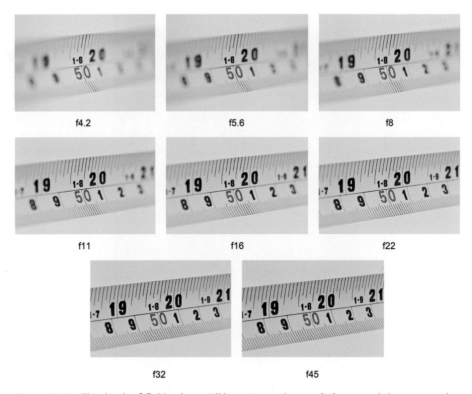

f4.2   f5.6   f8

f11   f16   f22

f32   f45

Figure 2.10   The depth of field using a Nikkor 105 mm lens as it is stopped down, note that the angle of the scale is approximately 45° to the camera.

the answer is no. The closer we get to the object, the smaller our depth of field range becomes (Figure 2.10). Because the DOF is so small, it is actually better to focus partially into an object rather than focus on its surface, for example.

Always try and use the smallest 'optimum' aperture available to optimise the DOF, this may require the use of a tripod, adjusting the shutter speed or ISO, or using auxiliary lighting. This will be dependent on your lens, but remember the smallest aperture marked on the lens is not always the sharpest when working in macro, so it is worth checking the manufacturer's guidance for the optimum aperture.

There is a depth of field preview button located on the front of many DSLR cameras. When depressed this closes the diaphragm to the selected aperture, allowing you to see if the depth of field is correct. However, when this is used at anything over about f11 so much light is lost that you can't see if the image is in focus or not! I can't remember the last time I actually used this. It is easier to take a test shot and check the preview screen.

Auto focus (AF)   As I have explained already, auto focus just didn't really exist when I studied photography, it was all manual. Now nearly all DSLRs have some form of auto focus controlled by the camera. Some use motors within the lens, others use a mechanical link to the body of the camera. Some cameras have a fixed auto focus point indicated in the middle of the viewfinder (check your camera manual) others allow the selection of the focus point. On my D80, any one of nine points can be selected.

There are number of different types of auto focus techniques used to perform the focusing split into two groups, Active AF is where ultrasound or infrared is used to measre the distance and this is then used to triangulate the distance. In Passive AF, focus is achieved through passive analysis of the image entering the optical system, these generally use phase detection, as used in the Nikon D2x, and contrast detection, which is generally used video cameras.

There is no doubt that auto focusing has come a long way since its inception. In most cases it is now faster than hand–eye coordination can work. There have even been systems that track where the human eye is looking in the viewfinder and focus on that position. Or can track an allocated target, like a footballer, and keep them in constant focus; even I may be converted in the long run.

So how do you know if the AF is having trouble with your scene? Generally you will hear or feel the lenses continuously racking back and forth looking for something to lock onto. This is often the case with large areas of mono-tone colour, like interior walls. There are a couple of options if this happens. You can focus on another object at roughly the same distance away and then push the AF lock button if you have one (some cameras will do this by half depressing the shutter button, this will lock focus at that position and will not refocus until the button is released) or you can switch to manual. As stated above, it may also fail in low light, or where you have a strongly backlit scene, which may confuse the camera. Where you have a near and far object very close together near the centre of the viewfinder, again the AF will struggle to separate them.

There is nothing wrong with the forensic photographer using auto focus, as long as you know when and where to use it.

2.12 Lenses

As I commented at the start of the chapter, the issue around sensor sizes also has a direct effect on our choice of lenses. The advent of the APS-C sized sensor now means that any 35 mm or FX full frame lens used on a DX sensor will create a cropping effect, as it will change the field of view, in effect adding a magnification factor; in other words a FX lens will acquire a longer focal length than it states on the barrel (Figure 2.11).

Nikon and Sony have a 1.5 multiplier ratio on their sensors. Cannon has 1.6. So a FX50 mm lens would become equivalent to 75 mm on the Nikon and Sony and 80 mm on a Canon DX camera, and a FX200 mm telephoto would become a 300 mm on the Nikon and Sony and a 320 mm on the Canon.

Figure 2.11   A 300 mm lens fitted in (a) to a FX sensor and in (b) to a DX sensor, increasing its focal length to 450 mm.

As can be seen, this can have some benefits, which can and are exploited, such as in surveillance or wildlife photography. Here the shorter light telephoto lenses can be used rather than the longer heavier ones further up the range.

However, for the wider angles, it becomes harder to use FX lenses, as even a 24 mm would be roughly equivalent to a 35 mm. Hence many departments have a mix of both FX and DX lenses on their shelves.

Although most FX lenses can be used on DX cameras, the converse is not true as the coverage of DX lenses is generally not sufficient to cover the sensor fully, causing vingnetting (Figure 2.12). This is where the coverage of the

Figure 2.12 An 18 mm to 135 mm DX lens, set to 18 mm, fitted to a FX sensor. Here we can see severe vingnetting around the edge of the image, where the coverage of the lens was not sufficient to cover the whole of the sensor surface. This effect can also sometimes be seen to a lesser effect when wide-angle lenses are fitted with lens hoods.

light passing through the lens is not sufficient to cover the whole of the sensor surface.

There is now a lens for nearly every focal length, with over 50 lenses in both the Canon and Nikon ranges, split into DX and FX types, with every application catered for, plus a vast number from independent manufacturers.

So what directs our choice of lens and why pick one over another?

2.12.1 Focal lengths

All lenses are quoted by their focal length. The focal length being the distance between the optical centre of the lens and the sensor, when the camera is focused at infinity ∞.

It is important to note here that some older lenses change their physical size, as they focus on closer subjects (hence why they are measured when focused at ∞) but in newer digital lenses only the internal optics move without any exterior changes.

Lenses are also often referred to as fast or slow, this is not referring to the speed of focus of the lens, but the maximum aperture available, which in turn affects the maximum shutter speed. As we have seen above, the larger the volume of light available the faster the shutter speed you can use. For standard lenses (see below) f2 is deemed the critical point. If it is wider than that say f1.8, it is deemed to be a fast lens. These fast lenses are, however, more expensive and need not generally concern the forensic photographer, as we are more concerned about controlling depth of field rather than requiring faster shutter speeds.

Lenses fall within two main groups: prime focal length lenses and zoom lens. As the name suggests, prime lenses are those of a fixed focal lengths. Prime lenses tend to be of a superior optical quality and are usually faster (larger maximum aperture) they also tend to be sharper with fewer aberrations and distortions due to the limited movement and number of the internal lenses. This is particularly true of Macro designated lenses that are designed to work close up in the macro or near macro regions (these are lens designed to capture at a ratio of at least 1:1).

Zoom lenses, as the name suggests, are able to cover a variety of focal lengths, offering the photographer flexibility at a scene. For example, on my work D800 I have a 24mm to 70mm for general scene work which allows me to undertake close up and wide angle work without having to carry around a number of lenses. The downside of this flexibility is that they are generally slower than a prime lens (smaller maximum aperture) and heavier, which means that slower shutter speed or higher ISO will be required.

I should say here that optical zoom, which we have just discussed, and digital zoom should not be confused. With optical zoom the elements of the lenses move position to produce a new focal length, filling the sensor. In digital zoom the camera crops the images to a smaller size, to make it appear as if it was taken on a telephoto. This is in fact limiting the number of pixels used to capture the image, inevitably leading to image degradation, and should not be used.

However, this general advantage of prime lenses over zoom lenses has been largely removed as optic design and digital technology and digital enhancing software have advanced.

You will notice that in most photographers' kits there is a variety of lenses covering all eventualities. Press and sports photographers would tend to have longer focal lengths, as against the forensic photographer who will probably have a macro to mid-range selection.

So, why not just have one lens to cover all the range? Nikon make an 18–200 mm which would make a good all round lens, but sacrifices have to be made. As mentioned above, for normal crime scene photographs the 18–70 mm zoom is excellent, but I would not use it for the 1:1 reproduction of shoe marks, as it has unacceptable barrel distortion when used. I would swap to a prime 60 mm macro lens. So what actual difference does the focal length of the lens make?

The focal length dictates the lens's field of view. Simply put, the shorter the focal length, the wider the field of view. If we were to use the Nikon fish eye lens, so called because it looks like a fish, it gives 180 degree field of view. This would make everything within image seem further away. If, however, we were to use a 1200 mm lens, we would only have approximately a 2° field of view. This would act like a telescope and would magnify the area of interest to fill the frame. A 50 mm lens on a full frame camera would have an angle of view of 47° (Figure 2.13).

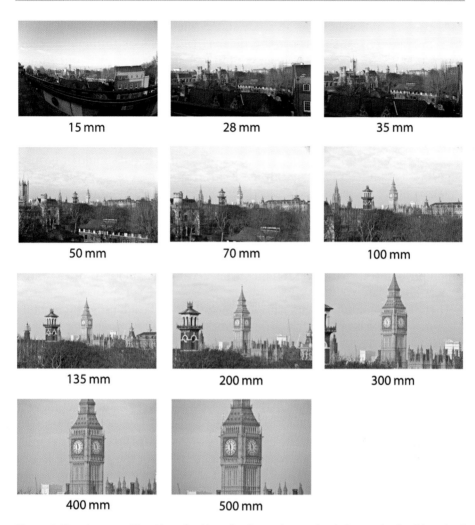

Figure 2.13 A range of focal lengths. Note the decreasing angle of view as the focal length of the lens is increased.

Lenses are also split in a couple of sub groups, that are referred to as standard lenses, wide angle lenses and telephoto lenses, plus there are a number of specialist lenses.

Standard lenses: knowing the correct standard lens for the camera you are using is vital, particularly in the forensic arena. In photography, a lens is a lens that reproduces perspective that generally looks 'natural' to a human observer under normal viewing conditions, as compared with lenses with longer or shorter focal lengths, which produce an expanded or contracted field of view.

A word of caution here: as all ready stated, the standard lens changes with the size of the recording sensor. This means that if we look through the camera and then look back at the scene nothing should appear different from a perspective point of view and items should still appear to be the same relative distance away from each other.

A I explained when talking about sensors, the traditional 35 mm standard lens was accepted as being 50 mm. This was based on the diagonal distance across the film negative, which was 24 mm × 36 mm. Technically, the Pythagoras theory of the hypotenuse of a triangle would tell us that it should be 43 mm, but camera manufacturers have always used 50 mm. This theory holds true for any size sensor, but as we saw earlier the DX sensor is only two-thirds the size of a full FX sensor or 35 mm film.

So, for example, the standard lens on my D80 with its DX sensor is 30–35 mm. The drawback with the standard lens is that although they give true perspective, they actually have a limited field of view of around 47°. So what happens when you need a wider field of view? You can either move backwards or swap to a wide angle lens.

There are a number of scenarios in which the standard lens is crucial in its use, one of which is fatal road accidents where you wish to record the scene of the accident as accurately as possible. The use of a wide or telephoto lens in this scenario would throw perspective out, making objects nearer or further away than they really are.

Wide angle lenses: these lenses have a shorter focal length than the standard lens. If you use these lenses you will notice a wider field of view, elongation of foreground to background distances and an increased depth of field. These are useful for interiors and allow the capture of a wider area in fewer photographs. The advantage is they can increase your depth of field, the downside is you can only normally get away with using up to around a 28 mm in a scene before barrel distortion (this is the bowing outwards of vertical lines at the edge of the image) becomes unacceptable.

Telephoto lenses: these are lenses with a focal length longer than the standard, they are often referred to as short telephotos, 85 mm, 105 mm and 150 mm, and long telephoto lenses of 200 mm and above. This magnification can be worked out by dividing the focal length by 50 mm (the standard) so a 100 mm would be equivalent to 2x magnification, a 400 mm would equate to 8x magnification and a 1200 mm would equate to 24× magnification. This allows items or people at distance to be magnified to fill the frame. The clear application for the forensic photographer is in surveillance work. The advantage is greater magnification of the target, the disadvantages are the narrower field of view, compression of background distances and shallower depth of field range. The other downside is that the longer focal lengths are heavy and require the use of high ISOs and shutter speeds.

Macro lenses: for small items such as a finger mark, some form of magnification is required to allow us to see the minutiae of bifurcations and ridge endings. You could be tempted just to use a 50 mm standard lens, which has a minimum focusing distance of anything between 80 and 300 mm. You could then try enlarging and cropping the final image on the computer, but that would give you an image only using about 1/7 of the sensor. Macro lenses are configured to focus at close distances and enable the viewfinder frame to be filled, if required, at 1:1. These types of lenses are invaluable for nearly all types of forensic work, but most importantly for finger, shoe and tool marks.

They are also available in varying focal lengths for various aspects of work, they are the 60 mm f2.8 GEDAF-S Micro Nikkor, the 105 mm f2.8 AF-S VR micro Nikkor and the 200 mm f4 ED-IF AF micro Nikkor. In the Canon range they have a 50 mm EF f2.5, 60 mm EF-S f2.8, 100 mm EF f2.8, 180 mm EF f3.5 and the MP-E65 f2.8 1.5x macro (often called extreme macro) which allows images greater than 1:1 to be captured. There are also a number of other camera companies and independent lens manufacturers. Of course, these lenses come at a cost, with the Nikkor 105 mm retailing at over £550 and Canon's Mp-E65 retailing at over £600. Many departments cannot equip all their staff, so is there a cheaper alternative?

Extension tubes: these work by moving the optical centres of primary lenses further from the film plane resulting, in magnification of the image. They are available in various thicknesses allowing different degrees of magnification and they can be stacked together. Because they contain no optical elements and are, in fact, just a spacer, you can purchase them relatively cheaply off the internet. For example the Kenko AEXTUBEEDGN DG AF Extension tube set 12-20-36 mm for Canon is approximately £100.

Extension tubes do have a number of drawbacks: because they are using the minimum focus distance to operate they produce a fairly narrow focus zone, they also reduce the depth of field – although this can be compensated for by stopping down. They tend to lose light through the system, so adjustments to exposure will be required. They also cannot be used on all lenses, particularly some wide angle ones, where the focus zone has moved in so close that the front glass element on the lens actually prevents you from getting close enough.

Bellows: as an alternative to using fixed extension tubes to create space between the optical centre of the film plane and the sensor, you can use a set of bellows. This allows a variable magnification to be achieved. Bellows originated from large format cameras where the front element was mounted on a moving rail and attached to the film plane with a light shield or bellows (Figure 2.14). This allowed the lens to be moved backward and forwards. Using bellows allows precise fine focusing, but they can be fiddly to use and are best fitted to a tripod. Again, there is a loss of light so compensation will be required to the exposure.

Close up filters and lenses: these are supplementary filters which can be screwed directly onto the front of the lens and allow magnifications of around

Figure 2.14   A set of manual bellows fitted to a macro Nikkor 60 mm lens.

1:6 to 1:2 depending on the manufacturer. They are normally designated $+1$, $+2$ and $+4$ and can be stacked in any combination.

From experience I would suggest always stacking the higher value closest to the lens and never using the three together as the image quality deteriorates. I would strongly suggest that for a forensic application they are only used as a last resort in an emergency situation.

Teleconverters: teleconverters are a handy tool if you only have limited room in your camera kit. These are generally fitted between the camera body and the lens. By the introduction of this secondary set of lenses the primary focal lengths can be increased. For example, fitting a 2x teleconverter to a 100 mm lens would be the equivalent of fitting a 200 mm lens. Fitted to a 200 mm would give you 400 mm, and so on. If this was then fitted to a DX sensor this could be stretched to 500 mm. The downside is that one or two stops may be lost in light absorption within the lens structure.

Shift lenses or perspective control lenses: these are specialist lenses that can be used to control perspective. The commonest application would be for the control of converging verticals, particularly where a wide angle lens has been used. You will notice that the top of the buildings seem to be coming together. These lenses allow the correction of that in camera, rather than relying on post-production software. They do this by allowing the front element to rise and fall and to tilt left and right.

Fisheye lenses: these lenses are extreme wide angle, the Nikkor 16 mm fisheye lens captures a 180° field of view. You may think that these haven't got a place within the forensic photographer's armory. Especially as they cost over

£500. But in fact the fisheye is crucial for the undertaking of immersive or 360° imaging, as we shall see later in the book.

In the past, Nikon made to order a 6 mm fisheye lens that had a field of view that was 220°: 40% wider than the 16 mm, which means it can actually see behind itself! In researching this book I came across a secondhand one on e-bay for $34 020 or a mere £21 000 at today's rate.

One last comment on lenses, you may have noticed that they now seem to have numerous codes on the barrels, not all of which are obvious.

- DX or FX: refers to the format of the camera sensor. FX is the full size 35 mm sensor and DX is the smaller digital format.
- VR: vibration reduction, this is designed to reduce vibrations that may cause blurred images if the camera is used at a slow shutter speed (my 105 mm macro employs this function).
- SWM: silent wave motor; Nikon's AF-S lenses employ this technology and it provides a fluid quiet focus.
- ED: extra low dispersion; Nikon developed this lens coating for its glass to provide precise colour correction, reducing chromatic aberrations.
- IF: internal focusing, this means that the lens barrel length does not change and focusing is done by internal moving of the lens groups.
- The number under the barrel of the lens refers to the diameter of the filter screw thread required for that lens.
- AF-S: an auto focus lens with integrated silent wave focusing. Some older bodies can't auto focus with them (N60, N8008). Some newer bodies (D40, D40x) can only auto focus with them.
- 18–135 mm indicates the focal length of the lens.
- 3.5–5.6: this is important as it shows the maximum apertures available across the lens. So, for the above 18–135 mm, the maximum at 18 mm may be 3.5 and at 135 it is 5.6. So it is worth checking before purchase that you have a lens which is fast enough for your requirements. Bear in mind that as the speed of the lens increases, so does the price.
- G: denotes that there is no aperture ring.

Lenses with VR (vibration reduction) and IS (image stabilisation): many of the lenses now being made use either VR or IS, often called 'anti-shake'. To accomplish this, the lens elements electronically move as the camera detects movement. This can be useful when hand-holding a telephoto lens where you cannot use a shutter speed reciprocal to that of the focal length of the lens. So, for a 500 mm you would need a shutter speed of at least 1/500th of a second. This may be difficult to achieve in low light, when undertaking surveillance for example. Conversely, you may just want to use a longer shutter speed for a proper exposure and so increase your chances of camera shake. Most VR lenses will eliminate blurring of up to around two stops slower than the correct exposure, but only when the movement is small and controlled.

I would suggest, if you find yourself in either of the above scenarios, increasing the ISO to compensate or using a tripod.

As an aside, and just to confuse issues, you should not use VR when the camera is mounted on a tripod; this is because they use pitch and yaw sensors to detect motion which is then fed to a couple of 'VoiceCoil' motors. These motors then react proportionally to the signal from the sensor. The VR sensors, however, work on a transducer principle, in that they actually cause the lens elements to move slightly in order to observe the feedback.

Important note: if the camera is on a tripod the lens oscillates, but doesn't move, thus causing its own blur. Therefore this function must be switched off when used in this mode.

Lens quality   Before I leave cameras and lenses, I need to just touch on the issue of optical lens quality. I am not going to go into any depth here, as there are plenty of books and web pages dedicated to these issues. For us, however, there are three main issues, that of aberrations, diffraction and distortion. Although you may not be able to control these, you should have an understanding of what they are and their causes.

When I was at college, the rule of thumb was that if you wanted to get the most from your lens, never use the two widest or the two smallest apertures. There was certainly some sense to this in early lens design, but today many original issues have been eliminated or reduced to being unobtrusive. Habits die hard though, and I still avoid the widest and smallest apertures on the lens if possible. Other lens problems include:

Aberrations or defects are when the lens fails to bring the light waves passing through the lens to a precise focus point on the sensor. The result is usually a softness of the image or loss of clarity. This comes in a couple of different forms.

Chromatic aberrations: these are caused by the wavelengths of red, green and blue light passing through the lens focusing at different points rather than coming together at one point. Blue focuses at the shortest distance and red the longest, and this produces a softness of the image, sometimes with a noticeable colour fringe. Longitudinal aberrations are caused by the light passing directly though on the lens axis and lateral aberrations involve the light coming in from the sides of the lens. Both cause the light to bend and refract to different degrees.

Spherical aberrations occur when the light refracted through the centre or edges of the lens elements does not focus at the same point. This causes the image to be in focus in different areas, producing a soft and slightly out of focus image.

Curvature of field: this is when areas perpendicular to the lens axis focus on a curved surface rather than a plane.

Astigmatism: this is when ray of light from a single point, which is not on the lens axis, fails to meet at a point causing it to appear as two sharp lines, one radial to the optical axis and one perpendicular to it near to the curvature of field.[16]

Coma: this effect is caused by single point of light coming from an off axis focused on different areas of the film plane, often appearing as a shaped blur.

Most modern lenses have almost eliminated the above problems for general usage, but they can still happen in certain circumstances. Wide apertures generally exacerbate most of the effects of the above, so stopping the lens down can reduce the risk.

Diffraction To some extent you could write a whole chapter around this subject. For us, in practice, diffraction occurs when light strikes an edge and the effect is loss of sharpness and clarity within the image. When the light travelling through the lens meets the aperture it begins to disperse or 'diffract'. Normally this is negligible, but with very small apertures, say to create a good depth of field, this creates a loss of resolution and sharpness and a general loss of clarity across the image. For forensic photography of critical evidence I would recommend that an f-stop of no more than f-16 should be considered. Although you may think that f-22 would give more depth of field, the effects of diffraction through the lens will outweigh this. The effects of diffraction are diminishing with each lens generation produced and will be different, depending on the lens in use. If you look at Figure 2.11 you will see that even at f45 the effects are minimal. So I would advise the undertaking of some simple lens tests to see which apertures are ok.[17]

> ## Case study: Re An Armed Robbery in Central London
>
> Some years ago, I was asked to attend an address in central London to record a witness viewpoint. The witness stated that they had stood in the bay window of their flat and observed two men in a car approximately 6–8 metres away transferring a blue bag from the back to the front. The bay window was slightly above ground level and was about 3 metres back from the pavement. The glass was clean and had an unimpeded view of the road, particularly of where the witness said the car had stopped.
>
> After discussing where the witness had stood, I prepared my equipment, in this case a Bronica 6 × 7 camera fitted with the standard 105 mm F3.5 Mc lens. This I placed on a tripod at approximately the head height of the witness. I then took a panorama of shots showing the view.
>
> Because the trial was already at court, I rushed the negatives back to our processing unit and had the images made into 10 × 8 albums, which I then delivered to the court. The next day, I received a call from the officer asking

---

[16] For a good in depth explanation see http://toothwalker.org/optics/astigmatism.html

[17] http://www.cambridgeincolour.com/tutorials/diffraction-photography.htm

me to attend the Old Bailey[18] immediately along with my negatives taken the previous day.

On arriving, the negatives were removed from me and I was directed straight into the witness box. After the formalities, I was asked to explain to the court what equipment I had used. I then explained the above scenario and equipment.

I was then shown an album of photographs taken by the defence's photographic expert. These had been taken from the same viewpoint that I had taken mine. But the perspective was wrong and was much wider than it should have been. This meant that any vehicle parked in the street now looked very small and any detail within the said vehicle would be almost impossible to see.

I was then asked by the defence to comment on what I could see, I explained that the perspective in the defence photographs was incorrect and did not match the human eye. The defence said this was irrelevant and their photographs had been taken correctly. The defence then claimed the reason mine were so clear was that I had used a telephoto lens. At this point he brought out *Langford's Basic Photography* [1].

He told the court, that I was using a 105 mm lens, which according to Langford's is a telephoto lens, when in fact I should have been using a 50 mm lens, and thus I had exaggerated the viewpoint of the witness by enlarging the field of view, and that in effect I was trying to mislead the court.

On answering, I explained that what he had stated was true, but only with regards to using 35 mm camera format, based on the diagonal across the film plane equalling 43 mm, but in reality 50 mm is historically the accepted focal length. But as already stated, I was using a 6 × 7 negative, the standard lens for which is around 90 mm but 105 mm is acceptable, thus mine in fact showed an accepted photographic representation of true perspective.

When I asked for my album and tried to continue on to talk about the defence images, the defence council cut me off. He said that what I thought of the artistic merits of the defence's photographs was irrelevant. Again I tried to say that in fact this point was crucial to the court's understanding and he again said that he was not interested in my thoughts. It was at this point that I noticed a note being taken from the chairman of the jury to the judge. The defence said he had no more questions and said I could leave the box. However the judge at this point intervened, explaining that the jury would like to know why I was so persistent in trying to explain the relevance of what a particular lens could have on the defence images they had been given.

---

[18]London's Central Criminal Court, named after the street in which it stands.

I was then able to explain about perspective and how we perceive it, the correct standard lenses for film formats and, most importantly, I was able to demonstrate that the defence photographs had all been taken using a very wide angle lens, probably a 24 mm or wider. Hence the barrel distortion of a tree at the edge of the frame and how, by using that lens, any vehicle in the road would seem to be in the distance. The judge thanked me for the explanation my thoughts and said that he was sure that the jury would take full note of them.

The two defendants were later found guilty of armed robbery.

The point to this story is that we never know what will be presented at court. The defence experts are not bound by the same rules by which we must adhere. It is after all their job to cast doubt into the minds of the jurors. If, in this case, the defence photographs had been allowed to stand unchallenged, the eye witness's evidence would have been viewed as weak, or even made up, which could have completely undermined the case.

Reference

(1) Sawdon Smith, R., Langford, M., Fox, A. and Sawdon Smith, R. *Langford's Basic Photography* 9 edn (2010) Oxford: Focal Press (Taylor and Francis).

3
The Use of Flash

Nearly every task we undertake as forensic photographers will require us at some stage to replace or increase the existing ambient lighting with a supplementary one. This can be for numerous reasons, overall low light levels within a scene, areas of shadow detail, or to increase our depth of field. The use of electronic flash offers a solution to many of these issues, providing a portable bright, daylight balanced light that can be manipulated and controlled as required.

3.1 How does it work?

I am sure we are all familiar with either using flash, or seeing flash being used, but do we understand the physics of the modern flash unit?

The requirement for an artificial source of light started back in 1839 with Ibbetson, who used Limelight, which was a ball of calcium carbonate heated in an oxygen flame until it became incandescent. This was followed in the 1860s by magnesium wire and then in the 1880s by flash powder. All created clouds of smoke and white dust making them unsuitable for studio work. It wasn't until 1929 that the first flash bulb was produced, called the 'Vacublitz', swiftly followed by the first mass production flash the 'Sachalite' made by GEC in the USA (General Electric Company).

In 1931 the first electronic flash tube was developed by Harold Edgerton and, unlike its flash bulb predecessors, it could be recharged and used time after time with repeatable results.

Most modern flash units (Figure 3.1) have three main parts:

(1) A power supply, in most units this will be batteries, although in studio equipment this will be mains.
(2) A gas discharge tube, which will produce the flash.
(3) A capacitor and circuits, which connect and control the flash.

Forensic Photography: A Practitioner's Guide, First Edition. Nick Marsh.
© 2014 John Wiley & Sons, Ltd. Published 2014 by John Wiley & Sons, Ltd.

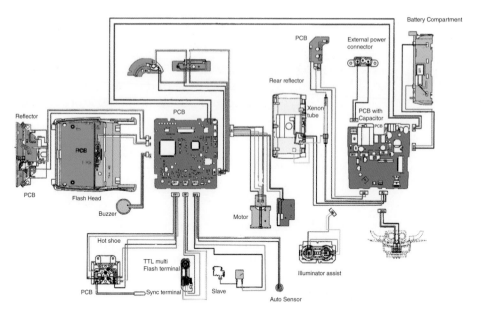

Figure 3.1   Illustration of a flash unit; image courtesy of Colin Inglis, Suffield Imaging.

When we switch the flash on, the power supply charges a photoflash capacitor, which stores the energy until required. Unlike standard electrolytic capacitors, the principle properties of photoflash ones are the high capacitance and working voltage, with equivalent series resistance, inductance and low working temperature.

The light energy emitted from the capacitor is proportional to the capacitance and voltage squared. Depending on the size of the unit it can have a range of 80 to 1500 microfarads (uF). Photoflash capacitors are designed to deliver a brief pulse of very high current, and are consequently sometimes used in railgun and coilgun designs.

(The charging of the capacitor often produces an audible low whistling effect.)

When a flash is required, the capacitor releases the electrical current through two connecters fitted to the ends of a glass tube filled with xenon gas. These connectors are attached together by a thin bar of metal or wire, which runs through the tube called the trigger plate. The idea is to energise the free electrons in the xenon gas; however, because there are very few free non-bonded electrons we have to introduce free electrons. This is done using the trigger plate, when a high positive charge is placed across it, it attracts negatively charged electrons in the atoms. If this attraction is strong enough it will pull the electrons free. They are pulled towards the positively charged terminal (the trigger plate) where they collide, ionising the gas, which becomes energised producing a flash of light.

To make this release of energy more effective and efficient, when the flash tube is fitted into the flash housing it is normally backed up by a polished metal plate, which acts as a reflector pushing the light forwards.

You may also notice, depending on your flash unit, that the tube has a slightly yellow coating. This is done to stop the unwanted light from the blue end of the spectrum from reaching the subject, giving the flash a more daylight balanced output.

It is worth pointing out at this stage that a new generation of flash is creeping onto the market, based around LED diodes. Unlike the traditional flash type shape, these tend to look like flat light panels, similar to those used in video illumination. This is because they are not constrained by using flash type tubes, technically meaning they could be made in any shape or size. The prototype ones I have tested so far have only been able to fire the flash at full power with no output control. But I am assured that by the time this book is published, a full TTL version will readily be available.

3.2   Guide numbers

One important question we need to ask when choosing a flash is: how much light will it actually produce? As a general rule, the more powerful the flash, the larger the scene it will light. Flash outputs, are measured by the flash **G**uide **N**umbers (GN) and all manufacturers use this as a reference. Historically, flash GNs were measured in 'feet' using 100 ISO. Although all manufactures now quote the GN in 'metres' and use 100 or 200 ISO as a standard, if you are purchasing a new flash unit to replace an old one, ensure that you are comparing like for like.

Why is the GN so important? Think back to Chapter 2 and our exposure triangle, aperture, shutter speed and ISO. We now have a new factor to be accounted for, that of distance. It is important to remember when dealing with flash exposures, that our exposure triangle is changed and is now aperture, distance to subject and ISO. Note that shutter speed has now been replaced, which we shall return to later in this chapter.

3.2.1   What is the guide number?

The GN is basically the maximum distance that the area of interest can be located from the flash and still be illuminated at f1 at ISO 100 (unless otherwise stipulated.) Provided the flash output is constant, the GN can be used to calculate the aperture.

$$Aperture = GN/distance.$$

For example, if the built-in flash on a digital camera has a GN of 12, this means that at 5 metres it would equate to $12/5 = f2.4$.

If a smaller aperture was required at 5 metres, say f8, we would either need to increase the ISO, move closer to the subject, or more realistically use a more powerful, externally mounted flashgun. To put that in perspective, here is a comparison of outputs between a number of flash units within the department, repeated at a 10-metre range.

- Nikon 5100 (built in flash), GN 12 at ISO 100. 12/10 = an aperture of f1.2.
- Nikon SB-900 AF Speedlight, GN 34 at 100 ISO. 34/10 = an aperture of f3.4.
- Metz 58 AF-2 Digital flash GN, 58 at 100 ISO. 58/10 = an aperture of f5.8
- Metz Megablitz 76mz-5, digital handle mount flash GN 249 at 100 ISO (with the 105 mm lens setting). 249/10 = f24.

The first three flashguns above are common types of flash used by most police forces. The Megablitz, however, is not as commonly used, but is a powerful professional flash that is capable of lighting up a large scene in one shot, or giving good depth of field at closer distances.

As we can see in the examples above, the relationship between the power output and the GN is clear. Don't forget, however, that the GN is only part of the exposure decision and in most circumstances a higher ISO of 200 or 400 will be used, thus giving you a least one or two extra stops.

It should be noted at this point that a common mistake made by amateurs is to try and change the shutter speed to compensate for an under or over flash exposure. Changing the shutter speed does not affect the power of the flash output or its given exposure. This is because the light generated by the flashgun only lasts around a fraction of second, so the shutter must be fully open to ensure that the subject is correctly illuminated.

All cameras have an optimum synchronisation speed (sync speed): this is the fastest speed that the shutter can be set to, which ensures that the shutter is fully open when the flash is fired. This is often around 1/60th or 1/125th of a second using a focal plane shutter, and up to 1/500th on a leaf shutter. On older film cameras this point was often marked with an 'x'. It should be noted that most digital cameras automatically set the sync speed if automatic or programme is chosen from the camera menu.

If you choose a shutter speed faster than the sync speed, the shutter will cross the film plane before the flash has exposed properly, meaning only half the frame will be exposed (Figure 3.2).

It is, however, possible to use shutter speeds that are slower than the sync speed. This is a useful technique when undertaking scene photography, as it allows the balancing of different types of illumination with the flash producing a more accurate image of the scene. For example, balancing an interior lit by flash, with an exterior view through a patio door. This is possible because although the flash output power is set to illuminate the interior, the camera is still taking an exposure using ambient light, coming through the door. This is

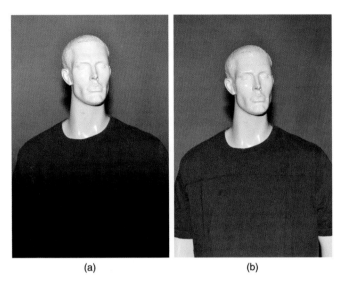

(a)   (b)

Figure 3.2   (a) The sync speed incorrectly set to 1/500th at f11. Across the bottom of the image we can see that the vertical shutter blades of the camera have not fully opened. (In older cameras, with curtain shutters, this unexposed area would run horizontally across the frame rather than vertically as in the example.) (b) The sync speed set to 1/125th at f11.

the standard technique used at crime scenes and we will explore this technique later in the chapter. Care must be taken, however, that this slower sync is not done accidentally. If too slow a shutter speed is set and you have movement in the frame you will get ghosting. This is where the flash fires, freezing the main movement, but the camera has continued to expose for the longer shutter duration (Figure 3.3). Therefore the object has moved during the exposure giving the blurry effect of movement. This is particularly noticeable if you are hand-holding the camera.

3.3   Flash modes

Like cameras, today's flash units are getting increasingly adaptable and more intelligent in ensuring that we achieve the correct exposure. It is impossible to cover all the modes in which they can work within this book, as these are particular to each unit, however I will cover the three basic modes in more depth: those of Manual, Automatic and TTL (Figure 3.4).

Many flash units also have the ability to swivel and/or tilt the flash head to direct the beam.

3.3.1   Manual mode

In manual mode, we, the photographer, set the power as a ratio of the output of the flashgun.

Figure 3.3   Here although the flash has provided the main exposure for the manikin, Greg's arm has also been exposed because the shutter was accidently set to half a second, and the ambient light generated by the modelling lights has exposed his arm causing it to appear in a ghost like fashion.

Normally on the back of the flash there is a panel showing the desired ISO and the power settings, this is usually along the lines of 1/1 full power, 1/2 power, 1/4 power, 1/8 power, 1/16 power, 1/32 power. There should also be a guide to the aperture and distance at which the flash will generate the correct exposure. On some units there is also another setting to adjust the angle of the flash, dependent on the lens being used.

If we look at the flash unit in Figure 3.5 we can see that the flash is set to M for manual. Below that is the ISO that is set to 160, below that is the distance scale, which shows 6 metres. Below that is zoom factor, at present set to 85 mm. Next to it is the aperture showing f11 and finally the power 1/1 (full power). So at present the flash would fire on full power giving us an exposure of f11 at 6 metres.

Note that no mention is made of shutter speeds; this is because, as I said above, shutter speeds are not part of our exposure triangle and are therefore irrelevant in terms of calculating flash exposures. However, as with our previous exposure triangle, if any of the above parameters is changed, the exposure will change. For example, if we change the aperture to f5.6 our range now changes to 13 m (Figure 3.6).

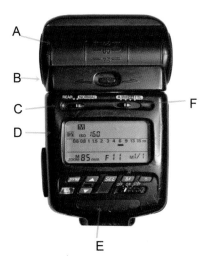

Figure 3.4   Here we can see the back of a generic type flash unit. Although each manufacturer has a slightly different layout, all display the same key features. (a) Shows that the head can be angled by set degrees allowing it to be bounced off the ceiling. (b) Shows that the head can be rotated in either direction allowing the flash to bounce off walls or other surfaces (c) Shows that the flash can fire at the end of the exposure 'rear' setting, or at the beginning 'normal' setting. (d) Shows the display readout. This one is digital display, many use a dial system, but both give the same information. (e) Shows the flash control panel; the orange light shows the flash is charged and ready for use. (f) Shows the function button for 'A' automatic, 'M' manual, three 'lighting flashes' strobe, 'TTL' Through The Lens metering.

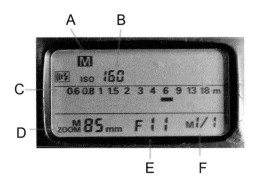

Figure 3.5   A typical digital flash display. (a) Function setting 'M' manual. (This would show 'A' for automatic and 'TTL' for Through The Lens.) (b) ISO 160 setting (when attached to the camera this will automatically change with the camera). (c) Distance and flash range indicated by the black bar. (d) Flash zoom setting (when attached to a dedicated camera fitted with a zoom lens this will automatically change as the lens is zoomed). (e) F-stop value. (f) Flash power 1/1 indicates full power.

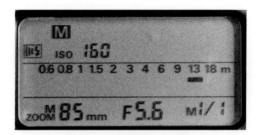

Figure 3.6   Changing the aperture.

If I change the zoom to 24 mm, the distance drops to 3 m (Figure 3.7) (this is because our light is now spread to cover a 24 mm lens setting rather than focused with the 85 mm lens setting).

If we increase the ISO to 400 then our distance moves to 9 m (Figure 3.8).

The flash can be set to give virtually any combination that is required.

There are of course a few problems with using the flash on manual, the most obvious of which is that the power of the flash output is set, regardless of the distance to the subject. Full power is full power, regardless of whether you are 1 m from the subject or 10 m. Of course, you can turn it down or down to $^1/_2$, $^1/_4$ or even 1/32, or open up or stop down the aperture, but you must physically do it, when there is already enough to consider at most scenes.

The other issue is around battery consumption. On manual setting the flash is discharging the same amount each time, and on full power, and this can rapidly deplete a set of batteries leading to a delay in recharge times. In Auto and TTL modes, the flash is switched off when the correct exposure has been given and thus saves battery consumption in the long term.

If you are using the flash on manual it is possible to achieve the correct exposure by remembering our exposure triangle of ISO, aperture and distance to the subject.

Let's look at this scenario; we are photographing an exhibit using a 50 mm lens and the camera set to ISO 200. The flash is set to full power, giving us a guide exposure of f11 at 4 metres (Figure 3.9).

Figure 3.7   Change of zooming factor.

Figure 3.8   The impact of changing the ISO.

Figure 3.9   Photographing an exhibit using a 50 mm lens and the camera set to ISO 200. The flash is set to full power, giving us a guide exposure of f11 at 4 metres.

However, because the output is set to full power, if I move forwards or backwards by a metre then this exposure will be incorrect. If I were to move closer, then I would overexpose the subject; to correct this I would need to change the aperture, the flash power, or ISO. In reality we tend not to change the ISO, and an aperture of at least f8–f11 is generally required to ensure a reasonable depth of field.

So let's look at the flash output options available (Figure 3.10):

- At 3 m we need to drop the power to $\frac{1}{2}$ power.
- At 2 m we need to drop the power to $\frac{1}{4}$ power.
- At 1.5 m we need to drop the power to 1/8 power.
- At 1 m we need to drop the power to 1/16 power.

If, however, we were happy to change the aperture whilst keeping the flash on full power

- At 3 m we would need to stop down one stop to f16.
- At 2 m we would need to stop down two stops to f22.
- At 1.5 m we would need to stop down three stops to f32.
- At 1 m we would need to stop down four stops to f45.

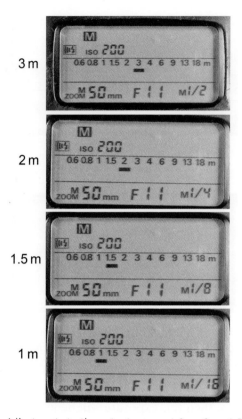

Figure 3.10 Adjustments to the output power at 3 m, 2 m, 1.5 m, and 1 m.

The above works if we move closer to our subject, but what will happen if we need to move further away and we are already at full power? Again, we could open the aperture or increase the ISO to make the sensor more sensitive, so our changes would be

- At 6 m we would need to open up one stop to f8 or increase our ISO to 250.
- At 9 m we would need to open up two stops to f5.6 or increase the ISO to 500.
- At 13 m we would need to open up three stops to f4.*
- At 18 m we would need to open up four stops to f2.8.*

(*Note that I would be wary of increasing the ISO beyond this point, it is dependent on your camera as it can produce unacceptable levels of noise.)

As we can see from the above example, there is a distance limit that the flash can be used at, the rule of thumb being the smaller the flash unit, the less power it outputs.

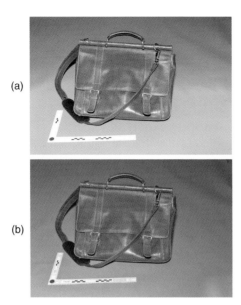

(a)

(b)

Figure 3.11   Shows an exhibit photographed from about 2.2 m. (a) With the flash on $\frac{1}{2}$ power at f11, overexposing the exhibit. (b) The same exposure, this time with single layer of hanky over the flash head. Clearly a reasonable compensation in exposure can be achieved in post-production; however, depending on the circumstances this is not always practical. It is therefore good practice to get the exposure right in camera when you, the photographer, are in control.

There are also a number of other ways to reduce the power of the flash without actually changing any settings, again thinking outside of the box. One is to use a single thickness of a white handkerchief over the flash head (Figure 3.11). This generally equates to approximately one or two stops. Don't be tempted to use multiple layers, as anymore than one thickness can create uneven illumination or reduce the power too dramatically. Also, don't use a coloured hanky or you will in effect be adding a colour cast to your image.

Another method is to hold one finger vertically in the middle of the flash head, as the light will still be reflected around the finger. This technique should not be used at close range as it may create uneven illumination if the light cannot spread before hitting the subject.

A third method is to bounce the light off a sheet of paper or card, by tilting the flash head vertically, or revolving it so it points upwards at 75° facing backwards. Then hold your card or white paper in front of it. The light will be reflected forwards; although it will lose around two stops, it does create a soft diffuse illumination, which is good for close up subjects.

It is worth noting that this bouncing of flash onto ceilings and walls is often employed to create soft overall lighting within scenes.

As an aside, subjects over around 12 metres away will probably need specialist flash to illuminate them, or another approach entirely, such as open flash, which we shall look at later in the chapter.

3.4   The inverse square law (ISL)

As this book is aimed a wide variety of experiences and knowledge I have included two descriptions of the inverse square law. A long one for those of you who like a deeper explanation, and a shorter version for those who just want a refresher.

3.4.1   The ISL (long version)

Whilst we are looking at manual flash settings, you may have noticed that when the distance was doubled or halved, the matching aperture or flash power wasn't. This is because f-stops, as mentioned before, are a strange group of numbers, and in the next few paragraphs I will attempt to explain all.

Strictly speaking the inverse square law states that as light travels from its point source it spreads out, its intensity varies inversely by the square of the distance it travels. Although flashguns are larger than the theoretical point source, for our practical purposes the theory holds good.

So what does this mean for us in day-to-day usage? As the light travels outwards from our flash, it does not remain in a straight line as, say, a laser beam would, but appears as a geometric expanding cone of light. As it spreads and travels outwards it gets relatively weaker the further it travels away. The inverse square law allows us to precisely determine its relative intensity at any given distance from the source.

Let's put that into practice. In Figure 3.12 you can see our flash emitting a rectangle of light (equivalent of the cone used in the theory).

You can see that at point 2, the light is now covering 4 times the area it was at point 1 and so is in effect only $\frac{1}{4}$ of the power that it was. To determine this, we can take the distance 2 and invert it (make it a fraction) so it becomes $\frac{1}{2}$. Square that $(1/2 \times 1/2)$ and the result is the intensity of light at that point 2 is a $\frac{1}{4}$: this can be expressed as the equation:

$$\text{Intensity} = \text{distance 1 squared, or } I = 1/D^2$$

For example, if at 2 metres our correct exposure is f11, then when we look at the diagram we can see that in fact the light is dimmer as it has spread. The question is by how much?

Because we doubled the distance from 2 m to 4 m $D = 2$. Intensity $= 1/(2)^2$. In this case Intensity $= 1/4$. If you remember in Chapter 2 we talked about f-stops being half or double the exposure of the previous one, each being

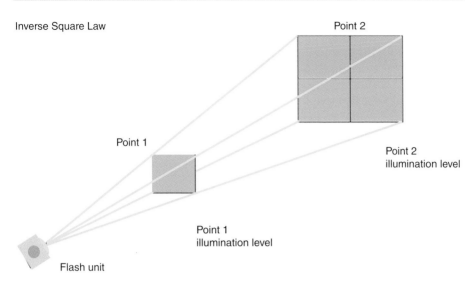

Inverse Square Law

Point 2

Point 1

Point 2
illumination level

Point 1
illumination level

Flash unit

Figure 3.12   Diagram showing inverse square law flash fall off.

equivalent to plus or minus one stop. So, in our example the light is only $\frac{1}{4}$ of what it was at point 1. Because $\frac{1}{2} \times \frac{1}{2} = \frac{1}{4}$, doubling the distance from 2 to 4 m means a two stop reduction in light. Therefore, to make the correct exposure we will need to open the lens two stops from f11 to a new setting of f5.6.

The equation $I = 1/D^2$ allows you to determine a new intensity for any distance change, and if the intensity is known you can use $D = \sqrt{1/I}$, the inverse square root being the intensity change. But that still doesn't answer the question with regard to the correlation between f-numbers and the inverse square law. Let's look at our diagram again. If doubling the distance the light travels quarters the light, at what point is it only one stop less? Logic would dictate that it's half the distance, or 3 m.

The equation $D = \sqrt{1/I}$ offers the solution. We know that at point 2 the light is $\frac{1}{4}$, therefore if we take $\frac{1}{2}$ the intensity invert that, it is 2/1 or 2, the square root of which is 1.4. So 1.4 × our known distance at point $D1$ 1.4 × 2 m (our known exposure distance) = our new distance, which is 2.8 m.

Let's repeat this again, but this time ask at what point is the light 1/8 as bright as at the original distance? Well, 1/8 is another way of expressing the equation $\frac{1}{2} \times \frac{1}{2} \times \frac{1}{2}$ or three stops less light. So, using our equation $D = \sqrt{1/I}$, the square root of 8 is 2.8 × 2 m (our known exposure distance) = 5.64 m. Do you notice anything yet? If we expand this rationale further, we would see that at the progressing distances we would get 1, 1.4, 2, 2.8, 5.6, 8, 11 m, and so on, each of which is exactly one stop and represents half the light of the previous number; and as we can see this is the basis for the derivations in f-stop numbers.

3.4.2   The ISL short version

In both photography and theatrical lighting, the ISL is used to determine the fall off of light as a subject is moved closer too or further from the illumination source.

As the subject is moved further from our lighting source, such as a flash, the light is spreading and getting weaker, and the ISL allows us to accurately determine this level of fall off using the equation:

$$E = \frac{I}{r^2}$$

Where E is the luminance and I the distance.

For ease of use, it is easiest to remember that doubling the distance reduces the illumination to one quarter of what it was. So if our flash was set at f22 and we double the distance, our new aperture setting would be f11.

- If you wish to halve the illumination, increase the distance by 1.4 (the square root of 2).
- To double the illumination, reduce the distance to 0.7 (the square root of $\frac{1}{2}$).

Fortunately, in the following modes the flash will do all these calculations for you in a fraction of a second; but it is important to understand what it is doing and why.

3.4.3   Automatic

In automatic mode the flash unit uses its own built-in light sensor to measure the flash being reflected from the subject. This sensor is mounted on the front of the flash unit, and allows the flash to switch itself off when it has delivered the correct volume of light to the subject. This mode has a number of advantages to us. Unlike the manual setting, the automatic setting only fires the amount of light that it thinks is required, conserving flash power and decreasing the recycling times. This is because only between 50 and 70% of the flash power is expended, rather than charging from empty. This also means that the battery lasts longer, which is particularly important if non-rechargeable batteries are being used.

Also, the automatic flash uses ranges rather than f-stops for different distances. Provided you do not step outside of the guidance ranges given, the flash should provide the correct exposure. Different flash units use various guides, so please refer to your manual for the specifics of your unit.

There are, however, a few disadvantages to using automatic mode. One is the sensor eye is mounted on the front of the flash unit. This means that the flash must be looking towards the subject, so unless the flash has a revolving head, it cannot be pointed sideways or onto an out-of-sightline surface. Another issue, in my experience, is that the sensor is also easily fooled about how much light is required to illuminate the scene. This is observed in a scene which contains highly reflective areas, such as windows, mirrors or even white walls. In these scenarios the flash will switch itself off too quickly, underexposing the scene. Conversely, overly dark scenes, such as fire damage, can fool the flash into overexposing. So we may need to consider using manual flash.

A handy tip if you are using the flash on auto, but then require full power for a particular reason, is to simply fool the sensor by placing your finger over the sensor window, it will fire on full power to try and generate a correct exposure. Conversely, always ensure that the window is never accidentally blocked.

3.4.4   Through The Lens metered flash (TTL)

Unlike automatic above, TTL flash is calculated using the light travelling through the lens. Originally with film cameras this was done by measuring some of the light reflected from the film surface into a sensor. Once enough light is received, the flash is switched off.

Because CMOS or CCD array chips are not reflective enough to use the analogue method above, DSLR manufacturers have introduced their own systems, for example Canon uses E-TTL and E-TTLII whilst Nikon uses D-TTL and i-TTL. These work in a slightly different way to analogue, in that before the actual exposure is made a number of 'pre-flashes' are fired. The light returning through the lens is then measured and the actual exposure is calculated. When front curtain flash is fired directly after the shutter is opened, the pre-flashes and main flash appear as one to the human eye. However, if you are using rear curtain flash, the pre-flash and main flash may be discernable.

Many camera manufactures now have dedicated flash units for particular models of camera, which they recommend. This pairing of flash and camera allows complicated exposure calculations to be carried out, improving the lighting of the subject. Often they are also linked to the focus, ensuring that where the camera is focused is correctly exposed. with the computer taking care of distance and power calculations. In general this give more accurate results than automatic.

With some of the latest models, such as Nikon's wireless Speedlight range, it is possible to link a number of 'slave' flash units together, with each flash being controlled by a central 'master controller' flash, allowing the exposure to be calculated by the TTL sensor in the camera. As pointed out above, this setting is only possible when the correct flashgun is used with a matched dedicated camera. So check that your flash is fully compatible with your camera. Some professional flashguns, such as the Metz range, can be purchased with adapters that let us take advantage of the TTL mode regardless of the camera in use.

3.4.5   Other settings

Rear and front curtain modes   This refers to when the flash will actually fire; this is either at the start 'front curtain' or the end 'rear curtain' of the exposure. In general scene photography we will be using the normal or front curtain flash. This means that the flash will peak once the shutter has fully opened, freezing any movement at the start of the exposure.

Rear curtain flash is fired at the end of the exposure, just before it closes. This is often used at the end of a long exposure when you want to freeze the action. For example, a creative shot of a slowly moving car shot at night with its lights on will leave a trail of lights in a long exposure. However, just before the shutter closes the flash is fired, freezing the movement and making the car appear sharp and in focus.

Strobe settings   Some flash units have the capability to fire very fast bursts of flash in a strobe effect. Although this is generally used in creative situations, to freeze movement within exposure or for creating multiply exposures during one exposure, it can be useful if you wish to paint with light but only have a short exposure time. For example, in Figure 3.13 I have set the flash to strobe at 9 Hz for 8 flashes to capture a specular shoe mark on a tiled floor. A single flash would not be able to create the desired effect, but using a strobe flash permits the light to be moved around, allowing the mark to be built up. If I was to set the flash to 1/64th power we could achieve 24 flashes at 50 Hz.

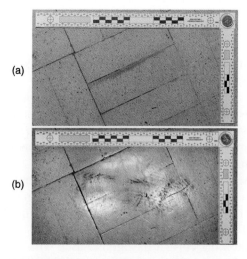

(a)

(b)

Figure 3.13   An example of strobe being used to illuminate a partial shoe mark on a tiled floor, using the strobe as specular illumination. Here the strobe was set to 8 flashes of 9 Hz at f13, with the shutter opened for 3 seconds.

Zoom function and diffusers Zoom function, as the name suggests, allows the flash unit to replicate a zoom lens when both are connected to a camera. This ensures that the flash is used at its most efficient, zooming with the lens so it only covers the area required. In non-zoom type flash units, the light will be emitted over an area of view, generally equivalent to a medium wide-angle lens. Fitting a diffuser to the flash head has the effect of diffusing the light, producing soft shadows rather than non-diffused harsh ones.

When set to manual, you can also use the zoom function to throw light down a corridor, to illuminate into the mid-distance or to throw a wide bounce flash off the ceiling.

3.5 The practical application of flash

Now we have an understanding of the flash modes, we need to be able put this knowledge into practice. This will fall into one of three flash modes:

- Flash only. In this scenario the flash provides the only illumination.
- Fill in. Here the flash is balanced with other forms of illumination. This is probably the most common technique used at most crime scenes.
- Open flash. Here the flash is the main illumination; however, unlike flash only, we are going to use a long exposure and position the flash by hand, so this technique can only be carried out in low light conditions.

3.5.1 Flash only

Here we are going to use the flash as the main source of illumination; this is often the preferred option for:

(a) Victim photography.
(b) Scene photography when the ambient illumination is poor.
(c) Studio photography for exhibits.

We will be covering the use of flash in victim photography later on in the book in Chapter 6, so here I would like us to concentrate on scenarios 'b' and 'c'.

In a typical scene, we often find that we are confronted with areas that are either poorly lit or have no lighting, such as arson scenes. For example, let's imagine we have a fire-damaged room. As normal, we need to set our camera on a tripod framing the area of interest.

When focusing, be wary of using auto focus, as described in Chapter 2, as it tends to hunt for mid-frame objects which may not be our prime point of focus; in these situations switch to manual focus. Using manual focus you have a choice of techniques. One would be to use zone focus by measuring the distance to the area of interest and setting that on the lens. Or, second, you point

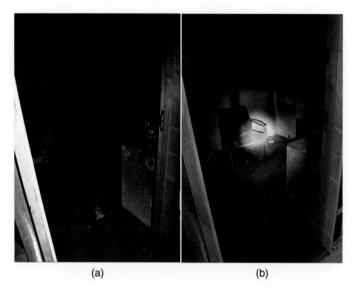

(a) (b)

Figure 3.14 (a) The area of fire damage and lack of ambient illumination. (b) In this case I was able to use the arm and seat of the chair as a point of contrast to allow visual focusing. The other alternative would have been to use zone focusing by setting the distance on the lens. Don't forget that you can zoom in if you are using a zoom lens to focus and then zoom out when you are ready to take the shot.

focus by illuminating the area of interest with a bright torch (Figure 3.14). In my experience, viewfinders are often too dark to see a beam, particularly if it is in the distance. An option to consider, if you are certain you are not disturbing or contaminating the scene, is placing a bright object at the point of focus. Here, again, the boat lamp is extremely useful as its outer casing glows, but an illuminated piece of paper works just as well.

Once focused, don't forget to remove the lamp or paper from the shot. The focal length of the lens and angle of view can also be chosen at this stage, but don't forget that if the photograph is meant to show true perspective, then the standard focal length for the camera sensor must be chosen.

Once we have focused we again have a number of other choices when using flash. We can use single on camera flash, multiple flash units or open flash.

On camera flash Most modern flash units will work reasonably happily on TTL, so technically we can set our aperture and take the exposure. (Remember in this scenario the shutter speed is irrelevant and in TTL mode will probably be set to the camera sync speed.) However, because our subject matter is very light absorbing, this may cause the flash to underexpose so don't be afraid to switch the flash to manual if required.

A more likely problem with a single flash either on camera or off is a drop off in illumination at the edges of the frame or behind the couch (our area of

Figure 3.15   Flash on camera creating deep shadows from the doorframe.

interest). As discussed previously, this is where the flash fails to illuminate the whole area (Figure 3.15). As an aside, this is often observed with full length post mortem shots, when only a flash on camera is used. Although the middle of the body is correctly exposed, the head and feet appear to be in shadow.

This brings us to the other flash options; multiple flash units and open flash.

Multiple flash, as the name suggests, is when we use two or more flash units together. One flash will be connected to the hot shoe, or preferably on a long extension cord to the flash synchronisation socket, whilst the second or third units are fitted with flash slave devices. These flash 'slave units' fire the flash remotely on seeing the flash discharge from the master unit. Modern flash units frequently have these devices built in, but they are readily available to purchase separately. The only issue is that they must be in line of sight with the master flash and are temperamental in bright sunlight. An alternative, but far more expensive, option to these simple flash slave units, is to use a wireless link, such as Pocket Wizard, which will fire the flash remotely regardless of the environment (other versions are available).

Using two flash units allows:

(1)   A greater area to be covered avoiding fall off.
(2)   Even illumination to be achieved.

Figure 3.16   As Figure 3.15 but this time two guns have been used. The diagram shows the approximate angle and direction of the flash.

If we now photograph the chair again, this time with two flash units, we have a number of options:

(a)   We can hold one on either side of the camera (Figure 3.16), pointing forwards but slightly towards the centre (this is to ensure they overlap), preferably at a good arm's reach to the left and right of the camera. Fire the shutter using a remote camera release; this will give us a much wider, even field of illumination.

(b)   We can hold one pointing directly at the chair but use the other to fill in the background, in this case by holding one flash down low and the other up high. Although reducing our field of illumination, it allows the light to fall on areas previously in shadow behind the couch.

Clearly any combination of flash positions is available and is not confined to two units. If three or four are available it is possible to create a virtually shadowless image. The important thing to remember in this scenario is to ensure that the flash units are set to the same settings and are balanced. We don't want one gun set to f4 and the other to f16 or we will create an uneven illumination.

A word of warning here: if you are going to use TTL, both guns must be compatible with the camera model. If not, the pre-flash (to allow the camera to determine exposure) will trigger the second unit early. In older flash units, such as my old Metz, the automatic or manual power setting will need to be used and this choice will depend to some extent on what you are photographing.

3.5.2 Open flash

What can we do if we don't have two flash units but we cannot achieve a satisfactory result using one flash? In Figure 3.17 you can see that I have tried to illuminate our scene using the camera's built-in flash. This, however, produces a poorly lit result, with fall off both behind the car and to the right of the image.

(a)

(b)

(c)

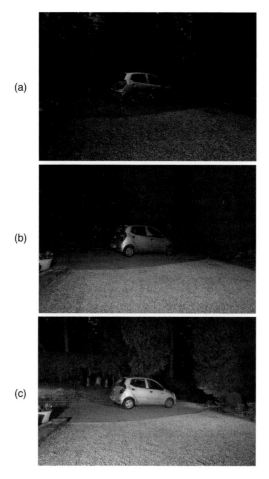

Figure 3.17   (a) The approximate ambient lighting conditions; the only light was a small interior light in the house, to the left in image. (b) One flash mounted on camera held beside the camera; this produces a reasonable exposure, but suffers from fall off behind the car and to the right hand side. (c) Multiple flash exposures around the camera; this produces a well-illuminated image with the car light from all angles. The important thing to remember is: what are we trying to achieve? Are we trying to capture the lighting, as, say, in the case of a fatal accident, when image (a) might be applicable? Or are we trying to see the scene so that all the evidence is visible, where image (b) or (c) might be the correct lighting?

If we are to try and light the whole scene so no evidence is missed, this is where we can consider using the open flash technique. This technique, however, is only possible in low ambient light conditions, as we will need to set the camera to a long exposure.

In Figure 3.18a we can see that I have been asked to photograph a motor vehicle in position at night. This is an ideal scenario for the open flash technique and we will set up the shot it as if it is in normal daylight.

Once we have set up the required field of view, we need to set the camera to 'bulb' or 1 min. This will depend on the size of area to be photographed; the larger it is the more time you will need to move round it. You will also need to set the aperture to f8 or f11 to give a reasonable depth of field. Again, this

(a)

(b)

(c)

Figure 3.18   shows an exterior shot of a car in position. The camera is set to f8 at 400 ISO. (a) 30-s exposure showing the ambient lighting conditions. (b) 2-min exposure (camera set to bulb) lit with five flashes on full power. (c) Approximate position of the flash. Note that I have slightly changed the camera position in (b) to include more of the drive.

will also be dependent on the distance to the subject, in this case because of the distance to the car a wider aperture can be chosen if required.

In this scenario the area is large, so I have set the camera to bulb. We now have a choice of whether to set our flash to automatic or manual, this will depend on our subject and how light or dark it is. In this case I will choose manual, because the paintwork of the car may reflect the flash causing it to underexpose the image. So, in this case I will use the flash set to full power giving me f11 at 4 m.

Do not attach the flash to the camera, as we are going to fire it via the test button on the rear. Trigger the shutter and then hold the flash in the desired position and fire the flash. Whilst it is recharging, move to the left or right of the tripod. Once it has recharged fire it again, this time covering the area not illuminated in the first exposure. Using this technique you can illuminate large areas. When the shutter closes, you will have all the flash fires in one exposure. This is a useful technique to use at scenes where there are low levels of ambient light, such as a vehicle collision at night. The downside is that a continuously open shutter will build up the exposure in the sky area, which we don't want. We can adjust the technique slightly by getting a colleague to hold a piece of dark card, like the back of a clipboard, in front of the lens. Then, just before you fire the flash, ask them to remove it. An important note here is don't be tempted to use the lens cap, as this increases the chances of moving the camera, creating a double exposure or 'camera shake'. It is important to block as much ambient light as possible, particularly in cities as the light pollution will cause an unnaturally light sky.

Care should be taken to ensure that the areas covered by the flash illumination are not repeatedly illuminated, as that will cause the area to be overexposed. It is therefore a good idea to have a mental picture of the scene and where the flashes are going to be fired. Again, if correctly used this can create a well-lit result as if it was taken in full illumination.

Be careful when using this technique with regard to your own health and safety, especially when moving around in the darkened conditions. However, if you are blocking the lens you can use a small torch to illuminate your path through the scene. You may be tempted to increase the ISO to compensate for low light levels, but that will only increase the risk of noise unless you are using the latest type of sensors; it is better to stick to a lower ISO and allow the flash to do the work for you.

Finally with regards to open flash, there is another issue, which I touched on above when I was talking about ghosting. The smallest light introduced into our scene when the shutter is open will leave a residual impression, and when firing the flash ensure that they are pointing away from camera out of shot, as can be seen in Figure 3.19.

The third scenario is when we have to use flash within a studio environment. I am not going to go into great depth around the use of studio flash, as there are plenty of books that are dedicated to it. Suffice to say that their use

Figure 3.19   A number of open flash faults. First we have the typical flash into camera; here it has been accidently pointed towards the camera on the extreme left and right, producing a starburst effect. This effect is often seen when small apertures and street lighting come together for long exposures and is formed by the aperture diaphragm. Second, the small green and red warning lights on the back of the flash can be seen, leaving long trails. It is a good idea to shield these with your body when moving around the scene within the viewpoint of the lens. Third are the unwanted and unintentional interventions of third parties, here it is Harvey our labrador who, just like any police office or bystander, is interested in what is going on.

should not be overlooked or thought irrelevant. One of the advantages of studio flash units is that they generally have built in modelling lights. Modelling lights produce a constant illumination (generally a normal 100 Watt light bulb) and although this is no reflection of the power of the flash, they allow us to see the effect of the light fall in real time (Figure 3.20). This is particularly helpful when photographing property. In these scenarios we can position the lighting to reduce the shadow areas. Often, three studio flash units are used, usually fitted with soft boxes or umbrellas. Soft boxes are large diffusers fitted in front of the flash head, whilst umbrellas are used to reflect the light. Both diffuse the light to soften any shadows or highlights they might otherwise create.

Also unlike portable flash units, which have complex exposure modes such as automatic and TTL, studio flash units only have a manual mode for power setting; this means that you have take a light reading to ascertain the correct exposure, and here we will use a flash meter (Figure 3.21). These devices allow us to take an incident reading of the light falling on our subject flash output to calculate the exposure.

To ensure that the lighting is even, each flash should be measured and adjusted individually. The final exposure should be calculated with all flash units switched on. This allows the light to be very accurately controlled for artistic purposes, for example to introduce a slight shadow in a portrait, by reducing one flash down by $\frac{1}{2}$ stop.

Figure 3.20   A basic studio lighting set up using four studio flashes, two fitted with soft boxes and two with umbrellas.

What can we do if the flash is already on full power but won't give us the aperture we require? We could move the flash closer giving us more illumination due to the inverse square rule, but that will probably change the effect. It is easier to increase the number of flashes given. For example, if our exposure were f11 with two studio flashes set to full power and we needed f16, we would need to fire each flash twice. If we then went to f22 we would need to double

Figure 3.21   A digital flash meter showing a reading of f11.6 at 100 ISO.

 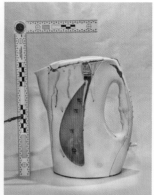

Figure 3.22   You can see in this illustration that I am using the corner of an office to photograph a blood-stained kettle. This has been laid out on brown paper, which I have taped to the side of a desk, acting as a basic infinity curve. Because the exhibit was on the floor I could simply have shot straight down. However, as the exhibit was a kettle, this did not look right when viewed through the viewfinder. I therefore decided to take it at ground level by mounting the camera on a gorilla pod. I originally photographed it from the front with two flash guns, however the shadows were harsh and strong so I changed the exposure to an open flash one. The lights were switched off and the camera set to a 20-s exposure, which was enough to allow me to fire the flash four times to illuminate the front, sides and behind the kettle.

it to fire each four flashes. This can be via the double exposure setting on the camera if it has one, or by the open flash technique using the flash test button to discharge the master flash unit.

What if we don't have a studio flash? For much of our casework, a prison cell or office will be our studio. There is no reason at all, however, why we cannot produce a perfectly good result with the minimum of effort (Figure 3.22). The first thing is the background: old sheets or purpose made background cloths are invaluable in these scenarios. Having a continuous tone background rather than floor tiles can make the difference between an amateur-looking photograph and a professional-looking one. Failing that, the plain brown back of an evidence bag is better than nothing.

As I have described elsewhere, never photograph the exhibit inside its evidence bag unless it is absolutely necessary or the object of the exercise. The exhibit should be laid out with a scale and an exhibit number if required. (See Figure 4.41 in Chapter 4.) Again, a tripod should be used as, once set up, exhibits can be rapidly replaced but the framing will remain the same, giving a sense of continuity between images.

Again, when using flash we have a number of options, with a single flash we can try bouncing it off a reflector or ceiling rather than firing it directly at the exhibit. Here we should be able to use the TTL setting, allowing for a good depth of field.

If we have two guns, we can provide simple copy lighting with the flash held at approximately 45°. Here we will probably need to select the auto setting, beware, however, reflective or very dark surfaces which may cause the flash to under- or overexpose. It is also advantageous to keep your exhibit as far from the backdrop as possible, as this will produce a shadowless background.

Another way to produce a shadowless background is to place your exhibit on a sheet of glass, placing a sheet of black card in the background. The further this is away from the glass, the deeper and richer the black it will produce; we use a glass topped stool for this purpose. Light your exhibit ensuring that no light passes through the glass onto the background and you have no reflections of the lights in the glass. This generally means using a light angle of less than 45° but it does depend on the light used. Meter for the exhibit and take your photograph, the exhibit should be correctly exposed and the black background should be underexposed, allowing the exhibit to float in space. It is important that any lights are switched off within the room as they can create highlights or reflections in the glass or produce grey in the background. If you have reflections in the glass which you cannot remove then the easiest solution is to get a piece of black card that is bigger than the area you have framed up. You then need to cut a hole for the lens to pass through. This is then mounted on the front of the camera; this should then block all other reflections.

If you wish to have a white background, you need to replace the black card background with a white card, or a light box. A light box is the simplest means to create a white field, as clearly it produces an even flat light. However, it is possible to do it using white card or paper. You must, however, ensure that it is evenly illuminated, if it is not it will show grey patches. The exposure should be equal to, or slightly overexposed to that of the exhibit, ensuring a crisp clean white. If it is underexposed it will produce an off white, which looks dirty, and if overexposed by more than a stop can produce white ghosting at the edge of the exhibit. This is, however, dependent on the type of exhibit, so some experimentation will be required.

If you are photographing an object with lots of sides or that has an awkward shape, don't be afraid of using the open flash technique to add illumination from multiple directions.

3.5.3 Fill in flash

This is probably the most used of the techniques and is when a combination of ambient illumination and flash is used to create your exposure. Probably 90% of scenes are lit this way, the art however is to get an even balance. I am often asked: why bother using a fill in flash when the sole use of flash can clearly illuminate the room with no problems? This is true, but I was trained to use any ambient light available to create a more realistic representation of the scene. The sole use of flash to illuminate a scene intrinsically changes that scene. For example, if the room was dimly lit with poor lighting, this may be integral to the case. If photographed using flash only, it will look brightly lit and possibly completely different. To me the control of flash in these situations is the mark of a professional at work. It should be used to infill shadows or cast light where there is none, yet it should remain unobtrusive to the viewer. If the scene has table or ceiling lamps, or an open window, we should allow for that in our exposure.

For example, if we have a scene as shown in Figure 3.23 we need to illuminate under the table and in the corner. If we take an ambient meter reading

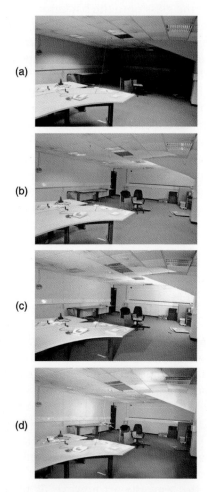

(a)

(b)

(c)

(d)

Figure 3.23   A room scene photographed using four different lighting techniques. (a) Under ambient lighting f11, 1/5th 800 ISO. (b) Using a fill in flash hidden around the corner of the right hand wall triggered by a flash slave unit, f11, 1/5th 800 ISO. (c) The room light with flash only f11, 20 s 800 ISO. (d) The room lit with only a torch 'painting with light' f11, 1 min 400 ISO. Note that the result in (d) leaves a slightly blotchy effect on the walls if the beam is too focused if kept in one place for too long.

we get 1/2 s at f11. Using this as our guide we can reset our flashguns on TTL or auto to f11. Using a cable release, fire the flash ensuring that one is pointed under the table, whilst the other is pointed into our shadow zone.

The important thing to note in Figure 3.23 is that both the position and output of the flash is critical to produce a pleasing overall effect. If we look at (b) and (c), we can see that in (b) the flash at the far end on the room has be positioned just to illuminate into the room area. But in (c) it has caught the far wall, slightly overexposing it. You should therefore not be worried about turning the flash down by a half or one stop, to keep a more natural feel to the lighting.

It is sometimes difficult to balance bright daylight with shadows if your camera has a limited sync speed (the exterior exposure requires a faster shutter speed than the sync speed); however, the problem can be lessened if the window is perhaps just at the edge of a shot by careful positioning. Or if, perhaps, the curtains are closed, which I think is preferable to an overexposed window. (Always check with the crime scene manager or Senior Investigating Officer before changing the scene.) If, for example, the reading from the window is 125th at f11, we can reset our flash to f11 and sync at 125 if possible. If you are limited to a 1/60th (X sync) then stop down to f16 (thus changing our exposure triangle) and increase the flash power to f16. Often you will find that the flash will be slightly overexposed, so if necessary repeat with the flash at f11.

The other common scenarios are areas of uneven illumination, such as corridors and halls. Often these have illumination at one end or the other, such as a pendant lamp fitting by the front door. This means that the end of the corridor furthest away will appear to be one or two stops darker. (Although visually our eye will adjust to compensate for this, so it may not be readily noticeable.) You could set up as normal and fire one flashgun down the hall; this, however, tends to create uneven illumination. There are now two ways we can deal with this issue, although if you only have one flashgun available the options are more limited. If you have two flashguns, there are a couple of options available to you.

Let's look at the two-flashgun option first. Here we will use the one gun to illuminate the end of the corridor closest to you. Whilst the other will need to light the far end of the corridor and, to achieve this, we need to change its focal length. So, instead of being set to wide angle spreading its light, it is set to telephoto. On some flash units you can remove the diffuser, reducing its spread, this will in effect send a beam of light down the corridor to the far end.

However the other, and my preferred, option, is to place the second flash at the other end of the corridor out of sight, but illuminating the area of concern (see Figure 3.23b). Again this flash will need to be fitted with a flash slave synchronisation device. This second flash is best held in place by a colleague and held high and pointed down, so when fired this gives the appearance of normal shadows and illumination. If the flash is held too low it can cast shadows in the wrong direction, which although not intrinsically bad, does look awkward to the viewer.

We now need to meter the light levels, for example $\frac{1}{2}$ s at f11. Both flash-guns can be then set to f11 when the camera is fired the $\frac{1}{2}$ s exposure will give an overall exposure and the flash will lift the shadows. Depending on the subject, I often find that by underexposing the flash by one stop (f8) the result is more aesthetical to the eye, as it still retains the subtleties of the original illumination. Any shadows created can be checked on the preview screen and the lighting can be adjusted as necessary.

If you only have one flashgun, I would suggest that it is held above the camera, again with the diffuser removed (or set to zoom), and let the flash illuminate the far end of the corridor letting the ambient light illuminate the area close by. Conversely, if the ambient light is at the far end, then reverse the process. Use the flash with the diffuser fitted to illuminate the area closest to you and allow the ambient light to expose the area furthest away.

From experience, beware of doorframes that are close to the camera position; these will pick up the light and will be overexposed and are very distracting to the eye. If possible, ensure that when you photograph into a room you are inside the doorframe or they are at the very edges of the frame.

3.6   Types of flash

Throughout this chapter we have looked at using standard hot shoe mounted flash units. There are, however, a number of designs of flash and it is worth taking a quick look at the other types available.

3.6.1   Hammerhead units

These types of flash are normally mounted on a bracket on the side of the camera, although not as popular as they used to be, these flash units are generally far more powerful than hot shoe mounted flash units. These types of flash are used when large areas or distances need to be covered, or a large amount of light is required.

Often these units can be fitted with external heavy-duty batteries, allowing fast charges that allow more photographs to be taken than with normal dry cell batteries. These are typically the flash used by ourselves when undertaking scene work.

3.6.2   Ring flash

As the name suggests, this specialist flashgun uses a circular flash tube, which sits around the lens. These types of units are almost exclusively used to provide soft, even illumination at close distances, such as macro photography. For us, they are very useful for the photography of ninhydrin and other chemical marks at scenes.

Ring flashes have traditionally been a very expensive outlay; today, however, a number of companies are producing adaptors, which turn a standard hot shoe mounted flash into a ring flash, by channeling the light into a circular reflector.

Although they lose one or two stops they have the advantage of being relatively cheap to purchase, yet produce a similar result.

3.6.3 Semi ring flashes

These flash units do not go all the way round the lens but are very small flash units mounted on the front of the lens. This allows a number of flash units to be mounted and allows some control over the lighting arrangement. (Rather than the ring flash which just produces even illumination.) Again these are primarily used for macro work due to the lack of overall power (Figure 3.24).

All of the above can normally be used in manual and automatic and, depending on the combination of camera and flash, in TTL mode.

Figure 3.24   Sigma ring flash.

Figure 3.25   Here we can see a studio flash fitted with a soft box being used to illuminate a piece of clothing prior to IR photography.

3.6.4   Studio flash

As mentioned above, these are the most flexible lights to use, as they come in a variety of shapes and sizes for all applications. They are, however, generally more expensive and not suitable for scene use. As can be seen in the Figure 3.25 these units are generally tripod mounted so they can be moved into position within the studio. You will also notice that they are often fitted with soft boxes or umbrellas to soften and diffuse the light, reducing shadows and producing an even illumination of the subject.

These types of light can also often be fitted with polarising or coloured filters, many also have outputs allowing their use for IR photography. This will, however, be dependent on your manufacturer. The use of these units should not be overlooked and make the photography of property type exhibits easier to undertake.

Before I leave the subject of flash, there is a perception that with the advent of more sensitive digital sensors the use of flash is not required or has limited application. It is true that many cameras now claim to shoot in the dark, or in very low light levels. This is fine if you have even levels of illumination and contrast in your scene, but it cannot place light where there is none, it can only lighten darker areas and, as we have talked about, this can bring forth extra issue. If you look at Figure 3.26 you can see that we have a scene with mixed lighting levels and contrast ranges.

(a) (b) (c)

Figure 3.26 (a) shows the area exposed for the surrounding area, with the interior of the shed in deep shadow. (b) shows the interior exposed for the marker, but note how the foreground is now overexposed losing all highlight detail. (c) shows the same area this time using a single Metz 45 to throw light into the back of the shed.

Case example

In this case, I was asked to photograph a murder in a motor vehicle that had been set alight. Although it sounded a straightforward scenario, as with all things it became more complicated when it turned out to be in an underground car park.

Although not extensively fire damaged, most of the overhead fluorescent strip light illumination was blown. This was an ideal opportunity to use the open flash technique, particularly for the long shots in the approach to the motor vehicle. Fixing the camera to a tripod, I framed up the image using a torch to find the point of focus and set the camera to f11 and its bulb setting. I then set two flash units (so I did not have to wait between recharges) to manual full power giving f16 at 4 m. This was to allow for the smoke damaged concrete to absorb some of the light. I then had the investigating officer stand with his notebook across the lens, as it was near pitch black. I fired the shutter and asked the officer to remove his notebook. Then, standing on either side of the camera I fired off the flash down the roadway towards the car. I then asked the officer to cover the lens again and, using a torch, I was able to move down the car park so that I could position myself behind a vehicle or pillar. On command, the officer removed his notebook and I fired the flash left and right so that there was hopefully an overlap of exposures. This was repeated until I reached the vehicle in question. In total, around 30 flashes were fired with an exposure of over 5 min. The resultant images showed a car park that looked as if it had full illumination. The reason for asking the officer to cover the lens was so that as I was moving with the torch it would not leave white streak trails across the image (see Figure 3.19 above).

It is worth noting that, for best results, keep yourself shielded by walls, pillars, trees and so on, and hold the flash up high, pointing down rather than at chest height, as this is more pleasing to the eye. Beware of either silhouetting yourself by firing the flash in front of you, with your back to the camera, or conversely towards the camera when you will create flare.

The second case is slightly unusual in that I was asked to photograph the inside of a brothel in central London. Here the standard technique of fill in flash was used and all was going well until I came to photograph the very large bathroom. This, unfortunately, was mirrored in every direction. No matter where I stood, every flat surface had a mirror including the ceiling and the back of the door. Thinking outside of the box, I had a brief conversation with the officer in charge and asked would he mind if I ran the bath! Emptying out the old cold bath water I started to fill it with steaming hot water. Within a few minutes all the mirrored surfaces had condensation on them. I was then able to frame up, placing the flash on the floor to bounce off the ceiling. Using an air cable release I was able to leave the room and fire the camera remotely achieving a good result without the camera or I appearing in shot.

4
Crime Scene Photography

4.1   Overview

There can be no doubt about the important role that forensic photography plays in today's investigations and legal system, whether you are working within the police or other affiliated agency. Yet, is the image we present or are presented with, really a reliable and accurate record for future reference? As we discussed in the opening chapters, never before has photography been so accessible, or so misunderstood, with anyone with a camera claiming to be a photographer. The issue is that owning a camera doesn't make you a forensic photographer; it just makes you a camera owner. So what is it that sets us apart from any other camera owner? To me there are two main considerations, first the attention to detail in the composition and second the technical delivery and understanding of those images.

In the first few chapters we looked briefly at the key technical skills we require to undertake our task. In this chapter I want to bring the knowledge and skills together in the crime scene. The concepts and ideas given below are for guidance, and your own force or agency will have its own standard operating procedures. For example, in some forces, large numbers of images are taken at postmortems, in others very few. The important thing to remember is we are the eyes of the investigating officers, prosecutors and defence teams, judges and juries, who will never attend that scene. We are in effect recording an event in pictorial form, allowing that scene to be presented in court in a professional, clear and complete manner.

Many books break the photography of crime scenes down into categories, such as fatal accidents, murders, and so on. However, to me these are really subcategories. I believe that, from a technical photographic viewpoint, there are only two types of scene you will ever come across: interiors and exteriors. In reality, all types of scene are only variants on these two options; fire scenes

Forensic Photography: A Practitioner's Guide, First Edition. Nick Marsh.
© 2014 John Wiley & Sons, Ltd. Published 2014 by John Wiley & Sons, Ltd.

are generally scenes that require more lighting. In the same way, in many cases a murder scene is only a burglary scene with a body within it.

There are, however, a number of technical issues and non-photographic factors that will change from case type to case type, particularly when dealing with:

- Motor vehicles
- Assault victims
- Property
- Prisoners
- Fire damaged scenes
- RTC (Road Traffic Collisions)
- Dead bodies/cadavers.

Later on in the chapter, we will look at some of the specifics that apply.

No matter what the assignment is, however, there are a number of questions that we need to ask and keep asking ourselves.

4.1.1   What are we being asked to photograph?

This may sound obvious, but isn't always. Investigators sometimes have an idea of what they want recorded; however, on other occasions there is no intelligence or information to indicate critical elements within the scene. In some cases they do not posses the technical knowledge or even the awareness to ask for it. It is our task to turn those thought processes into a visual record. For example, if they want the road layout photographed, is this best undertaken at ground level, or would an elevated or aerial view be better? There is no point in producing a well exposed, colour balanced image if it doesn't actually show what was required

4.1.2   When do I take photographs?

The question here is what we are trying to achieve; clearly if we are asked to take further photographs of a 'night, fatal' road collision scene, it may not be appropriate to take further photographs at midday if you are trying to replicate the conditions at the time, as this could mislead the jury in regards to the lighting, visibility, viewpoints or even weather conditions. Although it might be appropriate to do so if it happened at dusk and we arrive when it is dark, or if we are looking at producing a more detailed scene photograph. Clearly there are times when this will be inevitable, but reference should be made on your notes that the conditions may not be a true representation of conditions at the time of the event. In all cases the strategy should be discussed with the senior investigating officer or crime scene manager.

4.1.3 How will I take the photographs?

This covers the issues around the types of lenses and lighting required. For example, if you are asked to undertake the photography of fingermarks in blood, there is little point attending with only a wide-angle lens. Above all it is our responsibility as the photographic imaging expert to glean as much information from the investigating officer or crime scene manager as possible, to clearly convey the information required.

Before we start, though, we need to look at a couple of other issues over which we have no control.

4.2 Personal protective equipment (PPE)

At most crime scenes we will be one of the first people on the scene: the one overriding issue to be borne in mind, is that we are not exempt from the normal restrictions of working within that crime scene. Every effort must be made to avoid disturbing the scene or leaving cross-contamination, or conversely from the scene contaminating you.

At many scenes this is sometimes easier said than done, as they are often contaminated with blood or other substances and, once on the shoe or tripod foot, it is easily transferred around. For example, traces of blood may not be readily visible to the human eye, but under treatments such as luminol will become highly visible. Therefore the wearing of personal protective equipment (PPE) and protecting any equipment going into the scene is a given (Figure 4.1).

As you can see in Figure 4.1, I am wearing the full PPE used at a typical crime scene. The all in one suit is a Tyvec Classic model CHF5;[1] for personal comfort these are lightweight but water repellent. The mask is a disposable one and although this particular type is not designed for long-term usage, (some types are), we have found these paper type ones to be less restrictive.[2] At present we use the Tyvec type of overshoes,[3] which are embossed across the base with scene of crime. This, however, does not give you carte blanche to walk wherever you like, as even with these overshoes on your shoe pattern can still come through. It is therefore important that if you come into contact with the floor when stepping plates (see below) are being used, that the senior forensic officer, frequently the crime scene manager, is informed. This will allow your shoe pattern, if found, to be eliminated from the enquiry. Experience has shown that time and money would have been saved if staff had admitted that they had stepped on the floor and thus the shoe marks were theirs rather than the suspect's.

---

[1] Tyvec suits http://www2.dupont.com
[2] Mask: numerous suppliers are available on the Internet.
[3] Overshoes: via your scene of crime supplier

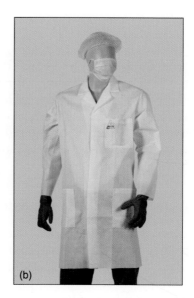

Figure 4.1   (a) Shows full PPE used for scenes and (b) the PPE for use within the DNA laboratories.

Single gloving is acceptable for fingerprint only scenes, but double gloving is a must for scenes where the retrieval of DNA is required. We wear either double layer of rubber or latex gloves.[4] At fingerprint only scenes, we often use black cotton gloves as these have a number of advantages:[5]

(1)   They are UV protecting (to meet internal H&S standards). These gloves block 98% of the UV emitted from our light sources. So other hand protection is not required.

(2)   We have also found the use of black cotton gloves over traditional white cotton ones advantageous, particularly when carrying out photography, or an examination, using UV or lasers. If you are using white cotton and it passes through the beam, they fluoresce brightly, thus reducing your effective night vision (Figure 4.2). The black ones do not, this also means that during long exposures, black gloves can be used to hold back areas such as labels.

(3)   They act as an absorbent barrier if worn under rubber or latex type gloves and stop the hands from sweating too heavily.

Black latex gloves are now available and can be used as a replacement for the standard brown rubber, or purple latex gloves, and give the same benefits as

---

[4] Latex gloves: numerous suppliers are available on the Internet.
[5] Black cotton gloves Southcombe Brothers, UK, http://www.southcombe.com/

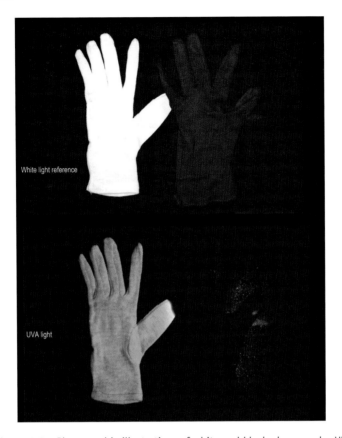

White light reference

UVA light

Figure 4.2   Photographic illustrations of white and black gloves under UV.

above.[6] Protective clear types of plastic safety glasses are generally not worn at scenes, unless there is a high proportion of airborne blood or other materials, or a chemical is being applied, but are available if required.

Note that at the end of every attendance, regardless of its length, these articles are bagged up and destroyed as contaminated waste. They are never reused, even if the scene is to be revisited the next day. Although rare, at some serious crime scenes these items may need to be exhibited and may be examined at a later date for a number of reasons. Again, this should be coordinated with your crime scene manager, in line with your force's policy.

Although above I mentioned the use of tripod socks in a scene to protect the tripod feet, any item that is taken within the cordon should be considered as contaminated. I say this because it is very easy to forget our kit bags, or other associated bits and bobs, such as extension cables, that we might use. All of these must be cleaned and disinfected to reduce the chances of

[6] Black latex gloves are available on the Internet or through your scenes of crime provider

Figure 4.3   Lightweight aluminum stepping plates, note the feet can be unscrewed for easy cleaning and, when stacked, the feet slot into the plate below.

cross-contamination, not only between the kit and scene or vice versa, but also the transfer between scenes. It is for that reason we use large, hard-shelled camera cases and never the material type, and plastic wheeled storage boxes for items such as the ball lights and so on.

Do not believe the TV presented scenarios of people wandering around in their normal clothing; this is bad practice, unacceptable and compromising to the evidence chain.

4.2.1   Stepping plates

In order to undertake the photography at many scenes we will working from stepping plates. These are available in a number of types, both in plastic[7] and metal.[8] At the present time we use plates of our own design. These are square and made from very lightweight aluminum, they can be stacked 12 to a carrying case without locking together.[9] They also have removable, easy-clean feet that do not slip (Figure 4.3). Finally, they are colour coordinated with non-slip paint, so that that the owner of the plates – photographic, scientific, crime scene manager, or forensic practitioner – is known and they can be returned at the end of a scene.

---

[7] Plastic stepping plates available from a number of manufacturers and suppliers including Sirchie's USA, http://store.sirchie.com/Transparent-Plastic-Stepping-Plates-Kit-Standard-P2370C603.aspx and Forensic Pathways http://www.forensic-pathways.com/products-and-services/forensic-stepping-plates

[8] Metal stepping plates are available from a number of manufactures and suppliers including Tetra Scenes of Crime http://www.tetrasoc.com/stepping-plates-aluminium-p-524.html and Scenesafe https://www.scenesafe.co.uk/index.php?route=product/product&product'id=172.

[9] Bespoke stepping plate http://www.Laserinnovations.com

Your force or agencies own personal protective equipment may vary from ours, but the concepts around its use will hold true.

4.3   The generics of scene photography

As discussed earlier, we are relied upon as the official recorders of the scene, but where do we start? In a small bedsit this may be an easy and straightforward decision. But what do we do at a large outdoor scene, or when priorities are changing or photographs need to be taken out of order?

No matter what the scene is, it is good practice to shoot in chronological order and to try and link photographs. This is clearly not always possible or practical, so notes should always be taken for reference at a later stage. Within our unit, shooting lists are kept by the photographer that document each photograph taken, in other forces notebooks or scene attendance forms are used. At one point, I used to use a voice activated dictaphone with a small lapel microphone.[10] I believe, unlike some book recommendations, that there is no longer a need to note every exposure value, as these values are now recorded in the metadata of the camera.

It is also appropriate at this point to mention the one element over which we have no control: that of weather conditions. Clearly depending on where you are in the world these conditions will vary.

4.3.1   Sunshine

This may sound obvious, but if possible avoid shooting into the sun; apart from the possibility of damaging your eyes, it will easily fool the built-in light meter creating a silhouette of the subject and causing flare across the image. Bright sunshine can also cause deep unwanted shadows or very harsh bright highlights and reflections.

If possible use a lens hood to shield the front of the lens or try 'flagging' the lens with your hand or paper.[11]

I would also suggest the use of a UV filter on the lens. These simple filters are cost effective and they will serve two purposes, one to reduce unwanted ultraviolet rays reaching the sensor and the other to protect the lens from dust and dirt.[12]

---

[10] Under disclosure any note made at the scene must be made available to be reviewed by the defence if required. If a dictaphone or other recording device is used then the recording medium must be retained for inspection.

[11] Flagging is when the hand or a piece of paper is used to shadow the front element of the lens from the sun, removing the chances of lens flare. This is normally done when shooting into the light and when no lens hood is available.

[12] UV filter both stops unwanted ultraviolet rays reaching the sensor and protects the front lens element from dust, dirt and rain. These are available at any good camera store.

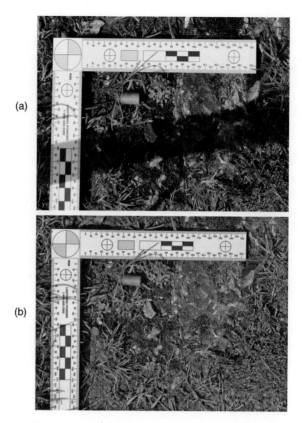

Figure 4.4   Here the distracting shadow has been removed, by shielding the area and using off-camera flash.

The other issue, as mentioned above, is the production of deep shadows; it is therefore useful to have an electronic flash to hand to fill in and enhance shadow areas (see Chapter 3 on the use of flash). In Figure 4.4 we can see a 9-mm cartridge case lying on the ground. In photograph (a) the shadow of the tripod leg is seen crossing the image from left to right. In image (b), the area has been placed in shadow by a colleague's coat and flash used to illuminate the area instead.

I have worked on a number of war gravesites in very bright sunlight. Here exposures at the graveside could be as high as 1/1000th s at f/22 using 100ASA film. Using a Bronica 6 × 7, I was able to sync at 1/500th and, by stopping the lens down to f/32 and using a Metz 60 on full power, I was able to infill the interior of the grave with flash, thus creating a usable exposure showing the deceased and the surrounding surface. A separate team working on another site without a professional photographer, returned with photographs just showing underexposed graves with no detail because the meter had been fooled by the surrounding graveside.

Don't forget: never leave your camera equipment lying around in a motor vehicle or other position where it can get excessively hot. The heat may or may not damage the electronics, but I have seen the glue on some parts melt or become sticky.

4.3.2 Rain

This can be an issue here in the UK, but probably not given much thought if you're reading this in Arizona or Abu Dhabi. The obvious and most important problem is damage to equipment. Although most modern DSLRs are weather proof to some extent, prolonged exposure to rain can lead to electrical or other failures. It is therefore a good idea to check with your manufacturer as to its possible suitability. Within the department we had over 50 Nikon D2xs (which had been in use for six years) and D700s (for the past two years), which are frequently exposed to rain and snow and yet rarely break down.

However, if you are in a climate that has heavy persistent rain, high humidity, or other airborne contaminates such as dust or exhaust emissions, you may want to invest in weatherproof housing. This is a sort of waterproof plastic bag that fits over the particular camera model you are using. You can also purchase completely waterproof housing.[13]

You can also protect the front element of the lens with a lens hood. Many of my scenes of crime colleagues use an umbrella attached to the tripod, a simple but slightly cumbersome solution. This option also normally avoids the other main irritation of rain, that of water droplets on the lens. These are often missed when reviewing the image on screen and are only seen when you review the images in post-production, as blurry dots on the image.

4.3.3 Wind

This may at first thought seem to be irrelevant. Yet, when working in low light conditions with long exposures, this can be a very real issue particularly if you are using a lightweight tripod. In these conditions, try using a sturdier tripod or hang weights from the centre column. (Many columns have a hook at the base for just this purpose.) Failing that, you can try parking your vehicle to act as windbreak.

The more obvious effect, and probably the most visually annoying, is the issue of movement within the image: if a tree or other plants are moving they appear as blurry shapes that can easily detract from the point of interest. Two options to reduce this effect might be to increase the shutter speed thus reducing the amount of movement, or alternatively changing your view point

---

[13] Waterproof housing seals the camera completely. These are bespoke to your particular camera, so refer to the manufacturer's website for the correct model and fit.

angle so the object is no longer prominent within the frame and thus is less noticeable.

4.3.4   Fog

As well as producing poor viewing conditions, resulting in soft and unclear images, fog is very reflective, so if direct flash on camera is used we will end up with a white out. Hence the reason cars have fog lights at a low level and you are instructed not to drive with full beam switched on. However, with care and consideration, supplementary flash can be used, but it must be fired at an angle of less than 45° to your subject. To find the angle, ask a colleague with a lamp or torch to walk in an arced line away from the camera (so as to keep the same distance between the camera and subject). Once the light falls on the subject, without directly reflecting into the lens, you can replace it with the flash. Use the open flash techniques as described in Chapter 3 on flash exposure.

4.3.5   Snow

The biggest issue with snow is that it can create extreme contrast, as with sunlight, and if flash is used it is often reflected more intensively than normal. When taking exposure readings through the camera the meter will read the surroundings as very bright. You must therefore nearly always overexpose by at least two stops to the meter reading, or take an incident light reading of your hand with an incident light meter. This is a similar effect to having an interior scene where the area of interest is close to bright light coming through a window. If you meter the brightly lit area, the rest of the room will be underexposed.

It is also worth thinking about what you are photographing. I was once asked to photograph a VW beetle involved in an armed robbery after a very heavy snowfall. When I turned up, the officer claimed he had 'brushed' the snow off the car, in fact he had just knocked the snow off the index plates, but the rest was just a white hump!

4.3.6   Cold

Cold creates a number of minor issues; firstly, kit left in vehicles overnight can suffer from the flash or other batteries being flattened, so if possible remove them to a warm place overnight. Cold air and, in particular, changing environments from inside to out and so on, can also create the issue of condensation. If possible, always allow time for your equipment to acclimatise before using it. If your first image is slightly soft, this probably means you have some condensation within the camera. Although kit can be warmed on a heater, beware that condensation doesn't form on the back element of the lens, mirror or internal IR filter. A good tip is to follow the example of many of my colleagues, who carry the camera bag in the driver's cab of their vehicles so that the camera and lenses can acclimatise before reaching the first job of the day.

4.4 Photographic equipment

Ok, now we have covered the bits and pieces over which we have no control. We are now in a position to look at photographing our crime scene.

The choice of equipment is often a personal thing, but the below is the standard equipment supplied to all of our photographers. It is also important to note at this point that, unless otherwise stated, and much to the disappointment of some, a tripod will be used at all times. Many forces do not support the use of tripods for all photography; but to my mind, if used properly, they offer a stable platform, enabling you to use any shutter speed or flash combination without the limitations of a hand held shot.

- A Professional Digital Single Lens Reflex Camera.
- 24–70 mm or similar lens (with lens hood).
- 105 mm macro lens (or similar).
- 60 mm macro lens (or similar).
- Cable release.
- Suitable tripod.
- Two flash guns and spare batteries.
- Forensic ruler.
- Boat lamp or similar.[14]
- Compass.
- Cross-polarising filters.[15]
- Spirit level.

This is a good place to mention the use of forensic rulers. Again, any form of scale is better than none, but careful consideration should be given to its reliability, as not all scales are equal [1, 2]. They should be included in any image that may need to be reproduced accurately, for example shoe marks or injuries, or that requires a physical guide as to an exhibit's size; failure to do so could mislead an investigation.

For example, in Figure 4.5 we can see in photograph (a) a large, dangerous-looking, offensive weapon in the form of a sword. It is not until we place a

---

[14] Lenzer torches are readily available on the internet.

[15] Cross-polarised filters reduce unwanted reflections and are available from any good camera store in both a circular and linear form.

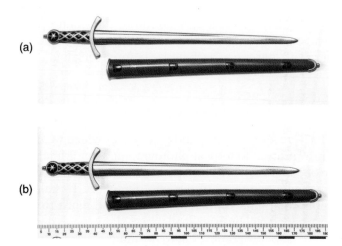

Figure 4.5   A toy sword with and without a scale.

scale within the image photograph (b) that it is clear that this in fact a toy, posing no threat. Yet all I have done is introduce a scale.

4.5   Composition

As I have already commented, we are the eyes of the investigating team, the prosecution, defence, judge and jury, and on some occasions the coroner or the Health and Safety executive. The way that we approach and record a crime scene could, if not handled thoughtfully, mislead or fail to capture all of the evidence.

In my mind it is easier to work out our approach and shooting sequence if we can split the photography into two processes: general shots – the long and mid range ones, and targeted ones – the close ups or points of interest. Although in reality these two will probably run together seamlessly, I will for the purposes of explanation within this book split them up.

General photographs are used to relate the scene to its surrounding environment, or key items within the scene to their location. These types of images are normally taken from a natural perspective and normally at a chest height position (comfortable tripod height) (Figure 4.6). This is because it is presumed by viewers of the images that this is what the photographer would have done. If you take photographs low down, say in a kneeling or lying position, or from above, say from a balcony, this should be clearly be indicated in you album index.

Unless otherwise directed, the prime lens for your camera should be always be considered first, this is particularly relevant for witness viewpoints or fatal accidents (Figure 4.7).

Figure 4.6   Here we can see the same view of our mock decapitation taken with a 50 mm (a) and 24 mm (b) lens. Although both images are acceptable as an overview, only image (a) has the correct perspective.

As we can see in the examples it is easy to accidently mislead the viewer simply by the choice of lens used. As you can see from Figure 4.7, the perspective within the photographs can be highly misleading. Indeed I have actually had this trick used against me at court with regard to a witness viewpoint in a very similar set of images as seen in Figure 4.7. In that case, the defence claimed that it would be impossible for the witness to recognise the suspect in a car at the distance seen in the photographs. It was clear on examining their photographs, however, that the images had been taken on an 18 mm lens, exaggerating the distance from the witness to the suspect's car. This I was able to articulate and show in court, proving that they had in fact misled the jury.

With outside scenes, try to ensure that your photographs are related to the environment around them. If possible, try to include road signs, telephone boxes or other references to show the position from which the photograph was taken.

In the metropolitan police, it is common to use street furniture such as telegraph poles or street light numbers as references to the photographer's position. (These are all individually numbered.) This is referenced to the points of the compass in the album index to indicate direction (Figures 4.8 and 4.9).

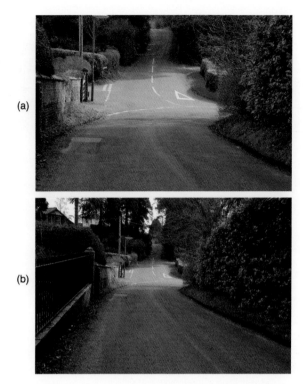

(a)

(b)

Figure 4.7   Here we can see the same choice of lens as in Figure 4.6. However this time, the change in perspective has grossly exaggerated the distance to the road junction, so that we now appear twice as far away as with the standard lens.

Figure 4.8   Shows view looking north along Ford Lane towards Aveley Lane from telephone pole 4. (Exposed at f9.5 at 1/180th 320 ISO.)

Figure 4.9   shows view looking north along Ford Lane towards Aveley Lane from lamppost 23234 (seen in previous photograph). (Exposed at f9.5 at 1/180th 320 ISO.)

In many countries it is common practice to photograph the street signs (Figure 4.10).

When framing up these scene-setting shots, remember that if you are in a large open space with lots of sky, any buildings in the distance could be under-exposed. So if they are of importance, meter off a grassy area or take an incident light reading. These general scene-setting type shots always take time, but in reality it costs very little to photograph up and down a street once you are positioned. So don't skimp on taking as many photographs as you think are required. In my experience, we are often asked to return to the scene later, because the officer or the prosecution want to show the view in the other

Figure 4.10   Show the intersection of Ford Lane, Middle Bourne Lane and Aveley lane. (Exposed at f9.5 at 1/180th 320 ISO.)

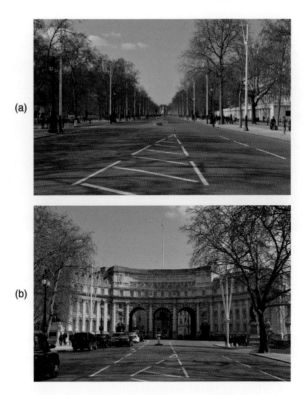

Figure 4.11   (a) The Mall looking west toward Buckingham Palace, from the pedestrian island to the west of Spring Gardens SW1. (50 mm lens exposed at f18 1/500th at 400 ISO.) (b) The Mall looking east towards Admiralty Arch from the pedestrian crossing to the west of Spring Gardens SW1. (50 mm lens exposed at f18 1/200th at 400 ISO.)

direction. Even in cases where the address is well known, as in Figure 4.11, accurate notes should be taken of the location. Some forces I know of now use GPS coordinates to accurately position their photograph, although within London I do not feel that is necessary.

The exteriors of buildings often offer another interesting challenge with regard to framing and photography. Photographing a building straight on causes converging verticals, which can be distracting to the eye, plus it is sometimes difficult to get the whole building in. One option is to consider a diagonal approach to the photography; this can, however, cause the building to form a wedge shape with one side nearer than the other. This is often compounded by the fall-off in depth of field. The ultimate choice is to photograph it with a perspective control lens (Figure 4.12), but in reality, due to the cost, we are unlikely to have one to hand. Generally the easiest and cheapest option is that the building should be photographed square on, but from a greater distance so we are not looking up, but across at it. In Figure 4.13 you can see the two alternative viewpoints, in this case both would be acceptable.

Figure 4.12 Converging verticals, photographed with a standard lens and then with a shift lens. Although only a minor issue, for our purposes it can be distracting.

Although the building might be a bit smaller in the frame, being square on also allows all the doors, windows or other areas of interest to be clearly seen, whereas the diagonal can obscure the view.

If we are photographing exhibits found at an outside scene, location photographs should always taken, preferably with a forensic marker in place (Figure 4.14). The important thing to remember is, if the item to be photographed is not indicated with a forensic marker, then it should be photographed with an easily identifiable non-movable (if possible) item in the frame. This is to stop any claims by the defence that the item has been moved.

When undertaking the close ups, think about the framing. How is the exhibit going to appear in the finished photograph? Is it actually going to show what the officer wants to see and what the court is going want to see? Even how the item sits within the frame is important (Figure 4.15). Consideration should not only be given to the positioning of the shot but the height at which it is taken. Would a plan view be better than an angled shot? (Figure 4.16).

Figure 4.13   Angles of view. Again, although the angle isn't a major issue, simply changing position has allowed the frontage of the building to be more clearly seen. This can be particularly seen on the lower photograph where the bushes and tress have blocked the view of part of the ground floor exterior.

4.5.1   Interiors

Intrinsically, the same rules that apply to our exterior scenes should apply to our interior ones. They should always be photographed as found; indeed we will probably be one of the first through the door. Before entering, we should be wearing our full PPE and if required stepping plates should be put down. If the scene is blood-soaked then it is recommended to use tripod socks[16] (Figure 4.17).

It should be noted at this point that all equipment going within the cordon should be cleaned to reduce the possibilities of cross-contamination. At most scenes there is a room or an area of space that is within the cordon but has been deemed to have little forensic value. This is generally used by the exhibits

---

[16] Tripod socks are available. These cheap devices protect the tripods foot area from heavily soiled scenes.

Figure 4.14 (a) The exhibit's relationship to both a forensic marker and non movable item (the building). (b) A positional shot of marker 'V'. (c) Close up of the exhibit at marker 'V'.

officers or crime scene manager (CSM) for writing or briefing purposes and this area should be used as your base camp. By that I mean that any photographic kit that is not required immediately is left at this point. There is no need to carry a loaded and full photographic bag into the main scene thus increasing the risks of contamination, particularly if DNA samples are going to be taken.

Again, a logical progression through the scene is advisable, although not always practical. This means that images may be shot out of sequence but rearranged into sequence when producing the album. A shooting list should be kept as you progress through the scene.

Figure 4.15   Poor framing and viewing angles. On the left, the firearm has been positioned poorly in the viewfinder at an angle. On the right, a landscape viewpoint has been chosen, but angled away from the observer.

Figure 4.16   Here the firearm has been correctly positioned so that it is square in the viewfinder with all the detail clearly seen.

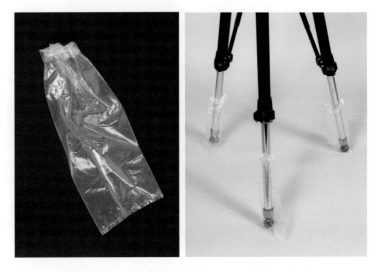

Figure 4.17   Photographic illustration of tripod socks.

Figure 4.18 15 mm (fisheye) lens.

Unlike exteriors, where a standard lens is often used, with most interiors this would give us a very limited angle of view, so a wide-angle lens can be employed.

Generally, however, extreme wide-angle lenses as used in Figure 4.18 should be avoided due to the distortions that can be present (see Figures 4.18, 4.19, 4.20, 4.21).

Never forget we are the eyes of the court and it is therefore good practice to photograph the exterior of the property, or corridor if it is an apartment (see Figure 4.22). This will then act as a reference point confirming the correct address and should be photographed as found.

If possible, I like to shoot the route to the deceased first and then undertake photography of the other rooms. (This means that is then possible for the other members of the forensic team to start dealing with the body.) In

Figure 4.19 24 mm lens.

Figure 4.20   35 mm lens.

most interior scenes this means that you are going to require supplementary lighting in the form of electronic flash. This will be used in one of two modes, complete exposure or fill in (see Chapter 3 on flash photography).

In the above example (Figures 4.23 to 4.30), I have used the minimum number of images to capture the scene. In reality, the complexity and importance of the scene will dictate how many images you need to take and of what. The important thing to remember is that we cannot go back, so it is always better to take more images than you require, rather than not enough.

4.6   Specific types of scenes

I said above that scenes fall into basically one of two types: interiors and exteriors. There are, however, a number of scenarios where other issues need to be taken into account. To look at this, I am going to break them down into bite-sized chunks using the guidance given by our own training section.

Figure 4.21   50 mm lens.

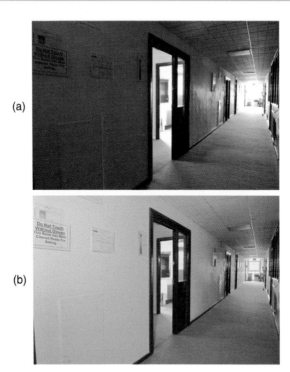

Figure 4.22   The entrance to the scene. (a) Illuminated with ambient lighting 400 ISO at f11 1.3 s exposure. (b) With two flash units, one illuminating the doorway one with the diffuser removed fired down the hallway (400 ISO at f11 $^1/_4$ s).

Figure 4.23   The kitchen area.

Figure 4.24   The living room area showing a knife.

Figure 4.25   The knife in position.

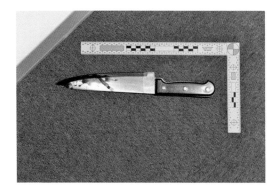

Figure 4.26   The knife.

Figure 4.27   The bathroom.

Figure 4.28   The view from the bathroom into the living room.

Figure 4.29   The bedroom.

Figure 4.30   The view from the bedroom towards the living room.

4.6.1   Motor vehicles

These are to all intents and purposes mini scenes, and should be recorded before any other forensic intervention takes place. As such, and unless otherwise instructed, full PPE should be worn if it is to be examined at later date for blood, fingerprints or GSR (gunshot residue).

(a)

(b)

Figure 4.31 The front 3/4 of a motor vehicle photographed (a) without fill in flash (b) with fill in flash.

The standard approach is to begin with a front $^3/_4$ view of the motor vehicle if possible, from both the near and offside positions, followed by the rear $^3/_4$ from the same positions. If possible these should be taken using a standard prime lens to avoid perspective distortions and using f11 or f16 to ensure a good depth of field. I know many forces do not consider the use of flash for the general shots of motor vehicles, but I believe that flash should be considered if possible, to illuminate the shadow areas, particularly along the skirt of the car, as this helps to lift the image aesthetically (Figure 4.31).

If space around the vehicle does not allow a standard front or rear $^3/_4$, then a wider lens is acceptable; but it should be noted and super wide lenses should never be used as they produce unacceptable distortions (Figure 4.32).

If there are areas of damage, these can now be located using a closer view-point and illuminated to highlight that specific area. In the case of dents or damage, careful consideration should be given before using flash, as this can easily 'flatten off' a dent or damaged area. I would try exploring the best

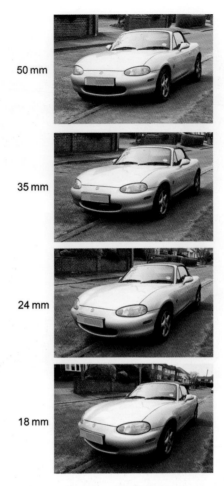

50 mm

35 mm

24 mm

18 mm

Figure 4.32   Front $^3/_4$ of MV using various lenses.

angle of illumination with a torch; if possible get a colleague to maneuver the torch whilst you observe from the camera position. You may wish to avoid using flash altogether if the damage is obvious under the ambient illumination (Figure 4.33).

This technique is particularly useful when it comes to broken windscreens or windscreen damage. Using a torch or lamp allows very small movements to be used in the angle of illumination, including back lighting from inside the vehicle, which can be critical in ensuring the damage is captured accurately.

Another option to consider, especially in the case of windscreens, is the use of a polariser filter. In Figure 4.34 you can see that when used it has the effect of reducing the reflections off the glass, particularly in regards to the large area of white in the lower right hand portion of the image.

Figure 4.33 Photograph of the damage to car door (a) when viewed square on – notice how the damage looks shallow. (b) As before, but this time photographed from the rear of the car looking forwards, illuminated with flash.

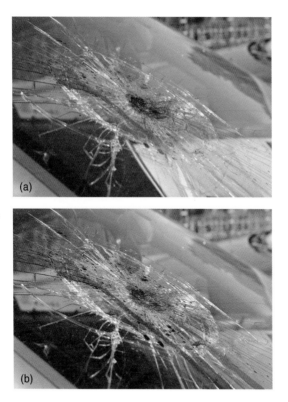

Figure 4.34 Damage to a windscreen. Although both are acceptable (a) shows the unpolarised image, whilst (b) shows the polarised image which appears cleaner and has more contrast, whilst the distracting white paper in the windscreen has been suppressed.

Figure 4.35   Photograph of VIN plate.

Dependent on the crime type, there are also certain other standard images required, particularly in relation to lost or stolen vehicles.

Engine numbers   Often these are placed in difficult or inaccessible areas with limited access. A short telephoto and mirror (either to reflect the number into, or to reflect flash or torch light for illumination) are often useful in achieving a usable result.

Stamped chassis numbers are usually found under an inspection panel on the doorsill. The photography is generally straightforward provided the plate is clean. Illumination should be at an oblique angle with flash or boat lamp with an aperture of f11 or f16 to ensure depth of field.

VIN numbers (vehicle identification numbers) have been standard across the motor manufacturing industry since 1981 and are a 17-number long list of information about the motor vehicle. The VIN plate can usually be found under the bonnet, normally near the bonnet catch (Figure 4.35). In many modern cars these numbers are easier to find and they are now positioned in the lower corner of the windscreen or in that general area. As an aside, they offer a wealth of information about that particular motor vehicle, hence their importance to an investigation.

If you are photographing a VIN plate, before photography ensure the plate is clean and all the numbers are visible. Slightly oblique lighting between 45° and 55° should be used to ensure that the raised number is enhanced.

If you are photographing one in the windscreen area, then it is often possible to use ambient illumination and a polarising filter (to remove reflections) (Figure 4.36). Direct flash should generally be avoided because of the chances of flare and reflections from the glass.

Etched windows and others   Many manufacturers etch vehicle indexes or other pertinent detail onto the glass of motor vehicle; again these can be useful identifiers and should be recorded if deemed necessary (Figure 4.37). These

Figure 4.36 Photograph of windscreen plate.

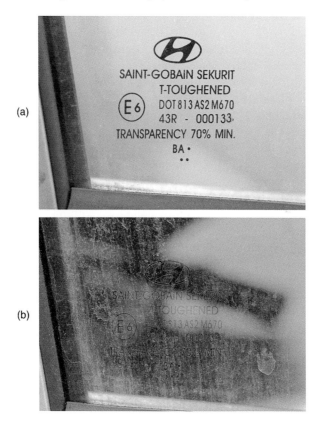

Figure 4.37 Window etching (a) with the door open using ambient lighting exposed at f8, 1/30th 400 ISO (b) with the door closed and illuminated with flash from the opposite side of the car, exposed at f8 1/60th 400 ISO, flash set to manual half power. Note in (b) although the etching is legible, the interfering background is distracting. This is often not seen until the exposure has been taken. It is not, however, always possible to remove them if the vehicle is locked.

are often clearly visible; however, supplementary flash can be used, but caution should be taken not to catch the reflection in the glass. Often back lighting the etching by placing the flash inside the car works well. If flash is being used on TTL, be careful that the flash does not overexpose as it will try and expose for the interior of the car. Conversely, if the flash is positioned inside the car, ensure it does not underexpose, as it could see the flash. Often it is easier to set the flash to manual, use ambient illumination or a torch or lamp, and then adjust the camera's aperture.

If any of the above have been tampered with or removed, the area should still be photographed to show signs or damage. If engine or other numbers have been removed, it is worth pointing the investigating officer towards the use of 'acid etching'. This technique uses nitric acid as a way of possibly retrieving them, and although this is dependent on the depth to which the number was pressed, I have seen it produce good results on a number of occasions [3, 4].

When undertaking motor vehicle photography, there are also a number of extra health and safety issues that need to be considered. If we are dealing with motor vehicles in position at an incident, then a high visibility jacket/tabard is mandatory. Even in daylight this is essential, as one may be easily distracted with the task in hand and not notice the movements of other vehicles around you.

Secondly, motor vehicles are full of highly corrosive, flammable or lacerating materials, many of which, particularly if the vehicle is in situ may spread across a wide area. Battery acid is highly corrosive at around 35% sulfuric acid, and can cause blindness and third degree burns if it comes into contact with the skin. It also can easily burn through most clothing materials and especially cottons, although polyester is naturally acid resistant. Even a mist of acid can cause irritation to the eyes, nose and throat and if breathed in can cause pulmonary oedema.

Petrol and diesel can offer a potential fire risk, but in reality by the time of our attendance most petrol fumes (the bit that ignites) will normally have evaporated away. (Although a check should always be made with the attending fire crews to ensure the area is safe.) Diesel is less likely to explode, but as it is oil based and can make the ground slippery and dangerous, caution should be exercised.

Within the engine compartment, some gaskets, rubber seals and wiring looms that have been exposed to temperatures in excess of 400 °C can produce hydrofluoric acid. This is a particularly nasty acid that is highly irritating to the respiratory tract and eyes. It is, however, more dangerous to the skin, as pain may not be immediately felt but may occur a number of hours later. If contact is suspected Calcium Gluconate Gel[17] should be applied as soon

---

[17] Calcium Gluconate Gel is applied to cancel out the effects of the hydrofluoric acid by combining with it to neutralize the powerful fluoride ion. The area should be washed if possible to remove surface

as possible. Failure to do so can cause further skin damage, which sometimes needs surgery.

Even the manmade fibres used in the seating, insulation and soundproofing can cause issues. These fibres can produce 'needle-stick' punctures to the skin, causing itching, inflammation and sore eyes.

Other obvious dangers are broken glass and twisted and ripped metal work, these all offer the potential to rip clothing or cut skin. Any injuries should be thoroughly washed and medical assistance sought.

4.6.2 Assault victims

Although I will cover this in far greater depth later, in Chapter 6 on the photography of injuries, here are some general guides and reminders.

When dealing with victims our communication skills are vital, as often they can be in a state of shock or conversely angry. Be aware of the situation, particularly if you are in their home, and continuously carry out a risk assessment. Best practice is always to avoid being left alone with the victim if possible and never undertake photography without a third party being present (preferably the police officer in the case).

For general injury capture, flash should always be used; however, as we shall see later on, this can be supplemented with a number of other techniques.

To ensure a reasonable depth of field, f11 or f16 should be selected, and if possible a short telephoto lens should be used, either a 85 mm or 105 mm in FX or equivalent DX focal lengths. Although this slightly foreshortens perspective, it allows stand-off room. Without this we can be on top of a victim, which can make them feel uncomfortable. It also allows better positioning of flash and so on.

Choose plain, non-reflective backgrounds if possible; if we are in the victim's home try to avoid light switches, pot plants or pictures appearing in the background or growing out of people's heads, they are all distracting.

If photographing multiple injuries, work logically from the top to the bottom.

Always use a scale, if possible a ridged one. Paper tape-type ones tend to bend and stretch and are difficult to rescale accurately.

With injuries to the eye area, take two photographs if necessary, one with the eyes open and one with them closed, to show the bruising to the lids and the other to show the damage to the eye itself (generally bloodshot).

If we are photographing swelling, say to a hand, photograph with the other hand to show a comparison.

Dressings should be removed to show the injury, if they cannot be removed then a note should be made to that effect and, depending on the circumstances,

---

HF acid then the gel is applied. It should be massaged in continuously and medical help should be sought immediately.

I would advise no photographs are taken. Avoid trying to show more than one injury per photograph (unless very close together).

Finally, it is best practice to use a same sex photographer to photograph intimate injuries if possible. Failing that, if the victim is agreeable, a same sex third party should be present. Always protect the dignity of the victim and only show the actual injury. See Chapter 6 for photographic guidance.

4.6.3   Prisoners

In the United Kingdom the photography of prisoners is covered by the Police and Criminal Evidence Act 1984 (PACE) [5] specifically sections 54A and 64A

Due to the fact these rules are subject to law they may change in the future.

Photographs may only be taken by an authorised and 'designated' officer.

To date, written permission/consent must be given and this is recorded in the custody record under section 54A (before you start photography you should ask to see the signed consent). If consent is not given, an inspector or above may authorise photography for a specific reason and this will also be recorded in the custody record.

If we are being asked to photograph an injury, follow the same procedures used for victims.

It should be noted that some prisoners will look down, or rock back and forth, to make photography difficult. A good tactic is to fire a spare flash just prior to the real exposure, or use the red eye reduction feature on the camera, if it has one. The prisoner, thinking that the expose has been taken, will then relax and generally look up and we can take the real exposure.

The best results for prisoner photography I have found are achieved when two flashguns are used. One attached to the sync socket and the other working as a slave.[18]

In our own department we have had a number of cameras damaged by suspects who would prefer not to be photographed.

Written permission is not required to photograph property or clothing belonging to the prisoner when it has been seized under statutory powers. If you have any doubts around the legality of the photography, speak to the custody officer.

If we are asked to attend the suspect's address, which is being searched, we are legally entitled to photograph anything the investigating officer may request.

Most of all be aware of your own health and safety and ensure that a police officer is present at all time.

---

[18] Flash slave units, many flash units now have these built in they are however readily available on the internet from your photographic supplier.

The above legislation is for the United Kingdom only and is liable to change, for non-UK readers, please refer to your own national legislation in regards to the issues covered by the above.

4.6.4 Property

Within many forces, the photography of low value items falls within the remit of the local investigation officer or is not recorded at all. A photograph is only taken of property when it is of high value, has been involved in serious crime, cannot be described, or requires specialist photography. This in reality means that you can be asked to photograph anything from a firearm through to a Picasso.

When undertaking photography it is useful to have a plain non-reflective background that is not distracting. For small items, brown paper evidence bags are suitable. For larger ones, I used to carry a large heavy-duty grey background cloth, which was the size of a double sheet. (These are unfortunately no longer available, but a double sheet in a neutral grey would work.) This ensures that distracting backgrounds can be removed with ease, producing a professional end result.

If possible, always include an exhibit label and scale, and preferably a solid ruler regardless of the size of the item. Always photograph identifying features, such as serial numbers and hallmarks, unless otherwise instructed. This is particularly relevant with firearms.

If you are photographing an item that is a particular colour or tonal range, or if the colour is important in the final result, such as a painting, ensure that a colour checker or colour register is within the frame.

If we are asked to photograph items such as cannabis plants, ensure that the whole item is photographed with a scale and then do a close-up of the leaves. If the item/plant is large or tall, consider using a person of a known size to act a basic scale within the photograph.

Finally, never photograph items whilst still in their exhibit bags, or forensic packaging, as this can easily mislead a jury as to size, shape and colour of the item (Figure 4.38).

Property photography is generally carried out at the police station in an office, prisoner cell, or storeroom and will require the use of flash. This will generally be in one of two modes dependent on the exhibit. For flat items, such as paintings or artwork, two flash units at less than 45° should be used, creating an even exposure and avoiding reflections from any glass (if fitted). If you have only one flashgun, try bouncing it from the ceiling or onto white paper (as described in Chapter 3 on the use of flash). Three-dimensional objects are best illuminated using bounce flash, again off the ceiling or a paper reflector, or by fitting a flash diffuser.

If we are lucky enough to have the use of a studio, a much better result can be gained using studio flash. These flash units are in effect scaled-up versions

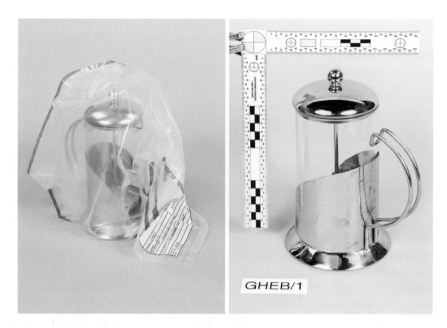

Figure 4.38   An exhibit photographed packaged and unpackaged.

of your hand flash, but they are more adaptable and can be fitted with soft boxes or umbrellas to soften and diffuse the light. Working within a studio also allows the use of neutral colour backgrounds to be used, which is particularly useful for the photography of clothing on manikins (Figure 4.39).

Figure 4.39   Clothing on a manikin.

4.6.5 Fire damaged scenes

The most important, overriding factor to be considered in fire damaged scenes, is our health and safety. As with motor vehicles, we must conduct constant risk assessments and ensure that we wear the correct PPE. Within the Metropolitan Police Service this will include steel toe capped boots and hard hats.

Scenes that have suffered structural damage should never be entered unless authority to do so has been given of the Borough Surveyor or the Fire Service.

The investigation of fire scenes often involves other agencies, such as in our case the London Fire Brigade or an independent fire investigation unit, into the causes of the fire. It is therefore good practice to work as closely with them as possible.

The scene photography should start with the exteriors first then the interiors room by room. If there is a specific seat of fire, then this should be covered with close-ups.

Particular attention should be made to burning patterns, smoke damage and spread, particularly if this is to neighbouring properties. Once the scene has been recorded, we may be asked to take 'clean up' photographs to show particular areas once debris has been cleared. If possible, refer to your earlier photographs to try and replicate angles and frame filling.

Photography can often be a challenge at fire scenes due to the high levels of contrast and flare often found; for example a window space next to an area of dense burning. If possible, mitigate these challenges by changing the framing angle. If it is completely unavoidable, we will need to sync our camera to its fastest sync speed and then take an ambient meter reading, changing only the aperture to control the exposure. Depending on the conditions, TTL flash may produce a usable exposure. If, however, it does not, you will need to set your flash to manual at a power setting equal to your given aperture.

Flash fall off is another issue to be considered; at close to medium range most small to medium sized flash units will be able to produce a reasonable exposure and depth of field. However, at greater distances a larger more powerful flash will be required, such as the Metz Megablitz 76.

In most fire scenes, lighting is limited at best, so the more common approach to photography is to use the open flash approach (Figure 4.40) (see painting with light Chapter 3 on flash photography).

The final issue is with regard to autofocusing. As already discussed, even when the lenses have assisted focusing by infrared or white light they can often be heard hunting for a point of focus. In Figure 4.41 you can see that I have manually focused the lens on the heating element of an electric fire. This was due to the lack of ambient light and contrast in the fire damaged area, meaning the autofocus could not distinguish the heating element of an electric fire, preferring to focus on the steel rod in the foreground or the metal plate seen behind the fire (Figure 4.41). From a practical point of view, in these situations it is far quicker and easier to focus the lens manually or use zone focusing.

Figure 4.40   A comparison between (a) flash on camera and (b) open flash technique. Although both would be acceptable (b) allows the area under the table to be illuminated removing unwanted shadows.

Figure 4.41   The lens manually focused on the electrical elements of a fire damaged electric fire.

4.6.6 RTC (Road Traffic Collisions)

RTC and exterior scenes can be the easiest, or sometimes the hardest, of scenes to photograph. Unlike interiors, which are constrained and protected, outside ones are often affected by all types of interference, not least the weather and lighting conditions (as previously mentioned).

As with many situations, your health and safety must come first. So high visibility jackets are mandatory. Because of the general size of these types of scene, you should also ascertain the forensic strategy required by the Collision Investigating Officer/Senior Investigating Officers to determine the shooting sequence. This will generally be around scene-setting long and mid-range shots, followed by the close-ups, whilst not forgetting to link frames as you go.

We must ensure road markings, signs and hazards are covered in our general views.

Skid marks should be photographed looking towards the scene; these can often be enhanced, particularly in wet weather, by the use of a polarising filter or try a high viewpoint. Or if possible try to gain access to an overlooking balcony or footbridge.

Within the Metropolitan Police Service it was a historically accepted rule to remove cordon tape just before photography was undertaken and then replace it immediately after. This practice will depend on your particular force's protocols; however, from an aesthetical point of view, it does offer a more realistic impression of the scene, rather than one dissected by fluttering blue tape. However, with the changing view around forensic protocols it is often now left in to show where the cordon was. I would now advise you to seek out your force's protocols with regard to best practice in this issue.

Unlike many other types of scene, RTCs should be photographed using a standard lens; this ensures that perspective is relatively correct (Figure 4.42).

Figure 4.42   The same road scene using a 28 mm, 35 mm, 50 mm and 70 mm lens.

Meter readings should be taken from mid-tone regions such as grass if possible, particularly if our road or pavement is dark tarmac (asphalt). Failing that, use the back of your hand, as discussed in Chapter 2. If you do take a meter reading off the ground, be sure that no major puddles are in view, or they will reflect the sky's exposure!

4.6.7   Homicides and postmortems (PM)

Although these can be seen as two distinct areas of work, there are a number of serious health and safety issues to be considered when working in the proximity of dead bodies. These include bacteria, disease and viral infections, which we can be exposed to both through contact and as airborne matter. PPE should always be worn and any equipment should be thoroughly cleaned and disinfected after use.

New photographers often get worried about the responsibility of photographing homicides or suspicious death scenes, but when considered rationally they are generally no more complicated than a burglary scene (they just contain a body).

As with all scenes, the photographic strategy should be discussed with the Senior Forensic Investigating Officer or equivalent, but the following are good main points to remember.

Treat the scene the same as any other: scene-setting shots then any close-ups.

The body should be photographed in position, full length, followed by the close-ups.

If the body has been hung or tied up, it is advisable to photograph any knots in situ before the body is moved, as their exact positioning may become relevant later at the postmortem or during the investigation.

Any drug paraphernalia present should be photographed, including any packaging.

It is recommended that all visible injuries be photographed in situ. It is also worth pointing out that it may be worth considering a light source examination at this point to enhance any visible injuries. This is because in the transportation and storage of the body, prior to postmortem, injuries can be lost or fade due to the redistribution of blood within the body over even short periods of time.

Any weapons or other implements found should be photographed with and without a scale if possible.

Finally, before we leave the scene, all equipment that has entered the scene must be disinfected using your force's chosen disinfectant. This includes cameras lenses tripods and so on. At scenes we use TriGene mixed at 1:10,[19] and within the laboratory Precept.

---

[19] TriGene Advance disinfectant cleaner

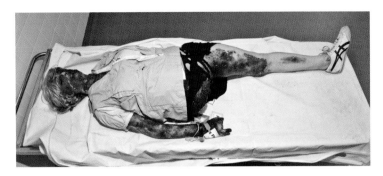

Figure 4.43   The full length clothed body taken above the table. This would be repeated for the back and then again when the clothes have been removed. Because we would use a tripod, each image is identically framed, keeping continuity between them.

In the United Kingdom, the forensic photographer at a PM generally has two responsibilities, to the investigating officer and to the home office pathologist.[20] Unlike most other situations, at PMs it is the pathologist who usually directs photography. (Although this can and does vary within each jurisdiction.) Also within the UK, there is also no general national agreement around how the images should be taken, but I would suggest the following as a rough guide: full lengths, front and back of the clothed body, plus any obvious damage to clothing and any rope ligatures that may still be in position. Don't forget at a scene these may have been overlooked or hidden from view. Some forces also photograph the body bag prior to opening, showing the exhibit label seal, but please refer to your force's standard operating procedures.

The full length photographs of the body used to be taken with the victim lying on the floor, but due to health and safety they now lie on an electrically elevating gurney. (These are used to transport the body from the fridge to the autopsy table.) If possible this should be set to its lowest point, and the full length should be taken above the body as close to 90° as possible on a wide-angle lens (Figure 4.43). This often necessitates using a small stepladder to gain height above the body, but the results are far superior to photographing the body from the side or even worse from the head end and then the foot end as this just produces untrue and misleading perspectives (Figure 4.44).

Again, I would suggest the use of a tripod, our scene of crime Manfrottos have no problem achieving the correct height. This also allows the use of two

---

[20] In the United Kingdom, Forensic Pathologists work within regional group practices which are independent of the Police Service and the Home Office and is provided to the Coroners and Police Authorities to investigate violent or suspicious deaths. They are currently structured in such a way that they can be self-employed pathologists or employed in a number of different organisations, including university departments, The National Health Service (NHS) or independent forensic science companies.

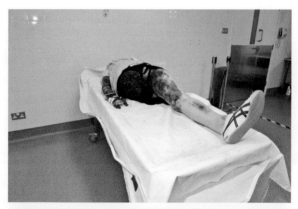

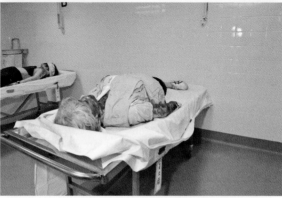

Figure 4.44   The body photographed from the feet and from the head. Neither viewpoint is useful and both produce distorted and unnatural viewing angles. This also often includes distracting background information.

flashguns to create even illumination and continuity between images, as the body is turned and undressed.

Sometimes it is impossible to get an elevated view over the body and it is necessary to shoot a side view. In these cases I would recommend asking the mortician to hold a mortuary gown or side of the shroud to create a backdrop, in effect blocking out unwanted views of the rest of the mortuary or surroundings (Figure 4.45).

The use of two flash guns will give you an even lighting effect, rather than one gun which will give flash fall off at either end. Some mortuaries are so bright that, if you are using a tripod, the available lighting can be used (Figure 4.46). (Be mindful, however, of any colour casts that may be caused by the fluorescent tubes, as this could alter the colour of any injury, so always undertake a specific white balance check.)

Whilst the body is on the low gurney is also an ideal time to photograph the face and any injuries, scars or tattoos on the top front surface of the body,

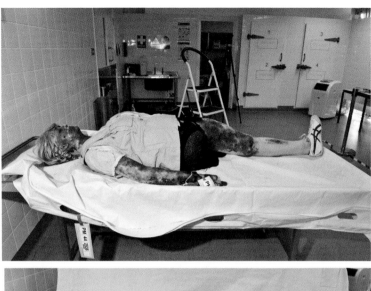

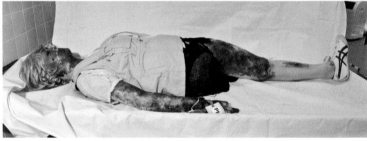

Figure 4.45   A side view of the body with and without a backdrop. Note that version with the backdrop has also been cropped, removing the superfluous part of the image.

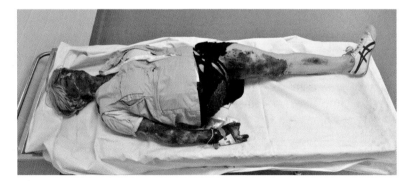

Figure 4.4?   Photograph of the body taken under available lighting. The issue to be wary of here is the length of exposure and areas of shadow that may require illumination.

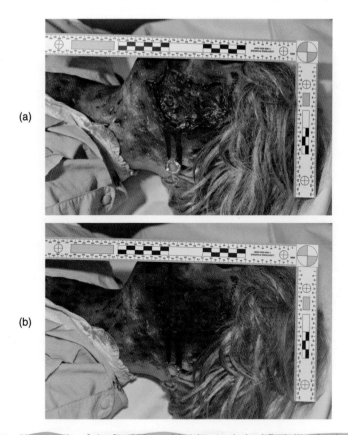

Figure 4.47   Photographs of the face taken with (a) un-polarised flash illumination (b) cross-polarised illumination.

such as the chest, stomach or thigh area if they are required (Figure 4.47). This is because once placed on the mortuary table for the postmortem you will no longer be able to get above them to look down.

From this point on the pathologist will dictate the images to be taken, which can range from a few to several hundred depending on the complexity of the case and the pathologist's reliance on images for the case notes.

Each photograph should be logged on your case sheet as you do it: never let yourself get rushed. This is particularly important when detailing small injuries, such as bruising, as it is very easy to get disoriented from left to right when you come to sorting out the injuries at the post-production stage. Some pathologists prefer to have the correct medical terminology used in the photographic index, if so ensure that you check your spellings with them prior to documenting. Others, however, are happy for more common names to be used. It is always advantageous to clarify this requirement at the beginning of the PM rather than halfway through.

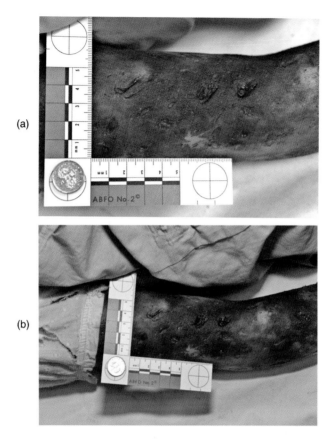

(a)

(b)

Figure 4.48 (a) shows an injury with no locating points (b) shows an injury in relation to the surrounding area.

The golden rule is to use the same skills as with normal victim photography and never shoot larger than life size unless requested.

At the present time we are still producing 10 × 8-inch prints of our images, therefore I would be thinking of how the image will sit aesthetically on paper whilst I'm framing the shot (Figure 4.48). In the near future we will move towards an electronic presentation and so this will become less of an issue, but we should always try to ensure that the injury is linked to another part of the body so its location can be confirmed, this also prevents similar injuries being confused from different parts of the body.

Always try to use ridged forensic scales, if possible, on the same plane as the injury. In my experience there is no general reason why they can't be used as they can easily be propped up or held in place.

Be mindful of the background to your shot. For example, if you are photographing a right leg from the left hand side of the table you will probably have a lot of superfluous background in the frame. Rather than leaving it there as a distraction, ask one of the attending officers to hold either a mortuary gown or shroud in the background (as we saw in Figure 4.45). This will give a clean result and the eye of the viewer will not get distracted from the point of interest. This is a quick and easy thing to do and yet makes the difference between an amateur undertaking the photography and a professional.

It pays to be thoughtful on the use of flash, as the target subjects tend to be highly reflective or of high contrast. Bounce flash or diffuse flash should be considered and it should never be used square on. Supplementary cross-polarisation photographs should also be considered for the photography of all injuries and in gross specimen photography.

Most of all be aware of the welfare risk to others around you. Postmortems and scenes with bodies in can be distressing or shocking. It is not uncommon for staff to feel unwell or even faint suddenly.

Finally, all equipment should once again be thoroughly disinfected before leaving the mortuary.

Case study

From a photographic point of view, many of the issues I have just been discussing where put into practice on the 24 April 1993.

At approximately 9 am a Ford Iveco tipper truck parked outside the Hong Kong and Shanghai Bank in Bishopsgate in the city of London. Shortly after, a bomb warning was given from a phone box in Forkhill Northern Ireland, warning the police to clear the area. The truck contained a one-ton fertilizer bomb, which exploded at 10:25 am, killing one person and injuring forty-one others. The blast also caused an estimated £1 billion pounds worth of damage with buildings up to 500 metres away being badly damaged, over half a million square feet of offices destroyed and over 500 tons of glass broken.

At the time of the explosion I was just returning to our offices in south London and heard the explosion across the river. I was sent to rendezvous at Bishops Gate Police station along with a colleague.

The enormity of the photographic task meant that after a lengthy discussion the scene had to be divided into sections. These were:

- The initial bomb crater, including any major areas of interest that could be identified.
- The direct surrounding area, the deceased and the subsequent post-mortem.
- The general surrounding area and any vehicle parts that were obvious.
- Then the wider damaged area and any specifics such as exhibits or parts of vehicles found in the buildings.

- Finally aerial or high level photography showing the radius of the crater and the damage circle.

There were also major health and safety issues, particularly from falling glass.

For example, some of the thick glass windows from the top of the National Westminster tower (Natwest), which were several inches thick, had actually fallen and embedded themselves in the concrete hundreds of feet below, rising from the ground like stalagmites. However, more dangerous were the lighter panes of glass that could aquaplane. This is where a window would fall out but, instead of dropping, actually fly sideways in the air due to the updrafts on the buildings. Before anyone was allowed to enter the site all staff had to ensure they had hardhats, steel toe and sole plated boots and high visibility jackets. We also had a minder to ensure that when we were undertaking photography our surroundings were being monitored for danger.

We didn't start photography until mid-afternoon when the scene had been declared safe from secondary devices, by this point the lighting was difficult with long shadows being caused. This meant that much of the photography of small vehicle parts exhibits and the deceased was carried out using flash in fill.

Once the deceased had been removed I attended the postmortem, working to the pathologist's guidance photographing the numerous injuries.

As I progressed around the scene over the following days, every film was numbered and logged and every exposure accounted for, often with a position direction using the compass points. This allowed the post-production, film processing and printing and the documentation to be carried out relatively smoothly. The photography of the scene continued for a number of weeks, with thousands of images being taken.

As an aside, by the time of recent London bombings in 2005 the department was digital, this meant that the photography and post-production could be undertaken far more swiftly and CDs of images produced rather than paper prints. In total over 14,000 images were shot by the department over the series of attacks.

4.7   Appendix 1: Trouble-shooting

No matter how well we think we have prepared for a job, if there is something to go wrong it will. So I have prepared a quick trouble-shooting guide for general issues.

Fuzzy images:

- Shutter speed too slow for moving subjects. This effect is often seen in trees and so on; it can be distracting, but is generally localised. Increase shutter speed or freeze with flash.
- Camera movement or shake during exposure. This will affect the whole image; the image may appear reasonably in focus but will suffer from ghosting at the edges of objects within the frame. The best way to avoid this is to use a tripod, and as a general guide never use a shutter speed lower than the focal length of the lens. For example a 60 mm lens should not be held with shutter speed of less the 1/60th of a second.
- Incorrect focus, affects the whole image. Generally the image will be soft and evenly fuzzy. This could be due to the camera autofocusing on the wrong area which, when combined with a shallow depth of field, will give reduced focus. Refocus the camera manually.
- Dirt or rainwater drops on the optics or the lens; this also gives a localised effect and appears as small spots, this can be corrected by cleaning. Ensure though that the moisture is completely removed rather than smeared across the lens. Consider protecting the camera with an umbrella or waterproof bag.
- Condensation on the lens, this may not be immediately obvious on observation at it may be inside the camera. A common problem in cold weather, when moving from central heated homes and offices to outside, or vice versa. Remove the lens and check. In my experience, to wipe it dry causes other material to stick to the damp surface so it is best just to let it acclimatise naturally. Common practice for us is to carry the cameras in the front of the vehicles rather than the rear and to remove them at night and put them in an office.

Picture too light or too dark:

- Incorrect exposure (under or over). Check your meter isn't being fooled by too much sky or foreground.
- Incorrect shutter speed (increase or decrease as required).
- Incorrect ISO film speed (wrong setting for the ambient illumination). If it is low illumination, increase the ISO; if, however, it is the height of summer, you may conversely find that the ISO is set too high. Check if the auto set ISO is selected in the camera menu and change if required.
- Flash failure, this can be due to a number of issues and often it is down to a poor connection with the camera. Clean the hot-shoe or check the 'sync' cables, which are easily damaged, so always carry a spare. Check your batteries are not dead. Also check the 'sync' lead connector as these often work loose and require crimping.
- Wrong power output on the flashgun. If the flash is not a dedicated type, ensure that the ISO is reset to match that of the camera. If it is dedicated

ensure that the camera is not reading off a highly reflective area within the frame, turning the flash off too quickly. Try setting the flash to auto or manual.

Blank or partial pictures on the review screen:

- Blank, not enough exposure to create an image. Camera battery too low to allow playback function. Check battery status. Partial picture, if flash is being used check the correct sync speed has been selected.
- Shutter did not open. Check battery status.
- Check the camera is fitted with a memory card; many cameras will not fire if there is no memory card present.
- Flash did not fire; check the contacts and sync lead connections.
- Lens cap or other obstruction in front of the lens. Check that fingers, lens straps, lens hood have not slipped and are obstructing the lens.

Red-eye effect:

- Flash too close to the lens axis; change to off axis flash if possible. If this isn't possible, try using the red eye setting if one is available on the camera settings. This fires a pre-flash that forces the eye's pupil to constrict, so when the main flash fire the eye appears normal.

Unwanted reflections/hot spots/flare:

- Remove items from the frame if possible. Change camera angle so that it does not reflect directly back into the lens. Try using a polariser.
- Flash aimed at reflective surface, try changing the angle of either the camera or object. Bounce flash off a reflector or ceiling.
- Flare from an ambient light source in or just out of frame, this is usually seen when shooting outside, ensure that the lens hood is used or the lens is 'flagged'. Again, try changing the framing point or angle.
- Lens pointed directly towards light source, if possible move position.
- Strong background colour creating a colour cast, change background colour to a more neutral shade.

Unnatural colour:

- Check the white balance setting on camera for the illumination type. If it is set to auto white balance. try re-setting to match illumination, fluorescence, flash and so on.
- Strong illumination by artificial lighting such as sodium streetlights. This can be corrected in Photoshop; however, bear in mind that if this is a witness viewpoint the colour of the lighting may be significant, so caution should be applied.

Unwanted perspective distortion:

- Wide-angle lens used. Motor vehicles and injuries should never be photographed with a wide-angle lens if it can be avoided due to this effect. This is a common fault when using zoom lenses, where the temptation is to change the zoom rather than the distance between yourself and the object of interest. Try fixing the zoom to a set point and then move backwards and forwards until the object is framed correctly.
- Limited content in general view, this is in general caused by too long a focal length of lens being used. Try changing lenses or move farther away from the point of interest.

References

(1) Payne-James, J. J. 2012. Rulers and Scales used in measurement in forensic setting: measured – and found wanting! *Foren Sci, Med Path*. 8(4): 482–483.
(2) Ferrucci, M., Doiron, T. D., Thompson, R., et al. *Dimensional Review of Scales for Forensic Photography*. US Department of Justice; Document 243213 ref 2010-DN-R-7121, August 2013.
(3) Steve Nunn and Jonathan C Wright. The Effects of Varying the amount of Acid in an Etching solution on the Restoration of Obliterated Serial Number. Department of Biological and Forensic Sciences, School of Science, University of Derby.
(4) Zaili, M., Kuppuswamy, R. and Harun, H. (2007) Restoration of engraved marks on steel surfaces by etching technique. *Foren Sci Int*. 171: 27–32.
(5) Police and Criminal Evidence Act (PACE) 1984 http://www.legislation.gov.uk/ukpga/1984/60/contents

5
Light as a Forensic Photographer's Tool

5.1   Overview of alternative light sources (ALS)

Photography in general, and forensic photography in particular, requires the understanding, control and use of light. Some types of light, such as electronic flash, may be used as a general illumination, whilst others, such as a laser, may have a more specialist role to play in revealing latent evidence. In this chapter I want to look at using these artificial types of light, or 'Alternative Light Sources', as forensic tools.

I am not going cover the actual photographic technique directly here, as this will be covered as we apply the illumination in different ways in subsequent chapters. I hope this chapter will provide bedrock of understanding for the range and diversity of lighting choices we actually have.

Although many forces own ALS, in my experience they often have little experience of using these types of lighting beyond the confines of the laboratory. This is a shame, as I believe they are at their most effective and cost efficient when deployed to crime scenes. For my part, I have spent the last 20+ years using and researching ALS to collect latent evidence, and am still amazed at what can be found.

So exactly what is an ALS? Most forensic books or guides take a traditional view on this. To many people, ALS are devices that produce filtered or coloured light in one form or another, such as a Crimescope or laser (see below). I believe, however, that the definition should be much wider; to me it should include any light-emitting device that we take into a scene or laboratory, which is not part of the standard light fittings. In its simplest form this could be a torch. My reasoning for this is that even white light (as we shall see later in the book) is available in many forms and, if used properly, can be just as effective at finding certain types of forensic evidence as any laser.

Forensic Photography: A Practitioner's Guide, First Edition. Nick Marsh.
© 2014 John Wiley & Sons, Ltd. Published 2014 by John Wiley & Sons, Ltd.

It is also argued by some that the use of alternative light sources should not sit within the role description of the forensic photographer. I strongly disagree; as already stated we, as photographers, have a strong affiliation with light and an understanding of how it can be used. More importantly, any evidence discovered can generally only be retrieved through the use of photography. It is therefore logical for us to be intrinsic to this process. I have also found that information about ALS is often listed in a dark and dusty paragraph in the back chapter of forensic photography texts, or just completely overlooked. However, I believe and would argue that this is one of the key topics that should be covered in a book about forensic photography and it should be right up near the front.

In this chapter I want to give a brief overview of the types of alternative light sources that are available, and in the following chapters I will show you the impact of their usage in everyday casework.

5.2   The Electromagnetic Spectrum (EMS)

If we are to achieve good, consistent results in our photography, we must have an understanding about the limitations of the human eye and the digital sensor in their relative abilities to either see or record, especially when the camera may 'see' what we, the operator, cannot. It is also important to have an understanding of what light is and why certain materials behave the way they do, particularly when we expose them to particular wavelengths of light (for example the phenomena of fluorescence) (Figure 5.1).

It is important, therefore, that before we start we have a general understanding of light and how we perceive it. The EMS is the range of all possible frequencies of electromagnetic radiation, extending from gamma rays at one end, through to radio waves at other. Within this is the tiny portion of the visible range over which most of us can see.

Figure 5.2 shows the small visible range of the electromagnetic spectrum plus ultraviolet (UV) and infrared (IR), which can both be exploited. Notice that the average person can only see radiation at wavelengths between approximately 400 and 700 nm. Although we are visually restricted to this small 300-nm section, with some electronic assistance it is possible to exploit wavelengths from 254 nm to 1100 nm (see UV and IR sections later in the chapter). (One nm (nanometre), is an SI unit of length, equal to 10^{-9} m (a billionth of a metre).)

It is important to remember that white light, as we see it, is actually a combination of various colours. We can see this using a glass prism or when the light is refracted to produce a colour spectrum, as in a rainbow.

When light is reflected off a surface, say a piece of paper, our brain identifies this stimulus and assigns a colour to it, for example 'white' if all colours are reflected. If no light is reflected back from the surface and it is all absorbed,

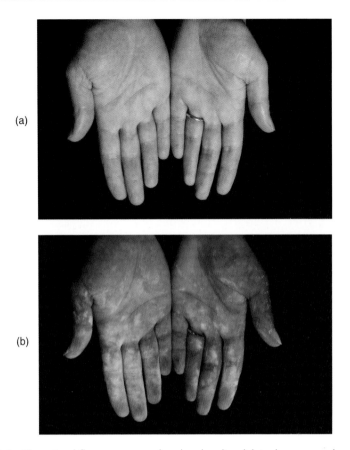

Figure 5.1   The natural fluorescence produced under ultraviolet when you peel an orange.

The Electromagnetic Spectrum

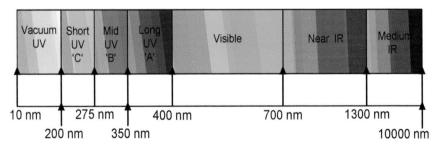

Figure 5.2   The small visible range of the electromagnetic spectrum plus the ultraviolet and infrared regions, which can be exploited.

the brain assigns the colour black. In reality black is the absence of colour, so technically isn't a colour at all.

Most surfaces reflect light to various degrees, which would equate to shades of grey depending on how much is absorbed/reflected. This 'shade of grey', of course, is effectively what the camera light meter is using to ascertain exposure. However, most items have some colouration to them; we see a green coat because the fibres in the coat are dyed green. When light strikes these fibres, green wavelengths are reflected back as what our brains have been trained to recognise as green. It should also be noted that light is not only reflected, some is also absorbed and some may be transmitted, all of which has an impact on the colour we perceive.

Since colour photography started, manufacturers of film and now digital cameras have tried to ensure that what our eyes see as being 'normal' is present in any subsequent captured photograph. This is why, as I discussed in the first chapter, digital cameras using a Bayer or mosaic filter have two green pixels for every one red and blue, because this mimics the relative sensitivity to these colours in the human eye.

Cameras, however, are not as forgiving as our brains; for example, if we photograph a scene in a living room we may encounter mixed lighting from two sources, for example, a window and desk lamp. The brain perceives this mixed illumination as generally white light, however the camera will see 'white' daylight from a window and a red or yellowish illumination from the table lamp (due to the spectral output of the tungsten filament bulb). In the days of film, this produced a reaction called 'crossed curves' in the final image. This is where a different colour balance was present in the shadow and the highlights, which couldn't be corrected in post-production.

It could, however, be compensated for during photography by using a film that was predominantly balanced to the main illumination source (daylight or tungsten balanced film) or by colour correcting the light with a colour correction filter.[1]

These colour correction filters have somewhat fallen out of favour with most non-professional users, as most people use the colour temperature settings built into all digital cameras. These colour temperature settings technically allow the camera to reset its white balance to reflect the dominant colour temperature within the exposure (also refer back to Chapter 1 on white balance within the workflow). Although these are not always accurate, as they only offer a generic factory setting, it is worth ensuring that your camera is adjusted to represent the major illumination source. You can also manually

---

[1] Colour correction filters. Traditionally photographic films were made for use with specific light sources, for example, 'daylight' and 'tungsten' film which were balanced toward those particular light sources. If, for example, you were shooting with daylight film (calibrated to 5600 K) under tungsten lighting, a bluish filter such as a Wratten 80A would be required to correct this colour balance shift into the warmer colours.

set the white balance in your camera for each scene (see your camera manu-facturer's guidance). All light sources produce a coloured output, which can be measured by its colour temperature in Kelvins.[2]

If you are capturing images as RAW files, this white balance correction can also be easily recalibrated when you open the files in a program such as Photoshop.

It is worth remembering that in many forensic applications, such as finger and shoe mark photography, any colour balance produced by the lighting may be irrelevant, if the final image is to be viewed and reproduced as greyscale.

In the first chapter we briefly covered the covered the importance of white balance and colour management, but it is vital at this stage to appreciate the above in terms of your scenes of crime or casework images. I mention this because if we are asked, for example, to photograph a plum-coloured jumper that needs to be replicated accurately for court (Figure 5.3) we need to ensure that the camera is adjusted to compensate for any colour balance shift in the illumination.

This need for colour accuracy can be assisted by the use of a known ref-erence, such as the colour checker passport[3] or greyscale. These are placed within the photograph giving a visual calibration reference point. There is lit-tle point in producing a final print for court if the jumper appears blue because you have not corrected for any colour shift that occurs.

This understanding of colour temperature is vital not only at the capture stage, but also at the post-production on-screen stage and the final reproduc-tion stage. A lack of colour calibration during the reproduction of images is one of the biggest issues I come across during my casework.

Although most off-the-shelf all-digital SLRs have been filtered to replicate roughly the same colour range response as the human eye. It means they can-not be used to record in the UV range, or into the IR beyond 750 nm, with-out some form of adaptation, although they can be used for fluorescent imag-ing casework, as any fluorescence produced will generally be entirely within the visual spectrum. Camera sensors are also generally more sensitive than the eye, so a very faint, visually fluorescent, response will often appear much

---

[2] Kelvins are used to state the absolute colour temperature of an ideal black-body radiator that radi-ates light of a comparable hue to that light source. Some types of lamps, however, such as fluorescent lamps, emit light through processes other than thermal radiation. This means that it does not follow the spectrum of a black-body radiation source. These are instead rated in terms of their correlated colour temperature and this is the human perception of the black-body radiator which most closely matches the colour of the lamp. Colour temperatures over 5000 K are called cool colours whilst lower colour temperatures are referred to as warm colours ('red hot' is a lower colour temperature than 'blue-white hot'). Colour film used 5600K as a white balance, whereas today's digital cameras, web graphics, DVDs and the internet use 6500 K to display the white point.

[3] Colour checker passport. This is a small calibration chart containing 24 colour and 26 assorted greys and warming and cooling white balance patches. Camera calibration and computer software is provided with the passport allowing custom Digital Negative converter (DNG) profiling as a plug in for Adobe CS5 and Lightroom. This software used in conjunction with the calibration chart allows colour calibration of the image for use on screen or for printing.

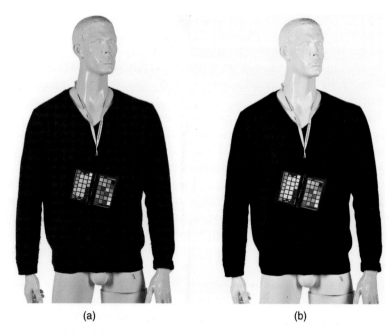

(a)   (b)

Figure 5.3   An item of clothing photographed with studio flash. (a) Shows the white balance set to flash. (b) Shows the cameras white balance set to Tungsten lighting. Failure to colour correct at either the capture or post-production stage can cause numerous issues, as we have seen above. Therefore, if we don't understand this task properly, nobody will.

stronger when photographed. At scenes this can produce problems, as you may photograph one particular mark that has been located and have another appear on the resultant image that has not been accounted for or documented. Any images captured will also benefit from post-production enhancement, in some cases using sophisticated tools, which is something our brains cannot do!

5.3   Fluorescence

There is another phenomenon we must look at whilst we are talking about light as a forensic tool, and that is fluorescence. This is the way that some materials respond when stimulated with energy. When this energy is in the form of photons emitted by high-powered light sources, some materials will absorb this light energy and then convert it into a longer but less powerful wavelength, re-emitting it in the phenomenon known as fluorescence.

Much of the casework we will look at in the following chapters relies on the exploitation of fluorescence and why and how we can induce it. To understand this we must have a basic understanding of the fundamental structure of the atom. In basic terms, this means a nucleus, containing protons, surrounded by electrons. The orbit of these electrons is always at their lowest energy state. However, when the atom is exposed to and absorbs energy in the form of heat or light, it pushes its electrons into an excited state. When this energy is lost, as the electron returns to its lowest state, it is transformed into light of a longer wavelength. An important observation is that the atoms can only absorb energy at certain discrete values (wavelengths), with all other energy (wavelength) values not giving excitation. Analysis techniques such as spectrophotometers use this effect by exposing the atoms to a range of energies and monitoring the response to measure where absorptions and emissions will occur. Planck's theory[4] suggests an electron will only get excited to a higher energy level if a photon of light possesses the appropriate energy to excite it to that level. Hence, molecules are selective of the particular wavelengths of light that they will absorb, with this selectivity determined by the electron energy levels each element possesses. In practical terms this is the reason why, when searching for latent forensic evidence at scenes, the search must be carried out by using light of more than one wavelength (Figure 5.4). This ensures that a wider range of fluorescent responses is made possible.

Once excited into the higher state, the electron does not remain there long and will quickly fall back to its original level, emitting light of a longer wavelength. This means that a continuous form of excitation needs to be used to ensure a continuous flow of emission from the atom (Figure 5.5). This differs from phosphorescence, where there is a slow release of energy ensuring luminescence continues for a period after the stimulus has been removed.

The optical brightness of any fluorescence induced is also directly proportional to the power of the excitation wavelength. This means a laser with an output of 5 Watts will detect marks where a filtered light source (which may only produce $^3/_4$ Watt spread across 40–60 nm) will not. This has to be tempered by the fact that in some very rare instances, the fluorescent response can become 'quenched' (burn out) and fades from view. This means that once the area of interest has been identified, it should not be over stimulated and if possible not illuminated again until the time of photography (this is particularly relevant to very faint latent finger marks).

The difference between the position of the peak excitation wavelength and that of the peak wavelength of the emitted fluorescence is referred to as the Stokes Shift[5] (Figure 5.6).

The important thing to note here is that when we are using fluorescence as a tool to find finger marks, we are not generally looking for marks

---

[4] Max Planck was one of the most influential scientists of the 20th century and is widely recognised as the founder of the quantum theory, which focuses on the tiniest subatomic particles. In 1918 he was awarded the Nobel Prize for physics.

[5] George Stokes was an Irish physicist. In 1852 he documented that that some materials will absorb light that strikes them and then converts them into light of a longer wavelength but of a lower intensity.

Figure 5.4   An example of why a number of light sources must be used to ensure all evidence is retrieved. (a) shows an area of wall under white light illumination. (b) shows the same area under a green laser at 532 nm. (c) shows the same area under a yellow laser at 577 nm. Note that even with a small difference of 45 nm the background is suppressed and the mark becomes visible. In (b) we can also see the phenomenon we refer to as 'the streaky bacon effect' as it looks just like it. The effect is caused when a thin layer of paint is applied over another layer of paint, which has a stronger autofluorescence, causing it to shine through where the brush has been applied.

predominantly containing natural sweat, although they may contain trace levels of naturally fluorescent compounds. In reality, most marks detected by fluorescence examination are contaminated ones. I mentioned above that many common substances, such as crisp fat, beer, some make up, orange zest and many other everyday substances, have some fluorescent properties,

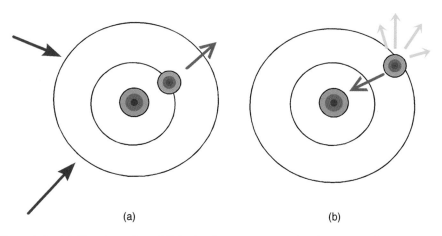

(a)   (b)

Figure 5.5   (a) The absorption of light by the atom causes the electrons to jump to higher state. (b) The emission of light by the atom causing the electron to fall back to its lower state.

which is what we, as forensic photographers, can try to exploit (see Figure 5.1 above).

The other important thing to note is that these fluorescent contaminated marks often do not develop with other traditional treatments, such as aluminum powder or chemicals. This is simply because they do not contain the relevant components that these chemical treatments target. In our own studies, looking at scenes over a two-year period, the use of ALS and ball lights (see specular illumination below) developed over 40% of the total number of marks recovered at all serious crime scenes.

The other factor that influences fluorescence examination is the surface or substrate the mark is on. For example, a mark deposited on a wall in a contaminate may be readily visible under UV. But when the same contaminate

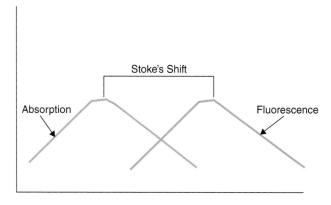

Figure 5.6   A simple illustration of Stoke's Shift.

is on, for example, a bare wooden surface, it may not be seen, due to the autofluorescence of the background being stronger than the fluorescence of the mark (Figure 5.7).

Autofluorescence is defined as the unwanted fluorescence of the substrate rather than the area of interest (i.e. the mark), increasing the background signal and blocking the fluorescence we are looking for. This may, to some extent, account for the fact that at some scenes many hundreds of marks are found, yet at others with highly autofluorescent walls they are not.

This autofluorescence, however, can sometimes be used to our advantage. As we can see below in Figure 5.8 the mark is in a dark contaminate which is difficult to see against the wood grain background. If this is exposed to 445 nm, we can see that we can produce autofluorescence in the background but the mark is adsorbing the light. This produces a strong contrast between the two, allowing the mark to be clearly seen. This phenomenon can be fully exploited on any surface that has been varnished, lacquered or polished and is nearly always undertaken using UV when examining laminate

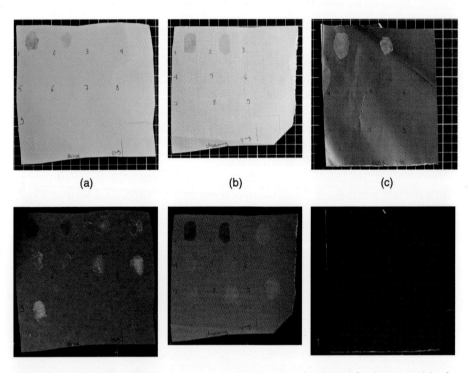

Figure 5.7 Along the top row we can see some test samples (part of a larger study) of a number of well-known types of make-up, applied to different coloured wallpaper surfaces. Below we can see the same samples illuminated by a 532 nm laser. This testing reinforces the impact that the substrate has on any subsequent fluorescence and is why it is important to examine surfaces with as many light sources as possible if you wish to reveal the maximum possible evidence.

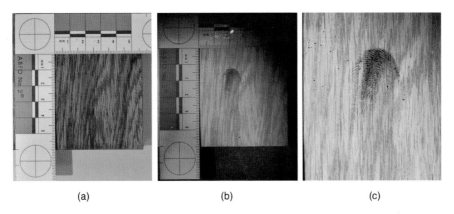

(a)   (b)   (c)

Figure 5.8   A contaminated latent mark on a wooden surface. (a) Illuminated with white light, note the background interference from the wood grain. (b)The same area illuminated at 445 nm, note that the wood grain has almost vanished whilst the mark has become much darker. (c) shows a greyscale image of the finished mark, note how although the top part of the mark was visible in photo (a), the core and the delta at the bottom were not.

wooden floors for blood contamination. (An example of which we will see in Figure 7.43, in finger and shoe mark photography where we separate blood from grease.)

It is possible to induce fluorescence anywhere along the electromagnetic spectrum, from ultraviolet to near infrared. At the extreme red end of the spectrum, the excitation wavelengths and fluorescent responses may remain invisible to the human eye (due to its limitations), and therefore some form of electronic assistance will be required to aid visualisation.

Many organic and inorganic materials, such as rock, soils and vegetation, have specific spectral absorption wavelengths and emission responses. For the forensic practitioner, it is more likely to be the use of particular chemicals that is important. Those in use for fingerprint detection include DFO, (1,8-Diazafluoren-9-one,)[6] [1] and the superglue dyes BY40 (Basic Yellow 40)[7] in the UK, or Rhodamine in the USA[8] (see Chapter 7 on finger, shoe mark and injury photography).

---

[6] DFO 1,8-Diazafluoren-9-one, also known as DFO, is a chemical that is used to find fingerprints on porous surfaces. DFO reacts with amino acids present in the fingerprint to form highly fluorescent derivatives. Excitation with light at ∼470 nm results in emission at ∼570 nm. [1]

[7] BY40 Basic Yellow 40 (Maxilon Flavine 10GFF) is a highly fluorescent dye stain, which stains cyanoacrylate-developed latent prints. When illuminated with an ultraviolet lamp or Alternative Light Source, latent prints fluoresce brightly, and weakly-developed latent prints that could not be seen under normal viewing conditions may be easily seen and photographed. Basic Yellow 40 is very sensitive to ultraviolet light and can be used with a simple long-wavelength ultraviolet lamp. It is often used by police agencies that cannot afford to purchase a more expensive Forensic Light Source.

[8] Rhodamine 6G is used to detect finger marks on non-porous surfaces that have previously been treated with CNA (cyanoacrylate /superglue). It will dye the CNA pink and will produce yellow fluorescence when illuminated with a blue laser and viewed through the appropriate goggles.

The most important thing to remember when working with ALS is that although the visual appearance of an object may be familiar to us under white light, the chances are that it will change once exposed to particular wavelengths and this can often be to our advantage.

As we can see above, not only are we, the operators, required to understand the responses of the human eye to the electromagnetic spectrum, we must also have an understanding of the use of light of different wavelengths and the interaction it has with the surface texture or the materials within it. We should understand how to produce either fluorescence or reflectance from the target evidence, depending on the results required. So the question is: how are we going to exploit the light sources available to us?

5.4   Alternative light sources

Here we are going to look at the main types of alternative light sources in use today, including fixed and tuneable output devices.

For me, the following pieces of equipment are vital to allow me to undertake my role as a forensic photographer correctly. I do, however, realise that the deployment of these sources may be a contentious issue in some forces, as these devices often sit within the forensic laboratory and rarely get deployed, whilst in other forces they are operated by scenes of crime personnel. For me, regardless of where these light sources sit, the forensic photographer, or those engaged in forensic photography, should be robust enough to request their use as and when required.

5.4.1   Ultraviolet (UV) light sources

Ultraviolet light is electromagnetic radiation with a wavelength shorter than that of the visible light at the blue end of the spectrum. The total UV spectral range covers the range 10 nm to 400 nm.[9] However, for practicality and

---

[9] The Ultraviolet end of the electromagnetic spectrum. Generally within the forensic arena, UV is split into UV 'A', 'B' or 'C' but, as can be seen below, this is a simplification and technically not correct.

Name	Abbreviation	Wavelength in Nanometers (nm)
Ultraviolet A, longwave or black light	UVA	400–315
Near	NUV	400–300
Ultraviolet B or medium wave	UVB	315–280
Middle	MUV	300–200
Ultraviolet C, shortwave or germicidal	UVC	280–100
Far	FUV	200–122
Vacuum	VUV	200–100
Low	LUV	100–88
Super	SUV	150–10
Extreme	EUV	121–10

 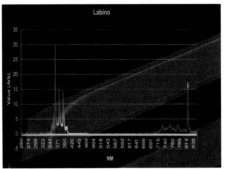

Figure 5.9 A battery powered Labino in use and a graph showing the emission wavelength, note the strong peak around 365 nm and the small ones from 740 to 848 nm, this accounts for the characteristic red hue that can sometimes be observed.

safety, the devices most commonly used emit light in the UVA region of the spectrum between 350 and 400 nm. Within the ERU we can also utilise UVC sources with output at 254 nm (see specialist photography). However, UVC of this wavelength has particular health and safety issues and is not required for everyday casework.

There are numerous manufacturers of UVA devices on the market, many of which I have been tested both in the field and measured in terms of their output with a spectrometer. There are two devices at the present time which I have found to give the most satisfactory results within the laboratory and at scenes. One is the Labino track pack series – a Swedish light available via Advanced NDT[10] – and the other is the UV 35-Watt hand lamp from the UK-based UV Products[11] (Figure 5.9). These systems are both based around a xenon gas discharge bulb (which has a very high UV output) mounted within a weatherproof housing. This is then filtered using a Woods type UV filter,[12] with both sources having a peak emission of around 365 nm (correct as of 2012).

It is important to note that the quality of the emitted beam is critical for finding latent evidence. No UV light should emit wavelengths over 400 nm, as

---

[10] Labino UV NDT: http://www.advanced-ndt.co.uk/

[11] UV products: http://www.uvlight.co.uk/pdfs/datasheets/35W UV Hand Lamp Datasheet.pdf

[12] Woods filter is the generic term for UV transmitting filters. Robert William Wood (1868–1955) developed the glass as a light filter for signal lamps during World War One. This 'invisible radiation' technique worked both in infrared daylight communication and ultraviolet night communications. The glass filter removed the visible components of a light beam, leaving only the 'invisible radiation' as a signal beam. Wood's glass is special barium–sodium–silicate glass. It is a very deep violet-blue glass, opaque to all visible light rays except the longest red and shortest violet. It is quite transparent in the violet/ultraviolet in a band between 320 nm and 400 nm with a peak at 365 nm. This makes the glass ideal for photography at both ends of the spectrum. The Kodak Wratten 18A filter is based on Wood's glass.

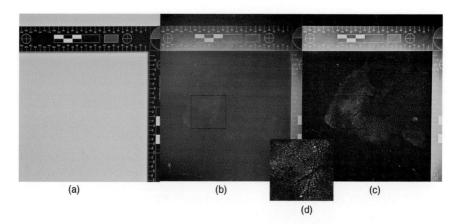

(a)   (b)   (c)

(d)

Figure 5.10   Comparison between the Labino and an alternative UV forensic torch. (a) shows the area under white light illumination. (b) shows the area under an unbranded UV torch; note the overall lack of contrast between the mark and background. This is due to the lamp emitting wavelengths beyond 400 nm. (c) shows the same area under the Labino. (d) shows the area shown within the black square seen on (c).

even the smallest emission into the visible spectral range can have a dramatic effect on any fluorescence induced (Figure 5.10).

It should also be noted that for some applications, such as victim photography, a continuous wavelength UV light source is not suitable because of the potential damage to skin. In these situations a UV flashgun (see injury photography) should be used.

It is also important to note that most UV devices have the potential to be a health hazard, so during their use you should be provided with and use personal protective equipment (PPE). All staff within our department are provided with full face shields, this ensures that the Maximum Permissible Exposure (MPE) limits are not reached as they block UVA, B and C radiation. These limits are defined by the Health and Safety Executive (HSE)[13] in 'The Control of Artificial Optical Radiation at Work Regulations'. These regulations actually cover all artificial lighting, not just UV, and therefore any light you are issued with should also have a risk assessment undertaken on it before use. We do not recommend the use of spectacle-type glasses for use with UV, as they only protect the eyes. For long periods of searching reflective surfaces, such as a white wall, the cumulative effect of reflected UV can often expose the skin of the face to more than the MPE. Always refer to your provider's health and safety guidance for safe operating times. A safe system of work should be devised taking into account the manufacturer's operating instructions, local working conditions and any measurements undertaken.

---

[13] http://www.legislation.gov.uk/uksi/2010/1140/contents/made

As I write this chapter, a number of UV torches have been made available on the Internet and, for their size, are very powerful. They also pose a possible risk to the eye, so some caution must be exercised in their use. In one case that I have seen reported, the exposure limits to the eye were exceeded after only 4 min at a light source distance of 100 cm during an 8-hour period. If in doubt, always protect the eyes and skin. Overexposure to UVA is cumulative over a given period and this can cause a number of issues, from something as simple as a headache, to photokeratitis, which is an inflammation of the cornea. Although painful, this fortunately is not long lasting. However, repeated exposure over the long term can produce cataracts and increases the chances of developing cancer of the eyelids, or other unprotected skin areas. Overexposure to UVB and C is far more serious and can cause burns, or even lead to the onset of skin cancer. If UV devices such as these are to be used regularly, I believe it is worth attending a one-day training course, to have a greater understanding of the dangers of UV in the workplace.[14] Conversely if, as the photographer, you have been given one of these devices, it is your force's or company's responsibility to ensure you are provided with the proper PPE and training on correct usage.

5.4.2 LASERs (Light Amplification by Stimulated Emission of Radiation) [15]

My first recollection (I guess along with many others of my age group) of seeing a laser in use was in Goldfinger.[16] Here a giant ruby laser threatens to cut Mr Bond in half. Later we had films such as Star Wars,[17] where light sabers and laser guns filled our screens. The practical realities, however, of using a laser in the early days for forensic investigation, was somewhat further from the truth.

---

[14] UV products run a very good one-day UV safety course which I have attended. UV safety courses: http://www.uv-light.co.uk/index.php.

[15] The Term LASER derives from the acronym, 'Light amplification by stimulated emission of radiation'. Laser light is notable for its high degree of spatial and temporal coherence which is unattainable using other technologies. This spacial coherence is often expressed by the output beam being a narrow or 'pencil beam' as they can be focused into tiny spots, or they can be launched into a beams of very low divergence in order to concentrate their power at a large distance. Albert Einstein, established the theoretical foundations for the LASER in the paper, *Zur Quantentheorie der Strahlung* (On the Quantum Theory of Radiation) in 1917, but it wasn't until 1960 that the first functioning laser was built at the Hughes Research Laboratory in California. Lasers are now found all around us in many electronic devices from computers to Blue-ray players.

They also use a multitude of lasering mediums from gases through to solid state lasers that use a crystalline or glass rod which is doped with ions that provide the required energy states. For more information, have a look on the internet, any search will bring up some good explanations on how lasers work.

[16] Goldfinger, Produced by Albert R. Broccoli and released in 1964, was the third film in the James Bond series, based on the books written by Ian Fleming.

[17] Star Wars was a 1977 film by George Lucas and released by 20th Century Fox.

When I joined the Metropolitan Police 25 years ago, the only laser in use was a Spectra Physics 2016 argon ion laser. It was so big that it had a room to itself. It needed mains water cooling, a transformer the size of a suitcase, a 50-amp three-phase input and cost £60 000 (at late 1970s prices). All of this was required to produce 2 Watts of light at 514 nm. In retrospect, this original system was very inefficient at producing light.

Over the last 10 years, technology has jumped forwards, lasers have got smaller, lighter, are air cooled and produce far more power, for a very low electrical input. Today we have a selection of lasers in use, including a number of 5-Watt Diode Pumped Solid Semiconductor (DPSS) Nd:YAG lasers[18] which emit a green excitation beam at 532 nm. We also operate the 'Tracer' 577 nm DPSS[19] (6) which has a yellow excitation beam and two 'Revelation 445 nm' solid-state diode lasers,[20] producing 6 Watts of light (Figure 5.11). The 'Revelation 445 nm' laser uses advanced Japanese diodes, adapted from those used in the digital cinema industry, and is in fact so small that the lithium battery is bigger than the laser head.

Lasers, unlike other specialist lighting, provide monochromatic coherent beams of bright, high-energy light, which is ideal for searching for latent evidence. Unlike other devices, lasers do not use a filter or a light bulb to create their light energy. Systems such as the Revelation and Tracer use high-powered diodes with emission at 808 nm, illuminated across a Neodymium-doped yttrium aluminium garnet rod to generate 1064 nm (Nd:YAG). This is frequency doubled, giving a resultant output of 532 nm (green). For 577 nm (yellow) the Nd:YAG rod is 'doped' with a semiconductor to give output at 1154 nm and subsequently frequency doubled. The neodymium, of which there is around 10% in the YAG rod, is the element responsible for lasing.

In my opinion, these lasers offer the greatest chances of finding latent evidence both at scenes and within the laboratory. This is a continuously developing area of research and, over the next few years, I am sure other types of technology offering alternative wavelengths and increased power will appear in this field.

---

[18] Laser Innovations http://www.forensiclaser.com/

[19] http://www.coherent.com/products/?1479/TracER-Compact-Forensic-Laser-System

[20] The laser diode is a laser where the active medium is a semiconductor similar to that found in a light-emitting diode. The most common type of laser diode is formed from a p–n junction and powered by injected electric current. The former devices are sometimes referred to as *injection laser diodes* to distinguish them from optically pumped laser diodes. The laser diode is formed by doping a very thin layer on the surface of a crystal wafer. The crystal is doped to produce an n-type region and a p-type region, one above the other, resulting in a p–n junction or diode. Forward bias in the electrical diode causes the two species of charge carrier, the hole and electrons to be injected from the opposite sides of the p–n junction into the depletion area. When the holes and the electron are present in the same region they may recombine, this results in spontaneous emission, creating photons of high energy light. The major practical difference in this new generation of laser is the size and power consumption. These diodes are no bigger than a grain of rice and in some cases smaller. I have a 445-nm version which runs on a 1.5 volt battery yet produces 1 watt of light.

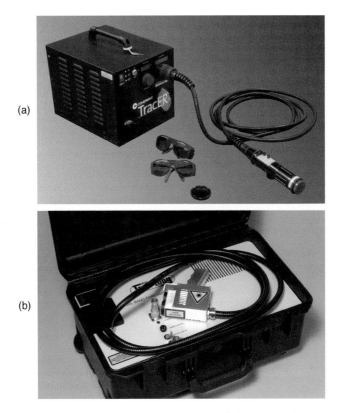

Figure 5.11   (a) The Tracer 577 nm. (b) The Revelation 'twin' 455 nm and 532 nm output laser.

As can be seen above, the laser comes with outputs at a number of fixed wavelengths. For general casework, however, the 532 nm green line has been found to be the most flexible for the diversity of evidence types detected. It is also a prime wavelength for the excitation of marks developed using the chemical DFO, so is also ideal for the laboratory environment. The 577-nm line has been found to be particularly useful for detecting evidence on poorly painted surfaces, whereas the 445-nm blue laser is particularly good for superglue marks dyed with BY40 and the detection of body fluids, in particular semen. All three wavelengths are used at scenes for the detection of latent evidence.

As with UV, taking health and safety into account when using these devices is crucial. They may look deceptively like coloured lights, but they are incredibly powerful and, although used as a diffused output as opposed to a focused beam, they have the potential to blind before the eye can blink. I have a 1-Watt 445-nm laser where the beam is reported to be visible at 20 miles, and on one online laser site they claim their 1-Watt krypton laser can be seen on the moon!

As these devices are becoming more prevalent in operational usage in forces, I would strongly suggest anyone intending to use them should receive some form of introductory safety training. Ideally an organisation using a laser would have a laser safety officer either on site, or one who regularly checks on the safety procedures. As an aside I, along with a number of my collegues, am a trained Laser Safety Officer.

Again, best practice is for the operator to be supplied with personal protective equipment in the form of goggles. The use of these devices is also covered by regulations for ICNIRP[21] (International Commission on Non ionizing Radiation Protection) and the HSE[22] (Health and Safety Executive) in the United Kingdom, so you or your organisation have a legal duty to ensure that you operate within the guidelines.

One of the questions often raised by forces looking to invest in new ALS is: why should I buy a 5-W laser when it is possible to buy 500-W tunable light sources? However, this direct comparison of the wattage is misleading. This is because with most devices you are talking about power consumption, as in the 500-W crimescope or a 60-watt light bulb. With lasers you are talking directly about their output power. The 'Tracer' 5-W laser emits 5 W at 532 nm only. A 500-W light source set to 535 nm may consume 500 W, but once this has been converted to white light and passed through a filter it is actually outputting a beam of a range of wavelengths, spread across a band of 40 or 50 nm, at less than three quarters of a watt (figures based on in-house testing). You cannot, therefore, compare lasers head-to-head with any other devices unless you take an output measurement, or record the energy over a set area.

5.4.3   Crime-lites

The advent of light emitting diode (LED) technology, has led to the development of other systems such the 'Crime-lites®' from Foster and Freeman[23] These are mains and battery operated, torch-like devices and offer a good alternative to the laser, with the Crime-lite® XL producing 40 W of light and covering a large search area (Figure 5.12). These diode-based lights emit light of set bandwidths. These bandwidths vary, but are generally 30–50 nm wide. They are also often sold in sets of 4 or 5, with a range of lights supplied covering the spectrum from UV to deep red. Because of the continuing development of these types of systems, it is worth checking with the manufacturers to see the latest versions.

---

[21] http://www.icnirp.de/PubOptical.htm Management health and safety guidelines
[22] http://www.hse.gov.uk/radiation/nonionising/optical.htm
[23] Foster and Freeman: www.fosterfreeman.com

The *Crime-lite®2* series offers...

- Good power to weight ratio making it ideal for initial crime scene investigations.
- Utilises single LED technology.
- 8W output.
- Even, shadow-free illumination.
- Precision, anti-glare camera filters and goggles.
- Up to 4 hours run time.
- Available in White, UV, Violet, Blue, Blue/green, Green, Orange and Red narrow band wavelengths.
- Available as cased sets or individually.

The *Crime-lite®82* series offers...

- High power to weight ratio making it ideal for detailed crime scene investigations.
- White light 'linear' version with filters for examining surface dust and locating shoe prints.
- 16 high power LEDs.
- 8W output.
- Even, shadow-free illumination.
- Precision, anti-glare camera filters and goggles.
- Battery or mains power.
- Up to 3 hours run time.
- Available in White, UV, Violet, Blue, Blue/green, Green, Orange and Red narrow band wavelengths.
- Available as cased sets or individually.

The *Crime-lite®XL* series offers...

- Exceptional illumination power for the complete and thorough recovery of evidence.
- 96 high power LEDs.
- Up to 40,000 mW of radiant optical power.
- Even, shadow-free illumination.
- Optically engineered anti-glare camera filters and goggles.
- Available in Blue, Blue/green, Green & Orange narrow band wavelengths.
- Optional trimming filters reduce background fluorescence.

The *Crime-lite®8x4* offers...

- 118 modes of LED illumination configured in a ring light, primarily used is for evidence photography.
- Seven narrowband light sources from violet to red.
- 98 color mix combinations.
- White light with 10 color temperature settings between 3000 K and 10,000 K.
- 10 white light intensity settings at the color temperature 6500 K.
- Battery option available for crime scene use.

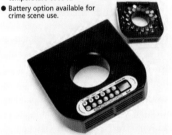

Figure 5.12   The Crime-lite® range. Note that a number of variants are available so it worth visiting the web site for up-to-date information.

5.4.4 Tuneable light sources

As the name suggests, this is a group of light sources in which the excitation wavelength can be varied. The three main models available in the United Kingdom are Crimescope (Figure 5.13), which is probably the most commonly used worldwide designed and built by SPEX in the USA[24] (10), the Polilight, designed by Rofin of Australia,[25] and the Quaser 2000/30 built by Foster and Freeman in the UK.

---

[24] SPEX: www.crimescope.com
[25] Rofin: http://www.rofinforensic.com.au/

Figure 5.13   A 500-W Crimescope CS16.

All of the above use a combination of band-pass filters, mounted in a wheel, to create the desired excitation wavelength. This is fitted in front of a bright white light source, such as a xenon arc or metal halide bulb. The wheel can be turned, so that a range of different 40–50-nm band pass wavelength filters are selected. (The Crimescope also has the ability to fine-tune this filter, by using the filter wheel, which I believe acts as a diffraction grating, allowing the filter to be narrowed to a smaller wavelength selection.)

Within the unit we use Crimescope for a supplementary lighting of scenes, as it is good for the enhancement of marks on coloured backgrounds or for oblique lighting along floors. It should be noted that the Crimescope is no longer used for the detection of latent evidence, particularly finger marks, as the higher output lasers have proved to be far more effective than a filtered light source (Figure 5.13).

There is also another issue that needs to be addressed with these types of lighting, particularly at crime scenes. All three of the above devices (Crimescope, Polilight and Quaser), use liquid light guides to deliver the light to the surface to be examined. These light guides are generally limited to two metres, this means that the device must be situated near the operator. This is often physically difficult to achieve, particularly when working on stepping plates, stairs and in small hallways. They also produce large amounts of heat and use air-cooling to control heat build up. This in turn increases the possibility, no matter how remote, of DNA or blood type particles being drawn into the device and re-emitted at another scene. This may result in cross-contamination of scenes [2] particularly where low template DNA analysis will be undertaken [3]. This is not an issue with the lasers, UV lights or some Crime-lites, as they either have long light guides or do not use fan-assisted cooling.

The most important thing to remember, whatever the ALS we are using, is that we are surrounded by evidence which is invisible to the human eye. Finger and shoe marks, saliva, body fluids, erased writing can all be made to 'glow in the dark' if exposed to the correctly filtered light.

'Just because you can't see it, doesn't mean it's not there.'

5.5 Filters

The correct choice of filter is just as crucial as the choice of light source, yet this is often overlooked in some books. Accurately cut, long band pass filters, whether in the form of safety goggles or photographic filters, could mean the difference between finding an identifiable mark or not. The filter ensures not only that the required wavelengths of light are transmitted, allowing the viewing of fluorescence, but they also act as a safety barrier against ocular damage. The quality of these filters is paramount and in the case of lasers a legal requirement. They must be of a robust enough construction to stand up to day-to-day usage and should ideally be tight-fitting to stop stray light from entering.

In some books I have read, sweeping statements are made regarding filter selection. For example, recommending 'orange' filters for undertaking fluorescence photography using a green 532-nm laser. Personally I believe this is misleading; to undertake fluorescence examination work properly, the filter needs to be carefully matched to the excitation wavelength. This should be selected to ensure all the evidence of importance can be detected and the user is fully protected from the light output. Even the small difference of 10 nm in the 'cut on' wavelength of the filter has been found to be the difference between seeing the mark and not (see Figure 5.14).

As we can see from Figure 5.14, the optical quality is all-important. At the present time (2014), all the filters we use have been labeled for use at specific bandwidths. Filters of this quality may cost upwards of £150 each, unlike an 'off-the-shelf' generic orange filter that may cost £20–30.

Filters come in three main types:

- Short band pass filters: these only allow light of wavelengths below their cut off point to be transmitted.
- Long pass filters: these only allow light of wavelengths above their cut on point to be transmitted.
- Band pass or interference filters: these only allow light of wavelengths with specific bandwidths to pass, an example being the Wratten 18A used in reflected UV photography.

For general induced fluorescence photography, a long band pass filter is employed, which has a cut on at a wavelength higher than the excitation

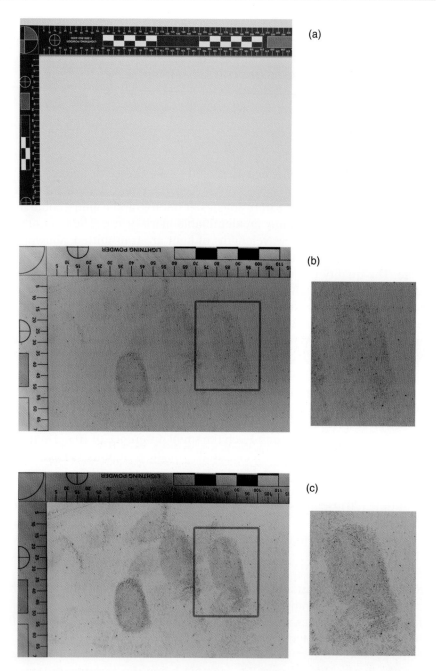

Figure 5.14   An area of wall illuminated under (a) white light illumination, (b) illuminated with a green laser at 532 nm, and photographed using an 'orange' filter, note the lack of contrast and definition within the mark. (c) Shows the same mark, this time photographed using a long band pass 550 nm filter, clearly showing the detail within the mark area.

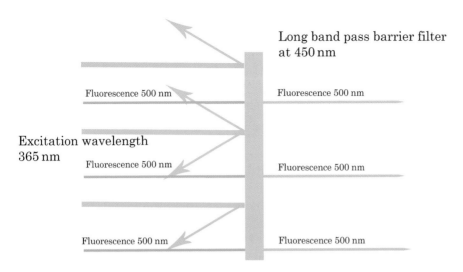

Figure 5.15 In this simple illustration we can see the excitation light at 365 and fluorescence at 500 nm reaching a long band pass filter at 450 nm. The short wave wavelengths of 365 nm are blocked, but the longer ones at 500 nm pass through (our fluorescence). In reality, some background fluorescence will also pass through but none of the original blue excitation wavelengths should. Indeed, if you can still see any of the excitation illumination through the filter, it is not working.

wavelength being used. As can be seen in Figure 5.15 the excitation rays at 365 nm, which are below the cut on point of the filter at 450 nm, are stopped, whereas the induced fluorescence at 500 nm passes through.

Most forensic light sources are expensive and therefore, to save on costs, some are supplied with mass-produced low-quality wrap-round type plastic

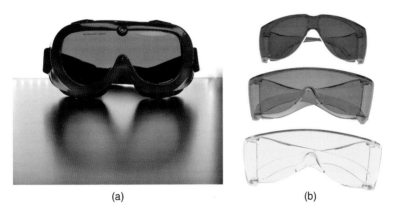

(a)   (b)

Figure 5.16 (a) The preferred type of goggles allowing no light leakage and clearly marked with a guide wavelength. (b) Wrap-around type plastic goggles, note that no wavelengths are indicated.

goggles of unspecified wavelengths (Figure 5.16) rather than more expensive tailored and specific goggles for the wavelength you are using. This is in my opinion a false economy, as they may be unsuitable for their intended use and should be avoided if possible. Goggles of this type may also not provide sufficient ocular protection and do not specify reliable wavelength values for cut on or cut off points. On some models I have tested, the wavelength cut off points varied from the left eye to right eye, and even in one case from the bottom of the lens to the top, depending on the thickness of the plastic.

It is worth noting at this point that a number of manufactures now supply spectacle type glasses for their equipment (rather than the goggles seen above in Figure 5.16a). Although these meet the current legal legislation, they were not designed with forensic purposes in mind. This means that, when used, there is light seepage around the edges; although this in not a direct health and safety issue, it does mean that you can lose your night vision capability. It is worth remembering when you are dealing with faint latent marks, rather than strong chemically enhanced ones, that goggle type of eyewear is preferable.

In choosing any safety glasses for use with a light source in fluorescence photography, it is essential that they have a cut on value of a greater wavelength than the excitation wavelength.

Photographic filters should also be chosen with care, and should if possible match the safety glasses. Both Laser Innovations (5) and Coherent lasers (6) supply correctly matched viewing goggles and photographic filters for use with their lasers. Foster and Freeman supply a complete range of matched goggles for their Crime-lite range. It is also possible to have bespoke filters made by companies such as Galvoptics.[26]

Before I leave the subject of fluorescence, there are a couple of points I should raise. When searching small exhibits it is best that they are searched on a non-fluorescing backdrop such as black paper. Otherwise you run the risk of autofluorescence from the background, overpowering weak marks. The other issue worth mentioning is that I have often been asked to look at equipment after the operator has said the laser isn't working properly. This is because they can't find anything fluorescing on an exhibit. Inevitably the exhibit turns out to be knife, or metal object, and the reason there is no fluorescence is because there is no contaminate to fluoresce! The safety goggles are absorbing all the reflected excitation light, and the exhibit has no fluorescent material on it. Simply shining the laser on the fluorescent flooring reassures the operator that the laser and goggles are working correctly. It is not unusual to get a negative response and it is nothing to worry about; after all, if a knife has just been through a dishwasher then you would it expect it to be clean and free from contamination.

---

[26] Galvaoptics Ltd: www.galvoptics.fsnet.co.uk/

5.6   Infrared (IR)

Unlike other types of ALS, the production of broad bandwidth IR radiation is much easier. Many forms of tungsten light bulb, electronic flash guns and daylight can offer rich sources of this type of radiation. If you wish to be more specific about the wavelength emitted, IR LED sources of a known wavelength can readily be purchased. Whatever choice you make, the best illumination is achieved when the light is soft and diffuse. Light sources producing a focused beam tend to overexpose the areas of interest.

Because our adapted camera is so sensitive to IR, exposure times for IR photography are generally the same as those with white light. For example, in the studio we use the modelling lights of two Bowen's studio flashes[27] which provide ideal illumination (flash switched off). This gives an exposure of about 1/15th s at f11 when the camera is fitted with a RG715 long pass IR filter, dropping to around a quarter of a second with an RG850 filter fitted.

IR photography is commonly used for the detection of altered inks, the visualisation of gunshot residues and the revealing of writing on burned documents. The surface or exhibit being examined may appear different in the IR region from the visible for a number of reasons:

- The substance or exhibit is absorbing IR radiation, turning it darker.
- The substance or exhibit is reflecting IR radiation, making it a lighter shade, or even white.
- The substance or exhibit is transmitting the IR radiation, which may cause the substance or exhibit to disappear revealing what is beneath it.
- The substance may also convert some of the IR energy to create radiation of a longer wavelength, creating IR fluorescence, although at the present time there is little published reference to this.

As we saw in the diagram of the electromagnetic spectrum, the human eye is visually limited to around 700 nm (deep red). Beyond this lies infrared (IR) and in particular the region we are interested in, that of IR-A (700–1400 nm). Digital cameras are intrinsically sensitive to IR to around 1100 nm, however IR is blocked from reaching the sensor on most digital cameras by IR absorbing filters bonded to the sensor, this ensures that any image recorded is correctly colour balanced.

If the quality of the end product you require is low, then it is possible to use a video camera with a 'night shot' mode. My Sony Handycam DCR-PC5E has this option. By flicking the switch the IR filter is physically moved from the optical path allowing the IR to reach the sensor. As we shall see in the following chapter, just like fluorescence photography the results obtained are

---

[27] Bowens: http://www.bowensdirect.com/

Figure 5.17   A self-adapted Nikon D70 with the IR filter removed.

dependent on the filter being used; it is, therefore, useful to have a selection available. I have attached a list of various manufacturers and the wavelengths available for guidance.[28]

As forensic photographers, we will probably require a high quality end result, so our options are more limited. We can purchase a dedicated camera, such as the Fuji UV/IR as mentioned above, or Calumet will supply an adapted camera of your choice. Or you can make your own IR sensitive camera by removing the internal IR filter. I have adapted an old Nikon D70; although this is a fiddly task, it is reasonably straightforward and simple with a little online guidance[29] (Figure 5.17). If you already own a Sigma SD1, then the filter has been designed to be easily removed to allow IR work. The advantage of using the sigma is that a full colour layer is used to capture the resultant image and therefore the quality is excellent.

---

[28] Filter makes and manufacturers

Wratten	Schott	B + W	Hoya	Tiffen	0%
#25	OG590	090	25A	25	580 nm
#29	RG630	091	-	29	600 nm
#70	RG665	-	-	-	640 nm
#89B	RG695	092	R72	-	680 nm
#88A	RG715	-	-	-	720 nm
#87	RG780	-	-	87	740 nm
#87C	RG830	093	-	-	790 nm
#87B	RG850	-	RM90	-	820 nm
#87A	RG1000	094	RM100	-	880 nm

[29] http://astrosurf.com/buil/d70/ircut.htm

5.7   White light

As I stated in my opening comments, I am deliberately including white light sources in this chapter. This is because when most people are asked to think of a forensic white light source, they consider the 'seek-and-search' type lamps, or electronic flash. For us the choice is far wider, clearly for lighting an arson scene, electronic flash is the perfect solution. But is flash the correct solution for a latent finger mark on a door frame? I doubt it. I feel it is very important to have variety of different light sources at your disposal, be it at a scene or within the laboratory.

Below I have listed the types of lighting we use on a day-to-day basis, both within the laboratory and at scenes. This is not exhaustive, but offers a good cross-section with a general description. Throughout this book you will see reference to their use in practical applications.

5.7.1   White light types

Ball light   These lights generally produce a soft diffuse light, which I will cover in more depth when we look at the specular photography of fingerprints. We use low-energy E27 electronic globe lights,[30] fitted into slightly adapted inspection light housings. They produce light at 2700 K (which is easily colour corrected in Photoshop if required). These lights are perfect for specular photography on most surfaces and can be used to enhance both finger and shoe marks (Figure 5.18).

The bulbs are generally mounted into an inspection lamp-type housing. These are often supplied with a metal cage to protect a normal light bulb from heat and damage, but these can normally be easily removed.

Although above I have quoted the E27, there are numerous shapes and sizes of bulb available, so it is possible to tailor your bulb to your application. Some manufacturers also produce a plastic globe rather than a glass one, which can be a bit more resilient to wear and tear at scenes. It is useful to note that bayonet type fittings should be avoided, as there is too much sideways movement in the bulb. Edison screw fittings should be used, these hold the bulb tightly and do not allow transverse movement.

Ring lights (sometimes referred to as bench inspection lamps)   These lights are more flexible than you might at first think. Used in one mode they allow flat, shadowless, even illumination to be produced. However, if turned at a slight angle, they are perfect for small areas requiring specular illumination. In their simplest form, they are simply a circular fluorescent tube. I would argue for most applications, but particularly for finger marks, a standard ring desk lamp

---

[30] Megaman 20-watt electronic compact globe light. Product number 933205

Figure 5.18   A low energy E27 bulb fitted into a standard inspection housing, with the metal cage removed.

is perfectly suitable. They are cheap, easily available and allow the operator to see any adjustment to the image in real time. All you need to do is remove the magnifying glass from the centre (if fitted) (Figure 5.19).

We rarely use ring flash, however a cheap alternative for a ring flash if required is to purchase a flash gun converter such as Rayflash.[31] Nor do we use purpose-built photographic LED ring lights, unless it is to photograph an injury or a finger mark developed using ninhydrin. This is because the ring light is generally fixed to the lens or camera. Although this is photographically correct to produce even illumination, it is often not the correct position for the photography of latent marks.

Soft boxes   Again these come in many forms, from a typical light box with a plastic or glass diffuser, through to the latest LED flat light panels, such as the Rosco litepad.[32] These lights are almost exclusively used for specular reflection work and allow large areas to be covered, again producing a large, soft, diffuse light (Figure 5.20).

Schott type inspection lamps   These are the type of lamps typically found on many microscopes and deliver the light via a fibre optic (Figure 5.21). These

[31] Rayflash: http://www.SimplyRingFlash.com/?gclid=CP3QhvWC96kCFXAMtAodF3ZN1
[32] Rosco litepads; www.rosco.com

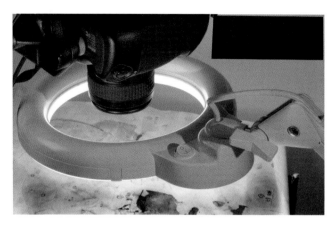

Figure 5.19 A ring light inspection lamp.

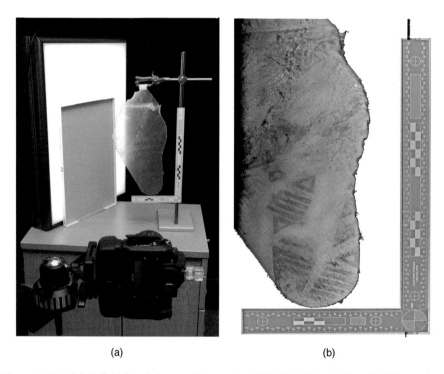

(a)   (b)

Figure 5.20 (a) A light box being used to create black field illumination. (b) The resultant mark reverse-coloured for comparison purposes. It is interesting to note here that, unusually, the sheet of plastic with the mark on it is hanging, rather than being laid flat. This was because it was not possible to achieve the right angle and distance to illuminate the mark properly when the plastic was laid on a glass-topped table.

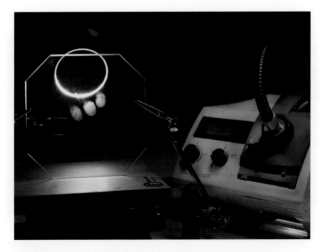

Figure 5.21   A Schott inspection lamp fitted with a ring light fibre optic. In this case it is being used to produce dark field illumination on latent finger marks on glass.

lamps are useful in the fingerprint laboratory for the oblique lighting of finger marks. They come in a variety of powers and with alternative fibre optic wand fittings including multiple headed and circular ones.

Pocket torches and collimated beams   Such has been the increase in LED technology over the past few years that traditional search torches have almost

Figure 5.22   A Kodak carousel being use to illuminate a vinyl floor.

been replaced by the new LED types. Many are entirely unsuitable for photography, due to their uneven beams. However, we do use the LED Lenser P7[33] which has an adjustable beam and is handy to have in your camera bag. We also still use a Kodak carousel projector to create a collimated beam of light for the detection of shoe marks at scenes or on lifts (Figure 5.22). Because of the lens configuration, it is capable of lighting the length of a hall or corridor.

5.8 Conclusion

I hope that in reading this chapter you have gained a greater understanding around the choice of illumination we can use for the detection and retrieval of forensic evidence both within the laboratory and at scenes.

In the following chapters, we will look at putting some of the above into practical use.

References

(1) C.A. Pounds et al. (1990). *J Forensic Sci* 35: 169.
(2) Rutty, G. N., Hopwood, A. and Tucker, V. (2003). The effectiveness of protective clothing in the reduction of potential DNA contamination of the scenes of crime. *Int J Legal Med.* 117(3): 170–4.
(3) Gill, P. (2001) Application of low copy number DNA profiling. *Croatian Med J* 42(3):229–32.

---

[33] LED Lenser P7: www.amazon.co.uk/ledlenser + p7 plus numerous other online sites.

6
The Photography of Injuries

6.1 Overview

The photography of injuries, like the photography of latent marks, can often be one of the most photographically satisfying in terms of results. Even the simplest of techniques, such as cross-polarised lighting, can have a dramatic visual effect on the clarity of the injuries being recorded.

However, with the advent of cheap, easy-to-use digital cameras, the role of the forensic photographer in the capturing of injury marks is often seen as less important or even unnecessary. After all, it is easy for an officer to pick up the office camera, point and shoot and get a usable result ... but is it? [1] Although the image captured may on face value appear to be correctly exposed and in focus, the real question is actually how useful it is. In other words, does it actually show them what they hope to see, the shape or pattern of a weapon or implement?

The reality is that many injuries hold information about their causation that is not always readily or easily seen [2] (Figure 6.1). It is our task as forensic photographers to make every attempt to unlock this information photographically [3].

The question for us is: what technique should be used to undertake the photography of the injury? Within this chapter we will look at the potential of some of these techniques to increase contrast and clarity, allowing you to deploy them with confidence and to capture far more than conventional photography can.

For a simple black eye type bruise, which has been caused by an amorphous shape (say a fist), a simple photograph from a camera with an integral flash may be more than adequate and all that is required. But what if that injury has

Forensic Photography: A Practitioner's Guide, First Edition. Nick Marsh.
© 2014 John Wiley & Sons, Ltd. Published 2014 by John Wiley & Sons, Ltd.

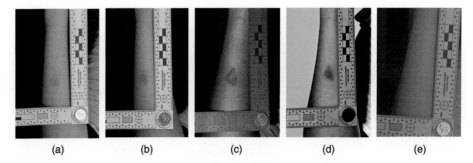

(a)   (b)   (c)   (d)   (e)

Figure 6.1 A burn to the arm photographed using (a) white light (b) cross-polarised light, (c) reflected ultraviolet, (d) induced fluorescence, (e) infrared.

been caused in another way, such as a bite, burn, welt, or what if the victim has suffered some form of previously sustained surface trauma? More importantly, what if it has been caused by an implement or weapon, something that may contain a pattern or shape [4]? Will a standard photograph really allow us to see and record the evidentially important features of the injury?

The taking of a 'standard' flash on camera photographs should not be seen as a criticism of anyone, as often this is the only option available. But with cases such as Baby 'P'[1] appearing in the press at regular intervals, it is important that other more advanced techniques should be available for use in cases which warrant going the extra mile.

Some of the techniques that we will look at, such as cross-polarised photography, require little or no investment on your or the department's part, whilst others will require dedicated equipment to be purchased. There is no doubt in my mind, based on my last 25 years of experience, that I have known decisions on whether cases are to be taken to court or not based purely on the quality of the injury photography. The techniques we will look at here work equally well within the studio on living victims, or at the mortuary on cadavers. Indeed some techniques, such as the use of cross-polarised light to reduce sheen on gross specimens, is worth the small investment alone (Figure 6.2).

I will explain and cover the equipment I am going to use, but again because of the massive diversity of photographic kit in day-to-day usage it is almost impossible to give hard and fast rules around exposure settings, so some trial and error will be required on your part.

---

[1] The Baby P enquiry involved Peter Connelly, who was a 17-month old boy who died in London after receiving over 50 injuries over an eight-month period. During this time he had been repeatedly seen by Haringey children's services and NHS professionals. Baby P's real first name was revealed as 'Peter' on the conclusion of a subsequent trial of Peter's mother's boyfriend on a charge of raping a two-year-old. His full identity was revealed when his killers were named after the expiry of a court anonymity order on 10 August 2009.

(a)

(b)

Figure 6.2 A kidney photographed with normal flash and under cross-polarised illumination. Although in this case the surface of the kidney is quite dry, the surface detail is lost under standard flash illumination, whilst under cross-polarised light the surface is clean and clearly defined. If this were a wetter, shinier surface, this effect would have been more evident.

6.2 The nature of injuries

Before we consider how to achieve the best result through photography, it is useful to have a very basic understanding of exactly what is happening medically with a bruise, bite or burn.

6.2.1 Bruises

Bruises are caused by a blunt impact that ruptures and haemorrhages the blood vessels within the underlying skin without creating an external wound. Vessels often bleed for some time and as a result bruises can often develop over a 24–48 hour window. The immediate reaction of the injured tissue is acute inflammation, and colour change is partly caused by the haemoglobin breakdown and partly by chromophore transport through the skin. The bruise then passes through a number of colour changes dependent on whether it is fresh or old, as the macrophages and neutrophiles engulf both the erythrocytes and the free haemologlobin molecules, producing bilirubin and hemosiderin. We always advise officers to check the development of the bruising on a victim over a number of days. Often, when fresh, the bruise will flare up and appear swollen and red. Although dramatic, it actually contains little detail; after a few days, however, this red inflammation often subsides, leaving the resultant bruise with more detail. This detail can then be fully exploited through the use of other photographic techniques.

6.2.2 Burns

A burn is the destruction of different layers of the skin and the structures within them, such as sweat and oil glands. This can produce a number of effects, from as little as a dry, pink patch to a full leathery or charred appearance. The actual appearance of the injury is dependent on the severity of the burn, categorised as 'first', 'second' and 'third' degree burns. See Table 6.1.

In my experience, most of the injuries that you will come across are on children, many of which will have been caused by either hot liquids, such as boiling water, or by hot metal, such as cigarette lighters or kitchen implements, being pressed to the skin. Although, as can be seen above, burns may lose much of their visible appearance over time, it may still be possible to detect them within the skin structure. The use of reflected ultraviolet (UV), particularly on

Table 6.1   The three categories of burns.

	First	Second (superficial or deep)	Third (full thickness)
Depth of burn	Epithelium	Epithelium and top aspects of dermis	Epithelium and dermis
How the burn looks	No blisters, dry pink	Moist, oozing, blisters, moist, white	Leathery, dry, no elasticity charred appearance
Causes	Sunburn, scald and flash flame	Scalds, flash flame, chemicals	Contact with flame, hot surfaces, hot liquids, chemical and electrical
Level of pain	Painful, tender and sore	Very painful	Very little or no pain
Healing time	2 to 5 days. May have peeling	Superficial 5 to 21 days.	Small areas may take months to heal. Large areas may need skin grafts
Scarring	No scarring but may have some colour discoloration	Minimal or no scarring may have discoloration	Scarring present

lighter European skin tones, is an effective way of visualising the injury. On darker Middle Eastern and African skin tones, the use of cross-polarised light is generally more effective, as the levels of melanin within the skin often mask the effects of reflected UV.

6.2.3 Cuts and abrasions

A cut is the separation of skin or other tissue made by a sharp edge, producing regular edges. This is distinct from lacerations (also called tears), which are generally made by force against the body, say from an implement or punch, leaving ragged edges. Depending on the weapon used, this can cause damage to the skin's structure, veins and arteries, causing bleeding and bruising. Abrasions or scrapes occur when the skin is rubbed away by friction against another rough surface. Both types of injury can have associated secondary bruising, which can initially mask the detail of the injury. More than one visit to the victim should be considered so that images can be captured once bruising has subsided.

6.2.4 Bites

These can take on any number of characteristics, from as little as a small bruise, caused by the pinching motion of the teeth, through to penetration of the skin leaving a laceration or cut. This is also one of the most requested types of injury to be photographed and we shall look at this in more depth later on.

When confronted with a case, it is important for us to know as much about the injury as possible. For example, if you were asked to photograph a six-month-old bite mark, it would be important to know the severity of the bite. If its cause was a gentle bite or sucking, hardly bruising the skin, then there is little hope that we could do much. If, however, the assailant bit through the skin, then reflected UV or induced fluorescence might be an option [5].

I should point out at this stage that some clinicians have reservations around the usefulness of the techniques that follow. They raise the concern that there is very little research into why reflected UV, induced fluorescence, or cross-polarised photography works. They feel that if they cannot see the injury with the human eye when carrying out an examination, they cannot comment on it, as it may be an older injury or another unrelated feature. [6] My answer is that all the techniques are based on known principles of science, the uses of fluorescence and cross-polarised lighting being well documented. [7, 8] If the application of a particular technique during photography can clearly show the causation of a mark, then that has to be a positive thing. If, by the same reasoning, the photograph proves that the injury was caused accidentally, showing the suspected party is innocent, should that information be ignored?

6.3   The photography

Clearly, the equipment we are issued with is often beyond our control and is driven by many factors, including cost. But, if you have a choice, I would strongly recommend the use of prime lenses or, failing that, locking the zoom to a fixed position. The use of prime lenses ensures that all the photographs are shot at the same focal length, thus adding consistency to multiple images taken of the same areas. Focusing is then accomplished by moving the camera backwards and forwards. If zoom lenses are used, the tendency is to use the zoom to fill the frame, which gives images of different magnification sizes. This creates a series of photographs where at best we have no consistency with the scaling; whilst at worst we can create false and distorted photographs.

Unlike medical photography, there is no national guidance for those of us employed within the police environment and it is left up to each force how to set its own standards. This I believe is unfortunate, as it leads to differing levels of quality and continuity across the country, giving somewhat of a 'post code lottery' to victims of crime. There are, however, a few rules which I believe we should try and adhere to:

- Try and use a standard viewpoint. (For example, in multiple images say, the reference and cross-polarised images should be taken from the same position.) (Figure 6.3)
- Never photograph an injury larger than life size. (Unless macro photography is required, and then a location shot must be taken. Otherwise this could unintentionally mislead a jury around the nature and size or even position of the injury.)
- Always photograph the injury so it is has space surrounding it, preferably showing its orientation to another body part. (For example, an area of a bite mark could be anywhere, back, chest, leg, this should not be open to

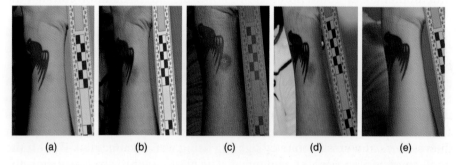

| (a) | (b) | (c) | (d) | (e) |

Figure 6.3   The above points in practice. Here five different techniques have been used to photograph a burn injury: (a) white light (b) cross-polarised light (c) reflected ultraviolet (d) induced ultraviolet fluorescence (these images are often left in colour to aid comparison due to the increased colour contrast) (e) infrared. Note: even though a number of different cameras have been used, all the injuries are taken at the same angle and orientation allowing easy comparison.

question and should be clearly located. I have seen hundreds of photographs where it is impossible to tell the actual location of the injury.)

- Check the lighting, is the injury actually lit? (If the injury is on the left side of the body then don't hold the flash on the right side and ensure that arms, clothing and so on will not cause shadows.)
- Always include a scale. [9] (If you are photographing the injury because it has shape or form then I would insist on using a scale, even if it's a face, as this will allow accurate reproduction at a later stage. This is particularly true in cases involving children, when it could be years before the case goes to court and feature sizes have changed.)
- Never be tempted to use a wide-angle lens to photograph an injury. (The use of these lenses, particularly at close distances, will distort your image and will therefore not be a true representation to the court. This makes such images open to question by a defence counsel.)
- Always try and choose an aperture that will give you the greatest depth of field possible.

Before starting photography, it is worth considering the final medium that the doctor or investigating officer is going view the images with. Within the Metropolitan Police Evidence Recovery Unit (ERU) most injuries are still at the printed to true (1:1) scale, on 10 x 8 inch paper. A handy trick I have found is to try and visualise how much space an injury will take up on the paper (when printed to scale), this allows me then to maximise the positioning for presentation. So many images I have seen are taken filling the viewfinder frame; this means that when printed life size they float in middle of a page, which I feel is neither helpful nor professional (Figure 6.4). If, however, you are exporting purely in a digital medium then this may not be a consideration.

We have all seen examples of poor injury photography, so accuracy and clarity is the most important thing to keep in mind. I find this is particularly true around children, as your image may either support claims of abuse, or equally dismiss them by indicating a natural occurrence.

The other issue we must look at before we start is the fact that the digital revolution has created a very real problem in injury photography. That is, the practical difficulty of gaining specialist results with the standard camera. With film, it was possible to undertake the control/reference, the reflected ultraviolet (UV) and the infrared (IR) image, all using standard cameras – the only cost being changing to different films. Now this once simple task is impossible; the latest digital cameras are designed to block unwanted UV and IR from their sensors. If you wish to undertake photography outside the visible region of the spectrum, an adapted camera must be used, generally costing thousands of pounds. This, I believe, has been a contributing factor in the demise of these techniques from many forces.

The visualisation of old bruising is probably still one of the most common requests made to the ERU. This is particularly relevant with regard to

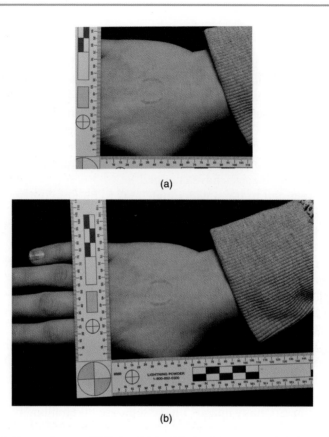

(b)

Figure 6.4   A bite mark to a child's hand (a) with the injury cropped tight in the frame, so its exact location on the body is not obvious. (b) The same injury with some surrounding area showing location. Both ways are acceptable but for different mediums; (a) would work well in a digital only form whereas (b) would be a more acceptable use of the frame for a print.

Child Protection Teams and those investigating sexual offences. [10] Often this casework is not brought to our notice until either the incident is weeks old, or after they have already tried to photograph the injury themselves. As we know, bruises can appear and disappear within a very short period of time, but in general have disappeared completely within six weeks. There are some reports of bruising being photographed using specialist lighting six months after the offence, but I am led to believe this is medically improbable and they are most likely imaging either something from a much later event, or another anomaly altogether.

There are occasions when the requirement for visual supporting evidence is crucial if a case is to progress; it is in these circumstances that we as forensic photographers must look at other alternatives, such as infrared, long-wave ultraviolet fluorescence, and deep blue fluorescence.

6.4 Before we start

I would strongly advise that photography is never carried out single-handed, both from a practicality point of view (holding rulers or flash guns in position and taking photographs is not easy) but also because the second person acts as an independent witness during the photography session. This is particularly important if you are dealing with a vulnerable or emotional victim.

The victim should be encouraged to sit or stand in a posture that they find comfortable. Not a posture, I would argue, which suits you. I have seen photographers trying to get people into positions that a contortionist would be proud of, trying get arms and legs in the same photograph, just to reduce the total number of photographs required! To my mind this is self-defeating; not only does this cause the victim unnecessary stress, but it also produces a photograph that is unnatural and contrived. It is far better to photograph each injury separately and carefully, ensuring it is recorded as accurately as possible. As already stated, I would always advocate the use of rigid rulers within a photograph, not only do they indicate the scale of an injury, but they also help with colour correction and contrast. The photographer must take responsibility for keeping the victim comfortable, however some thought must be given to ensure that the area of interest is roughly in the same position as when it was injured. For example, if an arm was bent when it was kicked, it should be photographed bent. If this is not the case the injury may appear unnaturally distorted. [11]

It should also be borne in mind that to produce a meaningful set of equivalent images, there is no point in having a control photograph if the cross-polarised one is taken from a different angle or position. This process of interchanging cameras/filters between different imaging techniques can be made easier by having a colleague assist you, handing over cameras and filters. Keeping consistent poses is a particular issue with children; therefore, within our studio, we keep a number of children's toys to hold their interest. The use of tripods is also encouraged, as it assures that the same viewing angles and distances are maintained. Clearly this advice needs to be balanced against practicality when you have a three-year-old running around!

Most injuries can normally be covered by one photograph, on one plane. The main exception to this is bite marks, especially when they are on limbs. [12] Here, great care must be taken to ensure that the upper and lower impressions are photographed square-on (Figure 6.5). This is important, as the injury may not be visible until the cross-polarised or reflected UV photography has been undertaken. In many photographs, I have seen the upper or lower set of teeth marks clearly visible, but somehow the opposite set has disappeared around a corner, or is so angled as to be of no help to a forensic odentologist. It is also worth remembering that a poorly angled image could also change any patterned injury, making its evidential value questionable.

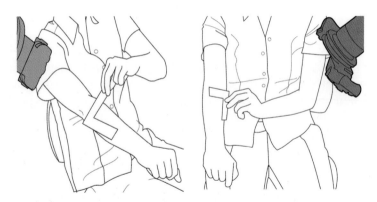

Figure 6.5   The arrangement of camera to injury. Image courtesy of Ruth Bowen, Cardiff University.

6.5   Techniques and equipment required

Before we start we should have a very brief look at the basic equipment required to undertake any injury photography.

6.5.1   Camera

The choice of this item will generally be down to your department or organisation; however, as already stated, I would suggest a good quality digital standard lens reflex (DSLR) with a selection of prime lenses such as a 60 mm, 85 mm or 105 mm. At the present time (2012) we are using a mix of Nikon D4xs and D800s. If you are looking to undertake induced fluorescence, the only cameras at the present time that seem to give consistent low noise results (as the ISO need to be set at least 2500) are those that are in the professional end of the DSLRs. Amateur models we have found tend to produce excessive noise, or have very little sensitivity to the particular wavelengths used.

If you are looking to undertake reflected UV or IR photography, then you will need a specially adapted camera, which I will talk about in the techniques below.

6.5.2   Illumination

I believe some thought also needs to be given to the illumination used to undertake even the reference or control photograph. In some organisations I appreciate that this is limited to the pop up flash in the prism head. Although these can be quite powerful for their size they are not ideally suited for the photography of injuries, as they can produce harsh direct lighting and fall-off at the sides when used in portrait mode. Also, because of the positioning of the flash, they tend to create reflections on the area of interest, especially if the skin is scabbed or tight.

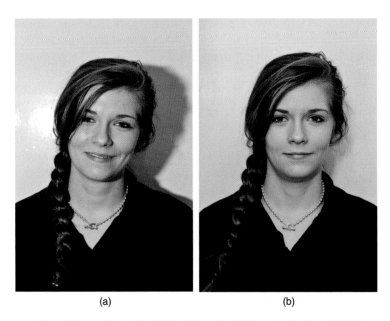

(a)   (b)

Figure 6.6   Shows the use of one flash (a) Lit from the left, producing harsh shadows and flare on the background. (b) Here the light has been bounced off the ceiling, producing a softer light with almost no shadows. Both images would show an injury to the face but (b), I would argue, is less distracting and more professional looking. This is one of the most common problems I encounter when looking at supplied images from other agencies. In scene photography the use of one flash does not present a major problem, as the distance to target is usually sufficient to ensure even illumination of the target. However, unless careful consideration is given in injury photography, it can produce uneven illumination, harsh highlights or flare that always falls across the injury under interpretation. Photographs taken at f11, at 1/ 125th at 400ISO using an SB-700 set to TTL.

The use of two balanced dual-mounted flashguns on either side of the camera is my preferred option if possible. This creates an even illumination, which removes harsh shadows and is considered an ideal for all types of injury. However, I appreciate this might be seen as a luxury. The use of one flash is perfectly acceptable provided you are mindful and aware of where the shadows fall (Figure 6.6).

A ring flash, by design, also provides soft, even illumination, particularly on body injuries. This is ideal for most surfaces as the light is projected from around the front optic of the lens. It can, however, suffer from drop-off in illumination if the injury is on a curved surface. In the past few years a number of ring flash converters have arrived on the market, such as the Coco CR-SB900 ring flash adapter for the Nikon SB-900.[2] However, most flashguns

---

[2] Microglobe, 3 Galen place London WC1A 2JR UK: http://www.microglobe.co.uk/catalog/product_info.php?pName=coco-crsb900-ring-flash-adapter-for-nikon-sb900-speedlight-flashgun

are catered for and suppliers are easily found on the Internet.[3] These adaptors clip onto the front of a normal hot-shoe mounted flashgun and deflect the light around the barrel, mimicking a traditional ring flash for a fraction of the cost. (See Chapter 3.)

Natural daylight should not be overlooked – it is, however, unreliable and is not easily controlled, although diffused sunlight can produce a soft, even illumination which can be useful. Desk lamps, light bulbs and other types of office lighting should be avoided if possible, as these generally produce coloured light, which although not noticeable to the human eye will produce a colour cast on any object photographed. This can be compensated for, to some extent, by resetting the white balance on your camera. If you are shooting in RAW file mode, lighting colour casts can be altered within software programs such as Adobe Photoshop, but in my mind this is adding unnecessary complications.

6.5.3   Polarising filters

These will allow the undertaking of cross-polarised photography. You will need at least two linear polarising filters, however only one needs to be of optical quality. We use the standard Cokin linear polariser on the camera and linear polarising sheets over the light source. (See cross-polarised below, although other makes are available.[4])

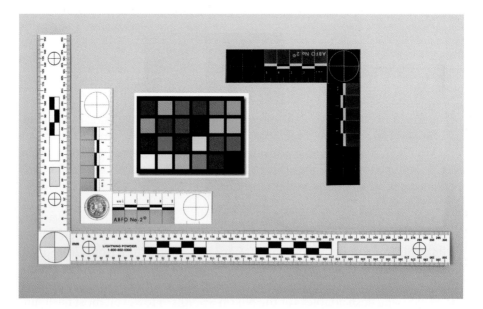

Figure 6.7   A selection of forensic rulers and a colour checker chart.

---

[3] Amazon: http://www.amazon.com
[4] Cokin filters: http://www.cokin.co.uk

6.5.4 Forensic rulers

We typically use two ABFO forensic rulers:[5] a small L-shaped one for close-up work and a longer straight version for general photography. These rulers tend to have a matt finish and are designed to be used with electronic flash. The use of commercial office-type plastic rulers is not encouraged, as the scales are often incorrect and when illuminated with flash create large hot spots (Figure 6.7).

6.6 The colour reference

The reference or control photograph is generally an image taken under white light and may in many cases be the only photograph taken. This photograph's critical role cannot be underplayed and the quality of image is all-important. A poor quality photograph can hinder a case or even lose one, especially if the area of the injury is not accurately illuminated or represented. This is particularly important to bear in mind, if your images are being reviewed by external experts, such as the UK NID (National Injuries Database),[6] to undertake physical fits, comparisons or other casework. The injuries must be clearly and accurately scaled, I would also encourage the use colour checker charts, or neutral forensic rulers. When in frame they act as a guide to the colour temperature and exposure.

Within the ERU, the photographers print their own images, but if in your organisation you do not, then these types of visual key are important to ensure that the images are reproduced as faithfully as possible by those responsible for printing.

The use of brightly coloured backgrounds should also be avoided as these can reflect colour casts onto any item close to them. Ideally a grey cloth or a portable backdrop such as a Lastolite[7] should be used, as this can be carried with us and offers a neutral backdrop regardless of location.

6.6.1 Cross-polarised photography

We are probably all familiar with polarised sunglasses and the effect they have on reflections. This technique takes the idea of singular polarisation one step further forwards. As the name suggests, this type of photography requires the light hitting the camera to be cross-polarised – this means the light has to pass through two polarising filters at 90° to each other before reaching the camera sensor. The result is a colour-saturated image that shows reduced sheen on the skin and enhanced pigmentation, which in turn maximises detail. This type of

---

[5] ABFO rulers via Tetra scenes of crime: http://www.tetrasoc.com
[6] National Injuries Database, which is part of the NPIA (National Policing Improvement Agency): http://www.npia.police.uk/en/6868.htm
[7] Lastolite products: www.lastolite.com

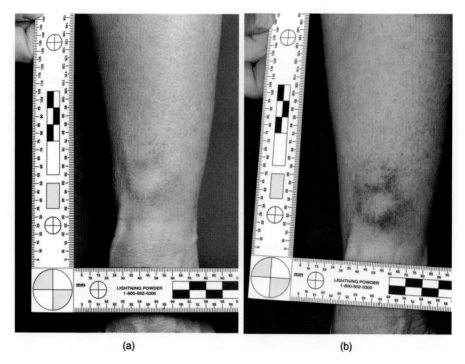

(a)   **(b)**

Figure 6.8   An assault injury to the wrist (a) under normal flash illumination (b) under cross-polarised illumination. Note the increased skin saturation and lack of reflections.

photography can be used for any of the following applications: bite marks, burns, injury enhancement, implement marks, strangulation marks, general bruising and gross specimen photography (Figure 6.8).

For me or any other forensic photographer, the carrying of a polarising filter in their kit bag is an essential. This will be used either to remove reflections, or to increase the saturation of colour. However, as I have seen the number of forensic photographers in many forces declining over the years, so has the use of the polarising filters.

To achieve the desired affect of cross-polarised lighting, you will require two linear polarising filters.[8] One must be of optical quality, which we will use in front of the lens. The other one, for the flashgun, does not have to be optical quality and we have found the plastic polarising sheets are perfectly adequate, as they can be cut to fit over whichever flash-head is in use.[9] Once

---

[8] Although circular, polarising filters are generally recommended for DSLRs because they do not affect exposure readings if the camera is using split beam metering. Linear polarisers are generally preferred to undertake cross-polarised photography, as it is a simple task to achieve the cross-polarised effect with each at 90° to the other. Linear filters often require an adjustment of two stops to ensure correct exposure.

[9] Polarising sheets: originally we had some difficulty getting supplies, however Flint are theatrical suppliers so this may be an option if you are looking to source this material. 43 cm × 51 cm (75 micron) yields approximately 50–60 filter strips for Metz flashguns.

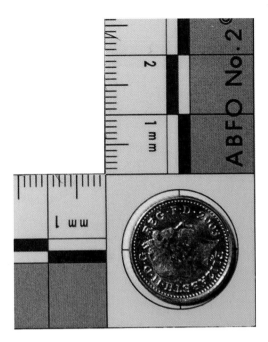

Figure 6.9   Here we can see a coin attached to the corner of the ruler; if you haven't got a coin to hand, then any highly reflective metal object will work.

fitted, the flashgun filter must be checked after every session for signs of burn out (normally the filter discolours or white spots appear) and replaced as necessary. This is because the light passing through these areas will no longer be polarised. They will normally last 40–60 flashes dependant on power output.

It is fairly easy to adapt most types of camera, enabling them to undertake cross-polarised photography. Even small compact cameras can be adapted by following the guidance below. In fact I have managed to demonstrate the technique at conferences using mobile phones. All you need is a few basic pieces of equipment: a small ruler, a small silver coin (such as a five-pence piece or dime), two or three polarising filters (depending on how many flashguns you wish to use) and correction fluid.

Step 1: Attach the small silver coin to the corner of the scale (Figure 6.9). This is important from both the photography point of view and for subsequent post-production later. Now we are going to photograph the scale with its attached five-pence piece. This will give us a control or reference photograph. To do this, place the camera on a tripod and place the scale in front of the lens square on at 90°. Make sure it roughly fills the frame and photograph as normal.

Flints also supply the black Gaffa tape we use. Flints Hire and Supply Ltd, Theatrical Chandlers, Queen Row, London SE17 2PX, Tel 0207 703 9786, Contact: John Joyce

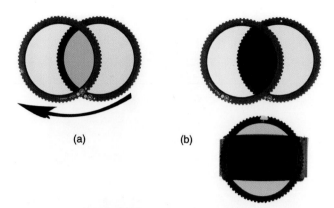

(a)   (b)

Figure 6.10   (a) The two polarising filters placed so they are overlapping, then being turned. (b) The filters in the cross-polarised position, using both a glass filter and using a sheet of filter fitted to a plastic flash diffuser. Although it may appear that there is no light passing through, only around two stops are lost in the process.

Step 2: We now need to find the point where the filters cross-polarise to have the maximum effect. This is easily achieved using either a window or a light box if available. Holding one filter in each hand, hold them over each other. Now turn the top one until it becomes black (this should require a turn of no more than 90° in either direction) (Figure 6.10). If you are using polarising sheet for the flash, you will need to cut it to the required size to fit over the flash head first. A word of caution here, try not to damage the sheet in any way when cutting otherwise you will have stress lines in the plastic reducing its reliability.

Step 3: Once the filters are oriented so that they turn black, they are cross-polarised. Keeping them in position, mark the 12 o'clock position of each filter with a dot of correction fluid or paint (Figure 6.11). (This is the tricky bit; notice that any small deviation from this position reduces the cross-polarised effect and this will be seen on any subsequent photographs.)

They are now paired, this ensures that whenever you use this pair of filters again, you will instantly be able to cross-polarise them when required. Note the process will need to be repeated with any new filters, to ensure that the pairs are cross-polarised. We now need to attach one filter to the front of the lens, with the dot at 12 o'clock.

Step 4: The other filter must now be fitted over the light source, with the paint marker dot at 12 o'clock. It is important to remember to place the polarising filter on the outside of the diffuser. Don't be tempted to place it behind the diffuser, as the light may be depolarised as it is diffused. It is also important to ensure that no stray un-polarised light can hit the subject, so the filter must wrap around the sides of the flash head or, if need be, the sides should be blocked off with black tape (Figure 6.12). Alternatively you may wish to make a small card box to fit over the flashgun head.

Figure 6.11 The top of the filter marked with a white dot.

If you are using a separate flash, the most important thing to remember is to ensure that the lens and the flash are on the same plane (Figure 6.13). This should be square to the target. If they are not, the technique will not work! It is also important to remember that some camera metering systems are fooled by the polariser and an allowance of approximately two stops may need to be given. This can be done by either opening the aperture, or preferably by increasing the flash power.

Step 5: Now photograph the ruler again. If the image capture system has been successfully cross-polarised, the silver coin should now appear black (Figure 6.14). If it is still silver or half silver, the filters were not correctly aligned and should be re-checked. The use of the silver coin also has the advantage at the post-production stage, in that the person printing can see that the image is meant to be cross-polarised and will print accordingly. It is worth noting that the difference between being cross-polarised and not can be a difference of only 1 or 2 degrees, so it is important to ensure that the filters are properly aligned during photography.

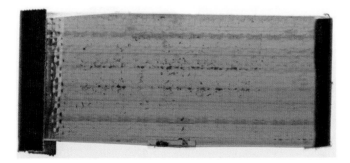

Figure 6.12 A sheet of polarising filter. As stated, the filter must be fitted to the exterior of the plastic filter; also note how the sides of the filter that are angled have been masked to remove unwanted un-polarised light.

Figure 6.13   The camera and flash ready to undertake cross-polarised photography.

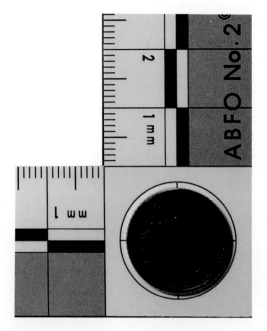

Figure 6.14   A correctly cross-polarised ruler. Note that the coin is devoid of any reflection. It is important to remember that, although this is a good indicator, if it is not exactly at 90° during photography, the rest of the photograph could be polarised.

6.7   Reflected Ultraviolet (UV)

This is a much more specialised technique and, as the name suggests, records the ultraviolet light reflected from the skin. In practicality the regions of the UV spectrum utilised here are between 300 nm and 390 nm. At these wavelengths many substances absorb or reflect in a completely different way than they would under visible light. For example, melanin, the tanning agent of the skin, absorbs ultraviolet very strongly between 330 nm and 400 nm (other epidermal chromophores do not). Therefore, any differences between pigmented and un-pigmented skin are exaggerated by the application of these wavelengths. Differences in skin tone, colour or pigmentation, which may appear slight in visible light, may become very clear under reflected UV. [13] This technique is particularly useful for the visualisation of old trauma injuries, such as bites, burns or those caused by implements.

Additionally, the UV at this wavelength has virtually no penetration of the skin, so there is no scattering of the light. This in turn leads to much sharper images, meaning that surface damage is more easily seen. The downside of this technique is that no guarantees can be given; results are variable and are influenced by the person's skin tone and healing speed. There is also some discussion around what exactly is being captured in the UV image, but the consensus is that it is the 'migration of the melanocytes', differences being due either to a loss of the melanocytes from the area of interest, such as a burn, or a build up in an area caused by a scar.

From my own experience with burn injuries, my general guideline would be the more northern European the skin type, the better the results with reflected UV are. For African skin tones, reflected UV tends to be less effective, but the cross-polarised results are generally better.

There are two ways you can undertake this type of photography, one is by using a specially adapted digital camera (and here I am afraid the choice is limited) or secondly by using a film camera.

Fuji make the Fuji UV/IR camera.[10] This camera is reported to be sensitive in both the UV and IR regions as it uses front-fitting filters instead of a blocking filter over the sensor.

I, however, have opted for an adapted Nikon D700, available through ACS (Advanced Camera Systems) in Norwich.[11] This adapted D700 is known to record as low as 300 nm and uses an internally fitted UV transmission filter, so focusing is much simpler. It cannot, however, record any visual light or infrared images. This is still not as good as film, which records images at wavelengths down to the UVC region at 254 nm. However, the adapted

---

[10] Fuji: http://www.fujifilm.com
[11] Advanced Camera Systems (ACS), Unit 10, Linmore Court, Threxton Road Industrial Estate, Watton, Norfolk, IP25 6NG
Tel 01953 889 324 Fax 01953 880 086 Email ACS_2005@BTconnect.com http://www.advanced cameraservices.co.uk

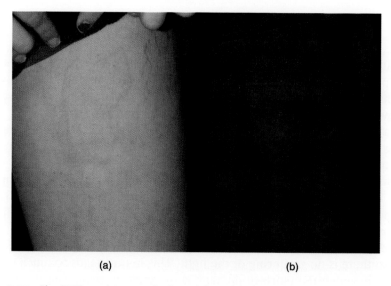

(a)   (b)

Figure 6.15   The D700 used to record a burn injury. (a) Shows the reference image taken on a D800. (b) Shows the reflected UV taken on the adapted D700. Note that due to the way the sensor works the UV image appears in the red channel. This is another reason why, for evidential purposes, the images should be provided as greyscale.

camera (D700) does give an acceptable result when directly compared to film (Figure 6.15).

As an aside, I have also seen results obtained from a UV-adapted Nikon D300 but I would strongly suggest that the D700 is chosen, as its result appeared far superior.

It is still possible to use a film camera; for that you will need a specialist UV transmitting lens if possible, although older conventional lenses with less effective multi-coatings work as well. We have used a twin lens rolliflex in the past with excellent results; this has another advantage in that you are focusing in white light. You will also need an 18A filter to cover the lens and a UV light source (see flash section below). You will also need film. I have for many years used Ilford Pan F rated at ISO 50[12] and achieved good results, other experts suggest T-max 100 pushed to ISO3200.[13] As you can see, there is a large difference in ISO ratings between the two. However, to some extent the overall ISO is somewhat irrelevant, as only the 'toe', a small proportion of the films characteristic sensitivity curve, is being exposed to the UV light. It also has a fine, tight grain structure so does not suffer from granularity which some other film stocks do.

[12] Ilford photographic; Ilford Pan
F http://www.ilfordphoto.com/products/product.asp?n=5#
[13] T-MAX 100: http://www.kodak.com/global/en/professional/support/techPubs/f4016/f4016.pdf

Photography is carried out in the same way as normal, using the adapted or UV flash as the light source. Before the photograph is taken you must place the 18A filter over the lens, if you are using a quartz lens then no focus adjustment is required (see section on lenses below). You will also need to do some calculations around exposure times. Once you have done some exposure tests, you can use the results to inform the correct camera settings in the future. Using our adapted Metz on full power we can achieve exposures of f11–16.

Normal digital cameras cannot record wavelengths below around 390 nm as they are produced with a filter in front of the sensor to remove the UV. This ensures that colour images recorded are recorded with a natural colour range. There are many articles on the Internet from photographers purporting to be able to record UV images using commercially available cameras. This is allegedly done by filtering them with a generic 'Woods filter'.[14] I believe this assumption is based on the fact that when they look at the colour channels in software, such as Adobe Photoshop, they see the blue channel exposed. This I believe is misleading, in such cases the blue channel contains overspill from the red channel. In reality the 'Woods filter', although designed for UV, also has a window within the infrared region of the spectrum. Because CCDs (Charged Coupled Devices) and CMOSs (Complementary metal–oxide–semiconductor) are far more sensitive to IR than UV, the IR response floods any information in the UV. In real terms the image seen is almost entirely formed of IR and gives a very different result than a properly exposed and reflected UV one. The easy way to check whether an image is truly UV is to look at the sharpness. If the image appears really sharp it is reflected UV, if it seems soft then it is more likely to be a variant on IR.

This is very important, because although for the amateur at home this causes no problems, for us as forensic photographers the use of an image with an incorrectly quoted capture technique could easily jeopardise a case. Indeed, I myself have been asked to review a number of so-called reflected UV images and have had to make several visits to the jury box to explain the recording of IR and UV images.

In recent years it has also become possible to see reflected ultraviolet in real time using ultraviolet based image intensifiers.[15] Working on the same principle as the more common infrared systems, they use a phosphor screen to convert UV radiation to visible light, and increase sensitivity to UV by many thousands of times. This has allowed increasing uses of this technique, as it is now possible to use the UV viewer to locate the mark so that it is possible to place the flash in the right place for optimum results. Although normally used

---

[14] Woods filter is the generic name given to most UV filters. During the First World War Robert Wood developed a glass made from barium–sodium–silicate glass with nickel oxide, to be used in signal lamps enabling the sending of invisible signals. This invisible radiation worked both in the infrared for daytime and ultraviolet for nighttime use. (See also Chapter 5.)

[15] Scenescope, RUVIS imager (Reflected Ultraviolet Imaging System): http://www.crimescope.com/march%2015/scenescope.htm

for the photography of finger marks, 'real time' viewers can be also be used to look at injuries at the pre-photography stage.[16]

6.8   Lenses

Here, I'm afraid, is another possible problem. Optical glass of the type found in camera lenses absorbs UV strongly at around 320 nm. Also, most modern lenses are multi-coated to block transmission of any unwanted ultraviolet light and they also suffer from a focus shift when using UV. [14] Focus shifts occur when the wavelengths representing different colours come to a focus at different points, any shift in these points is called chromatic aberration and the difference in focal point between visible and UV radiation can be considerable. If normal lenses are used, then the focus must be adjusted to compensate. Many authors make sweeping statements, for example 'just adjust in the opposite direction to infrared', however, due to the complexities of modern lenses this does necessarily hold water. Simple lens theory would suggest that a decrease in the lens-to-image distance will be required for ultraviolet and an increase for infrared. However, this is not the case for compound lenses, which have been achromatised. Indeed the focus shift may indeed be in the same direction as required for infrared. I would strongly suggest that you carry out some testing first; because of these difficulties many photographers just rely on using a large depth of field to compensate.

Although it is possible to undertake this type of photography with conventional lenses, it is recommended that if possible a specialist quartz fluorite lens should be acquired. The most commonly available lens is the UV Nikkor 105 mm macro. Using quartz fluorite means that the lens has around a 150% better at the transmission of light at 365 nm than glass lenses. Another major advantage is that the lens is deliberately manufactured, so that green and ultraviolet wavelenghts are brought to a focus at the same point over a wide range of magnifications. Thus, there are no achromatic focus shift problems when using this lens for ultraviolet photography. Although the original UV Nikkor is no longer made, they are still available in the second-hand market and Jenoptik[17] now make quartz lenses for medical and scientific application. Failing that, it is worth buying (or searching your store room for) an older 1970–80s type lens, as these older lenses were generally less well coated (if at all), compared to the modern types and therefore transmit significantly more UV.

6.9   Lighting

There is only one practical source of UV illumination for injury photography and that is the Xenon flash tube. However, most other modern flash tubes are

---

[16] I would strongly suggest reading 'Optical considerations' in *Medical and Scientific Photography*, which covers this issue in depth. http://www.msp.rmit.edu.au/Article_01/07.html

[17] Jenoptic Optical Systems (now called Coastal Optics): http://www.jenoptik-inc.com/

gold coated to remove the unwanted UV part of the spectrum, otherwise all our normal colour photographs would be unnaturally cold and blue. On some flashguns this gold coating is on the diffuser and can simply be removed, such as on the original Metz 45s – with others the coating is on the glass tube itself and cannot be removed. Therefore, careful consideration must be given as to the type of flashgun purchased. Some studio flash bulbs are still uncoated or can be ordered uncoated, such as the Quantum Q-Flash. Advanced Camera Services or Calumet via ACS will supply a dedicated, adapted Metz flash. This gun can be mounted on a bracket, beside the lens if required. Although this can cause shadows, the best arrangement we have found is above the lens. In the ACS reflected UV kit they supply a bracket that mounts the flash upside down over the lens (Figure 6.16). Although this works well, it is very unwieldy, so I have found it is easier just to hold the flash in position under the lens.

A legitimate question regarding UV photography, especially on live subjects, is whether the UV output from these flashguns could represent a health and safety risk. In the 1990s the Home Office Scientific Development Branch published a paper on the safety of UV flashguns. [15] This showed from

Figure 6.16   An adapted D700 fitted with a quartz 105 mm macro lens and adapted flash.

measurements that in practical applications, a person's maximum permissible exposure would not be reached and therefore the systems are safe to use.

Lastly, if film is being used, a UV transmitting filter will be required. The number of makers of these filters has declined over the years, but I believe it is still possible to acquire Kodak's Wratten 18A, through companies like Tiffen,[18] Schotts UG1, UG5 and UG7 filters[19] or Hoya's selection of UV-IR filters.[20] There are also a number of companies which will make a specific filter to order such as Galveoptics Ltd[21] or UQG (Optics) Ltd.[22]

6.10   Capturing the image

Once the control shot has been taken, the camera can be changed to one suitable for reflected UV. If film is being used, then you will need to focus the camera without the UV transmission filter in position, this only being placed over the lens at the last minute. This makes it impossible to see the subject area, so any movement by yourself or the client will produce unsatisfactory results. This is why a tripod and a comfortable position are so important for this type of photography.

For the best results with reflected UV photography, it was always suggested that you should wait at least one month, as it was thought that the process was recording the healing process know, as the 'migration of the melanocytes'. However, so many factors influence the healing process that I would now challenge this belief, as from my own experience we have had success with this technique after only a few days. American studies have also claimed that it is still possible to attain results up to one year after the injury occurred.

6.10.1   Induced fluorescence

There are a number of injuries which do not respond to cross-polarised light or reflected UV. Induced fluorescence of injuries relies on the same principle that applies to other latent evidence types, such as finger and shoe marks. That principle is that any differences in the material being illuminated, will result in different levels of fluorescence when exposed to an excitation source. Indeed the application of this technique has been critical in a number of cases over the recent years. [16] The difference here from scene or laboratory work is

---

[18] Wratten filter via Tiffen: http://www.tiffen.com/kpa.html

[19] Schott filter: http://www.schott.com/advanced_optics/english/our_products/filters/

[20] Hoya filters: http://www.hoyafilter.com/

[21] Galvoptics: http://www.galvoptics.fsnet.co.uk/

[22] UQG optics; http://www.uqgoptics.com/

that, in general, we cannot use continuous output light sources such as the Labino. These would expose living tissue (our customer) to excessive amounts of UV or laser illumination and pose a health and safety risk. Some UV light sources can easily emit more than the maximum permissible exposure limits in a short space of time and the laser provides both a thermal and optical hazard (although that is not to say lasers cannot be used in extenuating circumstances with appropriate precautions).

It is, however, possible to achieve good results by using electronic flash that is filtered. I have two versions that I can use, one is UV emitting, the other emits blue light at around 440 nm. To achieve a UV result, simply use the flash gun from the reflected UV set up described above, but instead of using the UV adapted camera, we need to use a standard DSLR (D700 or equivalent). A pale yellow long pass filter is also required, for example a Schott glass GG435 placed in front of the lens. To produce fluorescence further up the spectrum, we will need to acquire a band pass filter. I have a pair of filters by Galvoptics (made to order) with a band pass width of 420–460 nm (so we can use two paired flash guns). However, these filters also transmit IR though wavelengths above 750 nm, so they have to be used in conjunction with an IR blocking filter (Figure 6.17). In testing, I have found that the Quantum 5dR fitted with an uncoated bulb produces the best result.

(a) (b)

Figure 6.17 (a) Shows the adapted Quantum flash heads one fitted with the filter one with the filter removed, this emits between 420 and 460 nm. You can also show the orange Lp510nm camera filter on the left. (b) Shows our adapted Labino head fitted with a Quantum flash, which emits around 350–410 nm. As stated above the reflected UV flash can also be used if you have one.

A long band pass filter is also required above the excitation filter. In our cases we use a long pass filter transmitting wavelengths above 510 nm for the lens.

As previously stated above, you will need to use a professional DSLR; this is because the camera needs to be set to an ISO of around 2500. In my experience this technique with other cameras, some cameras did not achieve acceptable results due to the noise level. An ISO of 2500 is needed because most of the light emitted from the flash is lost by passing through the filter on the flash and then further reductions in light level occur when passing through the filter on the camera.

Induced fluorescence photography is undertaken in the normal way (i.e. with standard lenses and focusing), but the standard flash is substituted for an adapted one and the filter is fitted to the lens (Figure 6.18). As an aside, better

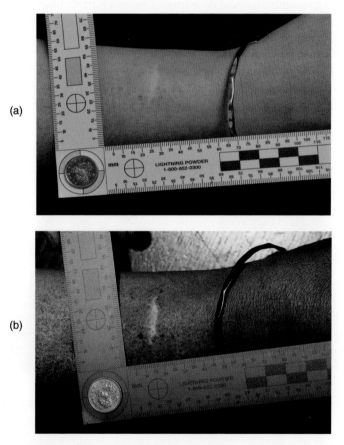

Figure 6.18   A burn to the forearm (a) under normal electronic flash and (b) under induced UV fluorescence. Converted to greyscale in Adobe Photoshop.

results will be achieved if the studio lighting is subdued, as strong ambient lighting may dominate the image and will affect the final result.

6.10.2 Induced fluorescence for cadavers only

As seen above, we are utilising electronic flash. This is both safe and relatively easy; however it is only practical because the victim can say where the injury occurred (if it is not readily visible). With cadavers a speculative search using flash isn't suitable and it is impractical to speculatively shoot the whole body in a random fashion. We therefore use continuous wave, Alternative Light Sources, as used in the detection of latent evidence (such as finger marks and shoe marks). In our cases we use a long wave UV source with output at 365 nm, and the 445 nm (blue), 532 nm (green) or 577 nm (yellow) lasers (see Chapter 5). It is worth noting here that even some of the small UV torches that can be purchased on the Internet can be a potential optical hazard. This is because the eyes have a much lower MPE than the skin – it is therefore advisable to wear readily available UV protecting glasses.

The use of continuous output sources is very useful and allows a body search to be undertaken in real time, allowing enhancement of any known injuries, or the detection of unknown ones, whilst the pathologist or Senior Investigating Officer is present. Best practice is for this to be carried out prior to post mortem (pm), not afterwards, as any areas of injury will inevitably be cut through at pm and the injury position and dimensions will no longer be accurate. For example, when the face is being peeled away it can result in rearrangement of the skin tissue, or may cause apparent impressions of artefacts which were not there before pm.

The body must be placed in area of complete darkness (if possible), generally the main mortuary room, but I have conducted examinations in the chapel of rest, or freezer rooms (any stray daylight will affect the result). If possible the body should be removed from its paper or cloth shroud, as these are generally white and have a tendency to be highly fluorescent (particularly when using UV), causing a sort of 'snow blindness' which may stop you from discriminating any injuries. To efficiently search a body it is advisable to have two operatives, one to hold the light source and one to move the body (these operatives should never swap roles during an examination as it will contaminate equipment). This also gives two sets of eyes with different perspectives to view the body during the search, as often being too close or too far away can stop the eye from detecting the true form of an injury. This is an acquired skill and the searching of a body can be slow and time consuming, especially as you may search with three or four different light sources. However, the results can be excellent and can certainly support a case, particularly where there is the possibility of impressions of shoe marks being recovered.

Any areas of interest should be recorded using the appropriate photo-graphic methods already described. It is important, though, to know your limits and I encourage working closely with the pathologist until you have sufficient experience to view the body objectively (as lots of unusual natu-rally occurring fluorescent patterns are often seen during these examination). I am not a medical expert, but I am expert in the use of light sources. Medical experts will be able to eliminate anomalies in the features observed, which may be down to hypostasis or general body deterioration. From my experi-ence, though, I would argue that it is better to photograph an anomaly that is not normal or natural, particularly if it is symmetrical, and dismiss it later. This is preferable to not photographing it at all, only to realise later it was the vital missing bit of latent evidence.

For example, in a recent case a small insignificant circle and two crossed lines found under UV, turned out to be two lines of stitching and a shoelace eye hole. In turn this undermined the defendant's claim of self-defence, as the only way for the mark to appear on the victims head was if he had been kicked like a football whilst he was on the ground.

I do not advocate the use of this type of light on a living victim, as unlike the above flash techniques where the exposure is milliseconds, here we are going to be using the light sources for much longer periods of time. This would easily exceed the MPE limits, within an 8-hour exposure period. It would also exceed the limits for the eyes within the natural blink response time of $1/4$ second and would cause retinal burns. However, as with all things there are clearly exceptions to every rule, such as erased writing on the skin (see Chapter 8). In these circumstances, health and safety must be your main concern, we use a special pair of blacked out goggles to give to the victim. They allow no light through, so are safe for both UV and the lasers. We are also aware of the thermal hazards, so the lasers in particular are never held in one position or close to the unprotected skin to reduce any possible risk.

6.10.3   Infrared (IR)

Infrared has long been used by the medical world because of two major ben-efits: first, it penetrates the superficial layers of the epidermis and reveals the structures beneath, and second, the reflection and absorption characteristics of tissue in the IR differ from those in the visible spectrum. Venous blood absorbs IR heavily, whereas oxygenated blood reflects IR, thus vascular dis-orders such as varicose veins can clearly be seen. However, although IR can penetrate the superficial layers it still has a limited penetration depth. Only the superficial veins can be clearly seen and unfortunately bruising tends to be at greater depth. We have recently carried out a field trial in collaboration with Kings College London into using IR for a standard response to injury pho-tography. However, the field trial showed that use of the technique was only beneficial in less than 10% of cases. This work and a number of other

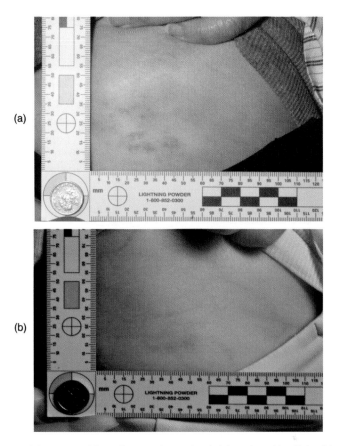

Figure 6.19   An injury caused by a flat metal coat hook (a) under white light (b) under IR. If you look carefully you can see the main shape, which is flat in the middle curving away towards the bottom of the image.

studies being undertaken across the country should be published by 2015 (Figure 6.19).

To undertake photography, you will require either infrared film or an adapted digital camera. If the image quality required is not high, then I suggest you look at the possibility of using a video camera with a night mode setting. This is normally a physical switch, which removes the IR filter from the optical path, thus allowing the camera to see into the infrared region of the spectrum.

A video camera already incorporates an IR source, so no other form of illumination will be required. However, if your illumination is a domestic light bulb or flash, then it is beneficial to filter it through a long pass filter on the lens. (Modern energy saver type bulbs should not be used due to their low IR outputs.) The best results are achieved if the infrared lighting is soft and bounced off reflectors rather than direct illumination, which can produce hot spots and can burn out vital information. If electronic flash is being used, try bouncing it off the ceiling or wall.

6.10.4   Summary

There is no doubt in my mind, based on personal experiences and those of my staff, that the clarity of the majority of injuries can be increased by using one or more of the specialist photography methods above (Figure 6.20).

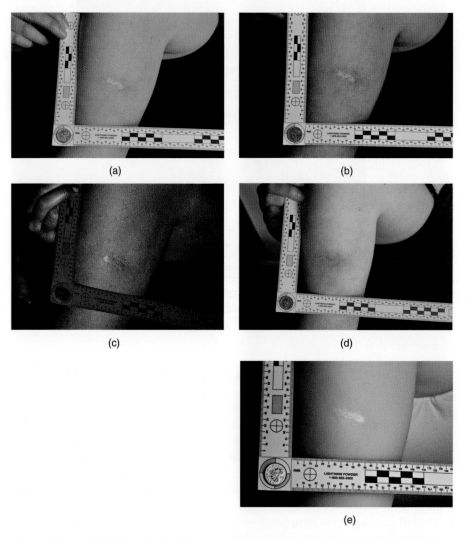

Figure 6.20   Shows an example of all five techniques used on a burn injury. (a) The reference image taken under standard electronic flash (b) cross-polarised image (c) reflected UV (d) induced fluorescence (e) infrared. Clearly the results of each technique will change dependant on the injury type, but this example shows the importance of trying all the techniques.

One of the most asked questions is around what technique is the most effective for what injury and over what time period. Unfortunately the answer isn't
quite as straightforward as the question. I hope by the time this book is published I will have published a technical paper, based on a study I am carrying
out, which may help to set some guidelines.

- Cross-polarised light: I believe that all injuries generally benefit from being
  cross-polarised, so this should be a standard enhancement technique for
  all injury types. This technique works well with bruising and general skin
  discolorations. In darker African Asian skin this will also enhance burns or
  other skin damage that reflected UV will not.
- Reflected UV: This works well where there has been substantial skin
  trauma, such as a burn or severe bite. It also works better on pale European type complexions than African or Asian ones. However if the damage
  is surface related then it will work on all skin types.
- Induced fluorescence: This works well on bruising and some underlying
  injuries such as burns; it is, however, reliant on the ability of the skin to
  fluorescence
- Infrared: Although IR should have a dramatic effect on bruising, from all
  of our casework and testing it appears it does not. It is therefore limited to
  a last resort technique. It can, however, in the right circumstances be very
  useful.

Effective time frames:

- Bruises: I have been reliably informed by a number of leading medical
  practitioners, that these types of injury are generally reabsorbed into the
  body within 6–8 weeks. There is talk of deep muscular bruising lasting
  longer, but none of our techniques mentioned above would have the depth
  of penetration to effectively reach it. I have noted on the Internet that there
  are a number of people who have reportedly photographed bruises after
  6 months. I would advise caution over these examples, as they would go
  against medical guidance and my practical experience. Unfortunately, it is
  very simple to create an anomaly through poor lighting, or having other
  contamination on the body that creates a false positive reaction.
- It is worth noting that anyone requiring specialist injury photography must
  remove his or her make up before photography, as this has been found to
  create false positives or mask injuries, thus radically affecting the validity
  of the results.
- Burns: Here we know that reflected UV could reveal a result for months if
  not years after the injury has been caused (Figure 6.21). In the photographs
  we can see a second degree burns case, caused by boiling water. The first
  four photographs of the injury were recorded approximately 9–10 weeks
  after the incident. However in image (e) we can still the outline of the burn

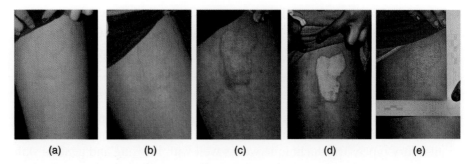

Figure 6.21 Shows (a) the reference image (b) cross-polarised light (c) induced fluorescence (d) reflected UV (e) reflected UV 24 months after the incident. Although the image in (e) is not as clearly defined as the original RUV image (d), the outline of the shape of the burn is still recognisable. The best results are seen on paler European skin, as there is less interference from melanin within the skin. In African and Asian skin tones we have found using cross-polarised light above can recreate the injury to good effect.

 24 months after the incident using reflected UV. In my own in-house testing we still detected faint scarring from burns injuries over 10 years old.
- Bites, cuts and lacerations: Unlike burns above where it is still possible to visualise the injury for perhaps years afterwards, the imaging of bites, cuts and lacerations is more dependent on the healing processes of the individual and the severity of the damage inflicted. In-house testing has shown that some injuries rapidly heal and disappear whilst others are visible after long periods of time.

In my experience the old adage 'nothing ventured nothing gained' has served me well with often surprising results being found.

 All of the above techniques I have found to be useful over the years with each one offering a different reaction. When searching the Internet there are a number of variations on the above techniques, which may or may not work, but I have found none to be as repeatable as those given.

Case study

This relates to a death of a 3-year-old girl, who had died in her sleep. The post mortem results had been inconclusive and the cause of death was not found.

 However, after burial, allegations came to light that the parents had been beating her, which was denied by the parents. We were asked to examine the exhumed body for possible signs of injury. The body showed little sign of decomposition and was duly examined using white light, UV and 532 nm (green) laser.

Under UV two areas of interest were detected, both in the area of the lower back. At first sight these areas displayed similarities to a cigarette burn and were photographed. When the negatives were processed and printed, it became apparent that they were not solitary injuries, but part of a larger pattern which the film had brought out. This revealed a horseshoe shape about 3 cm long and 2 cm wide, with one of the supposed 'cigarette burns' at the end of one of the horseshoe arms. An acetate sheet was then used to draw the outline of this shape. This was placed over the other 'cigarette burn' and again the pattern was seen, but in another direction. This process was then repeated in four more areas. Clearly what we were seeing was a repeating pattern, of the same size and shape but in multiple directions. After consultation with the officers and pathologist, further post mortem work was carried out on the areas of interest, revealing bruising.

Officers then carried out a search of the address and seized a number of items including the strap from a broken 'over-the-shoulder' ladies handbag. When examined closely it was found that the buckles at the end of the strap were of a brass horseshoe shape and were attached to the leather via two small screws. This was then photographed and a scale overlay made. When compared to the injury they made an apparent physical fit, with the screw heads now in alignment with our supposed cigarette burns. After further work by ourselves and the National Injuries Database, the parents were re-interviewed with this new evidence to hand. The mother admitted that both she and her husband had been consistently hitting the girl with the strap over the past year, as punishment for being naughty. At trial this was used along with other evidence and both were found guilty of assault and given prison sentences. There is no doubt that without being able to undertake this type of photography, this case would never have progressed to the point it did.

To pick up on an earlier point I made about framing up; rather than fill the frame with the cigarette type burns, I used the 10 x 8 imaginary frame. This meant that all the surrounding tissue was recorded, allowing the four areas to been seen (photographed with the painting with light technique). If I had not done this, they would in all likelihood have gone under undetected.

Case study 2

The second case is of a young girl who had been abused and tortured and I think clearly defines the reasoning for using a forensic photographer in casework.

The girl had suffered repeated and sustained attacks over a period of time by her guardians and subsequently died. She was originally photographed during the mortem by the scenes of crime photographer, but it became clear on viewing the images that the injuries were not particularly visible, as many were very faint or small. They had also been photographed in groups and many had no scale, or points of reference.

After consultation with the Senior Investigating Officer and Crime Scene Manager, my colleague and I re-attended the mortuary and carried out a full light source examination of the body. Using UV, Crimescope on 515 nm setting (blue/green) and cross-polarised lighting, over the following two days 128 different injuries were photographed and documented using a number of techniques. It subsequently emerged that these injuries had been caused by various implements including cigarettes, a bicycle chain, a hammer and length of wire. All the photographs were printed life size for the various experts, doctors and the court. Also taken were a number of entirety photographs, showing the injuries marked by small yellow arrows, in relation to their positions on the body. These images were subsequently reproduced as black and white line drawings by all the national papers at the time.

I have no doubt in my own mind that if this time consuming and difficult task had not been undertaken, the prosecution case would have been undermined to some extent by the lack of quality and clarity of the original photographs.

References

(1) Payne-James, J. J., Hawkins, C., Baylis, S. and Marsh, N. P. Quality of photographic images provided for injury interpretation: room for improvement? *Forensic Sci, Med Path.* 2012 8(4):447–50.

(2) Cameron, J., Ruddick, R. and Grant, J., Ultraviolet photography in medicine *Forensic Photogr.* 1973 2(3):9–12.

(3) David, T. J. Recapturing a five month-old bite mark by means of reflective ultraviolet photography. *J Forensic Sci.* 1994 39(6):1560–7.

(4) Peel, M., Hughes, J., Payne-James, J. J. Postinflammatory hyperpigmentation following torture. *J Clin Forensic Med.* 2003 10(3):193–6.

(5) Ruddick, R., A technique for recording bite marks for forensic studies *Med. Biol Illustr.* 1974 24:128–9.

(6) Marshall, R., Evaluation of a diagnostic test based on photographic photometry of infrared and ultraviolet radiation, reflected by pigmented lesions of the skin *J. Audiovis Media Med.* 1980 3:94–8.

(7) Eastman Kodak Company *Ultraviolet and Fluorescence Photography* (Publication M-27) Rochester, NY: Eastman Kodak Ltd. 1987.

(8) Krauss, T. and Warlen, S., The forensic science uses of reflective ultraviolet photography *J Forensic Sci.* 1985 30(1):262–8.

(9) Payne-James, J. J. Rulers and Scales used in measurement in forensic setting: measured – and found wanting! *Forensic Sci Med Path*. 2012 8(4):482–3.

(10) Rowan, P., Hill, M., Gresham G. A., et al. The use of infrared aided photography in identification of sites of bruises after evidence of the bruise is absent to the naked eye. *J Forensic Leg Med*. 2010 17(6):293–7. doi: 10.1016/j.jflm.2010.04.007.

(11) D. R. Sheasbury, D. G. McDonald 2001, A forensic classification of distortion in human bite marks. *Forensic Sci Int*. 2001 122(1):75–8.

(12) Mustakallio, K. and Korhonen, P., Monochromatic ultraviolet photography in dermatology *J Investig Derm*. 1966 47:351–6.

(13) West, M., Frair, J. and Seal, M. Ultraviolet photography of wounds on human skin *J Foren Ident*. 1989 39(2):87–96.

(14) Nieuwenhuis, G., Lens focus shift required for reflected ultraviolet and infrared photography *J Biol Photogr*. 1991 59:17–20.

(15) Revised Guidelines for the use of Flashguns Emitting Ultraviolet light for Photography of Evidence July 2001; Police Scientific Development Branch July 2001 Guidelines for the use of flashguns: Kent & Hardwick.

(16) West, M., Barsley, R. and Hayne, S. The first conviction using alternative light photography of trace wound patterns *J Forensic Ident*. 1992 42(6):517–22.

Further useful reading

DeMent, J. and Culbertson, R., Comparative photography in dental science *Dent Radiogr Photogr*. 1951 24(2):28–34.

Frair, J. and West, M., Ultraviolet forensic photography *Kodak Tech Bits* 1989 2:3–11,

Krauss, T., Close-up medical photography: forensic considerations and techniques, In: *Legal Medicine* Wecht, C. (Ed). Stoneham, MA: Butterworths 1989.

Marshall, R., Infrared and ultraviolet reflectance measurements as an aid to the diagnosis of pigmented lesions of skin *J Audiovis Media Med*. 1981 4:11–14.

Marshall, R. Ultraviolet photography in detecting latent halos of pigmented lesions *J Audiovis Media Med*. 1981 4:127–9.

Ray, S., *Applied Photographic Optics – Imaging Systems for Photography, Film and Video*. London: Focal Press 1988.

West, M. H., Billings, J. D. and Frair, J., Ultraviolet photography: bite marks on human skin and suggested technique for the exposure and development of reflective ultraviolet photography *J Foren Sci*. 1987 32(5):1204–13.

West, M. H., Frair, J. and Seal, M., Ultraviolet photography of wounds on human skin *J Foren Ident*. 1989 39(2):87–96.

Williams, A. R., Reflected ultraviolet photography *J Biol Photogr*. 1988 56(1):3–11.

7
Finger and Shoe Mark Photography

7.1 Overview

The accurate recording of finger and shoe marks has traditionally been one of the key duties for the forensic photographer and its significant input into an investigation cannot be underplayed. In no other area of photography do other experts look so critically at the quality of our work to enable them to undertake theirs.

It is also one of the most rewarding areas of work to be engaged in and can bring a great deal of personal and professional satisfaction, especially when a suspect is identified because of your efforts. In many books or articles I have read, the photography of finger and shoe marks is often mentioned only in passing, or in the case of fingerprints they only refer to their capture. Many police forces almost exclusively use automated systems such as Foster and Freeman's DSC4,[1] the Integrated Rapid Imaging System (IRIS) produced by the Home Office[2] or FISH (Forensic Information Scanning Hub).[3] However, when confronted with key or critical marks, particularly those at, or recovered from, serious crime scenes, a more bespoke approach is I believe required. Therefore I will not be covering the use of automated capture systems within this book, as there use is comprehensively covered in their own user manuals.

---

[1] Foster and Freeman DCS4 camera system; http://www.fosterfreeman.com/index.php?option=com_content&view=article&id=50:dcs4&catid=4:fingerprint-examination&Itemid=47

[2] IRIS imaging system; http://dbroker.co.uk

[3] FISH (Forensic Information Scanning Hub) is a digital transport/ imaging system for crime scene evidence submissions. FISH is designed to send crime scene marks to head office quickly and efficiently. See http://www.crime-scene.com/store/A-FISH.shtml.

Forensic Photography: A Practitioner's Guide, First Edition. Nick Marsh.
© 2014 John Wiley & Sons, Ltd. Published 2014 by John Wiley & Sons, Ltd.

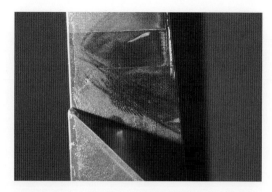

Figure 7.1   A dust mark on a piece of car cowling, lit obliquely with a scenes of crime torch. Some friction ridge characteristics are clearly visible, but the mark is probably not identifiable.

In this chapter, I want us to explore the techniques that we can use to capture marks before and after lifting or chemical treatments are deployed, both within the laboratory and, more importantly, at scenes. I should also point out these techniques, once mastered, are also applicable to other forensic applications, such as photography of tyre or tool marks.

Within the Evidence Recovery Unit (ERU), we the photographers carry out most of the searching for latent evidence at serious crime scenes, using a technique we refer to as 'UVL', Ultraviolet, Visual and Laser. This is because, as discussed before, we have an intrinsic understanding and affinity with light. I point this out because I hope this chapter is as useful to those of you reading this who are non-photographers searching for marks, as it is for those undertaking the photography.

In the United Kingdom there is a non-numeric standard for the identification of fingerprints which has been in place since 2001, with both finger and shoe marks being identified through direct comparison relying on the expertise and experience of a fingerprints officer or scientist. For us as forensic photographers, it is critical to ensure that any marks are captured to the highest quality, using the best techniques available. More importantly, we must ensure that the whole mark is captured and revealed, not just the apparent visual ridge characteristics. This may seem an obvious statement, but in many scenarios, marks often have hidden features that need to be enhanced through the correct use of lighting. For example, a dust mark lit obliquely may show the impression of a finger, but when lit by specular lighting hidden ridges or pore detail may be revealed (see Figures 7.1 and 7.2).

7.2   The nature of finger marks

Before we go on to look at the photography of marks, we should have a very brief look at how they are formed and how they are identified.

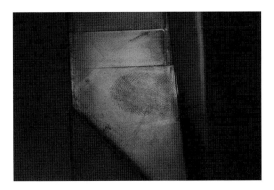

Figure 7.2   The same mark, this time lit with specular illumination using a ball light, revealing the greasy contact area of the mark.

The raised areas of the epidermis (the skin surface) are called friction ridges and are found on the hands and feet and are formed whilst in the womb. The patterns on these regions are unique to the individual, even identical twins (who have the same DNA) having different fingerprints. Some animals such as apes, monkeys, lemurs and koala bears have fingerprints.

Fingerprints in the crime scene context are formed when the friction ridges come into contact with other surfaces, leaving a trace of this contact on the surface. The impressions of these 'ridges' left on the surface help to create a unique means of identification for the person leaving them. The friction ridge skin on the fingers consists of ridges (the raised areas) and furrows (the areas between the ridges). The flow of the ridges on the finger forms patterns. There are three main types of pattern found in fingerprints: arches, loops and whorls (Figure 7.3). Small features within the general flow of the ridges are used for individual identification. There are two generic features: ridge endings are where a ridge finishes and bifurcations are where a ridge splits (Figure 7.4). There are also a number of subsets of classification of these features, most being combinations of ridge endings and bifurcations, but for our purposes this is sufficient.

Fingerprint features are also split into three levels that are used for visualisation, which are referred to as first, second and third level detail.

- First level detail refers to the pattern of the mark, for example a loop.
- Second level detail refers to the discontinuities in the ridges within the mark, such as bifurcations.
- Third level detail refers to position and shape of the ridges and the location of the sweat pores or other fine characteristics if they are visible (Figure 7.5).

All these points are taken into consideration when a fingerprint expert makes identification, along with scars or other defects that may be present.

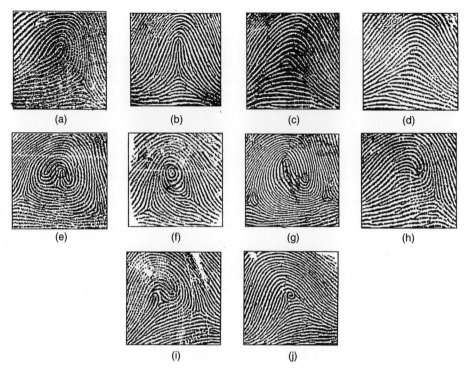

Figure 7.3 Photographic illustration of fingerprint patterns that shows the main fingerprint pattern types: (a) arch (b) approximating arch (c) tented arch (d) loop (e) nutant loop (f) twinned loop (g) whorl (h) composite (i) lateral pocket (j) accidental.

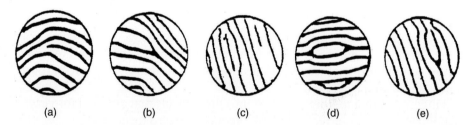

Figure 7.4 The main fingerprint characteristics: (a) ridge ending; this is where a ridge stops short and flanking ridges converge to take its place; (b) bifurcation; this is where a single ridge divides into two and the flanking ridges diverge to make room for it; (c) short independent ridge; this is a portion of ridge lying between two other ridges, which end in both directions; (d) lake; this is where a ridge diverges into two and then converges again within a short distance; (e) spur; this is a combination of a spur and short independent ridge.

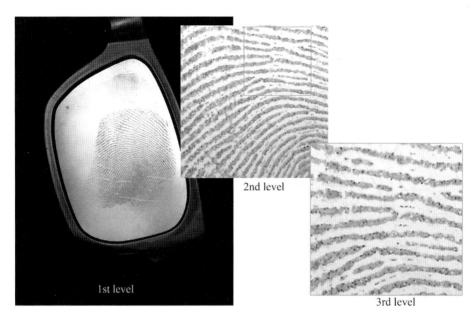

2nd level

1st level

3rd level

Figure 7.5   First, second and third level details.

The fingerprint pattern can then be compared manually, against an ink set taken from a suspect or a photograph of a mark in situ. Alternatively they can be compared against the national database using an automated fingerprint identification system (AFIS). In the United Kingdom IDENT1[4] is used. Once a pattern is loaded into the system, it can be searched against over eighteen million marks. Fingerprint identification is known as dactyloscopy, which uses their pattern and shape to classify them. Many countries use the 'Henry classification system'[5] although a number of others are available.

You will note that up until this point, I have referred to these ridge characteristics as both fingerprints and finger marks. The term fingerprint is usually only used in reference to '10 print sets' from fingers that have been inked and placed on paper or retrieved using a 'live scan' system. For day-to-day usage, the term finger mark is more applicable to marks left at crime scenes and covers the making of the mark by whatever means.

---

[4] IDENT1 is the national fingerprint database for England Scotland and Wales managed by Northrop Grumann Technology (NG) who are under contract to do so until 2013. As of April 2010 the data base holds over 18.6 million sets of ten prints (so called because each finger is inked, thus ten prints.) This database can be searched with an Automated Fingerprint Identification System (AFIS). NPIA, National Policing Improvement Agency http://www.npia.police.uk/en/10504.htm

[5] Developed by Sir Edward Henry in the late 1800s, it allows fingerprints to be sorted by physiological characteristics. http://static.ibgweb.com/Henry%20Fingerprint%20Classification.pdf For more information about fingerprints try http://en.wikipedia.org/wiki/Fingerprint http://www.finger printing.com/fingerprint-classification.php

The contact of friction ridges on a surface may cause three types of mark to be left: those deposited in natural compounds, those deposited in contaminates, and physical impressions.

The natural compounds are the components left behind by the skin's physical processes of sweating. This consists of around 98% water, but these deposits also contain many other components, for example minerals, lactate, fatty acids and urea. These are the types of marks that chemical finger mark enhancement techniques, such as cyanoacrylate (CNA),[6] diazafluoren-9-one (DFO),[7] physical developer and of course aluminium powder,[8] [1] are designed and targeted to work on. Other properties of the mark may also be of importance, for example the widely used aluminium powder adheres to the moisture in the mark or any physically sticky substances present. We shall look at the photography of this in more depth later in the chapter. Contaminated marks those are where the body's secretions have either been mixed or masked by another material, say blood, chocolate, milk, or make up and so on. These types of marks may or may not appear visually to the eye. Physical marks are where the ridge features have left a visible physical impression, say in a bar of chocolate or wet paint, these types of marks are much rarer and often offer their own challenges. Natural and contaminated marks are the types most often found at scenes, these can be enhanced using the techniques described later on in the chapter.

7.3   Shoe marks

Shoe marks form the other main form of physical evidence encountered at the scene, after all nobody can hover over the floor, so some form of general contact must be made. A shoe mark is made by the raised section on the soles of the shoe coming into contact with the ground or floor surface.

As with fingerprints, this can allow the identification of the individual shoe through analysis of the tiny distinctive features created by wear and tear or damage. It is worth noting that a visually strong shoe mark heavily soaked in blood is often not the best for identification. and it is often the third or

---

[6] Cyanoacrylate fuming is better known as CNA, or superglue. This treatment can be used on most non porous surfaces such as glass and plastic. The glue is warmed to produce fumes which react with the latent fingermark residues and atmospheric moisture to form a white polymer, Polycyanoacrylate. To enhance clarity of faint ridges or interfering backgrounds the developed marks can be stained with fluorescent dyes such as basic yellow 40.

[7] Diazafluoren-9-one is a chemical which reacts to the amino acids present in eccrine sweat and body proteins in a similar way to ninhydrin and fluoresces when exposed to green light between 500 and 550 nm.

[8] Aluminium powder here a very fine aluminium powder is physically applied to the surface of an exhibit using a specialised fingerprint brush (often glass 'zephyr'). As it is 'dusted' on it adheres to the residue left by the fingerprint ridges, allowing the mark to be seen. Aluminium powder is the most frequently used in the UK as it is cheap and easy to apply. However other types of powder are available in a variety of substances and colours.

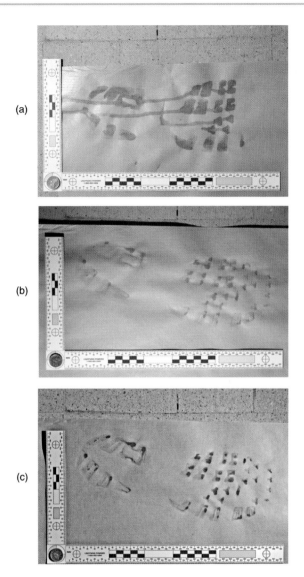

Figure 7.6 A shoe mark in blood like contaminate made on paper. (a) shows the first step (b) shows the fourth step. (c) Shows b converted to greyscale to aid the scientist in identification. Note that shoe marks are provided in either colour or greyscale, depending on the contrast between the mark and substrate.

fourth step, which may appear much fainter, that reveals the most detailed information (Figure 7.6).

As with finger marks, there is no numerical standard for shoe marks, identification is carried out by a direct comparison method between the mark left at the scene, an impression taken from the sole of the shoe and the sole of the shoe itself. Therefore the quality of your photography is the only thing that matters in this type of casework.

Shoe marks are also left in one of three ways. The shoe may be contaminated with material, such as dirt or blood, which is then deposited. Conversely, when the floor is contaminated, say with dust, the shoe may remove it leaving a negative impression of the shoe in the dust. Thirdly there is the case where a physical impression is left behind, for example in soil. These three methods will create either a positive or a negative impression (Figure 7.7).

The capturing of marks at the crime scene, and particularly serious crime scenes, is still probably one of the most important areas of work in forensics,

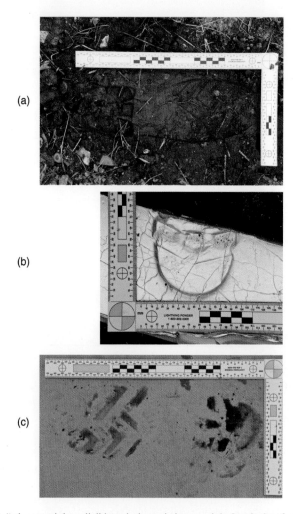

Figure 7.7   (a) A shoe mark in soil (b) an indented shoe mark in insulation foam board (c) shoe mark left in wet varnish.

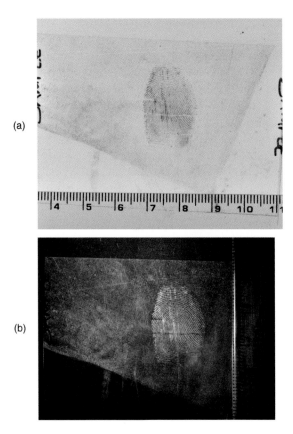

Figure 7.8 An aluminium powdered lift (a) scanned and (b) photographed with oblique lighting.

as a fingerprint match is still the fastest, easiest way to make identification of a suspect. Yet whether you are being asked to photograph the marks someone else has found, or you are doing the searching, this is also probably one of the areas of work where the skills and experiences of the forensic photographer is generally underused.

The recovery of most finger marks found at scenes within the United Kingdom is predominantly carried out using aluminium or black granular powder, both of which are relatively cheap and easy to deploy (Figure 7.8). Most marks developed using powders are generally lifted. If marks are photographed in situ at a scene they tend to be in blood or dirt and standard oblique lighting is used. In the United States coloured and fluorescent powders[9] are also used, supplemented by cyanoacrylate fuming.

---

[9] Fluorescent powders, Powders such as Redwop and Greenwop (Lightning Powder Company, Oregon, USA) are very fine powders, which are designed to fluoresce when exposed to a laser or alternative light source. http://www.redwop.com/download/flpowder.pdf

One of the commonest phrases I hear at scenes is 'Oh, that will powder!' referring to the likelihood of subsequently enhancing the mark using aluminium powder. This statement, in my experience, should never be taken at face value. We would have lost many marks if we had followed this advice without first photographing it using the range of lighting techniques at our disposal. Our own in-house review of two years of serious crime cases, has shown that at a conservative estimate of 30–40% of marks are retrieved using the UVL technique that would have been missed using conventional methods.

The other phrase readily used nowadays with regard to police photography in general, is 'fit for purpose'. With a stolen car in the police station car pound, I would agree to some extent that it might not require our professional photographic skills. But to my mind there is only one quality suitable for both finger marks and shoe marks and that is to achieve the best possible result.

So what do I mean? Under the above premise of 'fit for purpose', an untrained camera operator may photograph a mark which might show eight characteristics of in agreement after a database search. This would allow the fingerprint expert to identify a 'would be' suspect. However, if a trained photographer, using different lighting or angles, photographed that mark, it may have been possible to reveal extra information allowing the fingerprint expert to find ten characteristics instead. These extra two characteristics may show areas of disagreement with the suspect's mark, thus proving that it is not our suspect at all (Figure 7.9).

Although the above may seem a far-fetched scenario at first, at major crime scenes the marks found (particularly those in blood) are often poor quality. They are clearly highly relevant to the investigation, but could leave the fingerprint expert open to cognitive suggestion.[10] [2]

Hopefully, if we all have the same goal of trying to achieve the highest quality image at the start, it will help to ensure that misidentifications such as Brandon Mayfield,[11] the suspected Madrid bomber, and Shirley McKie[12] are not down to the quality of our photography.

---

[10] Cognitive suggestion is when an opinion may be biased towards an outcome when other factors are subconsciously known. This could mean that our fingerprint expert could lean towards an identification based on his or hers background knowledge of the cases or suspects.

[11] Brandon Mayfield was wrongly identified and arrested as a conspirator in the Madrid bombings in 2001, after his fingerprints were searched and wrongly identified by the FBI as a conspirator to the bombings. Later, Spanish police correctly identified the marks to an Algerian National, Ouhanne Daoud. In November 2006 Mayfield settled a lawsuit for a reported $2 million dollars and a formal apology.

[12] Shirley McKie, is a former Scottish police officer, who in 1997 was identified by the Scottish Criminal Records Office (SCRO) as leaving her thumbprint at the scene of a murder. She denied ever being there. She was initially suspended then sacked and then arrested by Strathclyde police for perjury in 1998. She was tried and acquitted in 1998 which led to a subsequent scandal in the Scottish SCRO and police and led to a public enquiry which became known as the 'Scottish Fingerprint Inquiry'. For the full enquiry see http://www.thefingerprintinquiryscotland.org.uk/inquiry/CCC_FirstPage.jsp For an in depth article by Champion magazine. http://www.nacdl.org/public.nsf/0/9090373de4fa9c7 d85256f3300551e42?OpenDocument

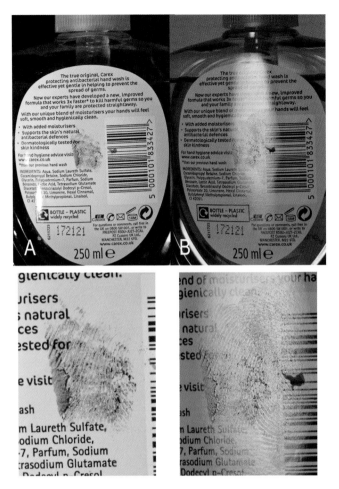

Figure 7.9 A blood mark on the label of a bottle. (a) shows the mark lit with oblique lighting (b) shows the same mark lit with specular or coaxial lighting using a ball light.

7.4 Equipment

The photography of both shoe and finger marks is best undertaken using primary macro lenses and not zoom lenses for the reasons mentioned in previous chapters. For shoe marks, I recommend a 60 mm macro and for finger marks, a 105 mm macro lens. Nikon, Canon and other independent makers all produce similar, suitable lenses. The camera also needs to be fitted with an electronic cable release; this minimises the vibrations caused by physically firing the shutter button. This may be a small point, but when using slow shutter speeds at macro type magnifications, any movement is clearly seen.

You will also require appropriate lighting equipment (see below), our good friend the tripod and a spirit level for shoe marks. Hot-shoe mounted spirit

Figure 7.10   A white, plastic bag stretched over an embroidery hoop.

levels can be easily obtained for only a few pounds on the Internet[13] and are invaluable in ensuring that you are square on to your exhibit.

It is also useful to have the following to hand:

- Embroidery hoops in various sizes and shapes (for the stretching of plastic bags in the laboratory or studio)[14] (Figure 7.10).
- Assorted rulers (within our own laboratory, a separate scale is not used for finger mark photography as the exhibit label contains a scale line).[15]
- Retort stands to hold items.[16]
- Small mirrors, preferably front silvered, but small dental, cosmetic or inspection types are all acceptable. These are used both for reflecting light and, on occasion, marks.
- Assorted scraps of paper and card, these are used for deflecting and reflecting light or making masks or windows.

---

[13] Amazon sell a wide range of hot shoe mounted sprit levels from £3.95 for one from Kaavie, through to the top of the range Manfrotto at £25.48 (September 2011) http://www.amazon.co.uk/s/?ie=UTF8&keywords=spirit+level+hotshoe&tag=googhydr-21&index=aps&hvadid=7517191385&ref=pd_sl_9m57a5eu52_b

[14] Embroidery hoops, these are available in a number of sizes, shapes and materials. Examples can be found at http://www.stitcher.co.uk

[15] We use the Macrography revisable scales and on occasions the 150mm self adhesive ruler label, available from WA products http://www.waproducts.co.uk.

[16] We use Fisher scientific retort stands which are metal rather than the plastic one. These are available in a number of sizes and shapes. https://extranet.fisher.co.uk/insight2_uk

Figure 7.11 One of the photographers at work.

There is also an interesting discussion to be had around how you physically work. Many forces have limited designated studio space within their finger-print laboratories. I would argue that a large studio space is preferable, as you will see that some of the techniques are impractical without it. Within our studios we are able to either use a horizontal photographic set up, (Figure 7.11) or a vertical set up using a copy stand (Figure 7.12). The horizontal photographic set-up in effect is an electric table[17] fitted with an infinity curve,[18] this table can be raised and lowered as required. For a tripod we are using either a Foba[19] or Cambo[20] studio camera stand.

As can be seen in Figure 7.11, using the horizontal set-up means that both the table and camera can be placed at a comfortable working height for each individual operator, with the exhibit horizontal to them. This also alleviates the issues of many photographers, some of whom may suffer from bad backs caused by continually leaning over tripods or low level photographic set-ups. Exhibits can then be positioned, either free standing or in a retort stand, inside

---

[17] Electric table available from Linak: http://www.linak.com/deskline/

[18] Cove lock II, Infinity curve. Originally provided by Colorama, although no longer listed on their website: http://www.colorama-photo.com

[19] Foba camera stands: http://www.foba.ch/eng/programm/programm.htm

[20] Cambo camera stands, USB range: http://www.cambo.com

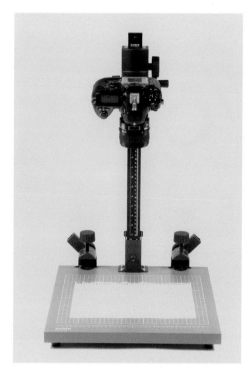

Figure 7.12   A conventional copy stand set-up. These are good for flat copy work, but they do not allow three-dimensional objects to be illuminated or positioned as required, due to the limited camera position.

the infinity curve. The use of this set-up allows a variety of lens and illumination types to be deployed.

With the vertical photographic set-up, the floor space required is much smaller. As the name suggests the camera is mounted vertically on a copy set-up. However this is very restrictive, as it ultimately limits both the distance the camera can be from the subject and, more importantly, it limits the distance and angles the illumination can be placed from the subject, particularly when transillumination or specular lighting is required.

We also have at our disposal an old metal stool that has had the seat removed and a glass top fitted, which is suitable for backlighting objects and is a fraction of the price of a proper glass topped forensic table.

In the photography of both shoe and finger marks, I would argue that the camera is actually less important than the choice of lighting we are going to use. Before we look at lighting techniques or photography though, we need to look at how we physically observe marks. When searching for marks we use binocular vision; this is logical, natural and allows a wide field of view to be examined at the same time. Clearly, however, a camera is a monocular device, as it has only one fixed position lens. Therefore, if marks are to be photographed successfully, only one stationary eye should be used to make the visual assessment. This does not preclude marks that vanish with monocular vision from being recorded, but it does offer us the photographers more of a challenge.

Provided the above guidance for monocular vision is adhered to, there is a simple rule of thumb that can be applied to visually found marks: 'If you can see it you can photograph it.' The challenge for us is to implement this!

When examining induced fluorescent marks, whether to use one or two eyes is normally irrelevant as the fluorescence of the mark is induced by the energy of the light source and not by the angle of the light.

7.5 Lighting techniques

In many forces the standard working practice, particularly for scene work, is to issue staff with some form of 'seek-and-search' lamp or bright torch. These are great for general observation, but not, I would argue, for finding or lighting finger marks, as they tend to be very directional and produce a bright, high-contrast beam of light. In my experience these are particularly not suitable for the detection of latent marks[21] on many non-porous surfaces found at scenes, including door and window frames, light switches and surfaces of electrical appliances such as fridges and cookers. In fact, on such surfaces we need to use soft diffuse light, in our case we use standard inspection lamps, fitted with low energy bulbs or soft boxes (see Chapter 5).

Unlike torches, which are generally held at 45°, the inspection lamp is held and used in a coaxial or specular mode. This means that the light is reflected straight back into the lens. Don't worry, I will explain and demonstrate what I mean by this a bit later in the chapter.

There are, however, a number of other ways to use white light and it is worth spending some time mastering the various techniques below, as each has proved invaluable over the years. As with all photography, taking an extra five minutes to get the lighting right and a correct exposure in camera will mean the minimum of post-production processing in the office later.

7.5.1 Copy lighting

Here the object of the exercise is to create flat, even illumination across the surface of the subject. Conventionally, as the name suggests, this form of lighting was used to photograph flat artwork. This is achieved by using two lights of the same power and output which are placed at an angle of 45° to the surface of the subject (Figure 7.13). It is important that each give exactly the same

---

[21] Latent finger marks are marks left at the scene of a crime, which may not be immediately visible to the naked eye.

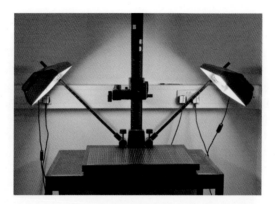

Figure 7.13   A variant of Figure 7.12, fitted with balanced 45° lighting.

exposure, so each light will need to be independently metered and then moved backward and forwards, or have their power turned up and down until they are equal.

Copy lighting has virtually been lost as a technique for many types of flat art work due to the introduction of scanners, but it is still a good technique for capturing chemical marks such as ninhydrin.[22]

7.5.2   Bright field illumination

In bright field illumination the object is directly lit from the front. This is the typical type of lighting used for photographing many chemically developed marks, such as those enhanced with CNA. Unlike copy lighting, which provides flat, even lighting, here the light can be directed onto the surface from any angle between 1° to 89°. (Below 1° you would be backlighting and at 90° you would be producing coaxial or specular illumination.) (Figure 7.14) One of the easiest and cheapest ways to achieve this, in my opinion, is by using a standard office ring light with the magnifier removed. This allows the lamp to be positioned around the lens and, more importantly, allows the contrast of the mark to be controlled by moving the ring light backwards or forwards towards the subject.

When using this type of light in the lab or at a scene, a tripod is a must. This allows both camera and light source to be independently moved by millimetres. This may not sound like a distance of any significance, but if you look at the images below you will see the impact that these small changes have on the quality of the results (Figure 7.15). Bright field can also be achieved by the use of electronic flash and more conventional directional sources such as

---

[22] Ninhydrin solution is commonly used in the detection of latent fingerprints on porous surfaces such as paper. The ninhydrin turns the amino acids contained within the deposited fingerprint purple, allowing their recovery generally through photography.

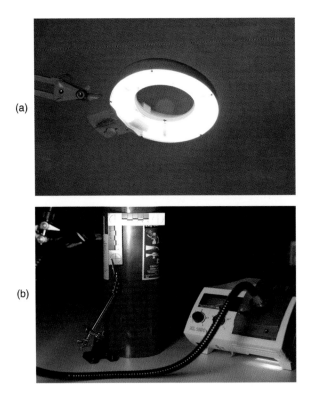

Figure 7.14 (a) Shows a standard office ring light with the magnifier removed. This can then be positioned around the lens to produce shadowless bright field illumination, or used behind a translucent surface to produce dark field illumination. (b) Shows the Schott light fitted with a standard fibre optic. Note that the display on the front of the Schott light is showing the colour temp of the light. Although generally not important for finger marks, which are traditionally converted to a greyscale, it could be important if used to light an exhibit for reference purposes.

the Schott microscope light[23] (as discussed in the previous chapter). This technique is often used for lighting marks in blood or other contaminates, or for marks developed using CNA.

7.5.3 Dark field illumination

Dark field illumination requires the subject to be illuminated from behind, but with the light positioned so that no direct light can be seen and the object appears on a black or dark background. Again this is a really good application for the ring light, as it produces a soft, even illumination that surrounds the area of interest. It is, however, also possible to use a torch, boat lamp or even the sun if you need to create more contrast in the mark. Dark field

---

[23] Schott lighting: http://www.schott.com

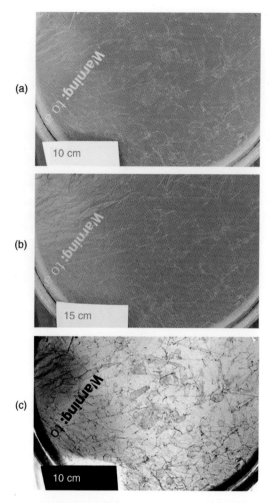

Figure 7.15   A CNA mark illuminated with a ring light at (a) 10 cm from the surface (b) 15 cm from the surface (c) shows (a) after post-production conversion.

illumination is the best form of lighting for untreated finger marks on glass, or marks developed using CNA on clear plastic bags (Figure 7.16).

Often these marks are found on plastic bags which are creased or folded. This makes them difficult to fix into a retort stand, or to keep flat. To assist in creating a flat surface we use an embroidery hoop, to which the plastic bag is fitted and stretched tight like a drum skin. This has a number of advantages in that it removes creases and allows a number of different lighting techniques to be used, such as ring, ball and induced fluorescence. A word of caution here, you must ensure that when fitting the bag into the hoop that the securing hoop does not pass through another mark, as it may rub it off or otherwise damage it.

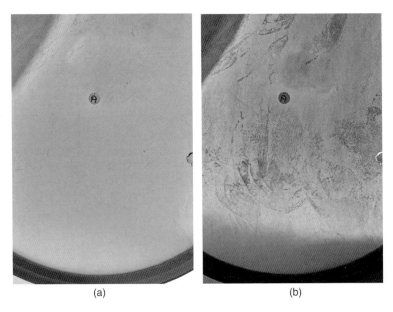

(a)   (b)

Figure 7.16   (a) The mark illuminated using bright field illumination. (b) The same mark using dark field illumination.

Alternatively, you can make a window mount. A window mount is simply a piece of card with a window cut in it. The area of the bag or exhibit with the mark on it is then taped or pinned gently across the window. The card can then be used as a holder in the retort stand or if preferred on a glass topped table (Figure 7.17).

A variant on the embroidery hoop for more fragile plastics is the magnetic board. For our purposes we use a magnetic board with a hole in the middle; this allows both bright and dark field illumination to be undertaken. Here the mark is laid across the hole and the magnets are used to stretch the bag into place. In Figure 7.18 we can see the photography of a faint CNA mark on an orange plastic bag, which has been lit from behind using a fibre optic.

You can see that once lit from behind the mark is visible but is the wrong colour for comparison and also has writing passing through it, perhaps hindering identification. In post-production, the blue channel was selected with the green and red channels being discarded (Figure 7.19). The remaining blue channel was greyscaled, inverted and adjust via curves.

Dark field illumination is also an excellent way to record aluminium powdered lifts on clear acetate. To achieve this we use a black void, say a large box with a window cut out as described above. The box should be lined with black or dark paper. The lift is laid across the window and the camera mounted above it looking down using an aperture of no more than f8 (this ensures the background will be out of focus). A directional light source, such as a

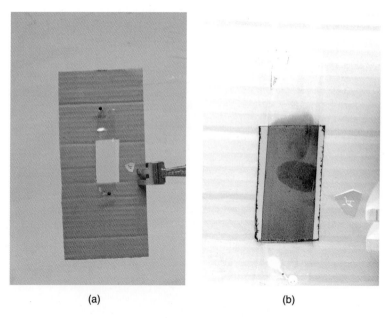

Figure 7.17 (a) Shows a mark on tape window mounted and held in a retort stand. (b) Shows the photographed mark after postproduction through Photoshop.

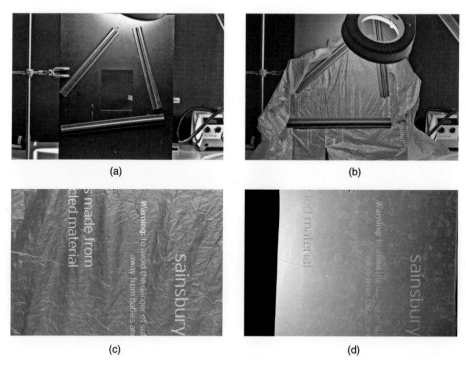

Figure 7.18 (a) The magnetic board (b) the bag roughly positioned (c) the bag just before the magnets are moved to stretch the bag (d) the magnets stretching the bag, removing wrinkles with the mark lit from behind.

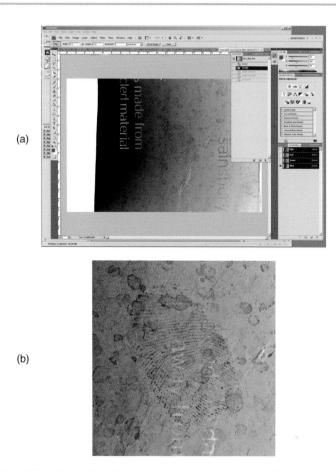

Figure 7.19 (a) Selection of the blue channel only removed most of the background writing. (b)The final enhancement once the red and green channels had been removed and the mark had been inverted and adjusted using curves.

Crimescope or electronic flash, should be used to illuminate the surface of the lift at 45° (Figure 7.20). Unlike scanning the lifts on a flatbed scanner, this will give a clear background without dust, scanning lines or interference. Within the Metropolitan Police a version of this technique was still used until 2011 to record the lifts straight onto rolls of photographic paper using a 'Propak' Sprinter (no longer made). As only a simple lens is used, the lift is placed over the black void face down and when projected onto the paper is the correct orientation. This technique allowed 200–300 lifts to be photographed an hour, these rolls are then processed in a 'JEM' black and white processer, producing a very high quality photographic print.

Another practical example of dark field illumination in use is for capturing marks on glass. How many times have you been to a scene and found finger marks on a windowpane? Your first instinct may be to powder them, yet that

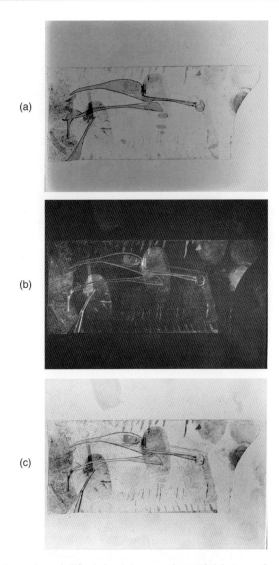

(a)

(b)

(c)

Figure 7.20   A faint and poorly lifted aluminium powder mark (a) scanned on a flat bed scanner. Note how the image has degraded, as the tonal range was adjusted allowing the mark to be seen. (b) Shows the same mark, but this time photographed using dark field illumination. Note the increased clarity of the marks on the right hand side in comparison to the scanned version. (c) Shows the lift after post-production conversation.

doesn't always give the required results. It is, however, possible to photograph them in situ, using the daylight as your backlight. With one eye closed, align the mark with a distant rooftop or tree to create your dark field backdrop. Once the correct position is achieved, replace your eye with the lens (Figure 7.21). Using this technique you can achieve some excellent results without

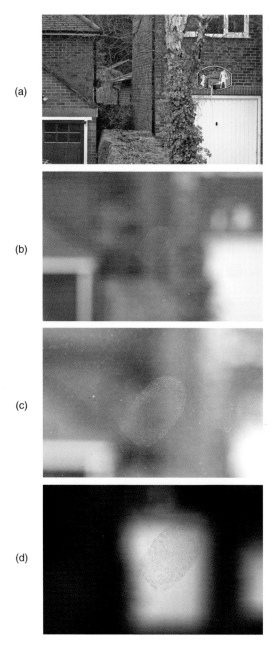

(a)

(b)

(c)

(d)

Figure 7.21 A greasy mark on a double glazed window. (a) shows area directly behind the mark across the street. (b) shows the mark in focus but not aligned properly. (c) shows the mark after being aligned with the brickwork to create dark field illumination. (Note that the mark would normally be reversed coloured before submission to the fingerprint bureau.) (d) shows the mark aligned with the garage door to create bright field illumination.

Figure 7.22   A Kodak projector being used to illuminate a latent dust shoe mark.

any risk to your critical mark. If there are no suitable 'backdrops' within the field of view, you can ask a colleague to hold a coat or dark material around one metre away on the other side of the window to create the same effect (just ensure you don't block off all the light!). As a rule, always use a wider aperture than normal to ensure that the background is out of focus. Again, always use a tripod.

7.5.4   Oblique lighting

This is the most commonly used light source techniques, and often the only one that people are familiar with, particularly for shoe marks. Here the light is projected at the surface to be examined at an angle of 45° or less and, in the case of latent shoe marks, nearer 1° or 2° off the floor. For this technique a collimated beam is best, we use an old Kodak Carousel projector,[24] with an 80 mm lens, although the Crimescope or Polilight are equally as effective (Figure 7.22). Torches and 'seek-and-search' lamps can also be used but tend to produce uneven, divergent illumination. Whichever light source you use, beware of the light fall off across the area containing the mark, in some cases this can be as great as one or two stops producing a poorly illuminated result.

This technique is useful for latent finger and shoe dust marks, or indented writing. In some cases where faint oblique shoe marks are located, it has been found that Electrostatic Lifting[25] may achieve a better result than photography (Figure 7.23). However, this should be tested on a similar area of no importance to the case before a decision is made not to undertake photography.

---

[24] Kodak Carousel projector, this professional slide projector had interchangeable lenses and a top loading rotating slide holder. Although no longer made, it is still available second hand on the Internet.

[25] Electrostatic lifting is a technique which uses a special lifting foil to be laid on the floor. A static charge is then passed through the foil causing the dust particle to stick to the underside.

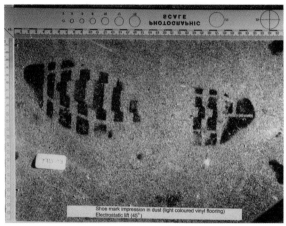

Figure 7.23 A dust lift before and after electrostatic lifting (ESL). Note that the ESL version has been reversed for comparison purposes.

7.5.5 Specular or coaxial illumination

This technique is probably the most useful technique there is to know and understand, but one of the hardest to master or explain. For the best result you should use soft, diffuse illumination such as the ball or panel light (Figure 7.24). The idea is that we need to create a reflection of the light source perpendicular to the subject's surface. In other words, if we hold the light in front of our face looking at the surface of our exhibit and move both in opposite directions, we can now see down the side of the light. Looking at the surface we should now see the reflection of the light source, and within that pool of light any contamination left by the fingermark will appear dark.

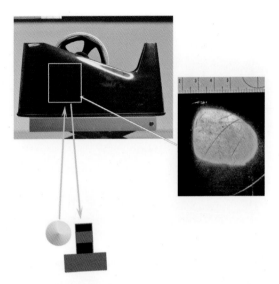

Figure 7.24   An untreated latent mark on the side of a tape dispenser. The ball light is generally held so that it is on the same axis as the lens. In effect you are looking at the reflection of the light. Any contaminate, for example, the greasy finger mark, will not reflect and will appear black against a white background.

This technique only works well on smooth glossy surfaces and not flat dull ones. If mastered correctly, however, it will allow you to photograph marks which will not subsequently powder and lift (Figure 7.25). This is why it is so important to use a soft, diffuse light source, such as the inspection lamp or soft box, as any fine detail would be visually lost in the brightness of the reflection from more focused sources such as a torch.

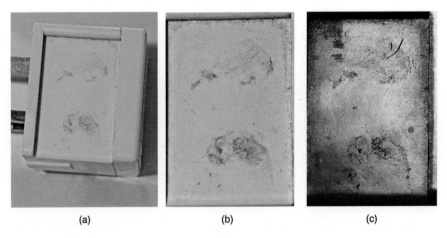

(a)   (b)   (c)

Figure 7.25   An untreated latent mark on an electric plug, (a) General shot, (b) Oblique lighting (c) Specular lighting. Note in the specular version 3rd level detail such as the pores, are clearly visible. Note that when powdered, no usable marks were retrieved.

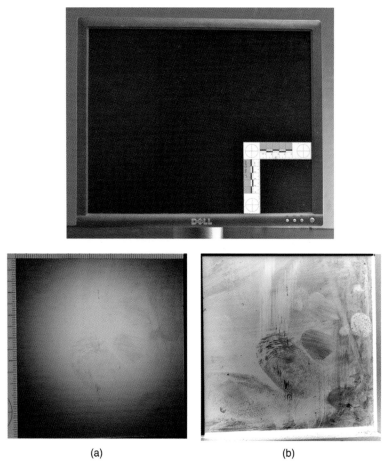

(a)   (b)

Figure 7.26   A latent mark on a television screen (a) Using a ball light. Note how the mark is pale and lacks contrast out due to the surface of the screen. (b) Illuminated with a Schott fibre optic, note that in many circumstances these marks clog when powdered or do not powder at all as they are 'baked onto' the glass.

There are a number of caveats, however; one is photography of the front of the television or computer screens where specular illumination with a point source type torch is more efficient (Figure 7.26), but as you gain experience you will be able to adjust the light sources and lighting conditions to the situation as required.

Coaxial illumination devices are also commercially available. These place a 45°, semi-silvered mirror in front of the lens. This allows the illumination source to be placed at the side, so that the camera axis and the lighting axis merge when they hit the subject's surface (Figure 7.27). Although these devices are convenient in principle, they are of a fixed geometry so do not offer the same advantages of versatility as the ball light inspection lamp or soft box.

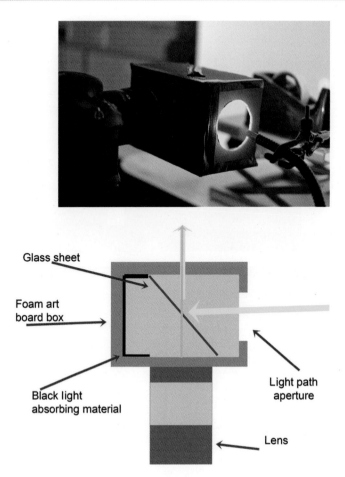

Figure 7.27 My home made coaxial device, which can be screwed onto the front of the lens. Using a sheet of glass rather than a front-silvered mirror loses around 50% of the light; however, it can still produce very acceptable results.

This technique is useful for photographing marks on non-porous, shiny surfaces that would traditionally be powdered, such as lacquered or laminate flooring

Although above I have spoken about using the ball light to create specular illumination, it is possible to create the same type of effect using other materials on occasions when the ball light is not available. This is simply done using a Crimescope, torch or Schott light and a piece of paper. In this scenario we project the light from the side or from behind the object into the paper held in front of the object or surface. This reflected light will then fall softly on the required surface, revealing the mark. This is a very useful technique where space might be limited or where the mark is in a recessed or confined position. The downside to this technique is that it tends to produce a softer more

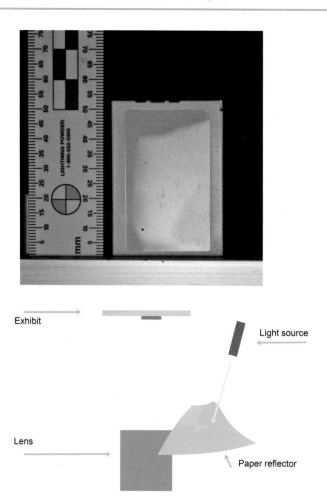

Exhibit

Light source

Lens

Paper reflector

Figure 7.28 A latent mark on a phone battery illuminated by light reflected onto a sheet of white A4 paper. Note how the mark disappears on the edge of the battery where the surface is not smooth, but textured.

diffuse light than normal, so you generally see a reduction in contrast within the mark (Figure 7.28).

7.5.6 Photography of specular marks

Once you have found your mark (with one eye closed, using monocular vision) you need to mentally estimate your height and distance from the mark. You can then place your tripod and camera at the equivalent position to where your eye was. Again, I would suggest using the 105 mm macro lens, as it gives sufficient stand-off distance to use our ball light. Move the camera back or forwards so that the mark and label fill the frame. Now introduce your specular

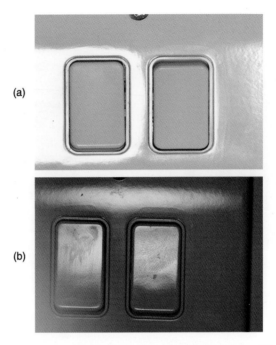

Figure 7.29   A latent mark on a light switch using (a) oblique lighting (b) using a ball light.

illumination source. Once it is positioned so that the pool of light is covering the mark, you need to move it backwards or forwards, as this controls the brightness and contrast (Figure 7.29). Generally, the nearer the light source is to the surface the less contrast the mark contains, and the further away the more contrast it contains.

It should be noted that every surface is unique and each mark will require bespoke illumination. Once in the right place, an exposure reading should be taken. If you are using spot or centre-weighted metering the area may be correctly exposed, but the mark will be underexposed. You may have to underexpose from the reading by three to four stops to correctly expose for the mark.

If the correct position of the light cannot be achieved, then change the angle of incidence between the camera and the mark by 1° or 2°, if you are using a 105 mm lens this will not be noticeable due to the focal length. Then try positioning the light again. In some cases we may use the 200 mm macro lens to get further away, and don't be afraid of holding the light at a variety of distances from the surface of the exhibit. In a number of cases I have had the light up to two metres away. The selection of a wider aperture than you may normally use is advantageous. On some surfaces, the use of small apertures can bring the reflection of the ball light into focus causing a hard edge to the reflection, which sometimes intrudes upon the mark, when in fact you require a soft edged reflection.

Figure 7.30   The author using a ball light to examine a door and door frame.

At scenes all shiny surfaces, such as gloss painted door frames, will be examined with the ball light and any marks found will be photographed prior to aluminium powder being applied (Figure 7.30). If this technique is used in the examination of motor vehicles, it has been found to increase the number of marks retrieved by up to 50% (in-house figures).

7.5.7 Transillumination or backlighting

This technique requires the light to be directly behind the subject, so that it passes through it. Normally a simple light box or an inspection lamp is used. If no light box is available, you can use a piece of white paper. This should be held behind the surface that requires illumination, well outside of the depth of field being used, to ensure it stays out of focus. The illumination source is then used to light the paper, creating a bright backdrop allowing the mark to be seen (Figure 7.31). This is useful for marks developed using CNA, VMD (Vacuum Metal Deposition)[26] marks on clear plastic bags or glass, and for the copying of x-rays. This technique is often used in conjunction with our glass-topped stool.

---

[26] VMD, here the exhibit is exposed to evaporated gold and zinc in a vacuum chamber. The resultant finger marks are generally dark in colour.

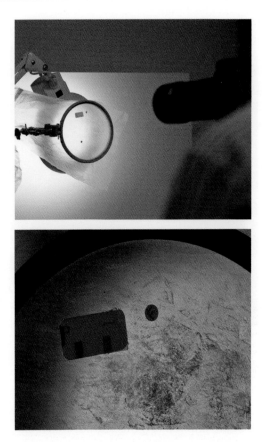

Figure 7.31   A CNA mark on a plastic bag being illuminated by a ring light bounced off a white card. (Note that when the ring light was used directly behind the bag, it failed to reveal the mark correctly.)

7.6   Chemically enhanced marks

As discussed earlier in the book, to fully exploit all the forensic possibilities within the laboratory and at scenes, the use of ALSs – particularly lasers and UV lamps – is equally, if not more, important than the use of chemical developers (see chapter on light as a forensic tool). In the sections above we have looked at generic white light techniques, but within the laboratory most marks are chemically enhanced, so I am going to look at these chemical treatments first. Nearly all police forces and forensic providers in the UK follow the sequential chemical treatment guidance given by CAST (Centre for Applied Science and Technology) in their Manual and Handbook.[27] [3]

---

[27] CAST, the Centre for Apllied Science and Technology was formally known as HOSDB the Home Office Scientific Development Branch.

Chemical treatments fall into two main groups, those for porous and those for non-porous surfaces.

- Surfaces falling into the porous category include paper, card and some types of untreated wood.
- Non-porous surfaces include plastics, glass, ceramic tiles, painted wood, and treated finished card such as the outside of cereal packets.

7.6.1 Treated marks on porous surfaces

Within the Evidence Recovery Unit, two main chemical treatments are carried out to develop latent marks these types of surfaces.

DFO (Diazafluoren-9-one) This chemical reacts with amino acids present in sweat to produce a fluorescent reaction product. DFO is carried out sequentially before ninhydrin. Marks developed using DFO need to be stimulated by a light source emitting green light between approximately 500–550 nm to enable any finger marks to be seen. We use the 5-W 532-nm ND-YAG laser, but a number of alternative devices are available. Because the viewing goggles and photographic filter has a cut on around 550 nm, we see the fluorescence produced by the marks as orange. (See Chapter 5.)

For photography, the camera should be mounted on a solid tripod or copy type stand. When excited by the light, the fluorescence generated by the DFO marks is generally quite strong, so an ISO of 200 should be adequate. A camera filter should then be selected that matches the excitation wavelength of the light source. For a 532 nm laser this will be around 550 nm long pass filter (e.g. Schott glass OG570), but your manufacturer may supply a filter matched to the laser excitation wavelength (see previous chapter in regards to filters) (Figure 7.32).

The item should then be placed in front of the lens so that the area of the mark and label fills the viewing screen. When you are illuminating the mark with the light source, don't forget to refocus the camera as there will be a focus shift. When metering, be careful not to meter directly from the DFO, as this will cause underexposure in the fainter areas of the mark; if in doubt bracket your exposures. Always check your camera display to ensure that it is both correctly exposed and in focus.

If using centre-weighted metering, you will need to allow approximately two stops to your exposure to compensate for the bright fluorescent reaction.

Ninhydrin (nin) Ninhydrin (2,2-Dihydroxyindane-1, 3-dione) is a chemical used to detect ammonia or primary and secondary amines, and like DFO reacts with amino acids in finger marks. This chemical reaction produces a deep blue or purple color, known as Ruehemann's purple, and any marks produced are clearly visible (Figure 7.33).

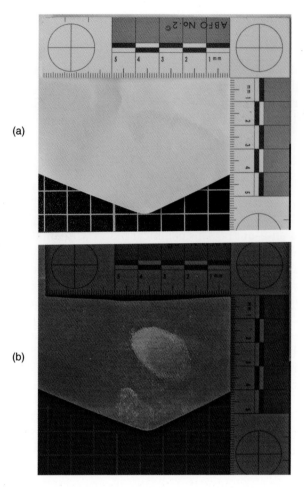

Figure 7.32   A DFO mark on an envelope exposed at 1/8th at f8 400ISO.

For photography, the camera can be mounted on a copy type set up or tripod with the mark positioned in front of the lens. There are two lighting arrangements that are suitable for nin photography. One is copy lighting, which provides an even illumination over a large area, or a ring light, which is suitable for smaller areas of interest. Within the laboratory we use a copy lighting arrangement, but at scenes it is almost exclusively the ring light or ring flash.

For the exposure, centre-weighted metering can be used, and as ninhydrin treated items are almost inevitably paper and thus flat, the aperture can be set to around f8. If the background is slightly reflective or if you need to increase the saturation of a weak ninhydrin mark, then a polarising filter can be used. If you are using correctly arranged copy lighting, it is

Figure 7.33 A nin mark on an orange envelope.

also possible to hold crumpled paper or fold paper flat by using a sheet of thin glass.

Physical developer Physical developer is an aqueous solution containing both silver and iron ions that reacts with lipids, fats and oils present in the finger mark. Physical developer is the last process in the chemical development sequence used on porous surfaces. Here the developed marks contain small particles of silver and appear as dark grey or black. These can be recorded using the copy type light for flat items or front lit for three-dimensional ones. Photography of these marks is generally undertaken using the ring light, oblique lighting or copy lighting. If the substrate has a reflective shine to it, a polarising filter can be used to remove this and increase the saturation of the mark.

If the developed marks are very faint, they may be enhanced by UV or laser excitation of the background. Here the mark will stay black, but the light will cause the substrate to fluoresce, increasing the contrast.

7.6.2 Non porous surfaces

These include most plastics, shiny card, magazine covers and painted surfaces.

Vacuum Metal deposition (VMD) VMD is a two stage technique. The process is effective on both the eccrine (aqueous) and sebaceous materials normally found in prints, making it one of the most effective processes with 'fresh' evidence. It has also been shown to develop marks on evidence that is 20 years old. Because it can detect films of fat only a molecule thick, VMD is able to recover marks containing only trace amounts of the substances that

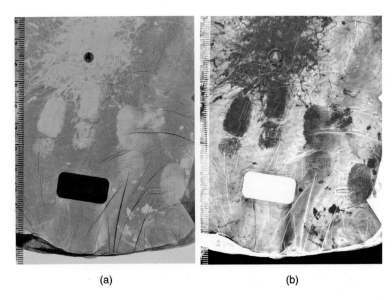

(a)   (b)

Figure 7.34   (a) shows VMD mark on a plastic bag (b) shows conversion to inverted greyscale.

compose every print. In stage one, a very small amount of gold is deposited under vacuum onto the exhibit, which deposits all over the surface and adheres to the latent finger mark. The gold clusters formed differ in size and distribution between the mark and the background. This is then followed by the deposition of zinc over the gold layer. The zinc grows at different rates on the mark and the background, leaving marks visible either lighter or darker than the background (Figure 7.34).

Photography of this type of mark is often undertaken in the horizontal mode, with the exhibit placed on a tapestry ring and then held in a retort stand. The surfaces bearing these marks are grey and slightly shiny and they fall into two camps for photography. Generally, marks on clear plastic require some form of transillumination, whilst those on solid or opaque items require oblique or specular lighting.

For transillumination, a number of techniques can be used, the simplest is the light box, but often this does not provide enough contrast in the mark. The other option is to mount the mark on the tapestry hoop and use the ring light or Schott light for illumination. This provides a more directional beam and increases the contrast in the mark.

For marks on solid exhibits, the marks are generally best illuminated with the ring or ball lights. However, if you are using the vertical camera set-up (copy stand), it can often be difficult to achieve the desired angles or distances.

For photography, the camera should be set up as with ninhydrin or DFO. The difference here will be that the exposure will be dictated by the light source. If the ring lamp is used, then a meter reading is generally accurate.

However, if back lighting or specular lighting is used, then the camera will underexpose as it sees the light directly. You will need to overexpose by up to four stops to achieve the correct exposure for the mark. When dealing with specular marks, always use the zoom controls on your reviewing screen to ensure that it has been properly captured.

It should be noted that VMD marks can fade through oxidisation, so they should be photographed as soon as practical and preferably within 24 hours.

CNA Cyanoacrylate, or superglue fuming, is probably the most common chemical treatment in use today. Any marks developed by this technique are white and, as with VMD, can be lit either with transillumination, oblique or specular lighting, depending on the substrate the mark is on (Figure 7.35).

The photography of marks on plastic bags can again be greatly helped by the use of the embroidery hoops, which can be used to stretch the mark as tight as possible. This will often enable the mark to be photographed in several different ways. Photography is carried out in the same way as ninhydrin or VMD.

BY40 (Basic Yellow Forty or Panacryl Brilliant Flavine 10 GFF) is used as a chemical dye for articles that have been developed with CNA. Again like DFO, the chemical needs to be stimulated by a light source in order to see its effect. In this case, the excitation needs to be in the blue area of the spectrum. BY40 has a wide response range from UV to around 480 nm; this is advantageous as it allows the filtering out of some background autofluorescence and interference, by careful selection of the excitation wavelength. If you are using a light source such as a Crimescope you can start at the UV band and work your way through the blue wavebands up until around 515 nm, looking for

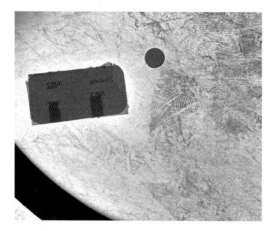

Figure 7.35 A typical CNA mark on a white plastic bag, in this case illuminated from behind using a ring light.

(a)

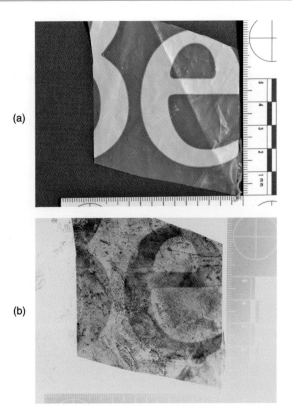

(b)

Figure 7.36   (a) a mark on a plastic bag treated with BY40 illuminated at 445 nm with the laser exposure of 1/4 s at f8 400ISO. (b) Shows the adjusted inverted greyscale conversion.

the filter that gives the best contrast between the mark and the background (Figure 7.36).

Unfortunately, BY40 has a habit of staining the surface of the exhibit as well as the mark and this can create problems when photographing faint marks. It is always worth checking the mark with a ring or ball light before undertaking fluorescent photography. This is particularly relevant for marks on plastic bags. Here, once stretched, they are often improved when photographed with the ball light rather than photographed under fluorescent lighting conditions (Figure 7.37).

For photography, the set up as used for DFO will work. In this case, however, we are going to use a blue excitation wavelength, so a yellow filter of the appropriate wavelength will need to be fitted to the camera.

Many other fluorescing enhancement chemicals are used around the world, such as Rhodamine 6G – another dye treatment for CNA – and 'Red wop' and 'Green glow' fluorescent powders (Figure 7.38). These are used as an alternative to aluminum powder on textured, patterned or multicolored surfaces and are designed to react with a variety of different wavelengths dependent on

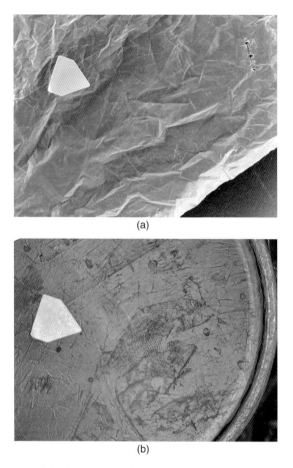

(a)

(b)

Figure 7.37 A BY40 mark (a) bag treated with CNA and BY40 (b) stretched using an embroidery hoop, then photographed as a specular mark using a ball light.

the requirement. In the UK, however, these are not in general usage in many police forces.

7.7 Latent marks

7.7.1 Fluorescence

Unlike treated marks, these 'natural' fluorescent responses to light are completely unpredictable and solely reliant on the type of contaminate present and the difference in response between the contaminate and the surface it is deposited upon (Figure 7.39). Many household products have a natural fluorescent response when exposed to the right wavelength, including cosmetics, oil, some greases, beer and milk [4].

In a recent in-house analysis (to be published 2014) it was found that around 10% of marks on exhibits submitted to the laboratory for fingerprint

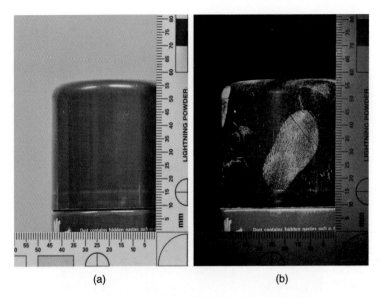

(a)   (b)

Figure 7.38   (a) A lid of a can treated with green glow fluorescent powder (b) after excitation with UV exposed at 1/15th s at f8 600 ISO.

enhancements were only recovered using an UVL examination and never developed using chemicals. At scenes, this figure rose in some circumstances to 50% of the marks retrieved.

At scenes, surfaces such as emulsion painted walls and gloss paint tend to provide a good surface to yield fluorescing marks. However, these marks are on the whole much fainter than those seen after chemical treatments such as DFO or BY40, so they generally need overexposing from the given exposure by one or two stops. Indeed it is often found that when a mark is photographed

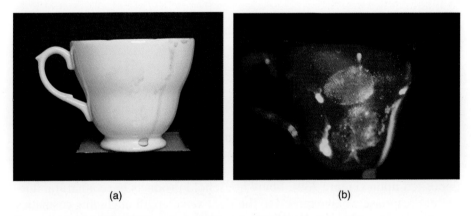

(a)   (b)

Figure 7.39   (a) White light control photograph. (b) Naturally induced fluorescence using an excitation wavelength of 532 nm and a 549 nm long pass viewing filter.

at a scene, a mark from an adjacent, previously unseen, finger will appear. This is because the camera is generally more sensitive than the eye, so exhibit labels should never be firmly fixed to the surface in case they cover up as yet unseen marks. With some surfaces, a reverse effect is seen in that the background fluoresces (autofluorescence), rather than the mark; this is typical of blood marks on glossy paint or plastics, when searching with UV or a low blue wavelength. Here the blood strongly absorbs the light (it does not fluoresce as is generally assumed). The background then fluoresces brightly, increasing the contrast between the marks and the background allowing them to be more easily seen. (Figure 8.8 in Chapter 8 shows an example of blood mark under ultraviolet.)

For the photography of marks the camera should be mounted on a tripod at 90° to the mark framing both the mark and the reference label. If the mark is to be fluoresced, then the appropriate filter needs to be fitted to the camera (don't forget that in an emergency you can use the filter in your viewing goggles as a camera filter). Don't forget to refocus once you have switched the lights out, this is particularly noticeable at the UV end of the spectrum. Use centre-weighted metering and overexpose by at least one stop.

For non-fluorescing marks at scenes, the ball light is the preferred first option for illumination (as discussed above in specular and coaxial illumination). If possible, use the 105 mm lens because this allows the camera to be moved off axis at a greater angle than is possible with a 60 mm macro lens, allowing greater maneuverability in the lighting position.

For the specular lit marks you may have to photograph the mark at a slight angle, as getting the correct lighting position is the important issue here rather than the camera. Exposures are as above for studio work.[28]

Sometimes with specular marks, because of the nature of the surface they are on, it is not easy to see the desired effect using only one ball light. This could be because the field of illumination may be too small, or you may need to illuminate two surfaces at once. In such situations there are a couple of tricks that can be used.

Double or triple ball lights: here we utilise more than one source of specular illumination. For example, a palm mark on a doorframe could be on two faces of the frame at once. A single ball light can illuminate only one angle, so by using a second one we can illuminate both parts of the mark at once (Figure 7.40). This is another reason for using a cable release, you can either hold it in the hand with a ball light, or preferably give it to a colleague who can fire the shutter when you tell them the lighting is in the correct position. If possible, use two identical bulbs so as to give consistency with the exposure.

---

[28] In recent in house UKAS validation testing, it was found that marks photographed at up to 20 degrees off axis, could still be identified on Ident 1.

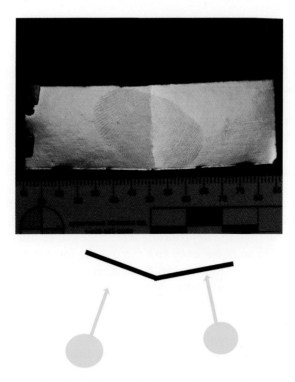

Figure 7.40   The use of two ball lights to illuminate a latent mark on a thin strip of metal. Note that the distance of the two lamps from the mark is different to optimise the contrast in each side of the mark.

Multiple exposures: this can be used when you have an exhibit with more than one surface face, as in Figure 7.40, but using multiple specular ball lights is not practical. Most DSLRs allow the selection from a menu of multiple exposures; this in effect allows you to take two, three or four images on the same frame, using a single ball light or even a mix of lighting techniques. As with all things there is a trade off, generally when using this technique there is a loss of overall contrast, particularly if the exposures overlap at any point.

Open exposure: this is particularly useful for specular marks on shallow convex surfaces, such as a mug or glass. Often marks will be seen as you move the light across the surface, but not in a single area, and these marks would therefore appear at first sight not to be suitable for illumination with the ball light (Figure 7.41). However, using the open exposure technique it is quite possible to utilise the ball light in specular lighting mode. The first thing we need to know is how long it takes us to move the light across the surface to illuminate the mark, and to mentally take note of the path it takes. For example, it

Figure 7.41   A latent mark, on a typical surface often found at scenes. (Area enclosed by red box.)

may take $\frac{1}{2}$ s for the light to cross the surface moving vertically. We now take an exposure reading, in this theoretical example say 1/8th at f8. For photography of the mark, manually change your length of exposure to 1/2 s and stop down to f11 to help compensate for the effects of overexposure. When you fire the camera, move the light across the surface as you have already mentally noted. The exposure may need some adjustment as the light will overexpose some areas on its journey; however, this is normally just by one or two stops (Figure 7.42). This overexposure can be rectified by either moving the light faster along its path, or by stopping the lens down, or by decreasing the ISO. When undertaken successfully, open exposure photography provides a useful technique in your armory.

It should be noted that all the above techniques must be carried out in a subdued lighting environment or if possible total darkness; this is to eliminate any ambient light that may interfere with your carefully controlled lighting conditions. In some scenarios, it is also helpful to build a shield around the ball light, this helps reduce flare and the spread of light (Figure 7.43). The shield is simply a piece of black paper placed around the rear of the bulb, thus shielding it from our view. On other occasions, this black shield can be replaced with a tin foil one creating a very soft, diffuse light.

Figure 7.42 The areas above photographed using the open exposure technique. Note that this took a number of attempts to get right, as the dimples in the bottles surface became very pronounced and affected the mark if the light was held too close.

Figure 7.43 A ball light with and without a black paper shield.

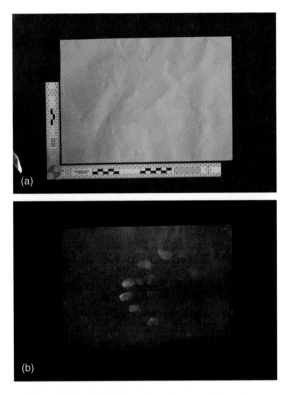

Figure 7.44 A DFO hand mark on an A3 envelope.

7.7.2 Painting with light

This technique is generally used in combination with UV and laser illumination, although it can also be used for some types of white light. Here we are going to move the light during the exposure to ensure that the light is applied evenly to the whole area. This allows a whole hand or shoe mark to be illuminated without a noticeable loss of quality (Figure 7.44).

To photograph, set up the camera as normal, and aim to have an exposure which is at least 1 s long. For practicality, the longer the exposure the larger the area you can cover. This is not normally an issue with marks or other latent evidence at scenes. Now take your exposure but, as you expose, move the light rapidly across the entire area of the mark. In effect you are building up the exposure conditions in the frame as you go. So if we have a mark that is highly fluorescent at one end, we can deliberately give that less exposure to the light as we take the exposure. It is possible with this technique to produce an even illumination across the whole mark. This technique is particularly important for photographing shoe marks, but is most often used at post mortem during fluorescence photography. Here we can have a long exposure time, allowing us to illuminate not just the injury but the whole surrounding area so that it is seen in context with its surroundings. Using this technique will also remove any effects of laser speckle (the small moving pattern that can sometimes be observed) and issues of poor or uneven beam quality in other light sources. A word of caution: as you will be working in the dark be careful not to accidently touch or knock the tripod during the exposure, otherwise the result may appear as a double image or soft.

There is one problem that occurs frequently at scenes, particularly when undertaking photography of fluorescent marks, which is that of highly fluorescent exhibit labels. Within the ERU we use a number of different coloured arrows or dots to indicate where the mark is, these have been carefully chosen not to fluoresce under either UV or 532 nm illumination. However, the exhibit labels are a standard issue yellow 40 × 12 mm rectangle. Although each batch of labels may appear to be the same yellow visually, their dye mix varies considerably and often they fluoresce very brightly.

If these appear in the same photograph as a very faint UV fluorescent mark, say, we are given the choice of either correctly exposing for the label but not the mark, or conversely exposing for the mark with the result that the label will be overexposed. The remedy to this situation is, however, straightforward and simple if you think outside of the box.

Although the label is important, clearly correct exposure of the mark must take precedence. Therefore we will expose for the mark, for example 4 s at f11, with the label requiring only 2 s to be correctly exposed (Figure 7.45).

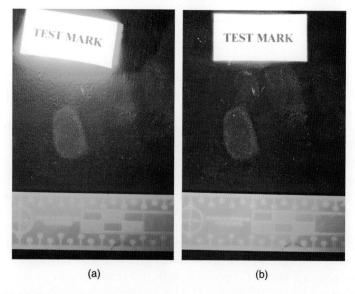

(a)   (b)

Figure 7.45 A fluorescent mark photographed (a) with the label in for the full exposure (b) removed after 2 s. By overexposing the label in photo (a) not only has the flare interfered with the main mark, but the mark to the right has also has very little information when photograph (a) is compared to photograph (b).

There are two options depending on your circumstances: the first option is to remove the label after 2 s. Here you would fire the shutter and illuminate the label for 2 s, turn the light in the opposite direction (so as to remove the illumination source which would otherwise cause ghosting as you remove the label) and physically remove the label, then carry on the exposure as normal. This removal technique can be used because we never use the full adhesive backing of the label, only exposing the adhesive on one corner to tack it down.

The second option relies on having black gloves, as previously discussed in scene of crime photography, or having a piece of black card in your kit bag. Failing that some black tape folded on itself and attached to the end of forensics ruler as a flag also works well.

Here the exposure is started as before, but after 2 s the glove or card is introduced into the frame blocking the light falling on the label (Figure 7.46).

Both techniques will ensure that now both the mark and the label are correctly exposed.

When counting seconds in your head, continuity of the timing is important, as we want to ensure we can repeat the exposures. For ease, I mentally count using, 'a thousand and one elephants a thousand and two elephants' and so on, rather than glancing at a watch or other device.

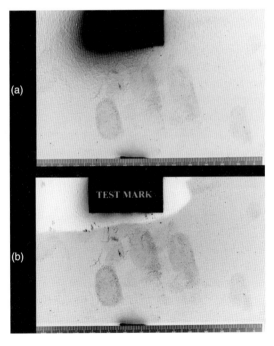

Figure 7.46   A latent fluorescent mark under 532 nm after post-production. (a) With the label left for the full exposure (b) with the label covered after 2 s. Again the mark in photograph (a) is less defined due to the flare caused by the overexposing label.

7.8   Shoe marks

Although there are some similarities in how we approach shoe marks and finger marks in some of the techniques we might use, there are also some big differences. First, shoes do not produce sweat, therefore the majority of the chemical treatments described above will not be effective in enhancing the mark and alternative methods must be used. Second, the area of a shoe mark is generally considerably larger than finger mark and careful consideration must be given to its even illumination. Third, unlike finger marks, which may only appear at a single point of contact, with shoe marks it is often the second or third mark made in a series of steps, which gives the best image (see Figure 7.6 above).

Some thought must also be given to your photographic equipment and camera settings. A prime lens should always be considered over a zoom lens, as this will avoid any issues or barrel or pin cushion distortions. You should also ensure the camera is set to its highest quality setting.

The types of shoe marks found at a scene will fall into one of the categories below.

7.8.1   Latent dust marks

Latent dusk marks are commonly found at scenes and can appear in either a positive or negative form, that is the dust may either be left by the shoe, or conversely removed by the shoe. They are relatively easy to find using an oblique light such as a projector or torch at an angle of between 1° and 5° from the floor (as seen in Figure 7.22). With this skimmed light it is then possible to see the disturbances in the dust layer. This technique works best on laminates and stone flooring, although it is equally useful for chairs and worktops. When searching for these types of marks with a projector type light, it is prudent to have two operators. One to look down the beam across the surface away from the light and one to look straight down the beam towards the light. This is because, in my experience, many marks are actually mono directional (due normally to the surface structure of the flooring) responding only to one direction of illumination.

Once latent dust marks have been found, they should be photographed as they are of a generally delicate nature. It is also common practice to electrostatically lift (ESL) not only the marks but the surrounding area as well. ESL works by applying a static charge of several thousand volts (but very low amperage) to a thin film of special lifting material, which is placed over the mark (see Figure 7.23 above). The static then causes the dust to stick to the underside of the film. The special lifting film is silver on one side to aid the conduction of the static charge and black on the other (to which the dust is attracted) to increase the contrast in the mark (Figure 7.47). These ES lifted marks should be viewed with standard oblique and specular lighting.

Figure 7.47   A pathfinder ESL being used.

If possible they should be photographed as soon as possible, preferably at the scene, any time delay can increase the chances of extra dust attaching itself to the surface, or dust being lost as it is rolled or boxed up.

It is worth noting that on some surfaces if can be incredibly difficult to see the mark when the camera is in place, although from an oblique angle the marks may look clear. In these cases it is worth discussing with the scientist or other personnel going straight to ESL, by carrying out a test on a nearby poor mark that contains little detail. This is not a 'cop out' but a logical position. If we are going to take a long time to achieve the required conditions to photograph the mark correctly, but they will easily lift to a high standard, then time, energy and money is saved by doing so. This is the only scenario where I would advocate not photographing the evidence first, but only because we have wasted many hours photographing marks which have been equally good once lifted.

7.8.2 Contaminated marks

The most common type of contaminated marks recovered from scenes are those deposited in blood. Here it is important to remember that bloody shoe marks tend to leave a trail, so it may be that the second, third or even fourth mark may show more detail than the first heavily soaked mark (see Figure 7.6

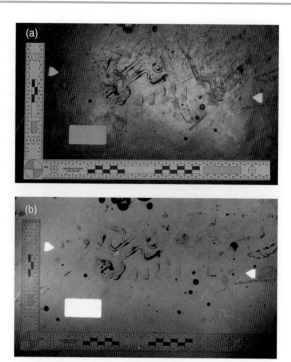

Figure 7.48 A mark in blood (a) under white light (note the background interference from the greasy surface deposits). (b) Under UVA – the use of UVA is an easy quick method for searching for blood on laminate and wooden floorings.

above). Blood does have one characteristic that we can exploit, in that it will strongly absorb certain wavelengths of light. This does not make it fluoresce, but the strong absorption causes the mark to appear black. For example, many laminate floors have a plastic coating or varnish to make them hardwearing. When exposed to UV they often turn a milky white colour. Therefore, if our blood stained shoe mark is on this surface and we expose it to UV, we will increase the contrast in the mark considerably (Figure 7.48).

The same principle can be applied to many other surface types, such as varnished doors or coloured wallpapers, using either UV or one of the different wavelengths of laser.

Devices such as the Crimescope can also be used as a coloured light source, (normally using wavebands around 445 nm) on surfaces like carpets. In this case, the light is used in neutralising the background colour, which can also dramatically improve the contrast in blood marks. This colour neutralisation will not be filtered, during photography to induce fluorescence but merely recorded as it is a coloured light. However, if you are using UV illumination you will need to filter the camera, otherwise you can cause the camera lens or even the sensor to autofluoresce.

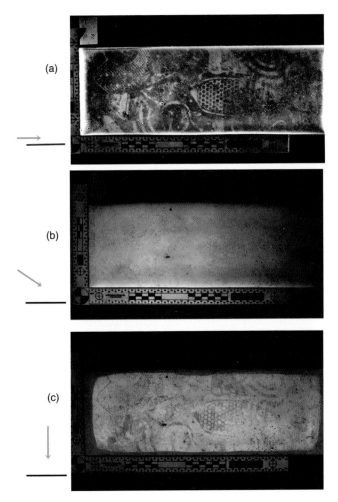

Figure 7.49 A gelatine lift illuminated from (a) a low oblique angle of approximately 2° (b) an oblique angle of approximately 45° (c) as a specular mark. Note how each lighting technique reveals a different part of the shoe mark. It is therefore very important that they are examined under controlled, darkened lighting conditions. So if this is not available at the scene, they should be packaged and re-examined within the laboratory.

Clearly we can have many other contaminates on our shoes other than blood, but the same principles apply: the floor should be examined by UV and laser to ensure that there are no fluorescent marks and then a specular examination should be carried out with the ball light. Marks in grease are often found by the ball light and once photographed can be lifted using a gelatine lifter. The gelatine lifter has a black gel surface on one side, which is slightly tacky. When it is pressed onto a surface, smoothed in place and subsequently removed, the contaminate adheres to this tacky surface and the resultant lift can be photographed in the same way as an ESL (Figure 7.49). Gelatine lifts are commonly used at scenes for the retrieval of many types of contaminated marks.

In some forces, such as our own, a Gel scanner[29] is used to photograph some retrieved marks. This enables specular photography of the gel to be carried out automatically and to a very high quality. However, the gels should always be examined with oblique lighting as well to ensure no information is missed.

7.8.3   Physical shoe mark impressions

These are shoe marks that are found in soil or other soft surfaces that produce a three dimensional pattern. Some of these types of mark can be particularly difficult to record accurately, especially if they are deep and at angles; in these cases directional lighting is required. If these are found outside in daylight then the choice is often limited to electronic flash or even ambient light. Marks in substances like snow which have a low contrast range (Figure 7.50) can be enhanced by the application of black paint or a wax spray. Black spray paint can be used to increase the contrast in the mark by gently spraying from one direction across the surface. This is not a particularly good technique for capturing the fine detail, but will give overall patterns. This is not without risk, as I have seen powdery marks almost disappear as they are sprayed. Wax spray, on the other hand, is generally applied in a two-stage process. First it is sprayed from just one direction, as with the paint this will build up a contrast range across the mark as the wax gathers, this should then be photographed. Stage two is to spray the mark from all directions so that all the vertical surfaces are covered. It should then be re-photographed. It is then possible to cast the mark, as the wax creates a barrier to stop the exothermic reaction of the casting compound melting the snow.

The snow itself also produces its own problems in terms of exposures. As excessive reflected light will tend to underexpose the mark I would suggest that you set your flashgun to manual and check your preview screen to review at each exposure.

7.8.4   Photography of shoe marks

Before setting up your camera the mark must be exhibited, normally in the form of a label, this will be in a format dictated by your force but generally it will show the date, place, job sheet number and identifying letter or number. A forensic ruler must be used to indicate scale, if possible the large right angle type, so the X and the Y axis must be included. This is important as without either an exhibit label or scale no subsequent scientific comparison can be

---

[29] Gel scanner; GLscan (Gellifter scanner) from BVDA in Holland is a purpose built scanner specifically designed to use specular illumination on the gel's surface: http://www.bvda.com

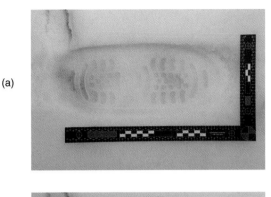

(a)

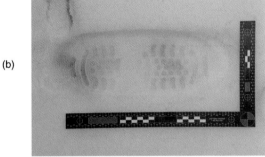

(b)

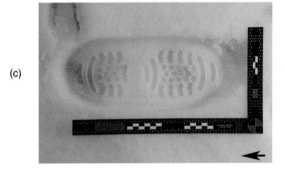

(c)

Figure 7.50 A mark in snow illuminated in three different ways. (a) Ambient illumination. Notice how the definition of the mark is soft. (b) Flash illumination pointed straight down, again the resultant image appears flat with few 3D characteristics. (c) Flash at 45° from right hand side. This was exposed at 1/125 at f19 with the ambient daylight being shielded by my coat. Note the fine lines on the instep part of the shoe, which are missing from (a) and (b).

carried out. You then need to position your camera at 90° perpendicular to the mark. It is always good practice to fill the viewfinder to the maximum; this ensures that no pixels are wasted on surrounding background information. The camera should be squared up using the spirit level across the front of the lens or with a hot-shoe bubble level (never across the camera back) provided the floor is actually flat. If the floor is sloping then it is possible to use an angle finder spirit level to find the new angle and then to set your camera to that. If you have forgotten your spirit level, get a colleague to look at the camera from a short distance away, looking in both the X and Y axis, and compare it to a known straight line within the scene, such as a door frame. They can then tell you to tilt or turn and so on until the camera is relatively straight. This will not be absolutely accurate, but will be closer than if you try to make adjustments from the tripod position.

A point of relevance here is that work undertaken by the National Injuries Database indicates that any mark or injury photographed at more than 15° from square will result in the mark being unacceptable and useless for direct comparison.

Again, ensure you use a cable release and more importantly check that any lens stabilisation is turned off. This is often overlooked but, as already discussed, will cause the lenses to vibrate in the barrel as they compensate against non-excitant movements causing blurred images. You can then introduce your light source and undertake photography.

Exposure will depend upon your light source, but it is worth remembering that when undertaking the photography of either finger or shoe marks, the correct exposure may in fact be an 'under' or 'over' exposure. For example, a bloody shoe mark on a black t-shirt may be helped by being overexposed by two stops, as we are more interested in seeing the blood on the t-shirt rather than correctly exposing the shirt itself (Figure 7.51).

When assessing the shoe marks on screen in post-production, don't forget to flip the image so it is back to front, as it will be compared directly to the bottom of the shoe and not another impression.

You will probably have noticed that I generally use a continuous light source for shoe marks rather than flash; this is purely a personal comment, but in my experience there are two disadvantages of using flash. Firstly, you cannot see the effect that the flash is having on your shoe mark and secondly the beam tends to be diffuse, spreading in all directions, and giving unpredictable results. There is, however, one occasion where flash does work and that is for an open exposure when using specular lighting. In this case you can set the flash to strobe effect, whilst physically moving its position around the mark (see Figure 13 in flash photography).

Other useful tricks are the use of filters and of post-production enhancements. In Figure 7.52 we can see the use of cross-polarisation in enhancing a mark on a plastic chair seat and in Figure 7.53 we can see the use of a red filter to remove an interfering pattern on a bag.

7.9   Tyre marks

The photography of tyre marks is very similar to the photography of a shoe mark. However, unlike a shoe mark, which may be 20–30 cm long, tyre marks can run for several metres. In practicality we need to only to record the

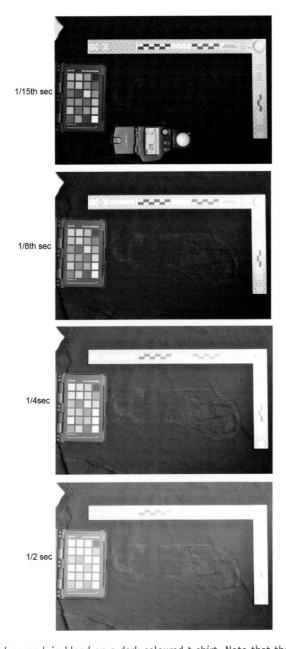

Figure 7.51 A shoe mark in blood on a dark coloured t-shirt. Note that the image at $\frac{1}{4}$ s is about the right exposure to reveal all of the shoe mark. Although it is possible to adjust the image to some extent within imaging software at the later stage, it is always better to get it right in camera, particularly if it is not you who is undertaking the post-production.

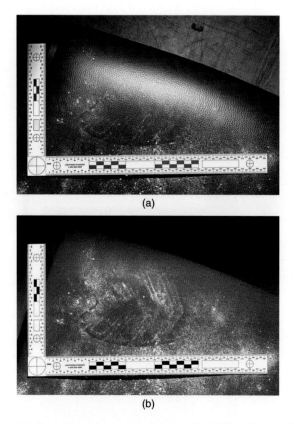

(a)

(b)

Figure 7.52   A mark in fire extinguisher powder taken under (a) flash illumination and (b) cross-polarised flash. To undertake this technique see Chapter 6 on using cross-polarised light.

circumference of one revolution of the tyre to ensure we have its full pattern, around 2.3 m. The first step is to photograph the mark in its entirety showing its position within the scene, preferably from above if possible. Next we need to segment the tyre mark into manageable sections, equivalent to roughly the length of the shoe mark (say 25 cm to 30 cm long), you should also allow for roughly a 2 cm overlap between adjacent sections. This is easily done by using a long tape measure laid in the soil beside the mark. Each segment is then referenced with a unique sequential number so as not to get confused as to its position in post-production. We now need to frame up on the first segment in our sequence; again I would suggest using the 60 mm prime lens and a sturdy tripod with the camera perpendicular to the mark (as with shoe marks). Once the area is correctly framed and squared up you need to ensure that the legs and head of the tripod are securely locked in place. This task is made easier if you have a right angle bar fitted to your tripod, as it allows the camera to be swung away from the tripod and directly over the mark (Figure 7.54).

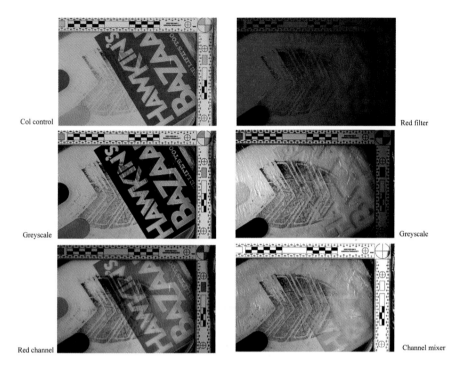

Figure 7.53 The left-hand side of the image shows a mark photographed conventionally, then converted to a greyscale and then as a red channel. On the right is the same mark photographed with a red filter, then as a greyscale, then after being mixed in channel mixer.

Figure 7.54 Shows boom arm attached to a tripod allowing the camera to be positioned at 90 degree to the mark. Photographic illustration.

You also need to add a forensic scale; this should be on the same plane as the actual mark. Note that the long tape we are using to segment the mark is probably on the surface, whereas the tyre tracks will have sunk in. If we use this as our scale, our magnification ratios will be incorrect when we reproduce it life size.

For convenience, this is one of the applications where flash is preferable and again we probably need to work with small aperture, giving us the greatest depth of field. If the mark is in direct sunlight we can get a colleague to block out the direct light, using a piece of black out roll or a coat to cast a shadow over the areas we are interested in. To even out the illumination, use a piece of white paper as a reflector to reflect some of the flash back onto the mark. Once the first area is photographed to your satisfaction, you carefully pick up the tripod and move it to the second section. Hopefully if the ground is flat,

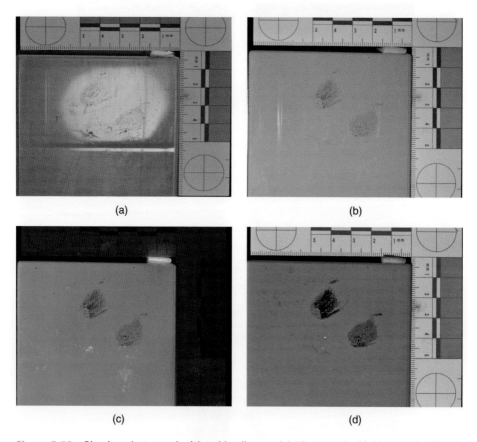

(a)   (b)

(c)   (d)

Figure 7.55   Blood marks treated with acid yellow 7. (a) Photographed with specular illumination prior to treatment. (b) Photographed under oblique illumination. (c) Photographed as a fluorescence mark using a 445 nm laser and 550 nm band pass camera filter. (d) Photographed using the 445 nm laser and no camera filter.

and provided that you locked the leg sections of the tripod, no alteration to focusing will be required. If the image does need refocusing, however, do not refocus the lens. Instead raise or lower the central column or legs as required, this will ensure that your magnification ratios remain the same between photographs of adjacent sections.

The resultant photographs can then be presented to your expert, either as a series of individual images laid out so that they overlap, or a very large digital file. Within our own department we also have the capability to print images of the full length of the tyre on a large format printer.

7.10 Blood enhancement techniques

As already stated one of the commonest and most important contaminates found at scenes, deposited as both finger and shoe marks and as spatter patterns, is blood. Although, as seen above, UV or other lighting may reveal some extra detail, there are a number of specific chemical reagents which can be used by us to enhance areas that are invisible. Although there are many used worldwide, the ones used within the unit are acid yellow 7, acid violet 17, Amido Black (Naphthalene Blue Black; acid black 1) and Leuco Crystal Violet (LCV) which are often applied sequentially. Acid yellow 7, acid violet 17 and acid black 1 can be applied in the form of different formulations: water/citric acid-based, methanol-based, and water/ethanol/acetic acid-based, according to circumstances.

7.10.1 Acid yellow 7

Before treatment with acid yellow 7 the mark in blood should be fixed with a 2% solution of 5-sulphosalicylic acid, this will stop the blood running and detail being lost. The acid yellow 7 dye solution is then applied, this stains the proteins present in the blood, staining the mark a pale yellow. However, once applied it can be enhanced by using a blue or blue-green light source, such as the Revelation 445 nm laser, causing it to fluoresce, although this is generally quite a weak reaction. This process is most useful for marks in blood on dark surfaces, but cannot be used on porous surfaces.

Photograph as normal for a finger or shoe mark. This time, however, you will need to use the blue laser or other light source, plus a matching long band pass filter over the lens.

In my experience these marks are often still quite faint, so an extra one or two stops may be required to achieve the correct exposure.

7.10.2 Acid violet 17

Treatment is similar to acid yellow 7, the difference here is that the marks will appear to be stained a deep purple colour. Once dry, the marks can either be

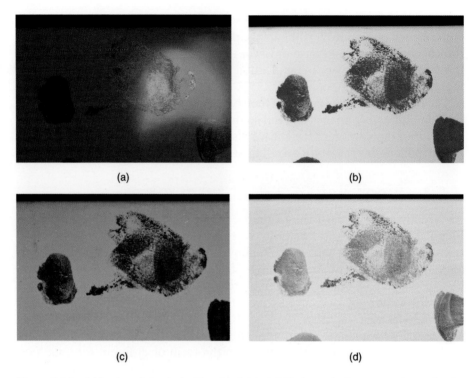

Figure 7.56   A blood mark treated with acid violet. (a) Photographed as a specular mark prior to treatment. (b) Photographed with oblique lighting. (c) Photographed using a 445 nm laser and 550 nm band pass filter. (d) Photographed using a 455 nm laser and no camera filter.

photographed in position using the relevant light source. Alternatively they can be lifted using a white gelatine lifter and will fluoresce red if examined using a laser (Figure 7.56).

These marks can be photographed as normal for a finger or shoe mark. This time you will need to use a green laser or other light source plus a matching long band pass filter over the lens.

In my experience these marks are often still quite faint, so an extra one or two stops may be required to achieve the correct exposure.

7.10.3   Amido Black (acid black 1)

This stains the protein present in the blood and other body fluids to give a blue-black product. This can be used on most surfaces provided blood is present. It will not, however, develop latent marks if only sweat is present and may damage some surfaces if the formulation based on methanol is used.

Photograph as normal for a finger or shoe mark; because the marks are dark blue or black the most suitable lighting for the situation can be used. Oblique, ring light or even specular should be considered (Figure 7.57). In some cases,

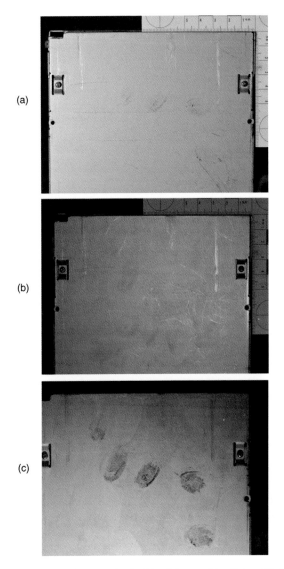

Figure 7.57   Blood marks (a) Photographed with oblique white light. (b) Photographed as a specular mark. (c) Photographed after treatment with Amido Black.

depending on the substrate, UV can be used to increase contrast and to separate the mark from the background.

7.10.4   LCV

LCV is a colouring reagent for blood that relies on the blood-catalysed reaction of the hydrogen peroxide with LCV, whereby the initially colourless LCV is oxidised to the purple crystal violet. This treatment is generally used for shoe marks on wood or solid non-porous flooring. Any marks found appear as dark purple.

Photography should be carried out as per any other finger or shoe mark. The choice of lighting will again be according to the situation, oblique, specular or even flash should be considered.

The one chemical that is often used at scenes to reveal blood is luminol; however, because its use is not generally specific to finger or shoe marks, I will cover its use in Chapter 8.

In my experience it is always worth photographing blood marks prior to any chemical treatment. If we look at Figure 7.55 it could be argued that the left mark is in fact better under specular illumination than the subsequent chemical enhancements, as the treatment has filled the core of the mark in.

7.10.5   Huffing and dead sets

There is another technique that I would briefly like to look at, that of huffing a mark. Although this was in common practice when I joined the department 20 plus years ago, it is used less often now, due to the reliance on DNA extraction. Huffing relies on exposing the mark to a flow of warm moist air, as commonly produced when breathing out or 'huffing'. It is a technique which is still extremely useful and when undertaken correctly and can yield excellent marks, particularly where only limited follow up chemical techniques are going to be deployed.

In Figure 7.58 we can see the technique applied to the surface of a CD. To undertake the technique you will require a soft skinned bottle, such as the wash or squeezy bottles used in labs. You could of course huff on the area, but this is not reliable particularly if the huffing has to be repeated. Next you need to set the camera up as if you are going to undertake specular photography. Finally, just before you go to shoot, you need to half fill the bottle with very hot water. Holding the bottle under you mark you now very gently squeeze. The rush of warm air will now flow over the mark, condensing on the background forming a layer. The contaminated area of mark will repel the steam and thus become visible against the background.

There are two important things to note when huffing marks; one is the air temperature of the studio. The cooler it is, the more impressive the reaction will be. If it is particularly warm in the studio, the effects will not be noticeable. To correct you can either cool the item down in the fridge, or switch the air condition in your studio to cold. The second issue is the rate of decay, or the speed at which the mark returns to normal. This is somewhat dependant on the surface and again temperature, some marks last for up to 5 seconds whilst others will be finish in less than a second. Therefore you will need to select shutter speed over aperture if you are to ensure that you capture the mark before it disappears. In Figure 7.51 the mark lasted for approximately 2 seconds.

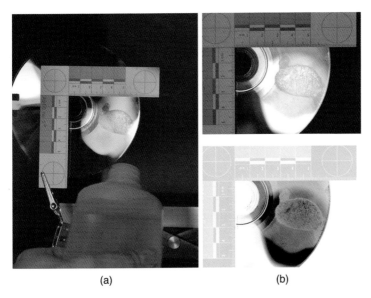

Figure 7.58 (a) Shows the CD in position held in a retort stand, with the squeezy bottle held just under the mark. (b) Shows a correctly huffed mark and the final reversed colour image after post production.

Clearly you cannot use this technique if the item is required for DNA later on but, if not, it does offer a simple yet very effective enhancement technique, which can also sometimes be used on glass and mirrors to remove unwanted reflections.

Before we leave the subject of finger marks, I would just like to touch on one aspect of work that is not commonly undertaken every day but does rely on good quality images, and that is of unidentified cadavers.

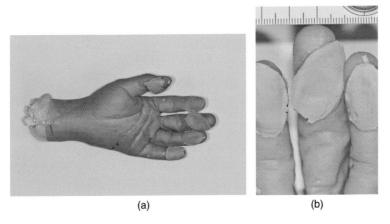

Figure 7.59 (a) Shows our dead set training hand. (b) Shows the use of the ring light (desk inspection lamp) to individually light each finger.

In the UK the standard approach is to ink the dead hands and take rolled impressions. However, in my experience, if the hands are decayed or have been immersed in water for any period, it is far better to attempt photography prior to inking.

The photography is best carried out using a ring light (the bigger the diameter the better the results), this is generally pushed down so that it is almost level with the skin surrounding the fingers one at a time. Do not forget that any images taken will need to be presented to your fingerprint expert in reverse direction.

We have found that photographing the marks in position produces a far higher chance of gaining identification than inking alone. If, however, you are not asked to attend the mortuary but are presented with a dental cast dead set, then there are ways of producing a good result as well.

Generally in the UK one of two colours of dental cast are used, white or purple, with white presenting the greatest challenge due to its natural lack of contrast. Before photography, you need to ensure that the casts have been properly autoclaved. This means that they are sterilised using heat, ensuring that there is the minimal possible health risk when handling them. This normally, however, does not remove detritus from the surface; so I would advocate a further clean with washing up liquid and a toothbrush using a gently scrubbing motion. If the cast has been properly set, then they are very robust and should come to no harm (if in doubt, try a test one first). This second clean will not only remove any residual rubbish from the surface but also any

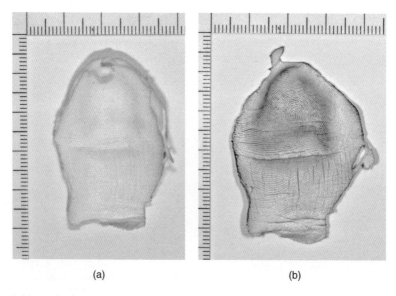

(a)   (b)

Figure 7.60   A dead set cast illuminated with a ring light (a) as received after sterilisation and washing (b) after the application of graphite powder.

greasy deposits. This still, however, leaves a flat white contrastless surface, as can be seen in Figure 7.60a. The next step is to reintroduce a contrast range. We have carried out numerous tests using most powders on the market and have found the best and simplest solution is graphite powder, applied with a soft paintbrush. Graphite powder is readily available, or you can make it yourself by taking the softest pencil you can find and rubbing it gently onto a slightly rough paper surface over and over again. (The inside is actually graphite and clay but will suffice for our purposes.) The residual grey dust can be then gently brushed with a paintbrush and applied to the surface of the cast (Figure 7.60b). This should be done slowly, building it up as you go, the idea is not to turn the cast black, but to get the dust into the furrows until the ridges can be clearly seen. Any excess powder can be removed with a clean paintbrush.

Again, the casts are generally photographed using a ring light held just above the surface. In Figure 7.60 the cast went slightly around the finger so was curved at the edges, to assist in flattening this out, the cast was photographed whilst it was under a sheet of photographic quality glass.

References

(1) Bowman, V. *Fingerprint Development Handbook*. 2nd edn. London: The Home Office Scientific Development Branch (HOSDB) Publication No. 1/05 2005.

(2) Sodhi, G.S. and Kaur, J. Powder method for detecting latent fingerprints: a review *Foren Sci Int*. 2001 120(3):172–6.

(3) Menzel, E.R. and Fox, K.E. Laser detection of latent fingerprints: preparation of fluorescent dusting powders and the feasibility of a portable system. *Foren Sci Int* 1980 25(1):150–3.

(4) Dror, I. E., Péron, A.E., Hind, S-L and Charlton, D. When emotions get the better of us: the effect of contextual top-down processing on matching fingerprints *App Cog Psychol* 2005 19(6): 799–809.

8
The Proactive Use of Light in Forensic Photography

8.1 Overview

In previous chapters we have looked at the use of photography within a 'scenes of crime environment' and although very important, it is in the main 'reactive'. That is to say the event has already happened. When we looked at the photography of finger, shoe and injury marks, we started to explore the use of specialist photography and alternative light sources (ALS) in a more proactive way.

In this chapter, I would like to develop this idea further and look at using a variety of ALS and photographic techniques to develop and capture other types of latent forensic evidence. Once you have an understanding of alternative forms of light and its possible applications, there is a wealth of latent forensic evidence all around us at crime scenes, waiting to be found.

It is argued by some that this work does not fall within the remit of the forensic photographer, but I would argue that who else within a scene is better equipped and trained to deal with light than us. Unfortunately, it is not possible to cover all the application of ALS within a book of this size. Although I hope that by covering the key applications, you will see that most forensic evidence can be enhanced in one way or another by the careful use of these techniques.

8.2 The detection of body fluids using an alternative light source

This is an area of work that allows a non-destructive search for body fluids to be carried out, which is particularly useful at large scenes. Importantly it can

Forensic Photography: A Practitioner's Guide, First Edition. Nick Marsh.
© 2014 John Wiley & Sons, Ltd. Published 2014 by John Wiley & Sons, Ltd.

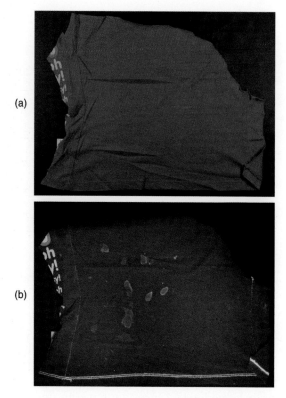

(a)

(b)

Figure 8.1   A t-shirt photographed under (a) white light illumination; (b) under the blue laser at 445 nm.

identify specific areas that can then be targeted for later AP testing[1] (Figure 8.1) without compromising a possible DNA hit. To undertake this work we will need an ALS emitting around 440–460 nm and or a UV light emitting 365 nm.

This is an area of work where I believe there is quite a bit of misguided information circulated, particularly on the Internet, around time lines and results. A number of MSc students and I have carried out many hours research, looking at both semen and saliva samples. We have found that it is possible to detect body fluids of all types, but there are a number of caveats that must be met before a search is practical or realistic. They are:

(a)   The time frame: testing and experience has shown that within the first six-hour window after deposition on a surface, semen/saliva samples generally have no noticeable fluorescent reaction. Any fluorescent reaction is

---

[1] An Acid Phosphatase (AP) test is generally used as a presumptive test for semen. The test targets the acid phosphates secreted by the prostate gland producing a purple stain.

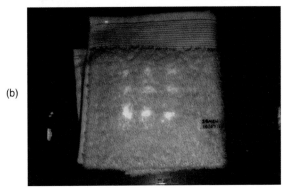

Figure 8.2   Various dilutions of semen applied to a yellow towel photographed two years after being applied. (a) Under white light illumination. (b) Under laser illumination at 445 nm.

first noted in the six to twelve hour window. This is because it is generally accepted that the fluorescence observed does not originate from the body fluids themselves, but by the products formed by resultant action of bacteria on them. However, once it starts to produce fluorescence, this reaction continues for many years. Indeed we have training samples that are six years old plus and now fluoresce very brightly. This means that the fact that a scene is historical does not preclude the use of the technique. In fact, in a recent pedophile case, fluorescence examination allowed samples found on a carpet dating back 10 years plus to be retrieved and identified (Figure 8.2).

(b) Wavelength: I often seen it written that long wave UV radiation should be used for the detection of body fluids; however, although it can and does work in some cases, it is not the most advantageous wavelength. This is because most body fluids have a peak excitation wavelength of around 440–460 nm. This means that depending on the strength of reaction with the body fluid and the level of background autofluorescence, samples may be missed if long wave UV is used. For example, semen on a white sheet can be easily missed during examination using long wave UV. This is due to the very bright autofluorescence produced by the high content of artificial whiteners used in the production of the white fabric and subsequent washing processes. As a consequence, the autofluorescence of the sheet will swamp the semen's own much weaker fluorescence. It is therefore better to use a more targeted approach; for this reason we use the blue line 445-nm laser, which does not induce the artificial whiteners to fluoresce, but is the right wavelength to induce a response from the body fluids.

(c) Power of the excitation light: as we have seen already in previous chapters, the fluorescent reaction is directly proportional to the excitation power. In our own in-house testing, we have found that samples revealed with the 5-watt 445-nm laser may not be found with other less powerful light sources because the reduced intensity of fluorescence produced in the sample cannot be detected by eye.

(d) Donors: one of the noticeable effects found during in-house testing was the variety of fluorescent responses found in semen, even when they came from the same donor, but at different times. This may appear to be a reflection of diet, or even medicinal drugs ingested in the previous twenty-four hour period. This is worth noting as it can lead to different fluorescent responses being seen at a scene.

It is worth noting here that there has been a long-running debate around the use of UV for the detection of body fluids with regard to the destruction of DNA. Although this might be true for short wave UVC radiation, I have used long wave UVA radiation for over 20 years and have had hundreds of positive DNA identifications after light source examinations from many types of surfaces, including grass, carpets, fabrics and concrete. I have never had any issues in subsequent testing, provided the normal DNA, personal protective equipment (PPE) precautions are carried out during examination and exposure times are kept to the minimum. There is, however, one point of caution with the technique. This is a visual inspection and is reliant on the operator's eyes and experience as to what a positive sample might look like, for example size, shape and colour. All stains that are thought to be positive should be tested in situ with a presumptive test. This ensures that negative swabs are not submitted to the laboratory for subsequent testing, which is wasteful of both time and money.

Although a general overview photograph of areas where body fluids are suspected to be present is not always undertaken, when the positioning of that stain is important and relevant to the context of a case, then the photography of that area should always be undertaken. In Figure 8.3 below we can see a general distribution of possible fluorescent stains, importantly note the possible hand shape at 6 o'clock and the 6–10 red fibres which are also present.

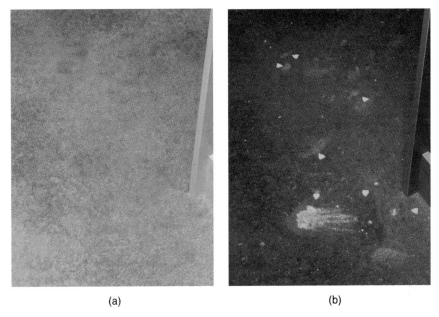

(a)   (b)

Figure 8.3   A possible sexual assault scene (a) under white light illumination; (b) under 445 nm with areas of body fluid indicated with yellow arrows. Note the hand shaped mark at six o'clock, indicating four fingers and a thumb. This could be important in the context of the case. Also note the 6–10 small red fibres, which can also be clearly seen fluorescing on the carpet. These may have been shed from the attackers garment and so may be important if fibre analysis is being considered at a later stage.

Photography of body fluids on areas of flooring should be undertaken as for photography of fluorescent shoe marks. The camera should be mounted on a tripod and fitted with the appropriate filter for the excitation wavelength being used. The aperture should be set to give sufficient depth of field to the area being recorded. Again, the long shutter speed and painting with light technique should be used, so that the whole area is properly exposed and not just the area of interest.

Photograph B in the example above was photographed on a Nikon D700 at 400ISO, with a 60 mm lens with an exposure of f11 for 30 s.

8.3   Inks

When I first started in forensic photography, the only work relating to ink we were ever asked to conduct, was the examination of altered documents using infrared reflection and infrared fluorescence. Although this is still a valuable technique, it has over time diminished in use due to the increase in electronic transactions and communications, which has reduced the number of physical documents being used.

However, a new avenue of work has unexpectedly appeared when we first started using the 532-nm laser instead of a filtered light source at scenes. It was noticed that we often found erased, removed or over-painted children's scribbles or writing on walls and doors. The relevance of these observations was often considered interesting, but not necessarily of forensic value. However, this viewpoint quickly changed after one particular domestic violence murder scene. A male suspect had been arrested on scene after his wife was found stabbed to death; he claimed that any injuries inflicted on his wife were in self-defense. During a subsequent search of the scene by officers, small amounts of pencil writing had been found on the wall. Thinking it may be of some potential interest we were asked to photograph it. Hardly a taxing task we thought; however, on attending the scene the writing proved to be very faint on dark, dirty, emulsion wallpaper and although readable, it wasn't particularly easy to distinguish. We immediately thought of using long wave UV to enhance the pencil or wallpaper but to no avail. However, when we tried the 532-nm laser we had a surprise. Although the pencil writing was more visible, the walls were now covered in writing with letters 3–4 inches high, saying how his wife was a cheat, how he hated her and how he would kill her. Over 30 such areas were discovered throughout the flat. Each area, although faint, was clearly legible but appeared to have been washed in an attempt to remove it, as the letters appeared soft with smudged edging. They had also then been over-painted using thin emulsion type paint (Figure 8.4). Although the words and text revealed during fluorescence examination could have just been written down, it would not have conveyed the impact that a set of images did, showing the walls covered in hidden writing. From a forensic point of view, the production of the photographs cast doubt on the defendant's alibi of self-defense and at trial he pleaded diminished responsibility, but was eventually found guilty of murder.

The second example is similar to the above; however, in this case a suspect was arrested for multiple murders around the St Pancras area of London. On his arrest his flat was searched and half a torso was found in his bedroom. When the rest of flat was treated with luminol in the search for blood, it was clear that there had been a lot of previous activity. When a light source search was carried out for latent finger marks to ascertain who else might have been there, in terms of victims or other suspects, a small area of erased writing was found, as in the above case. In this case, however, it was almost illegible even under the laser. As is standard practice we then repeated the search area using a tunable light source through the spectrum, starting at UV finishing at IR. To assist with the viewing of IR, a video camera with an IR viewing mode was used and this time the area showed a girl's name. The walls of the flat were then speculatively searched and videoed (as required) using IR and another four or five names were found. These names subsequently turned out to be the names of previous victims.

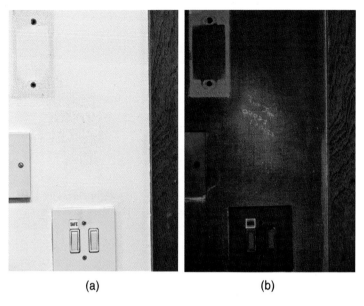

(a)   (b)

Figure 8.4   A section of wall under (a) white light illumination; (b) under the laser at 532 nm. It is important to note that the writing did not fluoresce under any other wavelength, due to the autofluorescent nature of the paint used.

There is also a third area of work with inks that is often overlooked, that of writing on the skin. At first thought it may seem to have little forensic value; after all, the person can usually tell you what is, or was, there. But in the following two casework examples, we can see the technique used to different ends. The first is generic in that many people write things on their hands, for example a registration of a strange car parked in the street. But what happens when a few days later it turns out that the car had been used in criminal activity? When the witness comes forward, the writing has been long washed off, or has it?

After extensive testing, we have found that using the 532-nm laser will retrieve erased writing up to ten days later, depending on the colour of the ink used (Figure 8.5). For example, our tests showed that if standard Metropolitan Police blue biro ink is used, then it was still legible around two days later under the laser. If black ink was used than it was still legible after four days, and if red ink was used it was still visible on our test subject up to ten days later. Although the time frames for persistence of fluorescence varied between different manufacturers of inks, fluorescence from most types of ballpoint pen ink and marker pens was legible after a number of days. Even when we deliberately tried to remove it using a nailbrush and soap, residual amounts of the ink were left on the skin.

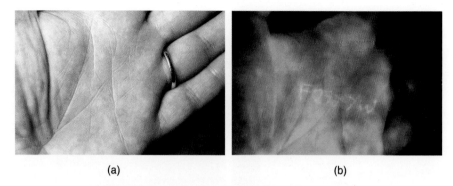

(a)   (b)

Figure 8.5   An example of erased ink on skin. (a) We can see the reference shot of my hand, 48 hours after the application of blue ink on the palm. Note that normal everyday washing has removed all visible traces of the ink. (b) Shows the same area under the green line 532-nm laser.

The second example is of a young girl who was approached at a bus stop by a teenage boy. After unsuccessfully trying to chat her up, he wrote his telephone number on her arm using a marker pen in the hope she would change her mind. Two days later the girl was walking home and claimed she was pulled into the alley and sexually assaulted. During the interview she described the boy and told the officers about the writing on her arm, which she had now washed off. We were asked to examine and if possible photograph her arm in the hope that some of the name or number could be retrieved. This was done using the 532-nm laser and clearly showed a boy's name and telephone number.

A number of days later we were contacted by the officer dealing with the case to be told that the number and name were correct. But the boy had a legitimate alibi and could not have carried out the attack at the time. It subsequently turned out, in a further interview, that the girl had made the whole story up and was attention seeking. She was subsequently charged with wasting police time.

Although the above cases do not necessarily solely rely on the use of forensic photography, it does highlight the importance of having an understanding of light and that each case must be treated in a bespoke fashion to ensure that the maximum forensic information is gathered.

The photography of inks on skin can be conducted as you would any other fluorescent mark; however, this is one of the few occasions when I would up the ISO to reduce the exposure of the skin to the laser beam. Although exposing the skin to the laser beam is not intrinsically dangerous if used correctly, it is always wise to reduce exposure to as little as possible, and the eyes of the subject should always be protected during such work.

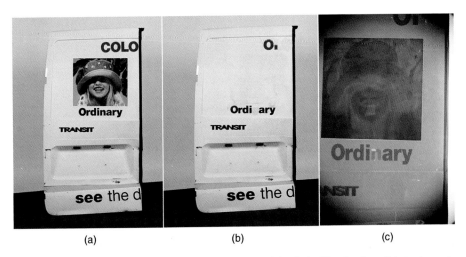

(a)   (b)   (c)

Figure 8.6   A van door with a sign on it. (a) Under white light illumination. (b) Again under white light illumination but with the signage removed. (c) The same area under UV light. Although you may think that you would only see a black square where the girl's face was, you can actually see the difference of where the stencil's colour has let through the light at different rates. Also note the returning 'n' in 'ordinary'.

8.4 Sign writing

It would seem logical that if we can detect erased inks, we may be able to detect traces of printing or other types of damage on different surfaces. For example, let us suppose that an eyewitness has seen a suspect driving away from a scene, in a white van with 'Fred Blogs the Butcher' written down the side. But when arrested the vehicle appears to have had a re-spray and is now green, or has had the sign writing removed or altered in some other way. At first glance you may think that there is little that can be done from a photographic point of view to assist the investigation, but this is not so. Paints, and in particular car paints, are designed to viewed with daylight. If we view the vehicle in a darkened room using UV at 365 nm we will be able to see through the paint to the original layers below. The original sign writing will show up a like shadow (Figure 8.6). This is due to two main factors: the degradation to paintwork caused by ultraviolet light from the sun, and polymer transfer between the vinyl stencils and the paintwork. In-house testing has shown that if a door panel with a stencil on the surface is exposed to ultraviolet light for a period equivalent to as little as twelve hours daylight exposure, then the pattern from the stencil will still be visible on the paintwork once it has been removed when viewed under ultraviolet light. It is worth noting that sometimes it is possible to see almost visible signs of removed sign writing in daylight along the sides of vehicles and this is usually a good indicator that UV will work.

(a)   (b)

Figure 8.7   A white van illuminated using UV, note that not only is the removed sign writing livery visible, but also that the side sliding door has at some stage been replaced. This technique would equally show up replaced mirrors, bumpers and bodywork repairs.

This technique also has the added benefit that any changes to the paintwork due to re-spraying or damage are easily seen (Figure 8.7). Although this is not an indicator of guilt, it does target areas to allow further investigations, such as the retrieval of paint samples, to take place. It is also possible to create the same effect using wavelengths up to and including infrared, with varying degrees of effect. It is also possible to use reflected UV in the same way and this, in the past, has allowed us to visualise and record two different layers of sign writing on the same vehicle.

To undertake photography of this type you will need a room that can be completely blacked out. Experience has taught us that even small amount of light can reduce the contrast in the finished resultant photograph. We are fortunate that our vehicle examination unit has a garage large enough to take a mid-sized van such as a security truck. Depending on the size of the area to be photographed, you may need one or two UV lights. For large vehicles I will use a UV spot and a flood lamp. The camera needs to be mounted on a tripod and the lens fitted with a long band pass filter with a transmission cut-on around 440 nm. This will have a number of effects:

(a)   Removing the slight violet cast given off by the Labino lights.
(b)   Increasing the contrast within the mark.
(c)   Ensuring that the image is now within the normal sensitivity range of the sensor.

An aperture of f5.6 or f8 is appropriate, as we are generally photographing a reasonably flat surface such as a car door. Again, there is a temptation to increase the ISO to make the camera more sensitive to the light; however, this can be counterproductive and can lead to increased noise. It can also have the disconcerting effect of making the area of interest float in space, as the background does not have time to be exposed properly. It is better to use a lower ISO of around 400 and a longer shutter speed, this allows you time to paint the area with light ensuring an even exposure. Depending on the size of the area to be covered, the contrast of the mark and the background colour, an exposure of between thirty seconds and two minutes is quite normal.

As mentioned above, if the area to be covered is large, than consideration should be given to using two UV lights. If possible I use a spot lamp to highlight the area of interest and a colleague will use the flood to cover the general area and give background shape and context. The longest exposure I have used was half an hour using Ilford technical PAN film rated at 100ASA, when photographing the side of an articulated lorry.

8.5 The detection of blood

As we have already discussed in a previous chapter, blood does not in normal situations fluoresce, and in fact absorbs over several important wavelength ranges. These include long wave ultraviolet, in the deep blue region around 445 nm and in the green region around 550nm, the strong absorption turning it very dark red or black. Although we can use this phenomenon to enhance marks, we can equally use it to find blood in the first place; this is a particularly useful technique when you are looking for blood on dark painted varnished wooden surfaces or when the surface colour is similar to blood (see Figures 7.43 and 7.44 in Chapter 7). It can also be used to find blood that might have been previously painted over.

If you are looking at painted surfaces, then you can also try using the blue or green wavelengths of a tunable light source or laser (Figure 8.8). Goggles are generally not used, as we are reliant on the blood absorbing the colour of the light used to search with and not a fluorescent result. It is therefore important to turn the power down on the ALS you are using so it is comfortable for a visual illumination.

If you are searching varnished surfaces doors and floors and so on, then long wave UV is a good starting point. See Figures 7.43 and 7.44 for an example where you can see the techniques used on a shoe mark.

Using long wave UV and deep blue wavelengths to induce fluorescence can also be a useful tool to find signs of possible clean up of blood at scenes, when chemicals such as luminol [1] (see below) are not suitable. Experience has shown us that when hard surface areas, such as a floor or kitchen units, have been washed or wiped down to remove blood, many types of cleaner can leave a fluorescent residue behind.

On other surfaces, such as walls that have been painted with a water-based paint such as emulsion, the application of cleaning liquids or water alone in combination with the rubbing action during cleaning, may remove a slight amount of surface colorant (Figure 8.9). When illuminated with UV or other lights, these cleaned areas absorb the light differently and this difference is

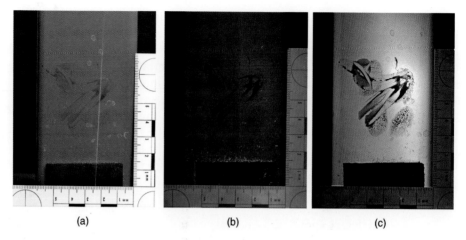

(a)   (b)   (c)

Figure 8.8   Blood on red metal tape dispenser. (a) Photographed using white light. (b) Photographed using UV. (c) Extraction of blue channel and green channels only, then converted to greyscale using Adobe Photoshop.

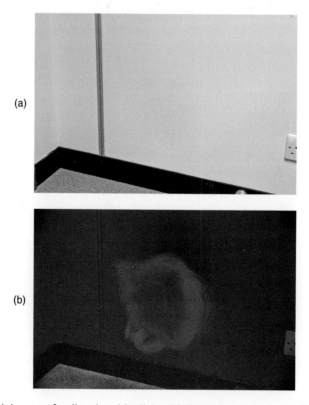

Figure 8.9   (a) An area of wall under white light. (b) The same area under UV illumination. The darker handprint in the middle is my original blood mark and the fluorescent surrounding region shows the area that I have cleaned with bleach and water.

exaggerated and becomes noticeable. Although this use of the lights is not a presumptive test for blood, it does allow the areas to be targeted with KM[2] or hemasticks.[3]

8.6 Luminol

For those of you unfamiliar with luminol, it is a chemical that exhibits chemi-luminescence when it reacts with the iron found in hemoglobin. For forensic purposes, it is sprayed in a fine mist onto the surface to be examined and when it comes into contact with blood it produces a pale blue glow. The use of lumi-nol allows the investigating scientist to detect blood that is no longer visible by any other means, whether this is the site of clean up or a blood trail leading away. The longest trail I have seen images of was over a half a kilometre long leading to a palm print in blood on a metal railing.

For the purposes of this book I will be looking at the photography of lumi-nol, although within the forensic community there is an ongoing debate in regards to its suitability against other products, such as 'Bluestar', which utilise the same fundamental reaction but contain other chemicals in the formula-tion to increase the intensity of chemiluminescence.[4] Indeed Bluestar has a reported optical chemiluminescence nine times stronger than luminol, but this has to weighed against our own findings within the Metropolitan Police that it not as sensitive and only has a detection rate to blood dilutions of 1:10 000, compared to 1:300 000 for luminol [2][2]. As an aside, from our own in-house tests, we have not found this lack of chemiluminescence in the luminol to be any issue with regard to photography.

Before we look at photography, we should give some consideration to the ambient illumination required to achieve the optimum results. All windows and doors must be blacked out with light-tight material, including the door edges. We have found that even the small neon illuminators in some plugs and electrical equipment can cause problems during a long photographic expo-sure, so these should also be covered or switched off. There is also another issue which people don't give much thought to, that is the dark adaption of the human eye. This varies from person to person, but in my case to fully adjust to the adaptation levels required to see the faintest luminol response, takes around 11 minutes. It is important to note that this dark adaption period should be used whenever latent evidence is being searched for, not just for

---

[2] The Kastle-Mayer (KM) test is a presumptive test for blood. The chemical indicator phenolph-thalein is used to detect the presence of haemoglobin, in the presence of blood. If positive, it gives a bright pink response.

[3] Hemastix is an alternative presumptive test for blood detecting peroxide-like activity of hemoglobin in a substance.

[4] Bluestar is a latent bloodstain reagent. It produces a chemiluminescent reaction when it comes into contact with haemoglobin.

luminol but also finger and shoemarks. The camera, of course, does not require acclimatisation time as it has far greater sensitivity that the eye, but if you can't see a faint response, you may not position the camera to photograph it.

There are a number of ways to work at a scene. One is to photograph every room to be examined and then apply the luminol, but we have found this to be time consuming if a negative result is found. For practical purposes we work the other way round; an area is lightly sprayed, if it produces a negative result no photographs are taken, however if a positive result is found we prepare for photography (Figure 8.10). Although the technique is not suitable for finger mark enhancement as it is too liquid and causes diffusion of the fine ridge detail present, on certain surfaces like carpets it is often used to find latent shoe marks. Here, only the smallest deposit of blood is required to create a reaction. This means it is very easy to contaminate a scene and hence the reason why stepping plates must be used until the floor has been treated with luminol (Figure 8.11).

For the photography, I would suggest the use of a sturdy tripod. I tend not to use the lightweight carbon fibre type in London buildings, as I have found they can be prone to vibration from passing traffic. You will then need to frame up the area of interest in the viewfinder based on the regions you have seen reacting during the initial light spray.

There are also a number choices in the way in which we actually take the photograph, and this will be dependent on the protocols within your particular force or the scientists you are working with, but they are:

(a) **Long exposure followed by flash**. In this technique the camera shutter is opened, and the area is sprayed with luminol. Once the correct exposure has been reached, a flash is fired to illuminate the scene causing the image to double expose. The result should be the correctly lit scene with the luminol visible. Although this is the easiest technique, we have found that any overexposure from the flash will quench out faint luminol reactions and therefore this technique is generally not used.

(b) **HDR**. In this technique a number of images are taken during the spraying of the luminol, plus a reference image captured under normal lighting. These images are then combined either by processing in camera (if your camera has the capability) or by combining the images through third-party HDR software at the post-production stage. Combining all the exposures allows the faintest reaction to be seen, it also reduces the noise content of the image.

(c) **Separate luminol and control exposures**. In this case two exposures are taken, one to act the reference image, which is exposed with flash or ambient lighting, the other is an open shutter exposure whilst the luminol is sprayed. During post-production these two images are combined using Photoshop layers, with the fill opacity reduced, until both the luminol and the control image are visible.

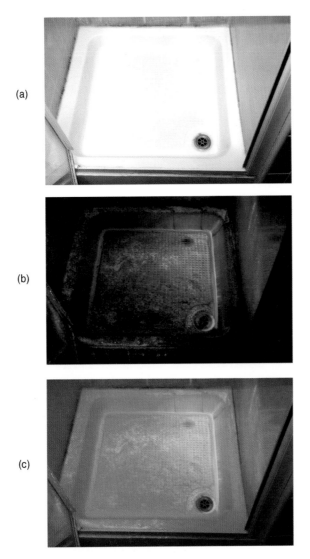

Figure 8.10 A bloodstained shower cubical (a) under white light illumination; (b) after the application of luminol, exposed for f8 for 30 s at 400ISO; (c) a Photoshop blended layer image of photographs (a) and (b) together.

Both options b and c are intrinsically the same and produce good results. They also have the added advantage that the luminol and reference images can be viewed independently. This can be particularly useful for allowing defence examination of results.

Guidance for the actual exposure time is difficult to give, as we will leave the camera open for as long as required. By that I mean that the scientist will spray

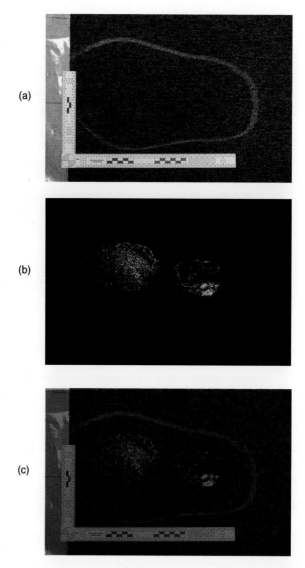

Figure 8.11   A carpet tile. (a) control image; (b) luminol image; (c) overlay of both images together.

and mark areas of interest as they go, so that the image is built up over time. In the past, I have photographed blood trails down a hall from an elevated position on the stairs where the exposure time was at least 10 minutes.

It is important to note that if the scientist, or whoever is spraying, uses clear spray bottles, they should be covered in black tape or other light tight material to stop the bottle 'ghosting' during the exposure. This is because the luminol gives off a very faint chemiluminescence from a reaction as it is shaken and although it is difficult for the eye to detect it, the more sensitive sensor in the camera has no problem.

8.7 Other uses of Infrared (IR)

In previous chapters, we have looked at the use of IR for the possible enhancement of injuries and above we looked at the detection of differences in inks. However, there are few less obvious uses where IR can be used to our forensic advantage.

One is IR on clothing: this technique is applicable in two situations GSR (Gun Shot Residue) and blood distribution. The other is for the mechanical fit of clothing that might have been previously identified on CCTV under IR illumination.

GSR is principally composed of burnt and unburnt particles of the propellant, which can travel distances of 1.5 m or further dependent on the firearm used. The patterns left on clothing or skin can be a useful indicator of the distance to the target from the shooter, or the type of weapon and ammunition used (Figure 8.12).

Both of the above techniques rely on the pigments in the clothing being transparent to IR and the underlying fabric reflecting it so that the clothing appears white. A number of different IR filters may need to be tried until the desired effect is obtained. In some cases the garment may absorb the IR, obscuring the GSR or blood, so other techniques such as fluorescence will need to be used.

As with GSR, it is also possible to use this technique to visualise blood on a garment; this can be useful to a scientist or expert when undertaking blood pattern analysis. It is important to note, however, that there is a difference in IR absorption and reflection between oxygenated and deoxygenated blood. This is because hemoglobin's reflection of red light increases as the number of oxygen molecules bound to it increase. For our purpose that means that there are two main absorption wavelengths: around 660 nm (deep red) for oxygenated blood and 940 nm for deoxygenated blood (Figure 8.13). This is a well-documented principle and is used in the design of blood oxygen saturation monitoring devices [3, 4].

Although the areas to be photographed are generally known, that is faint spots of blood are visible to the eye, it is possible, dependent on the garment, to carry out a non-destructive speculative search using an IR sensitive video camera. Again, for the best results a suitable long pass IR filter should be fitted to the camera. In house testing has shown that this is an excellent technique allowing a T shirt to be searched in less than a minute, using the IR video camera linked to a TV monitor. As compared to a visual search using a low powered microscope that may take 3 hours plus.

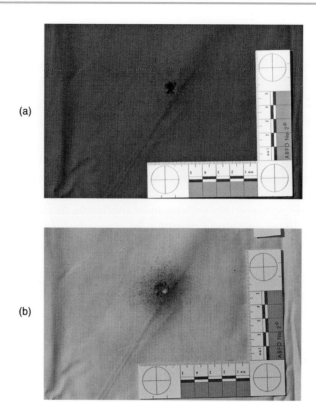

Figure 8.12 The visual damage caused by a self loaded 9 mm round, fired at a distance of around 20 cm. (a) Shows the reference photograph under white light. (b) Shows the same area shot under IR, here the particles of burnt and unburnt propellant are clearly visible. Photography was carried out using an adapted Nikon D70 fitted with a 730-nm long pass filter. The illumination used was the Bowens studio flash modeling light, fitted with a soft box, exposure f11 at 1/30th at 400 ISO.

8.7.1 Vein patterns

Whilst we are looking at the absorption and reflection properties of blood, it is worth commenting on an unusual case where this phenomenon was fully exploited and used. Not to find blood on clothing, but to identify a suspect by their vein pattern [5] (Figure 8.14).

In this particular case, the suspect had been covertly videoed by his victim, who he was allegedly sexually abusing. The victim had set the camera to 'night mode', using its own small IR led illumination, and then hidden it in a pile of washing opposite her bed. This unfortunately meant that it had a limited field of view at around waist level. When the suspect is seen entering the field of view he is illuminated by the IR LEDs, wearing a pair of cotton shorts. As he

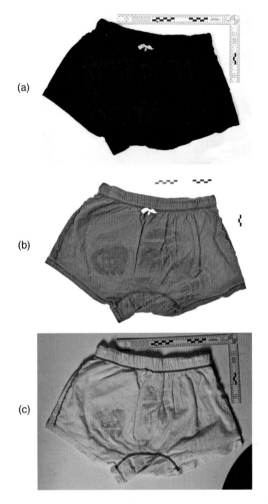

Figure 8.13   (a) Reference image of a pair of underpants exposed at f8, $^1/_4$ second 200 ISO. (b) Shows the above overexposed by three stops, at f8 2 s 200 ISO with the blue channel only selected and enhanced using highlight shadow command in Adobe CS5. Note how the shoe mark is now clearly visible but lacks detail within the minutia of the mark. (c) Shows the above using IR, illuminated with the Bowens studio flash set to modelling light and fitted with a soft box. Exposure was with an adapted Nikon D70, using a 700-nm long pass filter fitted to the lens and exposed at f5.6 at 1/20th second at 600 ISO. Note how the detail in the toe area is now clear and could be used for identification.

leans over the bed the vein patterns on the rear of his legs are clearly visible. Also visible in frame for around 1.5 s is his right arm, which shall become crucial to the investigation later on.

Thinking that it might be possible to identify the suspect by comparing the vein patterns, the officer contacted Derek Tremain, a Forensic

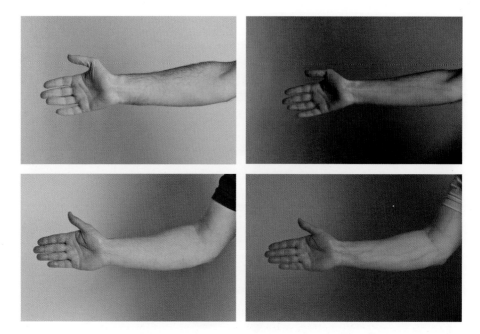

Figure 8.14   The effect of IR on an arm. Exposure was with an adapted Nikon D70, using a 700 nm long pass filter fitted to the lens and illuminated with a Redhead studio light. Exposed at f8 for 1/20th s at 400 ISO.

Medical imaging expert,[5] and after consultation had the suspect's legs and arms photographed. Unfortunately, they did not listen to the advice and guidance and photographed under standard flash illumination. As white light does not penetrate the skin to any depth, the vein patterns on the legs were not visible. However, the ones on the arm which are a lot closer to the surface could be just made out. This is important, as the defence would not let us re-photograph the legs under IR, arguing that it was not a suitable technique and he had already agreed to the previous photography and that vein patterns were not unique enough to allow identification.

Using the original video, I was able to extract a still frame showing the arm, this was then exported into Photoshop. This allowed some enhancements to be made to contrast, brightness and so on, enhancing the vein pattern. Working with Professor Sue Black,[6] and Derek Tremain, who are two of the country's leading experts in their fields, we were able over a number of days at court to show:

(a)   Vein patterns are as individual as a fingerprint.
(b)   That it is possible to use IR for the purposes of identification of an individual.

---

[5] Derek Tremain, Forensic Image Services: www.forensic-image.co.uk.
[6] Professor Sue Black, Professor of Anatomy and Forensic Anthropology, University of Dundee.

This was based on published research [6], supported by in-house research carried out in form of videoing 50 + volunteers arms for their vein patterns.

As far as I am aware this is the first time that the identification of an individual has been accepted in a UK court through the comparison of vein patterns.

8.7.2 Clothing

In normal situations, the photography of suspect clothing is a simple matter of placing the items on a manikin and photographing them as accurately as possible. There is a particular situation when this is not applicable and indeed could be misleading. This is when the clothing has been seen on CCTV lit by IR illumination.

For example, I recently was involved in a case where a man had been shot dead on the floor of a nightclub, within view of a CCTV camera. A suspect had been arrested and admitted being at the club, but denied any knowledge of being involved. This was because the CCTV showed a man dressed in a white coat crossing the dance floor and pulling out a gun, whilst the defendant had a black coat. Indeed, in other CCTV footage from the car park and reception area, the defendant could clearly be seen in a black coat. Just before trial, the defence team argued that because the CCTV showed a man in white coat, not black one, it was a case of mistaken identity.

I was then asked to look at both the CCTV and coat. On viewing the CCTV footage it was immediately clear that the CCTV was illuminated using IR. Knowing this, I replicated this IR illumination in the studio and re-photographed at the coat at the same angle it appeared in the CCTV images. It was immediately obvious that the coat changed from black to white when recorded under IR illumination and that they were in fact one and the same. At trial, the defendant was subsequently found guilty of murder (Figure 8.15).

This example raised another issue, which was not readily appreciated at the time but has been invaluable in subsequent cases in these types of circumstances. Officers often refer to the CCTV footage when submitting clothing for forensic testing. If there is any chance that IR illumination has been used, the clothing must be viewed in the same way. In one particular case, white training shoes seen in CCTV footage had been submitted to the lab. In fact, when they were viewed in normal light, they were dark green. This mistake not only cost valuable investigating time, but more importantly, in this day and age, money (Figure 8.16).

We have seen in other chapters and above that IR can be a useful, if a little underused, technique in the recovery of forensic evidence. There is one more use I would just like to touch upon and that is for burnt or heat damaged documents.

There are number of occasions over the years when we have been asked to retrieve writing on documents that have suffered fire damage. Although

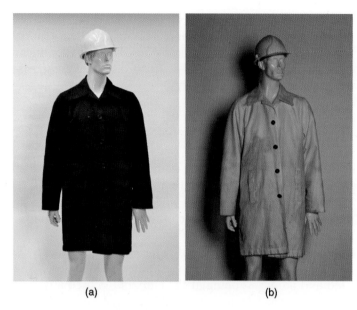

(a)   (b)

Figure 8.15   An example of how a garment can change colour depending on its reflectivity to IR light. (a) Shows a black coat under controlled studio lighting. (b) Shows the same coat under infrared photographed using a 700–900 band pass filter.

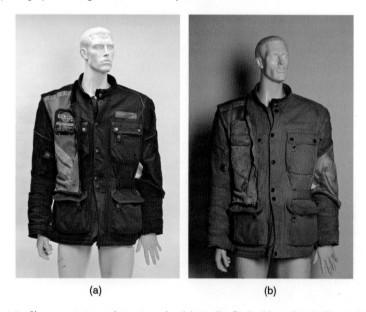

(a)   (b)

Figure 8.16   Shows a motorcycle coat under (a) studio flash (b) under IR illumination. Note how, under the IR, the distinctive bright orange reflective strip has disappeared, making it look like a different coat. Bowens studio flash modeling lights, fitted with a soft box, provided the IR illumination. Photographed with the adapted Nikon D70 fitted with an 840-nm long band pass filter and the exposure was f8 at 1/30th s at 400 ISO.

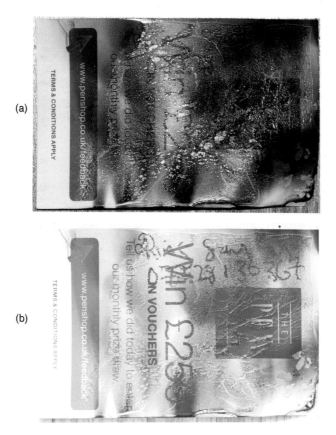

Figure 8.17 Shows a heat-damage document under (a) flash illumination using a Nikon D800; (b) under daylight illumination using an unfiltered IR adapted Nikon D70. Note that although some of the telephone number is visible in 'A', the six end digits are illegible.

the IR technique is the same as for any other case, the challenge is around handling the documents, which are usually incredibly fragile (Figure 8.17).

For photography I have again found that the studio flash modelling lights are very good, but any soft, diffuse IR-rich light source will suffice. Again you may have to test a number of filters until the desired effect is recorded. It is also possible to use this technique with faded writing, but that is dependent on the type of ink and paper used. With paper items such as faded till receipts, it is often possible to use the laser at 532 nm or UV as described in the above paragraphs.

It should be noted that for all IR casework the illumination should be as soft and even as possible. Harsh light sources, such as flash, should be avoided unless they are bounced or diffused as it is very easy to overexpose faint areas of interest. Unusually, in Figure 8.17, no band pass filter was placed in front of the lens meaning a broad band of IR light was received by the sensor. Helpfully, I have also found that although our DSLR has been adapted for

IR work, the exposure meter is still generally accurately to within a half stop for most subjects.

Throughout the book we have focused on using imaging to support police type forensic investigations. In this last section I would like to look at an associated field where forensic clues as to an item's true identity is equally important: that of Arts and Antiques.

In the past 25 years I have been involved in many cases were the application of forensic imaging has been crucial in finding the truth. This has ranged from paintings that had been changed or over painted to look like lesser pieces, to 3000 year old Egyptian relics adapted to look like copies (Figure 8.18). In essence all the techniques talked about throughout the book are applicable, provided one has the time and effort to apply them.

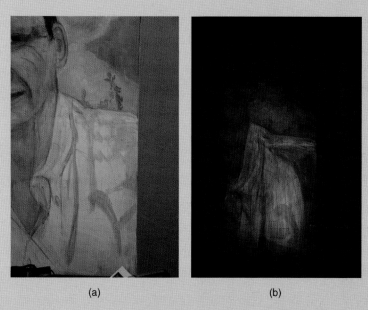

(a)   (b)

Figure 8.18   An example of over-painting, in the control shot (a) nothing is visible in, but in (b) we can see the shoulder has been repainted. Under normal circumstances IR or even x-rays might be used, but unusually this was found using the Crimescope at around 460 nm.

The case I would like to look at in more depth as an example is that of a Tudor broadsheet, circa 1555, a type of newspaper of the day. In this case there was no police involvement, this was purely a historical investigation being led by Anne Dillon with a fascinating outcome.[7]

---

[7] Anne Dillon is a member of the Lucy Cavendish College, Cambridge.

The black and white paper broadsheet depicts the 'The Martyrdom of the Carthusian Fathers' [7]. It was printed in 1555 from an engraving and its dimensions were 42.7 × 52.4 cm.

Anne was investigating the possible origins of the document, believing that it may have stronger historical significance then had been previously assumed. If it was of historical significance, as suspected, then it was believed that it should contain a watermark of the paper manufacturer, as was the norm of the time. It was also known that in normal circumstances any such mark should be near the centre of the sheet. Once unwrapped, the document was examined visually using white light and laid on a light box to allow transillumination, producing a negative result. The same process was then carried out under UV, 532-nm laser and IR. Under UV a very faint unusual mark could be seen just off centre, but unfortunately it was too faint to record with any clarity. At some stage in the past few hundred years the document had been stuck to a thin backing material, which was in places separating from the paper. The museum's conservator made a decision that the backing could be carefully peeled away from this area. Although when top lit the mark did not really improve, when laid again onto the light box and transilluminated it became clearer but it was still difficult to see the details. However, when it was laid out on a sheet of glass and transilluminated with UV and the laser, the mark became clearly distinguished from the background (Figure 8.19).

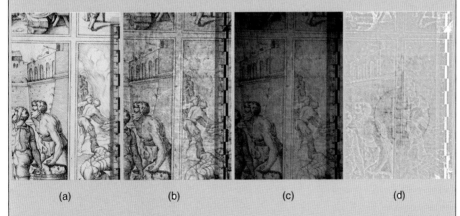

(a)   (b)   (c)   (d)

Figure 8.19   The area of interest on the manuscript. (a) The reference image, under white light. (b) The backlit image photographed on a light box. (c) A UV backlit image. (d) Shows (c) converted to a greyscale and reverse coloured. Image courtesy of the Metropolitan Police, first published in Dillon, *Michaelangelo and the English Martyrs*, Ashgate Press, 2012.

A number of photographs were taken with exposure times between a $1/4$ s to 5 s at f8 on 400ISO (dependent on light source).

Post-production was carried out within Photoshop using the raw files, allowing me to use the full range of the sensor to produce a variety of different versions of the image.

From a forensic point of view, we have successfully revealed something that had not been seen in over 450 years. But more importantly for all those concerned in the research, this proved that the Fabriano paper mills produced the paper in 1532, probably for a private commission. This paper, in turn, was thought to have been supplied to the workshop of a local Italian artist, who then produced the broadsheet: one Michelangelo di Lodovico Buonarroti Simoni.

If you wish to see further images or want to read the whole story then *Michelangelo and the English Martyrs* by Ann Dillon is available from Ashgate Press, ISBN 97807546675.

The use of alternative light sources for the enhancement of latent evidence is often overlooked or misunderstood. I have heard many operators say: 'Oh yes I used an alternative light source but it didn't work and was a waste of time'; they then restrict their use to purely chemically treated marks. I believe this attitude shows a lack of understanding and ignorance around their use and is denying the investigating officer and subsequent investigation a whole raft of proactive forensic photography, as exampled above.

I am also often asked: what ALS should I buy? I am sorry to say that the answer will depend on the casework you are involved in and the budget you have to spare. From my 20 plus years of experience, I would always advocate that the more powerful the device is and the narrower the excitation wavelength, the better the result you can expect to achieve.

I am often also asked, could I publish a list or guidance as to which light source to use on what surface? Unfortunately this is not practical, we have found that even two supermarket bags from different checkouts although looking identical, actually respond completely differently when placed under ALS, often turning opposite colours depending on the polymers used for their production.

Therefore the only guidance is, as I have said before, 'just because we can't see it, doesn't mean it's not there'. It's just a case of finding it.

References

(1) Adair, T. W. Experimental detection of blood under painted surfaces. Paper presented at the I.A.B.P.A. conference, 2006 http://www.iabpa.org/uploads/files/iabpa%20publications/March%202006%20News.pdf

(2) Larkin, T. The Sensitivity of Luminol and Bluestar™ and the use of a thickened luminol solution on non-porous surfaces. Paper presented at the I.A.B.P.A.

conference 2006 http://www.iabpa.org/uploads/files/iabpa%20publications/March%202006%20News.pdf

(3) Jawahar, Y. Design of an infrared based blood oxygen saturation and heart rate monitoring device. Electrical and Biomedical Engineering Project Report (4BI6), Department of Electrical and Computer Engineering, McMaster University Hamilton, Ontario, Canada http://digitalcommons.mcmaster.ca/cgi/viewcontent.cgi?article=1004&context=ee4bi6&sei

(4) Fuksis, R. Greitans, M., Nikisins, O. and Pudzs, M. Infrared Imaging System for Analysis of Blood Vessel Structure. Institute of Electronics and Computer Science, 2010. No1(97), Riga, Latvia http://www.ee.ktu.lt/journal/2010/1/09_ISSN_1392-1215_Infrared

(5) Kono, M., Ueki, H. and Shin-ichiro Umemura S.-I. Near-Infrared Finger Vein Patterns for Personal Identification. *Applied Optics* 2002 41(35): 7429–36 http://dx.doi.org/10.1364/AO.41.007429.

(6) Yi-Bo Zhang1, Qin Li2, Jane You2, and Prabir Bhattacharya1 Palm Vein Extraction and Matching for Personal Authentication. Paper presented at Advances in Visual Information Systems, 9th International Conference, VISUAL 2007 Shanghai, China, June 28–29, 2007 http://bcc.hitsz.edu.cn/homepage/resource/DigitalImageProcessing/DIP2/Palm%20Vein%20Extraction%20and%20Matching%20for%20Personal%20Authentication%20.pdf

(7) 'The Martyrdom of the Carthusian Fathers' by kind permission City of London, London Metropolitan Archives, SC/GL/PR/F1/CHA. Extracted from Dillon, A. *Michelangelo and the English Martyrs* ISBN 9780754664475 Farnham: Ashgate, 2012.

9
Specialist Equipment and Techniques

In the previous chapters, we have used a standard DSLR for the capture of our images. However, there are a number of applications and techniques in which the standard DSLR cannot be used and more bespoke equipment is required.

In this chapter I would like to look at the practical use of:

- Peripheral cameras.
- Object modelling
- Multi-spectral imaging camera
- High speed photography
- UVC photography.

9.1 Peripheral cameras

The photography of latent fingermarks on the curved surfaces of exhibits such tins and cups often offers an interesting photographic challenge. In the chapter on finger mark photography we looked at a number of options available to capture marks on these types of surfaces, such as multiple exposures or painting with light. Although these techniques work well on some surfaces, they have a number of drawbacks, especially when applied to a truly cylindrical surface. This is usually because the mark cannot be clearly seen in one exposure due to the diameter of the object, or because the mark cannot be acceptably captured in 'focus', using the effect of depth of field alone.

Peripheral photography allows the outer surface of a cylinder, such as a tin or cup, to be 'photographically' rolled flat. Indeed this technique was originally referred to as rollout photography, because of the final prints'

Forensic Photography: A Practitioner's Guide, First Edition. Nick Marsh.
© 2014 John Wiley & Sons, Ltd. Published 2014 by John Wiley & Sons, Ltd.

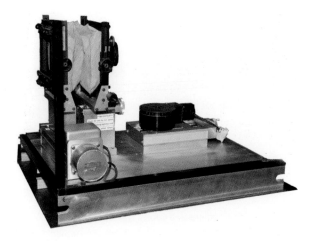

Figure 9.1   An original adapted 5 × 4 camera with mechanical slit.

appearance, or turntable photography, due to the fact that the object must be placed on a rotating turntable to allow its capture.

With the introduction of digital capture systems, the 'stitching' of multiple images together to produce a 'periphery type' image has become the norm in many forces. But the question is: does that make image stitching a forensically sound technique, when it comes to the photography of the minutia of a finger mark? I would argue that for this type of critical evidence, a continuous capture system is required. Peripheral cameras allow the outer face of a curved surface to be captured as one continuous image.

The original periphery photography was undertaken by placing the exhibit on a rotating turntable in front of a specially adapted 5 × 4 studio camera (Figure 9.1). In this camera, the dark slide has been adapted to have a mechanically driven slit, around 0.5 mm wide, which moves across the film plane during the exposure. (Using a narrow slit restricts the field of view to a limited amount of surface curvature.) As the turntable rotates, the slit moves in the opposite direction across the dark slide exposing the film, in effect 'unrolling' the exhibit.

In later 35-mm versions of the camera, the film was generally placed around a rotating drum, which again rotated in the opposite direction to the turntable. Both of these techniques allowed the capture of an image of the exterior surface in one seamless exposure.

Due to the demise of the readily accessible film supplies, and more importantly in-house film processing, these types of camera have faded from use. Unfortunately, there are very few true peripheral cameras in production at the present time. We have been lucky enough, though, to work closely with Seitz of Switzerland[1] and now have one of the first working Seitz Roundshot

---

[1] Seitz Phototechnik AG: http://www.roundshot.ch.

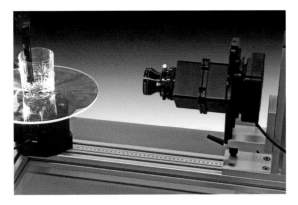

Figure 9.2   Here we can see the camera and turntable attached to the optical bench. As with all fingerprint photography, lighting is critical and here we see the mark being backlit through the glass.

D3 peripheral cameras in Europe. (This is a variant on their panoramic D3 camera.) (Figure 9.2) The camera uses 7500 pixels in a vertical scanner-type sensor array. This in effect gives it a restricted field of view, as with the original film versions that used a slit. As the vertical resolution of the scanner is fixed, the final size of the resultant image file is controlled by the diameter of the object. This means that on large diameter objects, files in excess of 2 gigabytes can be created.

As you can see, the camera is set on its own optical bench; this is important as the camera is initially focused by way of measurements, rather than optically. This means that before photography is undertaken, it is important to take some accurate measurements of both the diameter and the height of the object to be photographed. The camera can photograph objects with a diameter as small as 5 mm (see Figure 9.3) or as large as a car tyre.

The object is then positioned on the turntable either using the calibrated flat platform or using a special vice (used for small objects and used in Figure 9.3). These measurements are then entered into the software. The software in turn informs the operator of the distance from the lens to the sensor, to ensure the exhibit is captured at maximum resolution. This is achieved using the provided specialist macro tubes onto which the lens is mounted (see Figure 9.4).

The lens is set to an indicated focus point (Figure 9.5) and finally the whole camera is moved to a specified distance on the optical bench. Once these three measurements have been set, the camera should technically be in focus. This can be tested taking an exposure and watching the image appear 'live' on the computer screen, any minor adjustments to the focus can be done at this point by using the fine focus on the lens.

The camera has a built in exposure meter so it can work in automatic mode if required, once the operator has set the aperture. Alternatively, the camera can be manually set, allowing the operator to control the ISO, aperture and shutter speed. Importantly, it must be borne in mind that any changes to the

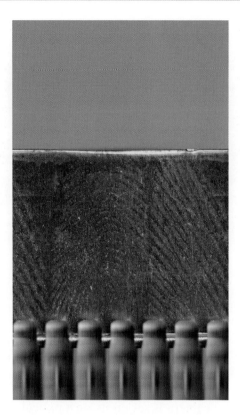

Figure 9.3 A 5-mm diameter .22 brass cartridge case. Normally these would not be pho-tographed for finger marks, due to the lack of attainable and usable marks. Here, however, we can see that with careful lighting, a latent fingerprint is visible. Note that the bottom part of the mark is covered with the teeth of the vice holding the exhibit in place. The vice is critical when working at macro levels and close working distances to ensure the exhibit is exactly centered. If this were a real case, the image would have been retaken. This time by turning the cartridge case upside down and placing it onto a small rod, which has a fractionally smaller diameter than the cartridge case, so that it snugly fits inside it. It is also approximately twice the length of the cartridge case, and this rod is then held secure in the vice. This technique was created due to the issues raised by this very image and now we have a selection of rods for a number of calibers. As an aside, longer rods can be used inside gun barrels, to ensure that they also rotate around their central point.

shutter speeds directly relate to the speed of rotation. Therefore, some thought must be given so as not to rotate the exhibit too quickly or too slowly, as this can cause movement issues, or excessively long exposures.

The captured 'DNG' raw files[2] can then edited in the Seitz proprietary raw processing software and can be downloaded into any format that is required.

---

[2] A 'DNG' (digital negative) file is an open raw image file format written by Adobe for digital pho-tography.

Figure 9.4 The 16 mm, 34 mm and 52 mm extension tubes.

The following examples are typical of the types of exhibit we are requested to deal with. Example one is a blue mug (Figure 9.6). We have a typical smooth surface, which is excellent for viewing specular marks. However, because of the curvature it is almost impossible to capture the marks without highlights, or even, for that matter, to examine the cup properly to ascertain if there was anything there in the first place.

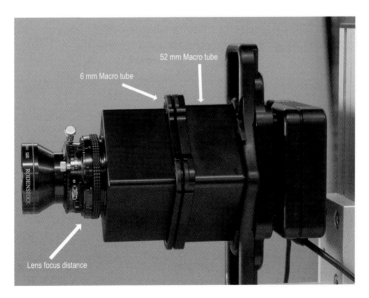

Figure 9.5 A 100-mm Rodenstock lens fitted to its own extension tube mount, attached to a 6 mm and 52 mm extension tube. The block on the right hand side attached by the Ethernet cable is the scanner back.

Figure 9.6 A blue mug that has been lit with the ball light, you can see that the reflection is limited both in width and in height and so is of no practical use in illuminating the mark.

Yet, if we position the lighting correctly, in this case using a fibre optic down the lens axis, by using the periphery camera to capture the image we can see that the ridge detail is clearly visible as a specular mark (Figure 9.7).

This type of photography also has another benefit, as it shows the position of the marks. That is to say, the distribution of the marks can be used to determine whether the object could have been held as a drinking vessel or possibly used as a weapon.

Example two shows a very faint finger mark on a correction fluid bottle. Here the mark has been in post-production within the Seitz software and converted to a greyscale image ready for a search on the UK fingerprint database (Figure 9.8).

Figure 9.7 This shows the result after post-production enhancement and conversion to a greyscale image.

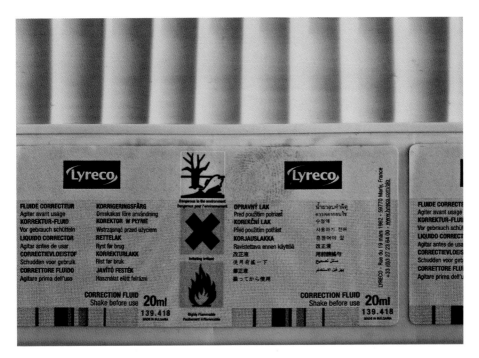

Figure 9.8   A finger mark on a correction fluid bottle.

Example three shows a Mont Blanc pen, here the diameter of the pen tapers to 8.8 and 8.6 mm. Figure 9.9 shows the colour version of the image whilst Figure 9.10 shows the image after post-production. In my experience I have not encountered another way of photographically recording the fingerprint on a surface such as this.

As with the photography of all fingerprints, the lighting is critical to ensure a clear result. In Figure 9.11 the glass is being lit from behind to increase the contrast in the mark, note however that a black pen has been placed inside the glass, directly in line with the sensor array of vertical pixels. This has two effects: one it creates the effect of dark field illumination behind the mark and two, it stops the logo and any reflected light reaching the sensor from the other side of the glass as it rotates.

If you would like to find out more about peripheral or rollout photography I recommend visiting Justin Kerr's website at FAMSI.[3] Although not directly forensically related, he demonstrates the use of a handmade periphery or roll out camera on ancient vases and pottery.

---

[3] Justin Kerr's FAMSI (Foundation for the Advancement of Mesoaamerican Studies http://www.famsi.org/research/kerr/rollout.html.

Figure 9.9   A Mont Blanc pen: colour version.

9.2   Object modelling

Although the Seitz offers a very high quality result, the end product is a flat rolled out, two-dimensional image. There is, however, increasing demand these days for exhibits to be represented in court in a more realistic and interactive way; the use of object movies allows this to be undertaken.

In its most basic form it requires the exhibit to be placed on a turntable, photographed and rotated. (The more photographs that are taken the smoother the rotation.) When played back, the object can then be rotated on screen for the court and any angle of rotation can be chosen and viewed.

Although this simple approach may work for a cup, what if you have a more complex shaped article, such as a shoe with blood on the uppers and sole? This

Figure 9.10 A Mont Blanc pen: the post-production image.

is where a more advanced capture is required; here the standard images are taken and then the camera is moved on an arc above the exhibit at an angle of around 25°, 45° and 75° degrees and the process is repeated. Finally a plan shot is taken and then a base shot by turning the exhibit upside down.

When all the images have been processed it is possible for the officer or court to view the object from any angle or direction.

It is possible to undertake the most basic image modelling using one angle of view, with nothing more complicated than a rotating platform on which to sit your exhibit. To create a more complicated complete 360° image requires some specialist equipment. Within the department we use the eme system (see Figure 9.12 and 9.13), which is a fully automated image capture system which

Figure 9.11 Here we see the view looking towards the exhibit from behind the camera. Note the simple insertion of a black pen held in a retort stand allows the light to reach the mark but provides a dark field for the photograph and stops the logo being exposed again once it rotates to the back of the glass.

Figure 9.12 The table, lighting and electronically controlled arm allowing a full 360-degree image of the object to be undertaken.

Figure 9.13   A fully interactive 360 example.

technically just requires the operator to position the exhibit centrally on the turntable and press go.

Although the above system can produce a 'SWF'[4] file automatically, we have found a more professional result is produced if we process the images through Object 2vr software, this allows us to add our own skins and functions.

9.3   Multi-spectral imaging camera

There are some occasions, when dealing with fingerprint evidence, when they present themselves on interfering or distracting backgrounds. This can be because the mark is a similar colour, or there is a repeating pattern. Here,

---

[4] A 'SWF' (Shockwave) file is an Adobe Flash file format used animating multimedia, vector graphics and action scripts.

Figure 9.14   Here we can see the camera fixed onto a copy set-up with the illumination being provided by Crimescope CS16.

traditional photographic techniques or post-production processes may fail to produce an acceptable image. For example, a ninhydrin mark on a bank note, where the colour of the mark is very similar to the colour of the substrate.

In these circumstances it might be possible to use a multi-spectral imaging camera to undertake the photography.

Within the department we use the Cri Nuance camera[5] (Figure 9.14), although other systems are available. The camera system was originally designed for medical applications, but it soon became apparent on investigation that it would lend itself nicely to a forensic one. Unlike a traditional camera, the system uses a 1.1 megapixel video sensor mounted behind a stack of LCD filters. These filters, when switched on and off, allow the camera to separate light into bandwidths as narrow as 10 nm wide, covering a range from 420 nm through to 720 nm. (Another version is available which goes into the infrared region of the spectrum.)

Although the camera was originally designed to fit a microscope or a c-mount video lens, we have adapted ours to take a standard Nikon 60-mm macro lens. This allows us to use a photographic quality lens and have greater

---

[5] Nuance camera from PerkinElmer Inc.: http://www.caliperls.com/products/microscopy-imaging-analysis/microscopy-imaging/.

Figure 9.15 Showing an area of multiple ink lines.

control over the aperture. For our purposes, the camera is securely fitted to a copy set-up, as it is important that all vibrations and movements are reduced.

It is also important to use a light source that has an illumination spectrum greater than the 420 to 750 nm range of the camera. Many do not, or have certain peak wavelengths, and this can cause problems with the extraction process in post-production.

Once the camera is set up with the exhibit, it is calibrated using its own software program. Once the exposure is started you will then take one photograph at each bandwidth and place them in a stack of images, called a 'cube'. This cube can then be analysed using the software provided.

This is not the same as photographing an item and then using software such as Photoshop or image pro plus to do the analyses. As in post-production, they can only analyse the image that has been captured, therefore any colour that appears is by default limited to the colour capture range of the image. Because the Nuance sees the image as a spectral response it can follow a defined colour of a particular spectral response as it passes through other colours, even if they are visibly similar, thus allowing its separation from all the colours around it.

If we look at Figure 9.15 we can just see that the area of interest in red has been covered with multiple lines of green and blue ink. Using the camera's own software it is possible to extract the ink colours from each other.

In Figure 9.16 we can see the end result after extraction through the software. Here we see the red ink after we have removed virtually all the traces of blue and green inks. Note, however, that it is not possible to remove all traces of black ink, as it generally contains traces of all the colours.

In the second example we have a green fingerprint on a £10 note (Figure 9.17). Because we have a repeating pattern, we could use techniques like 'FFT' Fast Fourier Transfer, but the technique is likely to remove the finger-mark as well as the background pattern. Figure 9.18 shows the area of the mark once captured and processed into 10 separate colours.

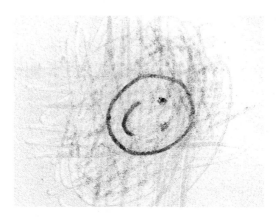

Figure 9.16   Showing Figure 9.15 after extraction.

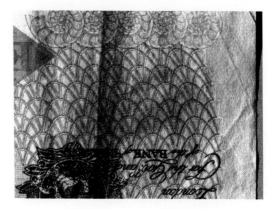

Figure 9.17   Here we can see the original control of the mark.

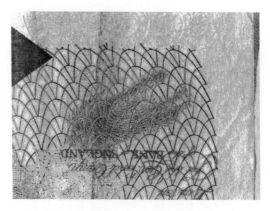

Figure 9.18   Here is the unmixed colour cube with each separate colour of the £10 note, now represented in one of 10 new colours.

Figure 9.19 Here we can see the final extraction and conversion to a 4.5 meg greyscale image. This is saved as a tiff file and can printed or imported into any other application, such as Photoshop, if required.

At this point it is possible to reassign colour values and remove or reassign the unwanted pinks and blues. (The choice of assigned colours is made by the operator in order to have an increased contrast between the mark and background.)

In Figure 9.19 we can see the final result after the extraction has taken place.

Note here that the selection of pure colours is critical, the system can select a single pixel of colour and any contamination by another colour will affect the result.

In the final example in Figure 9.20 we can see one of its more typical uses: that of a ninhydrin (nin) mark on a £20 note. Here the issue is that because notes are so frequently handled, many areas have sweat deposits and the nin develops all over the surface, not just on the fingermark, making photography

Figure 9.20 A nin mark on a £20 note, note how the nin stains all the background due to the constant handling.

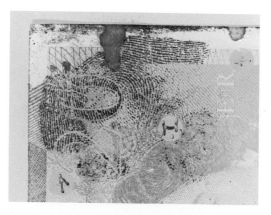

Figure 9.21 Here we can see the colour signal of the £20 note has been removed. Note that some interference is still visible, but compared to the original mark it has been greatly enhanced.

and extraction of colour spectra difficult. One of the advantages of the software is that it is possible to load a preset spectrum of colours. In this case we can preload the colours of a clean new untreated £20 note. Now, instead of trying to pick the colours we require, we can ask the software simply to extract all the colours that make up the ink spectrum of a £20 note. In effect, what is left should only be regions of the fingermark reacted with nin. See Figure 9.21.

9.4   High speed imaging

For us as forensic photographers, the use of high speed is limited mainly, but not exclusively, to one area of work: that of firearms. Here a few seconds can seem an eternity when capturing the discharge from a weapon, which can happen within a few thousandths of a second.

For example, we are sometimes asked for photographs which either show the gas discharge from a blank or converted weapon, (a single moment in time), or show a firing mechanism in action (continuous high speed footage). Both of these offer specific challenges and I would like to look at two possible solutions to these issues, one using conventional DSLR equipment, the other using a specialised high speed camera.

Let us deal with single moments in time first. In these situations we are asked to capture an action that happens too fast for the eye to see. For example, recording the muzzle flash from a firearm. We have had a number of firearms cases in the past where the weapon has been a converted blank firer, yet has been muzzle loaded to fire ball bearings. In these cases the defence have argued that because a weapon could only fire blanks, the muzzle discharge is low, with all the gases being discharged from the revolver chamber not the muzzle. Therefore the weapon poses no theat. Here the task is simple, to photographically capture the gas discharge from the muzzle.

Figure 9.22   In this image the muzzle flash provides the main exposure, with fill in flash providing illumination to the arm and hand. The main exposure was of several seconds, so it is clear that little or no gas or flames escape from the chamber area. As an aside, when the muzzle was loaded with a ball bearing and fired, the ball bearing travelled through one and a half telephone directories.

One way would be to simply place the camera on a tripod, select a long exposure (using available light) and get someone to fire the weapon. The results, however, would not be great, as the long exposure would cause the hand holding the gun and cartridge to be blurred. Plus, because of the ambient light levels we may not get the full extent of the muzzle flash, smoke and debris.

We could repeat the process in total darkness, so that our muzzle flash would in effect create the light for the exposure when it discharges. The problem here, however, is that although the muzzle will be lit, the rest of the firearm will not, so the gas discharge will appear to be floating in mid air. We therefore need to blend the muzzle flash with some form of flash to illuminate the rest of the firearm (Figure 9.22).

But how do we get the flash to fire when the action takes place in a few milliseconds? The answer of course is to fire the flash remotely via an electronic trigger device. This can be as simple as two pieces of wire that touch or a more sophisticated system based on sound or movement. For practicality within the firing range we have opted for a sound trigger. Again there are numerous models available, but we use the 'Shutter-beam'[6] system. (Figure 9.23)

It is important that before photography is undertaken the firer and the camera are aligned correctly, so that the flash units can be positioned correctly.

---

[6] Shutter beam system via Wood Electronics: http://www.woodselec.com/index.htm.

Figure 9.23 The front of the Shutter-beam device. The left side panel (out of sight) contains the power switch mains power socket, 2.5 phono socket (camera out) and PC jack for strobe out. The right panel (out of sight) contains the cameral pulse duration settings and the beam settings for Make or break, Steady or pulsed, and beam on or off. The rear panel contains the IR beam generator and receiver and the microphone.

Strategies like resting the firer's arm on the back of a chair or on the top of a tripod work well, as they ensure a fixed position for each shot. The camera can then be fitted to the tripod and positioned to frame up the shot as required. Don't forget that firearms are quite small, yet you need to leave enough space to ensure that you capture the gas cloud. These types of shot lend themselves to a bit of judicious letterbox cropping in post-production. The Shutter-beam system is now positioned close to the muzzle of the firearm, but out of shot.

Once the camera and firer are positioned the flash needs to be arranged to illuminate both the firearm and the gas cloud. These can be kept close and set to manual. If possible choose the lowest flash output as that will give a quick recycle time and keep the burst short. Often up to three flash units will be used, one connected to the Shutter-beam system on an extended cable release and two on flash syncs.

To allow us even greater control of the flash timings, we also use an ADDjust box (see Figure 9.24) this allows us to delay the firing of the flash from .0001 to 2 s after the noise is detected.

Once we are ready, we can dim the lights and on command open the shutter and the weapon can be discharged. The muzzle flash and discharge will be captured in the dark, with the flash firing once the sound wave reaches the sensor. On looking at the review screen you should be able to see the exposure and adjust as necessary. This will also give an indication of the delay required to be programmed into the ADDjust box. With good luck and deduction it should be possible to freeze the muzzle flash and ejecting cartridge (if you are recording an automatic) within the same shot. It should be pointed out that the Shutter-beam box, as the name implies, is also capable of being triggered by movement when its infrared beam is broken.

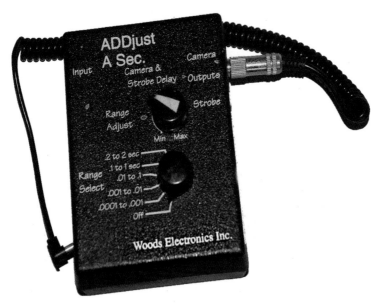

Figure 9.24 The ADDjust box, showing the increment changes that can be achieved.

If you cannot get hold of an automatic system such as the shutter-beam, it is also possible to build a simple trigger pad, using a flash sync cable with the sync end removed and the wires pared back and attached to small pieces of foil or similar. Simply closing the circuit will cause the flash to fire. This has many uses including camera traps or capturing a high-speed event such as a light bulb exploding.

In Figure 9.25 we can see the same technique of flash illumination used to capture a hammer smashing a light bulb. In this example the studio lights were switched off, with the only illumination coming from two studio flash heads fitted with soft boxes. These were connected to the Shutter-beam system through the ADDjust box. To achieve the final result took a number of attempts, adjusting the ADDjust box by tiny amounts each time.

For the image shown in Figure 9.26, the above process was repeated, this time capturing the water on the outside of a balloon as it bursts and collapses inwards.

Although the above technique offers high quality end results, it is clearly limited to a single moment in time. When we need to capture a sequence of images a different tactic needs to be employed and this is when we turn to a high-speed camera. There are a number of models on the market offering speeds of up to a million frames a second, some working in colour and some in black and white. In fact, like nearly all digital cameras, they all shoot in black and white (greyscale) and use a Bayer filter to add the colour rendition, this loses around one or two stops. So the choice is down to your application.

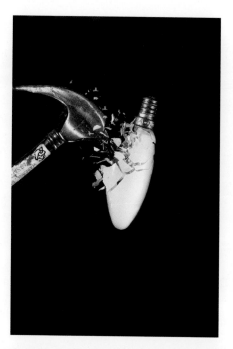

Figure 9.25   The point of impact as the hammer strikes the shell of the light bulb.

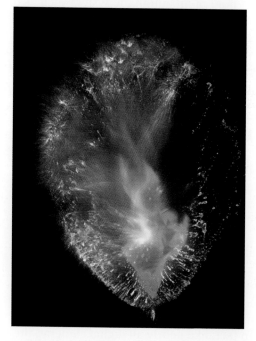

Figure 9.26   The outer surface of a balloon sprayed with a thin coating of water from an atomiser.

Figure 9.27   The NAC GX-1 preparing to shoot a blood droplet test.

We use a NAC GX-1[7] which is capable of shooting from 50 frames per second (fps) to 200 000 fps, although for most casework we use speeds of between 2000–5000 fps (see Figure 9.27). Unlike high-speed film or video with moving parts, the NAC GX- 1 is in fact a very high speed stills camera.

Clearly one big advantage over its film and video predecessors is that the footage can be replayed immediately, if required, allowing the action or lighting to be checked. However these files are large, a full capture cycle on our system is around 2 GB and this is what determines the recording time. I use the word 'cycle' as for this type of work we set the camera to continually record as a loop until we trigger it to stop. Once captured the inbuilt software allows films to be trimmed to required points and saved into various file formats, including 'AVI's'[8] as used in these clips.

In Figure 9.28 we can see a typical type of casework, the recording of a converted Luger pistol to show its unusual ejection and reload action. Again the typical defence is that the weapon is incapable of firing, although the film clearly shows the full movement during discharge.

The downside of high speed photography is that powerful lighting is required to achieve a correct exposure when using high speed recording and short shutter speeds. Although tungsten lighting can be used, these become hot, particularly for any subject standing in front of them! For that reason we use ARRi HDI[9] lights which produce no real heat but produce several thousand candles' power of light with no flicker.

We also use the camera in scientific research, and Figure 9.29 shows a preliminary test shot of a blood droplet as it falls.

---

[7] Nac GX-1: http://www.nacinc.com/products/memrecam-high-speed-digital-cameras/gx-1/.

[8] AVI files Audio video interleaved files were introduced by Microsoft and contain both video and audio files allowing synchronised playback.

[9] Arri lighting via: http://www.arri.com.

Figure 9.28   An automatic luger type pistol.

Figure 9.29   In this clip we can see a blood drop being dropped from a height of 500 cm during blood pattern testing.

Finally, in Figure 9.30, we can see the destructive power of a 7.62 round being fired from an assault rifle hitting a suspended water bottle.

9.5   UVC photography

In Chapter 7, we looked at the finding and recording of latent fingermarks using a number of techniques, including the use of the laser and long wave UVA radiation to induce fluorescence. These techniques are excellent at

Figure 9.30 A 7.62 round hitting a 5 l water container.

finding the majority of marks, but what if you have a key exhibit and every other lighting technique has failed?

Dependent on the surface material of your exhibit, it may be possible to use short wave UVC radiation. UVC, unlike UVA, consists of short wavelengths, found between 100 nm and 280 nm in the electromagnetic spectrum. This is often referred to as germicidal UV because of its use in sterilisation, and it is higher energy than UVA. Luckily for us, the ozone in the atmosphere blocks most of the naturally occurring UVC generated by the sun. However, when it is produced deliberately as required in this technique, it is a dangerous form of non ionising radiation. Prolonged exposure to radiation of this type may result in acute and chronic health effects, including the production of carcinogenic melanomas. Therefore extreme caution must be taken when using this type of equipment or using this technique.

UVC can be used in two distinct ways. One is to use it as another type of specular illumination, where we are relying on the mark to absorb the UVC, but for the surface to reflect it. This will give us a dark finger mark against a light background. This is perfect for smooth non-porous surfaces like magazine covers or plastics. On other types of smooth non-porous backgrounds you can get light scattering showing a light mark against a dark background.

The other way is to use it as you would UVA, that is to induce fluorescence, but this time not in the mark but in the background. This technique is, however, generally limited to smooth high quality white papers and card, used in the production of greetings cards or posters. Papers with heavy fibre contents will not work well with this technique.

Let's look at the absorption techniques first. As if the dangers of UVC weren't a problem enough, the other major issue is that the wavelengths are so short that our eyes cannot visually detect the result. We therefore need to use some form of electronic viewing and recording device. In-house we use

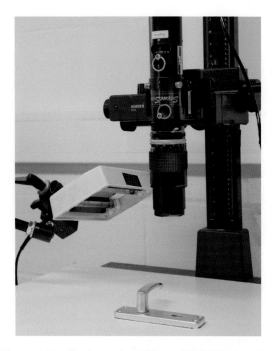

Figure 9.31   The image intensifier and UVC light housing.

the SPEX RUVIS UV image intensifier for viewing[10] fitted with a Nikkor 105-mm UV lens. This intensifier has been designed to only look at the UV wavelengths. To narrow the detection range even more, it has been fitted with a narrow band pass 254 nm filter. This ensures that we are only viewing UVC and no other UV wavelengths emitted by ambient lighting or equipment. The device is also fitted with a small video camera, which relays the images in real time on a TV monitor.

For illumination, we use two 4-W UVC tubes mounted in a hand-held mount. This allows the tubes to be positioned correctly, yet stops unwanted light from exposing the searcher.

UVC has the unusual and advantageous property that it is such a short wavelength it cannot penetrate any but the thinnest plastic surfaces. In effect, exposed to this wavelength of radiation, nearly all surfaces become opaque. This means that when searching with UVC you are only seeing deposits on the surface of the exhibit, including any marks in grease or dirt.

In Figure 9.31 we can see the image intensifier fitted to a copy stand, this enables the exhibit to be placed underneath and the light held in any

---

[10] RUVIS viewer via SPEX Forensics: http://www.spexforensics.com/applications/scenescope-advance-ruvis-uv-imager?utm_source=print&utm_medium=flyers&utm_term=scenescope&utm_campaign=spex-direct.

position required. It is possible to hand-hold and view directly through the image intensifier, allowing it to be used at scenes or on location.

To capture an image, at present, we have to replace the image intensifier unit with a film camera, using Ilford Pan F, generally exposing at f8 for 15 and 30 s and machine processing through an Ilford processor at 10% more than the recommended timings. Recently, a number of UVC enabled cameras have come on the market and, although expensive, allow the user to both view and capture with ease.

Although the above set-up is flexible, it does pose a number of health and safety issues, as the operator must wear a full-face shield and rubber gloves. In Figure 9.32 we can see a self-contained system built by the Center of Applied Science and Technology. This allows the operator to place the exhibit in a sealed cabinet protecting them from unwanted UV exposure.

Figure 9.32 A self-contained purpose-built UVC imaging system. Note that the light fitting inside the cabinet cannot change angle, with the device relying on swamping the exhibit with non-ionizing radiation to get a result.

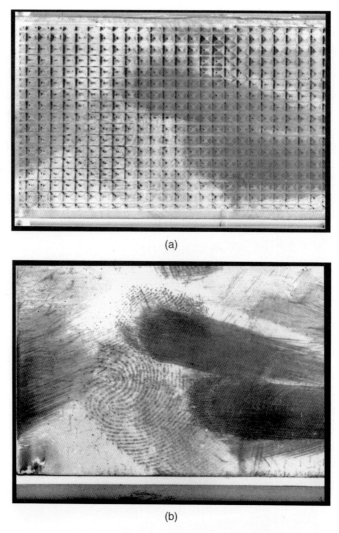

(a)

(b)

Figure 9.33   (a) shows a vanity light cover from a sun visor (b) shows the same area after illumination with UVC.

Within the department, we use much lower amounts of UVC, angling the direction of the light as required in the same way that we would use a specular reflection in the visible region of the spectrum.

In Figure 9.33 we can see our exhibit, a vanity light cover, from a sun visor from a suspect motor vehicle. If you look carefully you can just make out a finger mark pointing towards 6 o'clock. The small diffusing pyramids (the bases of which appear as small squares in the image) are on the reverse side of the plastic, yet contribute to the image and make the mark difficult to see. Because the UVC radiation cannot penetrate the plastic to any great extent, these

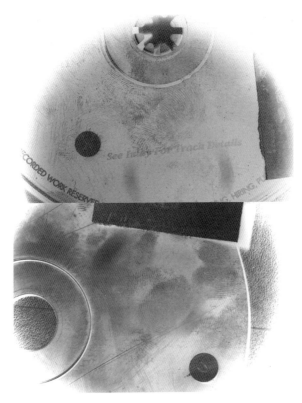

Figure 9.34   Here we can see two of the 20 + groups of finger marks retrieved.

distracting features are not present in the UVC image and the mark is clearly visible.

It is important to note here that the mark did not develop with subsequent chemical treatments, and thus would have been lost if this technique had not been used.

Figure 9.34 shows marks on one of a number of CDs which, due to the nature of their contents, were not able to be chemically treated (and thus destroyed). Therefore, only a visual examination could be carried out.

It is also possible to achieve a halfway house compromise if you own a UV adapted DSLR and UV flashgun. Although these cameras cannot detect radiation down to 254 nm, the adapted D3, for example, can still detect down to around 300 nm. This means that it will work best on faint CNA (superglue) treated marks on opaque backgrounds, depending on its thickness (this must be done if possible before BY40 staining). This is due to the surface topography changing with the application of CNA and the fact that the CNA absorbs the UVC. However, if you try to photograph marks on translucent or clear plastics/glass, the surface will appear transparent (Figure 9.35).

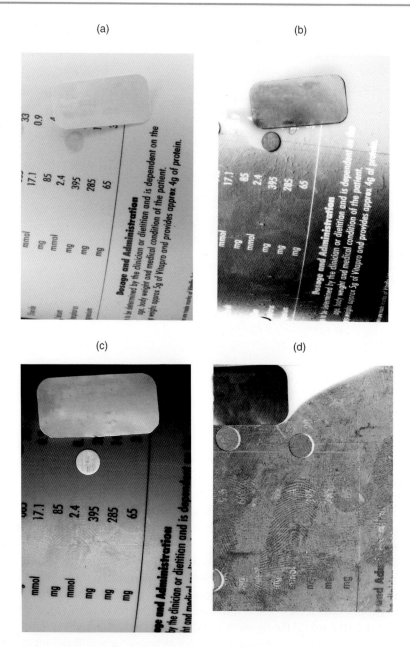

Figure 9.35 (a) Shows the position of an faint CNA mark, (b) & (c) shows the mark photographed using standard techniques (d) shows the mark under UVC.

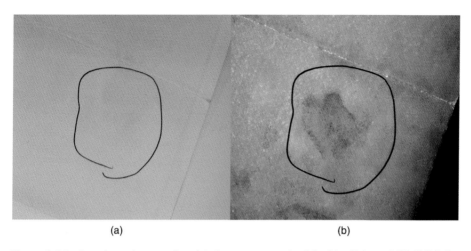

(a)   (b)

Figure 9.36   A mark on the rear of an A4 glossy poster under (a) white light and (b) UVC light.

As you cannot visually see at what angle the flash needs to be held to achieve the best results, a number of trial shots will need to be taken and reviewed on the playback screen. As a guide, marks on flat surface appear best when the flash is fired very obliquely across the surface.

Although the above reflection-based techniques require images to be recorded onto film or captured on a specialist UV camera due to the wavelengths involved, the undertaking of UVC fluorescence photography will work on any DSLR camera. This is because we are going to capture the image in the visible wavelength range, by filtering the camera with a pale yellow long pass filter at around 415 nm. Unlike the above technique, where the angle of the light is important, here it is not. In this technique we just need to flood the area with UVC, any contaminated marks on the surface strongly absorb UVC and will appear as faint black or grey ridges against a bright reflective and/or fluorescing background (Figure 9.36). These can be captured in the same way as you would capture any fluorescent mark.

Concerns have been raised that the use of UVC radiation can destroy any DNA present, which from an evidential perspective may be hoped to be retrieved from the item. [1, 2] In our own testing using the lighting at the normal distance or around 50 cm, no noticeable detrimental effect was found for exposures up to 5 min. However, to ensure that this exposure to UVC is minimised, the exhibits are searched as rapidly as possible and are only exposed to the lighting if marks require photography. Of course, this possible degradation of any DNA present must be weighed against the evidential value and the possibility of obtaining a usable finger mark.

If you wish to read more about reflected ultraviolet, a very good article is reflected Ultraviolet Imaging for Forensic applications written by Dr Austin

Richards and can be found at http://www.company7.com/library/nikon/ Reflected_UV_Imaging_for_Forensics_V2.pdf.

References

(1) Rammelsberg, A. How does ultraviolet light kill cells? *Scientific American* Aug 17, 1998 www%2Escientificamerican%2Ecom%2Farticle%2Ecfm%3Fid%3Dhow-does-ultraviolet-ligh&urlhash=ZDJ6&_t=tracking_disc.

(2) Wei, H., Ca, Q., Rahn, R. et al. DNA structural integrity and base composition affect ultraviolet light-induced oxidative dna damage. *Biochemistry* 1998 37(18): 6485–90. DOI: 10.1021/bi972702f http://pubs.acs.org/doi/abs/10.1021/bi972702f

10
Panoramic (Immersive or 360°) and Elevated imaging

10.1 Overview

As we have seen in previous chapters, we have photographed the scene in the same way for the past 100 years or so. That is to say: using a fixed camera point, aimed towards the area of interest. Although this produces a high quality result, it has a number of limitations. Not least of all is the fact that it is the photographer who is making the choice of what is in the image and what isn't. Clearly more than one image will be taken at the scene, but once captured we cannot go back and move to the left or right, or up and down. We can and do use video, but again the choice of viewing angle is limited to the photographer's experience.

In today's digital world we really want to be using technology to our advantage, indeed to some extent investigators and courts now expect this interactive approach. No longer are they happy with flat two-dimensional prints, they now want to make a virtual scene visit.

Within the limited confines of this book I cannot cover the principles of panoramic photography in any great depth, but a quick look on the Internet will provide ample supporting material for those of you who are interested. Originally, panoramic images, were created using single images panning across the scene. The individual images were then cut and pasted into a sequence; however, each would have a slightly different exposure or edge distortion issues making the joins look obvious. The alternative was to use a camera using a long length of film and a rotating lens or, as with later versions, cameras with a fixed lens but the film wrapped around a drum where the whole

Forensic Photography: A Practitioner's Guide, First Edition. Nick Marsh.
© 2014 John Wiley & Sons, Ltd. Published 2014 by John Wiley & Sons, Ltd.

camera rotated. Panoramic cameras with fixed lenses also have perspective characteristics similar to human perception. Whilst conventional fixed lens cameras produce flat images with fairly straight lines, rotating cameras or those with rotating lenses produce cylindrical images in which straight lines appear curved, and although they produce a 360° cylindrical view, they are vertically limited. Digital technology, however, has allowed the stitching of very wide angle, or fisheye, lenses to create a sphere of images. This means that if we were to stand inside the sphere we could look in every direction and see a projection of the image in front of us.

This is where panoramic, immersive or 360° photography comes into its own. Note that all descriptions are used by different agencies to describe the technique, but for the purposes of this chapter I will refer to it at immersive, as it allows us to enter our scene.

Although the images are still taken from a single point within the scene, it offers the possibility of allowing the investigator, judge or jury to look in any direction from that point, up, down, left or right. It also allows images to be connected to each other, so that we can move between rooms. Or we can embed other types of file, such as still images, video, or sound information, which can be activated by way of a 'hot spot'. It also allows the operator to produce high quality stills if required to support points of interest.

Many forces and agencies, including us, are using immersive imaging as the norm for serious crime scenes. If you look on line, you will find dozens of sites covering the production of 360° panoramas, using all manner of equipment. In fact it is possible to get a result from a mobile phone, or small pocket camera, and many don't even use a tripod. However, for us as professionals, we need a repeatable, reliable, quality technique that is still flexible and quick to use.

In this chapter I want to look at two ways we can create an immersive capture of a scene: one uses a self-controlled all-in-one system, in this case the Spheron VR, a bespoke panoramic camera, and the other uses a standard DSLR.

Note here that I am not going to cover the increasing use of 3D laser scanners, as they are not strictly photographic tools, although the latest generations of scanners now offer high quality images.[1] Clearly within a crime scene both systems have merit, but we have found that, at trial, the court would prefer to see true photographic images, rather than photo realistic ones.

3D scanners are also generally expensive and computer power hungry, whilst undertaking a basic photographic 360 is moderately cheap, quick and effective.

I also want to look at how the images can be put together and be used as a way of integrating evidence types. There are a number of systems available, so the choice is not limited to the options I am going to cover.

---

[1] http://www.faro.com/products/3d-surveying.

Figure 10.1   Shows Spheron fitted with the lighting option.

Technology is changing almost daily, and as I write this there are number of new self-contained systems being marketed, these offer one shot point-and-shoot methods of capture, so may be worth further investigation.

10.2   Spheron

The Spheron[2] camera is a German built, self-contained full-360° spherical imaging camera that captures a full 360° image in one scan. To achieve this it uses a vertical scanner array of pixels, rather than a traditional shaped DSLR 4×3 sensor. This allows the camera to continually capture a High Dynamic Range (HDR) exposure, giving range equivalent of to 26 stops (depending on the setting used), ensuring the correct exposure at all levels of illumination. The system is sold as a self-contained kit with lens, computer and tripod (Figure 10.1).

The system can be set from fully automatic, through to fully manual, and in a general scene will give exposure times between 5–10 minutes. However, in auto it doesn't allow the camera to save to a compact flash card and, although not an issue, this would be beneficial to us as it would sit within our audit trail.

Shooting a complete 360° image can generate a range of file sizes and types dependent on its quality setting. These files are generally saved as the equirectangular SPH (spheron raw) which can be processed to a floating-point

---

[2] Spheron: http://www.spheron.com.

radiance xml file[3] allowing the HDR (High Dynamic Range) file to be tone mapped in software such as Photomatix. These can then output as either equirectangular JPEG, or Tiff files, allowing them to be used by other post-production software.

As the Spheron system is self-contained, it is ideal for scenarios and scenes where space is limited, or an end result is required quickly. For very low lighting conditions, our system can also be fitted with its own dedicated LED lighting system and is widely used at arsons or other scenes where there is a diverse contrast range (Figure 10.1).

As with all things there is a trade off, in low light we have noticed that there are increased amounts of digital noise and if the system is set to shoot in HDR, the exposure times can be very slow.

As can be seen, this is a self-contained system that requires only a short period of training and experience. It is, however, not the cheapest option and can be slow in some circumstances. As such, some agencies with small budgets or requirements may need to consider a more flexible or cheaper option, and for that we can adapt our normal DSLR.

10.3   Digital Single Lens Reflex 360°

The alternative to a one-shot camera system is shooting the whole 360° image using a standard DSLR camera. Here, instead of one continuous shot, as with the Spheron, we will need to take a number of single images to create our immersive panorama. For many forces and organisations, this is probably the norm as this is a far cheaper option than an automated system. For this option you will need to purchase one of a multitude of specialist 360° heads available (Figure 10.2). These range from completely manual 360° heads such as the 360 Precision,[4] or Manfrotto 3035PH,[5] through to the Seitz VR2,[6] which offers a completely automatic process.

You will also need a wide angle or fisheye lens, for the purposes of this chapter I will be using a 16 mm on an FX (full frame) sensor. If you are using a DX sensor (three-quarter size), the equivalent will be a 10.5 mm lens, both of which are readily available (Figure 10.2). It is possible to use almost any combination of lenses but, as will be clear in a minute, the longer the focal length the more images you will require to create a 360° sphere.

I also recommend from experience that you use a heavy-duty tripod, to alleviate any movement between exposures.

---

[3] xml files: Extensible Markup language: defines a set of rules for encoding documents that are both machine and human readable; although designed for documents it is often used to represent data structures as it was designed to be simple and usable over the internet.

[4] 360 precision head: http://www.360precision.com/360/index.cfm?precision=home.home

[5] Manfrotto 360 head: www.manfrotto.com/panoramic-head.

[6] Seitz VR2 head: http://www.roundshot.ch/xml_1/internet/de/intro.cfm.

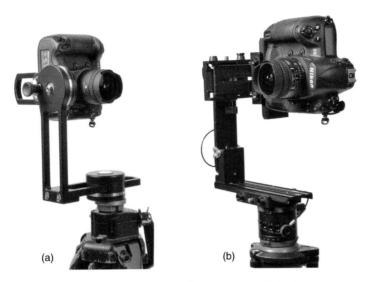

(a) (b)

Figure 10.2 (a) A fixed 360 head, which is dedicated to a particular lens and camera configuration fitted with FX DSLR and 16 mm lens. (b) An adjustable 360 head, which can be configured to any lens camera combination FX DSLR and 16 mm lens.

Before we even start to think about undertaking the photography, we need to calibrate our 360 head, by finding its No-parallax point (NPP); this will need to be found unless you have brought a dedicated fixed head (i.e. one designed for a particular camera and lens configuration). The NPP is often incorrectly referred to as the nodal point; technically, however, the perspective of an image is determined by the rays of light that formed it and because the aperture controls this, its location determines the perspective. The centre of perspective and the NPP are one and the same, located at the centre of the entrance pupil. Therefore, the position of the designer's front nodal point can be irrelevant. [1] Although in some cases this may be in a very similar position to the NPP within the lens, the NPP point is the exact point in the lens where the image is inverted, so that when images are viewed they are free of parallax errors. Although this sounds complicated, it is pretty straightforward once you get the idea.

I know some people do not think this stage is critical to carry out, but if not done correctly the resulting panorama will not stitch correctly. It will produce an image that is clunky and out of alignment and where objects within the viewable area will appear to move against the background. This is particularly noticeable when viewing foreground objects that are close to the lens. It should also be noted that although fisheye lenses are well suited to this type of imaging, as they cover a very wide angle, they unfortunately do not have a clearly identifiable NPP compared to normal (rectilinear) lenses. The location of the NPP in these lenses is based on the angle of incidence in the light reaching the lens. This means that the fisheye can never be precisely calibrated, although they can still be used, if the angle of rotation when setting the NPP is the same as the one used to undertake the photography. For example, if we shoot six images covering a 360° field of view we can use the same 60° (6 × 60° = 360°) rotation, to check our NPP.

In this example, we are going to use a 16-mm fisheye on a FX sensor and a Manfrotto head.

Unfortunately, lens manufactures do not generally provide information with regard to the NPP of their products, so we must do this for ourselves using trial and error. There are number of methods that can be used to find the NPP, many of which are demonstrated on the Internet. The one I will look at is the simplest, I think, as all you need to find is two vertical features such as a doorway and the edge of a wall. One of these should be close to the camera, the other further away; these will act as your references. If you are not using a preset dedicated 360 head, then you will need to mount your camera so that the centre of the lens is positioned directly above the rotation of axis. If you stand in front of the camera you should be able to adjust it left and right until it is directly above this point, this point is normal marked on the base plate (Figure 10.3).

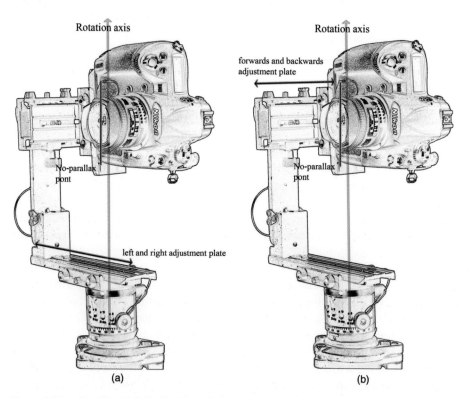

Figure 10.3   The set up of the Manfrotto head. Most 360 heads allow adjustments to both the vertical and the horizontal position of the camera and lens.

To find the NPP we need to move the camera backwards and forwards, left and right, until we can rotate the camera keeping our two reference points aligned (Figure 10.4), The NPP, unlike the axis of rotation, is generally close to the front of the lens.

Once the NPP has been found we can lock the head into position. Provided that it doesn't get knocked or moved and we stick to the same camera lens configuration, this should now be correct for all our photographs.

We will then need to position our camera in the scene; in standard two-dimensional photography, we would frame up looking at our point of interest. But for immersive imaging we need to position our camera so that it can see in every direction. As a rule of thumb this generally means placing it in the middle of a scene. Although clearly, if you have a large area or have areas that are hidden, a number of panoramas may need to be created. Also, if possible, try to avoid placing your camera close to large areas of wall or blank space, remember it is going to record a 360-degree image, so use it to your advantage.

It is also important to ensure that when you position your camera the area covered by the nadir (the area directly under the head that the camera cannot see) is not obscuring important information. Don't forget that if you do have areas of significant information or interest, such as a weapon, finger or shoe mark, or areas obscured by furniture and so on, they can be added as 'hot spots', still images, at a later date during post-production.

Unlike the Spheron I mentioned above, which automatically creates an HDR when taking the exposure, when using a DSLR the best plan is to use the 'mean' exposure point based on readings from the exposure meter. This means that the exposure metering system must be set to manual. Leaving the camera in automatic will cause each individual image to be taken at a different exposure, making the stitching process difficult and the final image badly exposed. Also, as we will be shooting in RAW, this will give us a degree of flexibility with regard to equalising our exposure range in post-production.

It is also possible to undertake full HDR using the DSLR; however, this can be a long process if done manually. Here again, systems like the Seitz VR2 will control the camera in HDR, allowing up to 7 stops in each direction, but we have found that if you are using the RAW file, this is only of real benefit in areas of great contrast.

In my example, we are using a 16-mm fisheye mounted on a FX DSLR; we are therefore going to take six photographs at 60° to cover the 360° around the camera, and one photograph straight up to capture the area above the camera. The taking of six photographs ensures we have a good overlap between images, which should in effect give us a better stitch.

In tight scenes or on stepping plates it is possible to use a system like the Seitz VR2, which will automatically do the seven shots required. It should be noted that when using this technique, the use of flash should be avoided as the light is very difficult to merge evenly at the next stage. If possible, compensate for the lack of exposure levels by increasing the ISO, increasing the

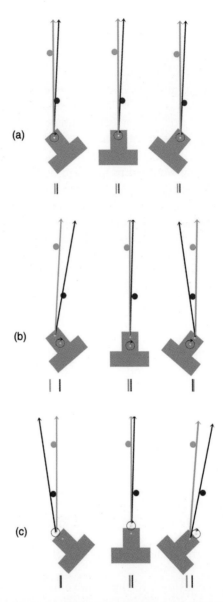

Figure 10.4   The relationship between the NPP and rotation axis of the lens. (a) The correct alignment of the nodal point and rotation axis. (b) The effect of rotating the axis forward of the nodal point. Rotating the camera away from the near object increases the gap width. Rotating the camera towards the near object reduces the gap width. (c) The effect of rotating the axis behind the nodal point. Rotating the camera away from the near object reduces the gap width. Rotating the camera towards the near object increases the gap width.

Figure 10.5   The seven images producing a panorama in PTGui.

aperture or reducing the shutter speed. It should also be noted that the focus should be set to manual, with the lens focused at the hyperfocal distance for the subject. If auto focus is left engaged each image will have a different point of focus, meaning that it will be difficult for the software to stitch.

Once we have set the exposure and the focus we can take the seven photographs required to produce a full 360° image. Once the images have been captured, we need to export them into a program such as Photoshop for postproduction. Here we can take the individual jpeg files (or post processed RAW files) and adjust the 'highlights' and 'shadows'. Avoid using extreme adjustments to the maximum or minimum, as the images may not blend properly, preferably use the midpoint only. These files can then be imported into a program such as PTGui[7] to create an equirectangular image file[8] and then be adjusted as required. An equirectangular image is when a complete 360-degree capture is presented as a long flat image (Figure 10.5).

PTGui will stitch the images using the principle of a one third overlap between images. This has the advantage of allowing an area to be masked. For example if there is a pedestrian in shot, who appears on right hand side third of one image (Figure 10.6). They may not appear on the one third of the left side of the second image and so the overlap will remove them. This makes

---

[7] PTGui stitching software: http://www.ptgui.com/.

[8] An equirectangular image is one that if wrapped around a sphere would be entirely seamless. As a photograph it captures everything around you, up and down. These are generally created by taking a number of very wide angle photographs and stitching them together within a software package.

Figure 10.6   An example of an overlapped image. On the left of the screen we can see two pedestrians have been masked. In the equirectangular image the software has overlapped the image, removing them from view.

the software easy to use and reliable and as such it will cope with 95% of all casework.

Although I am demonstrating here using PTGui, it is not the only stitching software available. Other companies such as 'Stitcher Unlimited'[9] have equally good products, using different algorithms, which look at the content of the image rather than pure maths as PTGui does. I would suggest trying a few, to see which works for you and is the easiest to work with. It is also worth saying that new software and updates are being produced all the time, yet the principals will remain the same.

Interestingly, there are some new automated 360 heads being released, which will undertake a full 360 plus vertical shot and control the camera in undertaking HDR. They also download an executable file, which can be imported into PTGui allowing very accurate overlaps, as the rotation information is automatically stored when the image is taken.

PTGui will also create a 'Quicktime' file, giving an instantly playable result. However these files cannot be opened by some Apple users, nor are they compatible with our own in-house court presentation system. So we need to look for an alternative to produce our end product.

For this we use PANO2VR,[10] again other programs are available, but this is probably the best known and most commonly used at the present time.

---

[9] Stitcher unlimited stitching software: http://usa.autodesk.com.
[10] PANO2VR software: http://gardengnomesoftware.com/pano2vr.php.

Figure 10.7   The skin editor; here we can see an example of our skin being created with inset information and still photographs.

Within this program we can create HTML 5[11] and Flash files[12] depending on your output requirements. This software also allows the introduction of 'skins'. Skins sit on top of each image and contain graphical information, for example maps, still photographs, arrows, plans, pointers and importantly for us 'hotspots'. These hotspots provide the link between the panoramas, or to other embedded images such as a shoe or finger marks, CCTV or even sound files, allowing a smooth transfer through the scene. Some forces use 'hotzones', rather than hotspots; these are just larger areas within the image, such as door or windows.

The skin also acts as a sort of reference page and generally shows information with regard to the address, date and so on (Figure 10.7). A map with embedded hotspots and direction arrows, often these are only visible when hovered over with the mouse. One of the most important things in our experience is to keep the content of the skin to a minimum, particularly if you have a lot of panoramas to join together. We use the skin to show an information page to show maps/plans, text, info boxes and stills (Figure 10.8).

Again, each panoramic presentation is bespoke, this allows the case to be worked on over a period of time. This is another advantage of having

---

[11] HTML files: Hyper Text Markup Language is used to display the information as a web page in a web browser.

[12] Flash files: Adobe Flash is a multimedia platform used to add animation video and interactive web pages.

Figure 10.8   The skin as it would appear to the viewer, along the bottom we can see the direction arrows, zoom and information. In the centre we can see a hotspot labeled firearm, which would take us to the still image seen in Figure 10.7.

individual images building your panorama as they can be re-edited and output as required, often as SWF[13] files.

Figure 10.8 shows a completed immersive image ready to be viewed. In this scenario we have a large scene under different lighting conditions. The images were shot on an FX sensor and processed via the route discussed above. For the purposes of this book, I have kept the panoramas to a minimum, but in a real case, these may be propagated with more links to other panoramas, stills, videos or even audio files.

This is fast growing area of our casework and one of the biggest and often-overlooked advantages of using the above immersive imaging within the judicial system, is the reduction in both court time and costs in transporting a jury to the scene. This is particularly relevant, as all the crown courts in the United Kingdom will receive electronic case files by June 2016.

In some cases, however, particularly exterior ones, the true size of a scene or positioning of areas of interest within the scene is not easily conveyed from ground level even using a full 360 capture.

As we shall see in the section, it is in these cases that we need to combine the above panoramic technique with an elevated platform to get the ultimate scene capture.

---

[13] SWF: originally used as an abbreviation for ShockWave Flash This usage was changed to the backronym *Small Web Format* to eliminate confusion with a different technology, Shockwave, from which SWF was derived. SWF can contain animations and applets and is the dominant format for displaying animated vector graphics on the web.

Figure 10.9 A ground level photograph of the body. As we can see the view just shows vegetation and the body remains hidden.

10.4 Elevated imaging

Although I have covered scene photography in general already, there is one area of work that has really come into its own since the introduction of lightweight digital cameras, and that is elevated imaging. Aerial platforms have been around for many years, but were fitted with film cameras or video; in reality they were not very user friendly and expensive. The introduction of digital capture has changed all that. Cameras can now be fully controlled via a laptop or iPad type device, enabling us to see what we are about to photograph and, more importantly, change the camera settings prior to exposure to adjust for local conditions. Indeed, there are a number of companies who specialise in this type of photography, particularly related to building works.

There are also a plethora of aerial drones now available, although within the United Kingdom these are not in common usage by police forces for imaging. For the purposes of this book I will concentrate on the use of ground-based devices.

I suppose the first question is: why is an elevated view so good? There have been many times over the past 25 years when I have taken photographs at ground level, knowing that an elevated vantage point would have been more beneficial (see Figures 10.9 and 10.10). This is often because of sightlines, street layouts or obstructions, where the ability to look over something from a higher viewpoint would have been advantageous not only to the investigating officers, but also at a later date the jury at court. Indeed in many circumstances I have photographed from buildings or cranes, and so on to get a 'birds eye'

Figure 10.10   The same scene, this time taken from an elevated position; note that in this shot an area of flattened grass is clearly visible around the body showing a possible safe forensic approach route.

view, which is especially useful for road traffic accidents, allowing skid marks or damage to the road to be seen in context with their surroundings.

Like many police forces, the metropolitan police operate a helicopter, which is capable of undertaking aerial photography. However its deployment is often hampered because of combination of weather and flying restrictions, particularly in built up areas. The other main issue is that the officers dealing with the case cannot review the images until hours or days later, so have no confidence that the particular angle or viewpoint has actually been recorded.

In the next few paragraphs I would like to look a number of options available that allow us to capture the scene from a more elevated viewpoint.

Within the department we have three different elevated imaging platforms, each has a number of advantages and disadvantages. In the first two systems the poles are commercially available either directly from the manufacturer or through third parties (who will sell you all the equipment required as a kit), whilst the third has been built in-house.

The highest platform is a 25-m mast that is mounted on the roof of a transit type van.[14] In its normal carry position the mast is laid horizontally along the roofline. When required it is swung into its vertical position and uses the van as a base support (Figure 10.11). Although the van also has stabilisers, which are deployed when the mast is erect, in practicality this means the mast needs to be deployed on a relatively flat, even and solid surface. This is because the

---

[14] 25-metre mast: http://www.clarkmasts.com.

Figure 10.11   An overview of an archeological dig photographed from the mast.

mast has very little maneuverability in terms of vertical adjustment, as it rises vertically at 90° from the rear of the vehicle. Therefore, if it is parked on a camber, by the time the mast is fully extended it could have massive deviation from 90° and. although this may not be a problem for simple still image, it would make 360° photography impossible as we could not achieve a flat horizon.

The top platform of the mast is fitted with a DSLR mounted on a pan and tilt remote control head cable connected to a laptop in the van. (This is in the process of changing to connect the DSLR via Wifi to a tablet device.)

Because of the above issues and the fact that the above cannot go off road, we also have a shorter, portable 15-m mast;[15] this can be fitted to a large estate car for either transportation or for deployment. Unlike its bigger brother, above, if the mast is used attached to a car, there is the ability to make minor adjustments to correct the vertical (Figure 10.12). However, because it is lightweight aluminum, it is easily detached from the vehicle and can be carried. This means it can be transported anywhere and then mounted on its own tripod. At the end of each tripod leg there is a vertical bar, which allows the tripod to be adjusted by up to a height of half a metre, so it can be levelled on the roughest of ground. However, because this mast is much lighter and smaller than its big brother, the platform will only cope with the

---

[15] 15 metre mast from SMC (South Midlands Communications).

Figure 10.12   The short mast fitted to an estate car, in the left photograph note the special fixing bar on the roof and then on the right the pole in the deployed position; note here that the car is acting as the tripod mount.

weight of a high-end compact camera and small pan and tilt head and again it is cable connected to a laptop (Figure 10.13).

This mast is probably the most versatile, because it can be deployed on any surface and in most weather conditions and has been used in casework from murders to fatal accidents.

Finally, for interior work we have two 3-m hand-held pole cameras; one is hand-held and used almost exclusively within scenes and allows the capture of a unique plan view of a body in position. The second is similar to the hand-held version but is mounted on a wheeled tripod. This is used for the photography of motor vehicles involved in serious or fatal road collisions.

Both are very lightweight and fully transportable systems but are not commercially available, as they were built in-house by my colleagues after hours of research. They are both fitted with a high-end compact camera equipped with a zig viewer[16] allowing the operator to position the camera very accurately within the scene (Figure 10.14).

For photography, the camera is fitted with a wide-angle lens, because of this we use the camera's built in flash (which is generally ineffective at lighting a scene from above when using the wide angle lens) to trigger external Metz 45s (Figure 10.15).

Very recently, a number of commercially available smaller masts have come on the market, these take advantage of Wi-Fi connectivity. One such product is 'Photomast'[17] (other similar products are available) which comes in a range

[16] Zig viewer: http://www.zigview.co.uk.

[17] Photomast: http://www.photomast.com or Colin Inglis: http://suffieldimaging.co.uk.

Figure 10.13   The pole mounted on its tripod. It is worth noting that it is almost impossible to push the pole over from the central position and is only possible if you physically lift one of the legs.

Figure 10.14   The G4 fitted to the 3-m pole; for ease of use it is generally braced against the ceiling, with the end placed under the foot for extra stability.

Figure 10.15   The ground level and then the elevated viewpoint.

Figure 10.16   An elevated 360 degree view of south London.

of sizes from 6, 8 and 10 metres. These are made of very lightweight carbon fibre and can support a lightweight DSLR.

Finally, if you want the ultimate in crime scene recording, you can combine the elevated platform with an immersive image. This gives an impressive overview of any exterior scene where a plan view of an area is required. The important thing to remember here is to ensure that the elevated platform is as close to 90° as possible, otherwise your 360 rotation will have a tilted horizon line (Figure 10.16).

Reference

(1) Littlefield, R. Theory of the "no parallax" point in panorama photography. Version 1.0, February 2006. Available at: http://www.janrik.net/PanoPostings/NoParallaxPoint/TheoryOfTheNoParallaxPoint.pdf [accessed May 2014].

Appendix 1
Tripods and Camera Supports

A.1 Tripods

With the introduction of digital cameras and their mass-market appeal, there seems to be a perception that tripods are no longer required and as such their use appears to have gone out of fashion.

People say to me 'oh I don't need one of those, they only get in the way'. I would say, however, that 95% of my work is shot using some form of camera support or tripod. For my part, the requirement within a scene or studio hasn't changed with the introduction of digital photography. Not only do they offer a stable support allowing slow shutter speeds to be used, they also offer continuity between images. Finally they have another benefit, which is often overlooked, that of where you put your camera in a blood stained room. The tripod is an ideal safe place for it to sit without the risk of it becoming contaminated by the scene, or vice versa.

The beauty of tripods is that they really are available in every shape and size, for every application. They range from the large studio types such mono stands, all the way through to small gripping tripods, which can be attached to almost anything. They also made from a variety of materials, from wood through to carbon fibre, so there is bound to be one to suit you or your application (see Figure A.1).

A.2 Scene tripods

This is often a personal choice and is a source of great debate amongst my colleagues. Clearly we don't want to carry a heavy tripod up 15 flights of stairs in a tower block, but we do require stability for a 30 s exposure with a laser

Forensic Photography: A Practitioner's Guide, First Edition. Nick Marsh.
© 2014 John Wiley & Sons, Ltd. Published 2014 by John Wiley & Sons, Ltd.

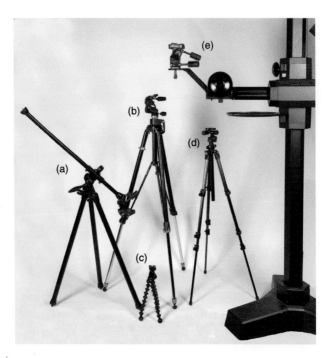

Figure A.1   Shows a typical assortment of tripods (a) Benbo (b) Manfrotto 058 (c) Gorilla pod 35 mm (d) Manfrotto 055 carbon fibre (e) Foba studio tripod.

when we get there. So we do need a variety of choices. Most of the tripods we use are Manfrotto[1] and for this book I will use them as the examples of what to consider when buying a tripod, although there are numerous other manufactures available.

A.2.1   The 058 Triaut Tripod

This tripod is the standard issue to all our professional photographers. It has a number of advantages over its smaller and lighter counterparts as its maximum height is 217 cm but it is still capable of going down to 44 cm. It also has a geared centre column, which means that it can be wound up and down using one hand and the column is self-locking, so it won't move once in position. The big advantage, however, when used at scenes, is that all three legs can be simultaneously released using your thumb, without the need to make individual leg adjustments. For example on stairs, the tripod can be held and the legs released via the release lever. Once pressure is removed from the release lever the legs lock at their new heights. This means that in operational situations the tripod can be positioned quickly and as it features a bubble level on the top plate, it can be levelled in a few seconds. It is normally fitted with the 3D super

---

[1] Manfrotto: http://www.manfrotto.co.uk.

pro head, but it will take the full range of heads available from Manfrotto or other manufacturers (b in figure A.1).

A.2.2   Manfrotto 055 fitted with the Manfrotto 322RCE head

We also use a number of these smaller carbon fibre Manfrotto tripods. These are useful particularly where the evidence is low down near to the ground, as the centre column can be reversed, allowing the camera to be mounted upside down. Being so light and small has a number of advantages, such as it is easy to pack and adds very little extra weight (around 2 kg) to your kit. Conversely its lightness means that it is more prone to vibrations than its bigger brother.

A.2.3   Benbo[2]

This is an unusual tripod. Unlike most tripods where the legs are fixed at a joint just below the camera platform, the Benbo legs have a pin running through them attaching them to the centre column. This means the legs can be moved in virtually any direction, including vertically to be braced against a wall. When used for the first time by the uninitiated, it has been likened to wrestling with an octopus. However, once mastered, these are excellent tripods allowing the camera to be positioned in difficult, awkward and small spaces.

A.2.4   Studio type stands

Generally studio type stands can't be really described as a tripod, as in reality they are mono pods using only a central column, with an adjustable cross-bar fitted with a pan and tilt head, the camera can then be raised lowered, turned or angled in any direction with ease. This means the camera can be moved to just about any position and offers a very stable platform allowing exposures of many minutes of even hours to be undertaken. With the department we use two main makes of studio mono pod, Cambo[3] and Foba[4]; these are used within the main photographic studios and within the DNA studios.

A.3   Other types of camera platforms
A.3.1   Gorilla pods[5]

These are extremely unusual tripods in that the legs are made up of connected circular leg joints, which can be moved into any position. The system is

---

[2] Benbo available through: http://www.warehouseexpress.com.
[3] Cambo: http://www.cambo.com.
[4] Foba: http://www.foba.ch/eng/programm/programm.htm.
[5] Gorilla pod by JOBY: http://joby.com/gorillapod.

specifically designed to be twisted or bent around any object with the environment. They are available in various sizes and load weights, but the 'Focus' range is designed for video or pro cameras cameras in particular and is able to take a weight of up to 5 kg. Not only do they make great camera supports, but also offer the capability of placing extra flashguns into the scene, directed to where they are required.

A.3.2 Monopods

Although clearly not a tripod, Monopods do have a role to play in some circumstances were it is impractical to use a tripod, but some support and stability is required. The most common example is when a long focal length telephoto is being used. Personal I own a carbon fibre Trekpod XL[6] that weighs just over half a kilo, including the head. It also has the unusual feature that the

Figure A.2 A Sachtler video tripod, note the central leg brace, which locks into place making the tripod extremely stable.

---

[6] Trekpod monopod: http://www.trek-tech.com.

bottom part of the pole splits into three feet so it can be used as a traditional tripod. But when closed it can also be used as a walking staff.

A.4   Video tripods

Video tripods such as the Sachtler video tripod[7] are extremely stable tripods and differ from stills tripods in that they have braced legs to give them extra stability (Figure A.2). Generally they are made out of either aluminium or carbon fibre making them very lightweight for their size. In normal usage they are fitted with fluid damped heads to allow smooth pan and tilt whilst filming. We use the tripod both for video and for the high-speed video camera.

A.5   Other types of clamps

Whilst on the subject of photographic supports, it seems a good place to introduce other types of supplementary equipment that is often used at scenes or within the studios.

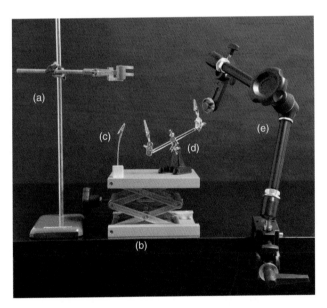

Figure A.3   (a) Standard scientific retort stand[8]. (b) An adjustable platform, which allows an exhibits to be moved millimetre by millilitre if required. (c) A wedding name card holder this simple set of crocodile jaws is very useful for holding labels and scales etc. (unknown manufacturer). (d) Helping hand (unknown manufacture but readily found on the Internet). (e) Manfrotto flexi arm fitted with friction wheel (a).

---

[7] Sachtler tripods: http://www.sachtler.com.
[8] Fisher Scientific: http://www.fisher.co.uk/.

Figure A.4   The Manfrotto flexible arm holding a ball light in position.

Within the laboratories and studios, we use a number of small retort stands and vices to hold a variety of exhibits. These are available in both plastic and metal and are easy clean. This is particularly important within the DNA laboratories, where the risk of cross-contamination needs to be eliminated between exhibits (Figure A.3).

Helping hands are cheap and small double-ended clamps that are extremely useful in studios for holding small items such as labels, rulers, and paper reflectors. A number of makers supply these and a good choice is available through online providers such as Amazon.

The Manfrotto arm is extensively used as a number of fittings can be placed on the end mounts, in our case generally two adjustable clamps. The arm shown in Figure A.3 is a friction-locking device but is also available as an on/off device, both of which allow the arm to be bent into any direction. Although in our experience it is not stable enough to support a camera, it can hold flashguns, fibre optics or other supplementary lighting.

The Manfrotto flexible arm, again as above can be used to hold equipment by simply bending it into positions. This is a very simple bendy arm, which again can be placed in any position. It is available in both light and heavy-duty versions and although it cannot support a camera it can be used for fibre optics or other accessories (Figure A.4).

The Manfrotto Repro arm is an extension bar that fits to the tripod head allowing the camera to be mounted at the end. This allows the camera to be given extra reach where a tripod cannot be positioned. This is often used for shoe marks that are tight against the wall where a normal tripod would not allow the camera to be positioned perpendicular to the mark.

Although I have used a number of specific suppliers in my illustrations, many of the above items are available via other companies at price ranges to fit your budget and application.

Index

Note: Page number followed by f indicates figure only.

Forensic Photography: A Practitioner's Guide, First Edition. Nick Marsh.
© 2014 John Wiley & Sons, Ltd. Published 2014 by John Wiley & Sons, Ltd.